MW01136945

Care for the Sorrowing Soul

Care for the Sorrowing Soul

*Healing Moral Injuries from Military Service
and Implications for the Rest of Us*

Duane Larson

AND

Jeff Zust

CASCADE *Books* · Eugene, Oregon

CARE FOR THE SORROWING SOUL
Healing Moral Injuries from Military Service and Implications for the Rest of Us

Copyright © 2017 Duane Larson and Jeff Zust. All rights reserved. Except for brief quotations in critical publications or reviews, no part of this book may be reproduced in any manner without prior written permission from the publisher. Write: Permissions, Wipf and Stock Publishers, 199 W. 8th Ave., Suite 3, Eugene, OR 97401.

Cascade Books
An Imprint of Wipf and Stock Publishers
199 W. 8th Ave., Suite 3
Eugene, OR 97401

www.wipfandstock.com

PAPERBACK ISBN: 978-1-5326-1770-6
HARDCOVER ISBN: 978-1-4982-4258-5
EBOOK ISBN: 978-1-4982-4257-8

Cataloguing-in-Publication data:

Names: Larson, Duane H. (Duane Howard), 1952– | Zust, Jeff.

Title: Care for the sorrowing soul : healing moral injuries from military service and implications for the rest of us / Duane Larson and Jeff Zust.

Description: Eugene, OR: Cascade Books, 2017 | Includes bibliographical references.

Identifiers: ISBN 978-1-5326-1770-6 (paperback) | ISBN 978-1-4982-4258-5 (hardcover) | ISBN 978-1-4982-4257-8 (ebook)

Subjects: LCSH: Suffering—Moral and ethical aspects | United States—Armed Forces—Chaplains | Military chaplains—United States | Psychology, Military | Military ethics | Healing—Religious aspects—Christianity | Pastoral care—Christianity | Counselling—Religious aspects

Classification: BV4012 L37 2017 (print) | BV4012 (ebook)

Manufactured in the U.S.A.   10/31/17

We dedicate this book to those in military service whose moral goodness was wounded in combat and to those who accompany the morally injured through their sorrowing toward emotional and spiritual healing.

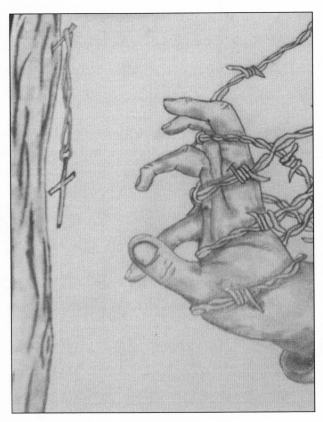

Image by MAJ. (Ret.) Jeff Hall

Contents

Preface

WE BELIEVE THAT IT is vital for military combatants to engage their brains in order "to listen to their hearts" as they perform their duties. This opening line may seem harsh to a reader unacquainted with military training and culture. Combat reflexes are trained to be autonomic, postponing moral processing. This conscience processing could mean the loss of the combatant's own life or the lives of friends. Nevertheless, today's primary mode of operant conditioning does not well serve the moral convictions that a young person brings into military training, what we in this book call a person's "moral voice." It also predisposes the combatant for a date with moral injury.

It is urgent that this imbalance be redressed. A soldier's use of his or her critical rational faculties—beyond simply following the dictates of one's primeval brain (the amygdala)—and hearing one's own moral voice is, in fact, vital for the responsible performance of one's duties. Soldiers' professional character and competence depends upon this union. So does their spiritual wellness. For soldiers of religious conviction, this union becomes a matter of faith, stewardship, and vocation.

In combat the divorce of head from heart produces a moral dissonance that morally injures soldiers and results in a soul sorrow that long haunts their lives. The military, our society, and our religious communities have a moral obligation to (1) prepare soldiers to navigate these risks in order to serve honorably and faithfully under duress, and (2) to accompany them with understanding and compassion during their suffering and healing from moral injury. Those who willingly take up the vocation of defending the common good must be better fitted indeed for a marriage of head and heart that will mean lives of fulfillment for them after their service. This is simply the right thing to do.

And so we invite you into this conversation about moral injury: what to understand about it and how possibly to help in healing those who suffer from it. We are indebted to many professionals from many different disciplines who have studied moral injury and worked long in the healing trenches. Using some of their work, we will present additional models for understanding MI that we hope will mitigate and heal moral injuries in combat veterans. The models we present are grounded in human character development, military training, and spiritual care. We believe this synthesis is necessary to allow veterans and healers together to shape new and meaningful life. Thank you for joining our conversation.

—Duane and Jeff

Acknowledgments

FIRST AND FOREMOST I want to thank my wife, Chom, and my children, for their patience, love, and encouragement. She has been my strength through the deployments and research hours behind every page in this manuscript. I couldn't have done this without them. I honor the leaders, soldiers, and families of the 2-2 Infantry Brigade Combat Team whom I served in Iraq. I also acknowledge all the soldiers with whom I have served for the last thirty-two years. Their thoughts, deeds, sacrifices and courage have focused the foundational questions for my research and writing. I thank the senior military leaders, faculties, and students of the United States Army Sergeants Major Academy and the National Defense University. During my assignments, our seminar conversations provided me much to ponder regarding what it means to provide spiritual leadership as a pastor and professional military officer to our nation's military. They have also been a vital resource in reviewing this work.

It has taken me years to make my contributions to this manuscript. I thank Dr. Albert Pierce, Dr. Max Stackhouse, and Dr. John Yaeger, Dr. Mark McGuire, Dr. Lynn Thompson, and Chaplain Ken Sampson, who were my teachers and academic mentors through the research and writing process. I also wish to thank an extraordinary Army healer, Colonel Stephen Bowles, a combat leader and veteran advocate, Major Jeff Hall, and two fine Navy Judge Advocates, Captain Mike Boock and Captain Pat McCarthy. They were my "battle buddies" and "red team" in working through the human and legal dimensions of moral injury. Finally, I want to thank my writing partner, Duane, whose wisdom and competence have turned many loose ideas into a manuscript.

All of these conversations will remain private because they are either privileged communication or academic non-attribution. However, these conversations were behind the public source material I chose to use in writing this book. The following material is my own work and does not

xi

represent the official views of the US Army Chaplaincy, the US Military, the United States Government, or the Evangelical Lutheran Church in America.

—Jeff Zust

THERE HAVE BEEN MANY readers, advisors, and supporters who have been of immense help during the long course of this project. First, I thank Jeff Zust, my collaborator, for introducing me to the growing problem of moral injury several years ago. I am deeply grateful for what I have learned from him and the friendship we have grown. We would not have guessed that a casual barbecue with theretofore unlikely collaborators would lead to this important work together. God's Spirit has strange ways of bringing people together and I am grateful for it. Dr. Kristine Wallace, professor emerita of Classics at Rice University, was an inestimably valuable help in reading our work and guiding me with welcome detail especially with regard to early Greek literature. Her clarity and perspicuity sharpened us; where our work here is nevertheless dull, that is due fully to our resistance to her whetting stone and implies nothing less of her than sheer excellence. I am also grateful to the dozen members of the 2016 Communiversity Class at St. Ambrose University, Davenport, Iowa, for their constructive readings of our first draft; to colleague members of the editorial board of *dialog, A Journal of Theology*, who encouraged me in this work; and to many chaplains, social workers, veterans, and faith communities, particularly Christ the King Lutheran Church in Houston, Texas, who heard presentations of this work and contributed many reflections to its maturation. We are notably indebted to Chaplain Eric Wester and Chaplain David Colwell for their exceptional vision, wisdom, and guidance, with many further associations, giving us keener focus so finally to complete this book. Above all, I have had no better cheerleader and patient prodder than my wife, Joen. She has supported me through the frustrations that are common to writing anything of importance; thereby she proves the more how blessed I am that she is in my life.

—Duane Larson

———

CHAPTER 1

Introduction to Moral Injury

"How do I square my sense of self with what I had to do? How can I lead a good life, given what I did—even if what I did was justified?" Reconciling war's paradoxes, without dismissing the humanity of those whose lives were taken or whose livelihood destroyed, involves dealing with moral injury.

—Lieutenant General James Dubik[1]

IT HAPPENS A LOT. It happens back at "the house" after a vet's funeral. Or at the VFW. Or at the assisted living center where a vet now resides. It happens anywhere. We discover that the conversation partner is a vet who served in WWII, Korea, Vietnam, or more recently in the Middle East. Some prompting may have been required. Sometimes it takes a couple of beers. Often no prompt is necessary. Once the conversation turns to religion—natural for funerals and such!—the vet often says, "God will never forgive me for the things I had to do," though the active duty combatant usually resists using the "God" word.

"Really? Never forgive? Is any healing possible here?" These questions and more are the most likely candidates to enter our heads when we wonder how to answer and converse with this person. How can we or anyone provide care for this person? How can we really understand what is going on?

And there we go. Often we discover that the vet has carried this burden for all that lifetime not measured in single digits or teens. She or he has been carrying the awful invisible wounds of war. The invisible wounds of war have likely been known since the earliest recorded histories. Many now believe that even Homer's famous *Iliad* and *Odyssey* thought about

---

1. Sherman, *Afterwar*, xiv.

these invisible wounds. As we will explore later in this book, we believe that Augustine was concerned about war's invisible wounds on combatants and this influenced his own further development of the just war argument. Augustine even provided his own unique term to identify what we know as moral injury. He called it "soul sorrow." And so the opening terms of this book's title.

Somehow in Western experience, military command and society at large began to neglect, if not forget, the reality of war's invisible wounds. We now recognize the natural course of post-traumatic stress (PTS) and the unnatural debilitating phenomenon of post-traumatic stress disorder (PTSD). But different and less visible than PTSD are wounds of conscience that erupt into unhealthy behaviors. These are the invisible wounds that so many think are beyond forgiveness. These are the wounds of moral injury (MI). With this book we present an argument for how to understand, mitigate, and heal MI. This argument will echo much of current research and treatment. It will also differ significantly from many theories about the causes and cures of MI. To begin to understand MI we must compare and contrast it to other hidden wounds with which popular culture is more familiar.

Since Vietnam, we are grateful to have regained the common social value and need to honor and care for our veterans and fallen heroes. But we still grapple with how better to care for our wounded veterans. Their hidden wounds make proper recognition and treatment difficult. One of the more famous incidents involving the improper handling of invisible wounds is General Patton's slapping a private during the Sicily Campaign of World War II. Patton believed the soldier was a coward. Patton acted with the intention of "shaming" the soldier back into honorable service.

Patton's intention to return the soldier to duty wasn't out of line with the developing medical practice to return "combat fatigue" soldiers immediately to their units. Patton's actions may have been well intended. But he was wrong in both his assessment and his treatment methods. Private Paul Bennett was an experienced combat veteran from the North Africa campaign who "broke down" after several days of intense combat and witnessing the wounding of a close friend.

Today we would recognize Bennett's invisible wound as the result of post-traumatic stress (PTS) or a combat operational stress reaction (COSR). We would attempt to treat Bennett with more understanding and compassion, with the post-trauma goal of returning him to duty.[2] In spite of the slapping incident, Bennett returned to duty in World War II, and later

2. Both terms are current concepts use in military models for treating soldiers.

served in the Korean War.[3] His resilience is an example of how the presence of PTS or COSR, maybe MI too, need not be the final diagnosis of one's mental and spiritual health.

But perhaps we have not fully learned the lesson exhibited in the Patton/Bennett case. In 2006 the United States "surged" additional troops into Iraq. This action extended the time of then deployed combatants by three months. This was not a popular decision. There were many news stories about the hardships placed upon the military and their family members. When a reporter asked a young infantryman about his reaction to the extension, the combatant replied, "Great, I get to relive today 90 more times."[4]

The daily exposure to combat stress wears one down physically. It also normalizes a high adrenalin state of mind that keeps one alert. Any traumatic stress the young infantryman might have experienced could be described as a *"terror of one's own vulnerability"*[5] and if severe enough might have become PTSD. We also must recognize that the young infantryman might have sustained wounds caused by *"the horror of one's own immorality."*[6] These two phrases help distinguish PTSD from MI, while they may also, but not necessarily, be related.

Two case histories from the Vietnam era make the point. In 1992, the commanding officer of the destroyer USS Morton disobeyed both direct orders and US policy by rescuing fifty-two Vietnamese "boat people" who were lost at sea. For violating orders in favor of obeying his conscience, the CO was decorated by the US Navy and thanked by survivors and their families for the rest of his life. Would he have been morally injured had he followed orders and policy? Perhaps the answer comes in the case of the USS Dubuque. In this case, the USS Dubuque's CO followed policy and orders by *not* rescuing 110 Vietnamese refugees lost at sea. He did provide them food and water. But the crew members witnessed the drowning of many refugees as they were prevented from climbing aboard the amphibious assault ship. Thirty more of the refugees were cannibalized after they died by the survivors. The CO was convicted of dereliction of duty, which is to say that his

---

3. Perzo, "Gen. Patton." There were two incidents: a young soldier suffering from malaria (Private Charles Kuhl) and a four-year veteran (Private Paul Bennett).

4. CH Zust witnessed this interview at Forward Operating Base Loyalty, Iraq 2006.

5. Janoff-Bulman, *Shattered Assumptions*; Shay and Haynes, "Understanding Moral Injury and PTSD.'"

6. Shay and Haynes, "Understanding Moral Injury and PTSD.'" Haynes' distinction between the "terror of one's own vulnerability" and "the horror of one's own immorality" is perhaps one of the best rhetorical distinctions between PTSD and MI that we have found in print. It is also a distinction that Chaplain Zust presented many times in military circles several years before Haynes' publication.

duty to follow his conscience was higher than his duty to follow orders. He resigned thereafter. His crew too had to live with their inability to follow their consciences by following his orders.[7]

The case of the USS Dubuque exemplifies how MI results when one's values are betrayed by another. MI also can happen when a combatant must make the choice to kill a non-combatant when it appears that the person may present imminent danger to the combatant's unit, or when a non-combatant is regarded as "collateral damage." We will consider such examples later in this book. Our point now is that moral injury until recently has not been recognized as a real factor in the debilitation of military personnel. *Further, and this is our primary point, moral injury is a virtually inevitable consequence for combatants because war requires transgressing personal values so to protect the same values on the larger social scale.*

In sum, we ask combatants to go against their personal consciences so to secure a country-full of personal consciences. We ask our military personnel to accept the "horror of immorality" to protect us from the "terror of vulnerability." We cannot understand moral injury in our veterans without accepting this foundational premise for the making of war. This is to say that war is one way (unfortunately, the most practiced way) of trying to settle conflicts of human values and that combatants are morally injured almost inevitably and almost necessarily in the conduct of war.

James Childs, a theological ethicist, and veteran/military chaplain Wollom A. Jensen instruct us again of the reality and purpose of the military as a moral institution.[8] They summarize how the US Army's core values of loyalty, duty, respect, selfless service, honor, integrity, and personal courage are present in all US military branches. These values are practiced by military personnel, especially for the crucial matter of mutual bonding and protection. They are assumed to cohere with the larger sensibility of a person's belonging to the human race, such that connection with the humanity of the enemy, too, is assumed to belong too to the combatant's moral universe. Indeed, the military's distinctive moral values are intended not only to cohere with, but to become part of the "braided identity" that every person bears, having been shaped morally by family, friends, mentors, faith communities, service agencies, political movements, great ideas and great traditions, and more. We will consider more closely the concept of "braided identity" with psychological and philosophical frames in chapter 4. Insofar as a human person carries in oneself these influences and values, one is a "braided identity"

7. These cases, again, are referenced in Haynes.

8. Jensen and Childs, *Moral Warriors, Moral Wounds.*

who brings a complicated and story-filled self into the arena of war. How one can then "know oneself" after moral injury can be daunting.

Combatants become morally injured from striving to uphold their values. Some people may argue that "war bastardizes the noblest virtues of humanity."[9] Others argue that war is a context for practicing values. And others argue that our values challenge our participation in war, and subsequently, the legitimacy of our identity. We do not here argue which is the right position. We are simply stating that different moral stances focus uniquely on war, such that the very existence of a military is itself a moral argument with many internally competing moral visions. Combatants know this well.

The men and women who wage war and who are caught up in it are living beings defined and motivated by values that come from many sources. Filled with many competing moral visions within itself, the military itself is not the only value source for the service member. The military is a value-centric organization that refines personal and social values into its habituated codes of professional character. Thus, members of the military serve with a "braided" identity derived from personal values interwoven with professional character. In war, the military champions these codes of professional character while deploying its members into conditions that can unravel their braided identity. Here combatants become injured by the very values that legitimize their existence. In so saying, we restate in different terms our (ironic) statement above that we require our soldiers to protect morality by engaging immorality. The resulting injuries are the devastating, invisible wounds that we currently define as moral injury (MI).

We therefore define moral injury as follows: *Moral injury is the complex "soul" wound that results from a person's inability to resolve the difference between one's idealized values and one's perceived experiences. This wound produces a chain of emotions and maladaptive behaviors that corrode character and damage an individual's capacity for living.*[10]

9. The authors cannot identify the original source for this sentence. CH Zust came across it in 1984 and included it in his study notes and Bible. It has served as a point of reflection in his ministry over the years.

10. This definition combines some of the authors' research conclusions with elements from Jonathan Shay, Edward Tick, Rita Nakashima-Brock, Gabriella Lettini, Brett Litz et al., Crystal Page et al., William Nash, Joseph Currier, and David Bachelor. Their specific works and contributions will be cited later.

Soul Care, Souls, and Their Stories

How might we attend to the healing of moral injury? We will argue that we help the morally injured toward healing by assisting them in the construction and sharing of their personal stories. Perhaps surprisingly to the reader, this is a spiritual task. The history of helping psychically scarred people to "tell their stories" is, in fact, the history of "soul care." The word "soul" has a kind of funny history. Throughout Western history there have been times when the "soul" was thought to be an independent reality residing within a human being. A dominant strain in early Greek philosophical thought, called Neoplatonism, uniquely held this understanding. One could read of the "immortality of the soul." Indeed, one might also think quickly of "soul" and "spirit" as two terms denoting the same reality. Some religions even held and still hold that the "soul" is the *only* really real thing and that everything "material" is both unreal and bad.

It may also surprise the reader, then, that the tradition from which we authors write, Christianity, as well as Judaism and Islam, do not have or support this understanding of an "independent" soul, as if some divine doctor could possibly someday perform a "soulecthomy" on a very special surgical table to set people truly free from the cares of this world. The "soul," rather, refers to the whole integrated and inseparable identity of a human being. The Hebrew word *nephesh* referred to the enmeshed inseparable wonder of dust and spirit called "human" ("Adam") created by God. The Greek word *psyche* was used in the Christian New Testament to mean the same thing. *Psyche*, of course, also means "mind." "Mind," too, can mean nothing without inseparable relationship to flesh and blood. "Mind" and "soul" both function as reciprocal terms with varied accents that refer to the same invisible core of what makes human being, well, *human* being. Psychologists and psychiatrists who share the same root term, however secularly, narrowly, and even materially they may think of themselves, practice "soul care."

We who trust in a larger spiritual dimension that transcends and includes our own material world share in soul care. Like psychologists especially since Freud, but also long before Freud recognized the essential need for self-storytelling (what he called psychoanalysis), Christians, Jews, and Muslims have recognized the need of narrative construction, reconstruction, and communal sharing of narratives so to have positive individual and communal spiritual health. We will see how this is so, too, with healthy Greek societies, from whom we also have inherited so much vocabulary and worldview so to understand our humanity. We will underscore the importance of this task with regard to healing the invisible wounds of our military veterans today. This justifies also our argument in this book that recognition however one might name it of a spiritual and/or religious character of a combatant's life and person is required for the healing of MI. Healing MI invokes the practice of soul care. Healing MI means that the caregiver and the patient both go deeply into the patient's recall and telling of her story.

The presence and extent of veterans' moral injuries are revealed in their narratives of military service. Veterans form their narratives from an ongoing comparison between their values and their experiences. These narratives also reveal the "braided identity" that links their understanding of their vocation with their identity as moral human beings. Here, professional ethics (commanded by values derived from military ethos) combine with personal morality (governed by the values derived from humanity). The product is a living narrative that defines veterans' lives. These stories can reveal veterans' great resilience and post-combat healing. These stories can also reveal veterans' deep sorrows and invisible injuries.

The injuries include wounds to the psyche and spirit that affect both physical and social well-being. It is our intention to present an understanding—a model, as it were—of moral injury that will aid combatants, their family members, and their extended caring communities in the mitigation and healing of MI. Our model is based upon two premises: (1) military combatants are moral actors who strive to uphold their values, and (2) military combatants are moral actors who cannot fulfill the high obligations imposed upon them by their vocation and humanity. The first premise is based upon an idealized "moral harmony" between value and practice that is inherent within the military ethos. The second premise is based upon a "moral dissonance," a disharmony between values and practices that results from combat. Both premises come together in veterans' combat narratives.

Combatants do not get to choose their war. Nevertheless they: (1) choose how they will act in combat, and (2) judge their experiences, their actions, and the actions of others. We believe that moral injuries form from unreconciled issues between veterans' ultimate values and their perceptions of combat experiences. Thus, our model is based upon a triad relationship between moral development, moral judgment, and moral reconciliation. The relationship between these three elements is built during military training, practiced during combat operations, and re-experienced during re-deployment. Each of these three elements has a specific history that is a part of every veteran's enduring war narrative.

These war narratives last and define a lifetime. They also link veterans from different continents and generations. This linkage makes it possible to build a model for exploring the specific causes and effects of moral injuries. Veteran Matti Friedman describes the enduring power of his war narrative: "So important was this ritual [describing his hyper-alert state prior to assuming duties at his outpost] at such an important time in my life that this mode of consciousness became an instinct, the way an infant knows to hold its breath underwater. I still slip into it often. I'm there now."[11]

War may "happen" at the strategic levels of government. However, most combatants experience it at a tactical level where the direct short-term result of their choices either traumatizes them or provides for their resiliency. Ironically, the same choice can lead to both results, because the values that lead to injury are the same values that guide healing. Our argument may seem simple in theory, but it is intricate within the concrete experiences of veterans. In combat, circumstances are never clear and outcomes are seldom certain. Therefore, combatants assume a "readiness" attitude where, "absolutely anything can happen."[12] Some combatants verbalize this attitude as "wherever, whenever, whatever."[13] This "readiness attitude" doesn't justify "anything goes," but it acknowledges the reality of assuming risk while serving in volatile, uncertain, complex, and ambiguous contexts. Often, the risks in these missions can only be mitigated, not controlled.

Most of us do not live this way. We would choose to avoid these types of situations if we could. However, military members voluntarily serve in environments that defy the imagination. They risk life and limb as well as their psychological and spiritual well-being. The modern battlefield is a fluid environment where there is not always a linear connection between causes and effects. Marine Corps General Charles Krulak introduced the "three-block war" concept to explain the fluidity within a given operating environment. On one block units conduct traditional offensive and defensive operations, while on the second block they lead peacekeeping operations, and on the third block they participate in humanitarian aid.[14] Missions differ on each block, and so do the conditions for using lethal force. However, deadly threats exist within each block. Combatants understand this, and so do their enemies. The coexistence of these deadly threats blurs the lines between combatants' ideal values and the moral valuation of their real actions.

It is vital to understand that these three blocks are not necessarily defined by time and physical distance. The condensing of time and distance narrows abstract strategic risks into concrete personal threats that shape what individual combatants perceive and practice. At the strategic and operational levels this complexity indicates what is classically labeled as the

11. Friedman, *Pumpkinflowers*, Kindle loc. 75–76.

12. Couch and Doyle, *Navy SEALs*, Kindle loc. 75.

13. This is not a quote from military doctrine. It is a slang expression soldiers express in various forms to convey the need to be prepared.

14. Krulak, "Strategic Corporal."

"fog of war." However, at the tactical level, closest to the violence, combatants experience this fog as the "chaos of combat." The chaos of combat can be defined as "the three-second war." Here combatants have one second to identify a threat, the next second to figure out a plan, and the third second to act.[15] They have the rest of their lives to live with the consequences.

Combat is full of choices where participants put their personal morality and professional ethics on the line. The moral and the ethical become one. Values and practice flow together in nonrational and noncognitive combinations. Combatants' moral agency is often instinctual and measured in milliseconds under duress. They must react with whatever experience and competence they can utilize from their education and training. In these complex situations, combatants' reactions may override their values, but they do not nullify them. Their values are embodied within the competencies that define their vocation. Their values guide combatants' choices and inform their perceptions.

The perceptions of a combatant after an injurious action create a fundamental difference between traumatic injuries (resulting from fear-based responses to physical threats) and moral injuries (resulting from value-based responses to physical actions). This is the more exact meaning of what earlier were called the "fear of vulnerability" and the "terror of immorality." Veterans' narratives often reveal wounds that are distinct from medical conditions such as PTSD and traumatic brain injuries (TBI). Both PTSD and TBI are conditions related to physical injury and "fear/adrenaline-based" combat reactions. The reactions do not necessarily indicate or lead to moral injury. However, veterans who qualify for PTSD and TBI diagnoses may also present further troubled behavior and anxiety and others without PTSD or TBI may be psychologically and spiritually troubled by their combat experience. These issues are "value-based." These struggles must be recognized and treated as moral injuries.

As veterans process their experiences in the construction of their war narratives, their emotions, perceptions and physical reactions to combat affect their perceptions and judgments. They measure their choices and the choices of others by using their values to judge between shades of "good/bad," "right/wrong," "better/worse," and "appropriate/inappropriate."[16] Inevitably they also judge their own identity. At times this judgment affirms a moral harmony between value and practice. It also results in a moral dissonance between values and practice manifested in a variety of related

15. From CH Zust's assignment with the 2-2 Infantry Brigade Combat Team in Iraq 2006–2008.

16. Kidder, *How Good People Make Tough Choices*. Kidder describes similar types of categories that people use for moral reasoning.

behaviors. Veterans' inability to come to terms with their moral dissonance results in moral injuries.

A Challenge

To understand how and why this happens is the goal of MI research. Since 9/11, MI has become a "growth industry" and has its own story line. The stereotypical description of MI reads this way: (1) soldiers go to war; (2) they are traumatized (physically, psychologically, and spiritually) by what happens to them; (3) they return home with a sense of horror, shame, guilt, and betrayal; and (4) they either seek to readjust their lives to achieve inner peace, or they continue into some pattern of maladaptive behaviors.

We agree with this basic story line. However, we want to challenge certain premises used to describe the veterans who express moral injuries. What happens to combat veterans is more than a movement away from naiveté toward a second naiveté that some label as either post-traumatic disorder or growth.[17] Some veterans do fit this story line and they return to civilian life. Other veterans continue to serve in uniform and look for healing with a new sense of vocation. Narratives from both groups of veterans describe a profound change to their identity based upon their wartime experiences. Sometimes this reaction is guilt. At other times it is anger, betrayal, hostility, isolation, depression, cynicism, or withdrawal. These feelings can then drive any number of subsequent behaviors. The common factor in these behaviors and emotions is that veterans express them as moral evaluations of their combat experiences.

Many of the veterans we have spoken with resist the stereotypes that others place upon them. They process their specific experiences using unique sets of values that express their desired self-identity over and against their perceptions of who they have become. The narratives they construct out of a wide range of events convey complex emotions and behaviors. Introspection as such is a positive practice, particularly when acceptance of reality can lead to forgiveness, hope, and positive behavior modification. But unaccompanied introspection, particularly, is a much more treacherous road to follow if the veteran can only see in her narrative blame and condemnation, thus forcing her to live with shame and guilt.

Combat veterans have expressed these stories and issues to us. Their narratives communicate deep senses of habituated values forming their perceptions of their actions, inactions, and associations in combat. For

---

17. We are borrowing from the clinical distance arguments of Paul Ricoeur, whose hermeneutics illumine the maturation process contained within life narratives.

reasons of privileged communication, we have refrained from using their personal stories, except where given specific permission. Instead, we have complemented their stories with examples gleaned from the human sciences, philosophy, theology, literature, and current public sources such as veterans, researchers, academics, and healers. These singular narratives reveal common expressions of the complex relationship between the moral development, moral judgment and moral reconciliation of veterans' personal identity and professional character.

In the following pages we will propose a model to understand how moral standards and moral judgments interact in injuring and healing combat veterans. For any model to be effective it must empower combat veterans to express and critically interpret their own narratives. An adequate MI model will allow all of us to listen to what they are saying. Further, an adequate model will aid in the mitigation of MI before it happens as well as help heal MI after it happens. Therefore, a working MI model must include a moral argument for what it means to train for war, and serve in combat.

Thinking about MI in veterans requires a different perspective. It is easier to understand the origins of MI from the perspective of a victim than it is to understand it from the perspective of a perpetrator. Nevertheless, the differences between victim and perpetrator are important for distinguishing MI from other post-traumatic wounds such as PTSD and TBI. One receives either PTSD or TBI from being attacked ("the terror of vulnerability"). Granted, being the victim of attack alters the victim's values and perceptions of self. Moral wounding can and does happen to anyone who experiences traumatic events that transgress their belief systems. Here PTSD may join with MI. However, there are important distinctions between the wounding that results from unwilling participation in an event and the type of wounding that results from one's own active agency by *attacking, aiding an attack,* or *perceiving* oneself as *part of the attack.*

Why Focus on Military

Soldiers are moral actors. The purpose of the military is to use violence in defense of national interests. These interests require military members to act, and these actions affect their identity. Therefore, we will focus upon moral injury in military members, with applications to a wider audience. We also focus on military members because their suffering status today compels our attention and care. The suicide rate of twenty-two active duty and veteran military personnel a day demands attention and care for their families and friends and for our society, though MI will not explain every suicide.

We also believe that the incidence of MI in our active and veteran military members signals a growing danger for society at large. Attention to MI can help in understanding treating MI in other growing non-military populations, too, as with violence against women and racial violence. We hope that the specific focus on the military, however, will enable communities like churches, synagogues, and mosques to discern how they can assist in the healing of MI for their own military constituents.

Throughout this book, we will use the words "soldiers," "warriors," and "pirates" as moral terms to refer to the professional obligations and conduct of all who serve in the military. When the context requires, we will identify specific military branches. We choose this language to construct a moral argument that differentiates the moral conduct of professional "soldiers" from the ethical competence of "warriors" and the self-serving values of "pirates."[18] Each of these nouns refers to both individual and group actions and character. The specifics of this argument are vital for understanding the formation of MI.

Character and Competence

The character of professional soldiers is integral to the competence of a warrior, but they are not the same. Character refers to adherence to a code of conduct defined by core values. Competence refers to proficiency in a set of professional skills. In our preparation for this book, we received some negative feedback for stating that the purpose of a warrior was to kill the enemy in close combat. Our statement was taken from current sources used in training recruits for combat. Another person correctly stated that the strategic purpose of war was to defeat the enemy's will and capability for resistance. However, what is planned at the strategic level is different than what is done at the tactical level. At the tactical level hands get dirty and consciences get soiled.[19] In the Marine Corps' Warrior Song and the Army's Soldier's Creed, recruits specifically affirm that they are warriors ready to engage and destroy their enemy in close combat.[20] Both the Marines and the Army champion

18. The language of "pirate" is used within some military units to refer to rogue individuals who endanger their peers, civilians, and their mission. The authors are borrowing from a statement made by Air Force fighter pilot Colonel Jay Aanrud, and ethicist Dick Couch, *Tactical Ethic*.

19. Grossman, *On Killing*. Grossman describes the physical relationship between physical distance and killing in combat.

20. The precise wording can be found at: The Army Soldier's Creed, https://www.army.mil/values/soldiers.html, and the Marine Corps' Warrior Song, https://www.mca-marines.org/leatherneck/video/warrior-song-hard-corps.

the competent use of force. But neither the Soldier's Creed nor the Warrior Song deal with the professional character necessary for guiding the use of that force. Soldiers and Marines must get that from some other source if there is to be any hope of restraining or resolving MI.

In conversations with veterans we used the example of a video showing Marines urinating on the corpses of Taliban fighters. One World War II veteran defended the actions of the Marines by appealing to his own combat experiences, commenting that he gladly would have urinated on a German tank after combat. We agree with this veteran's analysis of the emotional combat stress, and can understand the post-combat release of anger directed toward a deadly enemy. We also noted that this World War II veteran did not tell us that he would gladly have urinated on the corpse of a German soldier. The distinction demonstrates the existence of moral limits even in the midst of the emotional chaos of combat. These limits can be matters of professional ethics, human morality, or both. Therefore, we need to ask: who sets these moral limits, teaches them, and who judges the trespass?

One of the Marines (Corporal Robert Richards) who participated in the above "urinating incident" was a combat veteran voluntarily serving his second tour out of a deep "sense of obligation." Richards didn't justify that it was OK for him to do what he did. He knew that "Marines don't do this kind of stuff." But in the duress of the moment he made a choice. We weren't there, and we have no moral superiority to judge him. He judged himself, and so did his Corps. He was demoted in rank from sergeant. During his second tour, a roadside bomb wounded him. Tragically, he died after returning home, likely from complications in the medications he took for his injuries.[21] Corporal Richards was buried with honors in Arlington National Cemetery. His struggles exemplify the narratives of many hurting veterans. Given the complex relationship between his physical wounds, his moral sense of duty, and the aftereffects of his demotion—there are many variables that contributed to his wellness, and we only know a part of his story. The hidden parts of his narrative, or similar narratives from other veterans, may reveal the difference between healing or further injury. They may help teach better, too, how to train in such a way that incidents of MI are reduced and more effectively treated.

As stated earlier, the military is a value-centric organization that blends professional ethics with human morality in defining its vocation. We include the spiritual dimensions of these values, not as specific theological constructions, but as an admission that our values provide life purpose by including dimensions that transcend our physical existence. The definition

21. Waggoner, "Retired Marine Sniper."

and practice of these values is often referred to as a "matter of conscience" as much as it is a "matter of cognitive thought." Some refer to this transcendent conscience as "soul." Because of this, we can speak of conscience and soul as constructions of self-identity and character without confining them to a specific theological tradition. In the military, highly individualized as well as social values are practiced in a pluralistic community that connects individuals across spiritual boundaries. Marine Corps veteran David Morris describes his blending of personal religious and professional values:

> War has made me as I am. . . . To me, asking, *Do you regret going to Iraq? Or Do you regret going into the Corps?* is almost like asking *Do you believe in God?* It's a really big question, a question that many people can answer with ease but one that tells you a lot about that person, how they see the world, how they see the role that fate plays in human life. But when I think about it, what I usually say is this: I believe in nature. I believe in brokenness. I believe in wholeness. I believe in whatever it is that connects the one to the other. . . . To fully appreciate the joys of this world, one must understand how temporary they are, how fragile human existence is.[22]

In the military the religious preference data say nothing about the specific values soldiers hold, and the level that these values shape their vocational identity. Recent research implies that soldiers share similar transcendent values while expressing different spiritual orientations.[23] Within the close relationships that soldiers develop in combat, these transcendent/spiritual values communicate variations of meaning, purpose, and identity. Specialist Tony Lagouranis, an Army interrogator in Iraq, describes an important conversation he had with an officer:

> After he [the evangelical Christian officer] saw me reading a Bible . . . we launched into a series of long conversations about his faith and his service, and I always left deeply impressed with his

22. Morris, *Evil Hours*, 170.

23. Pew, "'Nones' on the Rise." Recently the Pew Research Center documented a growing population who are "less religious than the public at large on many conventional measures . . . [but] this group professes personal religious or spiritual values in some way." The Pew Foundation labeled this group the "Nones" (meaning no religious affiliation). In the military a similar group is labeled "No Preference" (from the religious preference choice military members list in their personnel records). A comparison of the Pew data with the military religious profile data shows that this group of nonaffiliated or no preference individuals makes up between 24–26 percent of the population of both military and civilian populations. The data also shows that both civilian and military populations have similar religious preferences with about 5 percent describing themselves as atheist or agnostic. See Pew, "U.S. Public Becoming Less Religious."

commitment to both, not to mention his patience with pointed questions from a committed agnostic. I needed this kind of conversation. I am not religious, or even "spiritual," but at the time I was struggling daily with how my duties often ran up against my morals. Franklin had thought deeply about how his service was in some ways incompatible with Christianity, and he was willing to talk openly about it. The chance to think about bigger questions for a while helped me prepare for what came next.[24]

In dealing with moral injuries we cannot separate the military from the human, the ethical from the moral, or the spiritual from the physical. Nor can we separate mitigation from healing. Moral injuries exist within the structures where combat veterans find purpose, and they reside in the narratives where they express meaning.

The paradox of war is embodied in two related myths.[25] The first myth states that fighting within the rules of engagement during a "just" war should not trouble a soldier's conscience. The second myth states that building a resilient conscience provides immunity from the effects of war. Veterans' war narratives directly challenge both myths. These challenges reveal the complex relationship between fighting well and resiliency to war's injurious effects. Ethicist Michael Walzer captures the essence of this relationship when he writes, "But the truth is that most of us want, even in war, to act or seem to act morally. And we want that, most simply because we know what morality means (at least, we know what it is generally thought to mean)."[26]

Soldiers go to war with a set of personal and professional values that form their morality and guide their conduct. Combat simultaneously stresses both their values and conduct, and in doing so alters their self-identity and community. A Special Forces soldier remembers his reaction after he killed a teenage enemy who was trying to shoot him: "He [the

---

24. Lagouranis and Mikaelian, *Fear Up Harsh*, 221.

25. The word choice of "myth" here is deliberate. Popular usage today equates "myth" with "lie." Technically, however, a myth is a dramatic untruth that communicates a larger truth, usually about the character of human existence. For example, an ancient myth prevalent in all Mideast-born primitive religions, especially focused in the Babylonian *Epic of Gilgamesh*, told of a global flood that wiped out the living things of land and air. Such stories are not to be taken as factual, but to represent, among other things, the seemingly impetuous character of "the gods" (a.k.a. nature) and the heroic resilience of human beings. "Myth" suggests the partnership of untrue facts and true meanings even when embedded in the same term. Soldiers have demonstrated a particular understanding and even a wry affection for the term in the cultural context of the military.

26. Walzer, *Just and Unjust Wars*, 20.

enemy soldier] just laid there. I dropped my weapon and cried."[27] Both of these emotional responses are linked with a deeper sense of morality that transcends legal codes and social permissions. Lieutenant General Dubik summarizes soldiers' moral challenge.

> War changes lives. War is the realm of the paradoxical: the morally repugnant is the morally permissible, and even the morally necessary.... War justifies—more importantly, demands—what, in peacetime, would be unjustifiable: the destruction of the lives and happiness of others. Those who fight live this paradox day in and day out. In a very real way, war is the abnormal ruled normal. Such a life begs important questions, questions that often don't arise until years after a war: "What kind of person am I to have done this?"[28]

Our Agenda

Soldiers are moral actors in a vocation designed to use violent force. Participation in combat creates ample opportunities for moral dissonance. Left unaddressed, this dissonance leads to moral injury. However, moral dissonance can also be the conscientious signal to seek paths of healing, because the conflicting values that drive both injury and healing are often the same. The sources of injury and the resources for healing lie within the braided identity of the human soldier.

The mitigation and healing of moral injury must include the transcendent, spiritual values that we use to give purpose to our existence and guide our lives. MI grows out of a challenge to the ultimate values that define character and identity. The last decade of war has demonstrated how political, cultural, vocational, human, and spiritual dimensions influence the formation of moral injury in soldiers and their families. Any model for working with moral injury needs to help us understand how these dimensions connect values (moral voice) with conduct (moral agency). This connection begins with a specific understanding of the development of moral conscience and professional ethics. Understanding this development begins by listening to the powerful values driving veterans' war narratives.

The content in this book is the authors' own work and does not reflect the official positions of our church or government. We have maintained privileged communication with those we consulted, unless specifically granted

---

27. Grossman, *On Killing*, Kindle loc. 1677.
28. Lieutenant General (Retired) James Dubik, as quoted in Sherman, *Afterwar*, xiv.

permission to use these conversations in our work. We are the first to concede that the model presented in this book needs to be the subject of future research and discussion, and we heartily invite open communication.

We seek to address those who experience moral injury and those who care for the morally injured. Our primary audience, as we have noted, is soldiers and those who lead and care for them. However, we also have a larger audience in mind. The moral injuries experienced by soldiers are also experienced within society. Soldiers are a sample of those with invisible wounds. Their experiences may serve as "the canary in the coal mine" to alert us to the moral wounding many others are experiencing in our larger culture.

In the following chapters we will present a model for recognizing, mitigating, and healing moral injury. This model will affect how soldiers train, operate, and regenerate.

- Chapter 2 further defines moral injury and introduces the authors' two-mirror model to understand how MI occurs.

- Chapter 3 surveys current practices for the healing of MI and draws from them to develop further the two-mirror model, as well as to establish the necessary roles of "moral voice," "moral agency," and "judgment" so to redress MI.

- Chapter 4 surveys psychological and philosophical theories of what it means to be human, to be *self*-aware, and to have a "conscience."

- Chapter 5 draws from military developmental theory and practice to chart the "ideal" development of military character.

- Chapter 6 introduces the acronym FRAME (fidelity, responsibility, accountability, maturity, effectiveness) as a criteriology for judging military character and shaping one's sense of vocation.

- Chapter 7 engages the theme of "The Centurion" in Luke-Acts as an example of how scriptures can inform vocation and provide symbolic purposeful content for the narrative reconstruction necessary for healing MI.

- Chapter 8 reviews several important theological themes—creation, human identity, sin, justification, the theology of the cross—that provide the mitigating and healing means for living realistically and hopefully.

- Chapter 9 concludes the book by reflecting on the necessary roles of confession and repentance, distinct from the category of reconciliation, finally to assay how spiritual language allies with adaptive disclosure therapy, within the context of a caring community, so that the sorrowing soul will again know the solidarity of God.

- The appendix is recommended for readers who wish to go further with two case studies, the My Lai massacre and drone warfare. They show how mission command causally effects formation of moral dissonance in soldiers.

So, we invite the reader into a serious conversation about moral injury beginning with how the character by which soldiers live is well or poorly constructed. We hope that our considerations will be incorporated into the practices of all who provide education, leadership, and care in the places where soldiers "live, work and have their being."[29] Further, we hope that the attention given here to one group proven to be so vulnerable to moral injury will also inspire care for the many people in society at large for whom moral injury looms even as a new pandemic.

29. The Apostle Paul used this quote borrowed from the Greek poet Epimenides to set up a similar public conversation in a pluralistic environment. Paul's use of the quote sets the scope of the human condition that he wishes to address. See Acts 17:28.

CHAPTER 2

The Two-Mirror Model of Moral Injury

An Interpretive Tool for Understanding War Narratives

It is a big step to take another human life. It is not to be done lightly. I know of men who have taken life needlessly in other conflicts, I can assure you they live with the Mark of Cain upon them.

—Lieutenant Colonel Tim Collins[1]

The people who survived the sword found grace in the wilderness.

—Jeremiah 31:2[2]

Can any of us imagine the path a veteran travels from the battlefield to home? Sometimes this is a seemingly endless journey littered by moral injuries that make travel unbearable. War narratives reveal the signs of these otherwise invisible injuries. Thus, war narratives are the most accessible way of learning about the hidden effects of combat upon soldiers and their family members. These narratives also reveal "touch points" by which veterans can reconcile their experiences with their identities in order truly to return "home."

The path from diagnosis to a helpful prescription is, even so, unclear. Definitive studies, legal medical diagnoses, and universal definitions of MI

---

1. "Tim Collins' Iraq War Speech," given by Colonel Collins to his soldiers prior to attacking into Iraq in 2003.

2. Jer 31:2 ESV.

do not exist. But we do know that moral injuries exist because soldiers who experience these injuries tell us about them in their stories. It is not difficult to find media sources containing veterans' war narratives witnessing to the powerful moral effects from combat upon their lives. These soldiers voice deep emotions driven by transgressed values that we must respect. The primary question is, "how do we interpret these narratives?"

Each war narrative includes common elements of moral voice and moral agency for things soldiers did, failed to do, or were associated with. It is not enough only to acknowledge that veterans are "hurting" from war. A suitable theory or model is needed to understand and help them deal with their pain. Such a model begins with a definition that guides one's understanding of what combat veterans are saying. Because a commonly accepted definition for moral injury does not exist, we proposed in chapter one our own hybrid definition. It combines elements from professionals who currently work with veterans who display signs of moral injury. *Moral injury is the complex "soul" wound that results from a person's inability to resolve the moral dissonance between their idealized values and their perceived experiences. This wound produces a chain of emotions and maladaptive behaviors that corrode character and damage an individual's capacity for living.*[3]

Current literature uses terms such as "morally injurious events" (MIEs), "moral pain," and "moral emotions" to explain the formation and effects of MI. We will argue that "moral dissonance" is an accurate term that allows us to describe the dynamic processes connecting MIEs with the formation of moral pain. One could almost propose a mathematical equation that displays how these terms and events relate, wherein MIE represents morally injurious event, MP is moral pain, and MD refers to moral dissonance. These are all discrete matters in the literature. Thus $MIE + MP \rightarrow MD$. And if moral dissonance is left unaddressed, and the damage compounds, then $MD \rightarrow MI$. Together these events and pain are elements of a destructive dissonance that results in moral injury.

As stated earlier, moral dissonance is the effects from incongruence between soldiers' values and practice. It is the opposite of moral harmony, but should not be considered as a simple lack of integrity or an act of hypocrisy. Moral dissonance is a complex reaction to the violation of values that define self-identity. Others can initiate this violation or it can also be self-inflicted. In the military, self-identity is enmeshed with professional character, which itself combines professional ethics with personal morality. Violations to this blend generate moral dissonance that can resonate

---

3. This definition combines some of the author's research conclusions with elements from Jonathan Shay, Edward Tick, Brett Litz et al., Crystal Park et al., William Nash, Joseph Currier, Rita Nakashima-Brock, Gabriella Lettini and David Bachelor.

throughout a veteran's life and affect multiple aspects of his/her existence. In this chapter we will introduce a model—the two-mirror model—for interpreting the moral dissonance in soldiers' war narratives. We will use this model to understand moral injury from the perspective of those who suffer its effects. With proper understanding, we can then examine ways to mitigate and heal moral injuries.

Morally injurious events (e.g., a sniper's tragic choice to kill a young child carrying a weapon) cause moral dissonance. MIEs evoke strong emotions resulting from practical conduct disconnected from the desired values that form a soldier's self-identity (e.g., soldiers do not kill noncombatants, and good human beings do not kill children). Values guide our behavior and help resolve ethical and moral questions. Sometimes values will conflict. For example, a good soldier may find that the absolute value of protecting one's unit from all threats might conflict with the value that good human beings defend their friends when the friend poses a risk to the unit, or vice versa. The dissonance from such events occurs for many reasons. Some moral dissonance is healthy and may actually serve as an alarm for a soldier to act differently. At moderate levels moral dissonance can occur without causing moral injuries.

However, moral injuries cannot occur without moral dissonance. Severe levels of moral dissonance are generated from significant separations between values and practice. These severe levels result in moral judgments that damage self-identity and social relationships. Severe levels of moral dissonance contain judgments and perceptions that cannot easily be overcome. These perceptions and judgments may come from inside or outside of the soldiers, and cannot be reconciled without addressing the original sources of the moral dissonance creating them. The damage from this process is moral injury, and moral dissonance is the causal agent of the injury.

Moral pain, also called moral emotion, manifests itself as the audible and visible expression of moral dissonance. It is a part of the symptomology of MI, but not the injury or the causal agent of injury. Significant emotions such as grief, anger, shame, betrayal cynicism, hostility, apathy, condemnation, and guilt are often linked with visible behaviors such as depression, chemical dependencies, antisocial lifestyles, relationship difficulties, and self-destruction.[4] However, this linkage says nothing about the source of the emotions or the cause of the behaviors. Moral emotions and the related behaviors are only the presenting symptoms (or outward expressions) of a hidden, complex injury.[5] To focus on the types of MIEs, forms of moral

4. Currier et al., "Role of Moral Emotions," 249–62.
5. Shay, *Odysseus in America*, Kindle loc. 3035.

pain, and categories of behavior is to disregard the source of the moral injury. The presence of moral dissonance begins the hurting, and it can generate and continue to drive a spectrum of enduring emotions that contribute
to a multitude of behaviors. The cumulative effects from this dissonance
determine the severity of a moral injury. Thus it is vital to understand the
formation of moral dissonance from the veteran's perspective, and this understanding is only possible through listening to the unique war narratives
of those who claim to suffer moral injuries.

An essential practice for healing MI is to accompany the injured
through the task of deconstructing and reconstructing their "war narrative." Deconstructing war narratives reveals veterans' perceptions of the
conflicting values and practices that generate their moral dissonance. The
deconstruction process also reveals core values and purposes that promote
healing through the construction of a reconciling narrative that restores the
soldier's genuine identity. With this book, we hope to guide soldiers, family
members, and healers through this process. The two-mirror model is a good
way to start.

The Two-Mirror Model[6] (TMM) of Moral Injury[7]

6. In the humanities and sciences, a "model" is much more than a mere example.
It is a guide or heuristic that trains one's thinking toward a certain end or understanding, after which the "model" may not be necessary any longer. In this respect, "model"
functions like "framework" within military culture. Were this book's readership only
military, "two-mirror framework" (TMF) would be the preferred term. Also, since
"two-mirror framework" could be confusing as a subset of larger frameworks (FRAME,
this book, etc.), "model" seems to be in this context a better choice.

7. Olson, *Counseling Teenagers*, 29–32.

The TMM is composed of three interactive processes: the development of moral voice, the judgment of moral agency, and the formation of moral dissonance. The relationship between these three processes forms moral injuries and enables moral healing. The TMM is based upon a clinical model used by Dr. Keith Olson to describe the comparative process people use in forming self-identity. Each mirror reflects a self-image or "selfie" that soldiers use to monitor their human identity and military character. These mirrors may reflect a snapshot of a particular moment in time, or they can reflect multiple frames of a video that soldiers replay. These mirrors do not reflect each other. They reflect separately the conflicting perspectives of the morally injured soldier. They simultaneously reflect images that serve as normative images of life as it "should be" (ideal) and life as it is "judged to be" (perceived). These "dual reflections" need to be considered as two perspectives by which a soldier understands his or her identity and character.

The first mirror reflects the moral development processes that compose the "ideal" self. This reflection is the product of habituated values and reasoning processes that obligate and guide conduct. The "ideal self" is a reflection of a soldier's moral voice.[8] Moral voice is developed over time from individual, social, cognitive, and emotional processes. Soldiers' moral voices consist of the core values that compose their personal identity and their military character. Images of the "ideal self" form as soldiers consider what they "ought" to do. These images reflect the "ideal" standards of life, as "it should be." Moral voice informs soldiers' moral agency, and becomes the basis for their moral judgments.

The second mirror reflects the moral judgment processes that compose the "perceived" self. This reflection is the product of reasoning processes, reactions, and choices that determine conduct. The "perceived self" is a reflection of a soldier's moral agency. Moral agency is the actual conduct of soldiers acting or failing to act upon their moral voice. Reflections of the "perceived self" form as soldiers apply the ideal standards of their moral voice to their specific conduct. These reflections are the products of soldiers' "real-time" choices as well as the historical consequences from what they did (commission), what they failed to do (omission), or what they experienced (association). The congruence between a soldier's ideal and perceived reflections results in a moral harmony or a moral dissonance that impacts one's self-image.

The origins and effects of moral dissonance contribute to the third TMM process. Differences and distances between a soldier's "ideal" and "perceived" images combine to form a fused image of self-identity. However,

---

8. Gilligan, *In a Different Voice*, and Gentile, *Giving Voice to Values*.

it is not an accurate reflection of a soldier's genuine being because this fused image is distorted by the tension between ideals and perceptions. From the positive side, moral dissonance is driven by soldiers' senses of fidelity, responsibility, accountability, maturity, and efficacy.

These five senses can be remembered by the acronym FRAME. Each sense represents specific values that are both normative and descriptive of soldiers' identity and character. All five senses are present in soldiers' war narratives as concrete ideals and perceptions of their moral voice and agency. *Fidelity* is the degree of "buy-in" to the core values and standards that define a soldier's moral voice. *Responsibility* is the level of ownership a soldier accepts for his/her moral agency. *Accountability* is the blame or culpability a soldier assigns to his/her agency. *Maturity* is the influence of experience and development that define soldiers' capacity for exercising their moral agency. *Efficacy* is interaction between context and empowerment that affect a soldier's capability to exercise moral agency. Together, these five senses form a way to name and understand the origins and causes of moral dissonance generated between a soldier's ideal and perceived self-reflections.

Moral dissonance causes moral injury, but MI is seldom the presenting problem. Continuing here with the visual metaphor, dissonance needs to be considered as a space between competing perceptions within one's own mind. It is vital to remember that moral dissonance is an active tension between voice and agency, between one's moral conviction and act, which can generate one's competing, even mutually hostile, perceptions of a given morally-laden situation. This tension also enables mitigation and healing.[9] Minimal separations between voice and agency cause levels of dissonance that can influence change.[10] Great separations between voice and agency cause severe levels of moral dissonance that can result in pathologies. At these extreme levels, moral dissonance can be the *cause* of PTSD instead of a symptom. Soldiers, continual "replaying" of their conflicting ideals and perceptions generates a continuum of dissonance that affects both their self-identity and their social relationships. Moral dissonance may be caused by MIEs, but it continues and amplifies in complex emotions such as guilt, shame, disgust, anger, hostility, despair and betrayal. These emotions manifest as: survivor guilt, demonic/evil guilt, moral/spiritual guilt, betrayal/abandonment guilt, and superman/superwoman guilt.[11] More noticeably,

---

9. Kashtan, "Moral Dissonance."

10. Olson, *Counseling Teenagers*, 26–32.

11. For an explanation of the guilt process in relationship with PTSD, see Huang, "Combat Exposure," 41–48; and Litz et al., "Moral Injury and Moral Repair."

these complex emotions may drive behaviors that lead to marital problems, isolation, depression, chemical dependency, anger issues, grief issues, suicides, PTSD or any number of "personal issues."

The insidious part of MI is that the linear relationship between cause and effect is "not there." What "is there" is a complex hidden injury that reveals itself in visible symptoms. This does not mean that the visible symptoms should not be treated. Just the opposite, they need to be treated by addressing the causes of soldiers' moral dissonance. The TMM provides a tool for identifying and understanding the moral dissonance that is present within soldier's war narratives.

The Formation of Damaging War Narratives

Soldiers' war narratives contain their ideals and perceptions of their combat experiences. Their spoken words, as well as their unspoken memories, reveal their moral dissonance in the form of their voice and moral agency stemming from specific events. War narratives reveal soldiers conscientiously wrestling with "conflicts and impediments that can frustrate otherwise successful action."[12] Often these wrestling matches result from specific events (morally injurious events) that are "crystallizing moments" where soldiers are active agents in choices that violate their moral voice. Author David Wood captures the essence of these crystallizing moments as soldiers "sense that their fundamental understanding of right and wrong has been violated and the grief, numbness or guilt often ensues."[13] Moral dissonance is life altering and produces deep injuries that are immune to social protests and quick absolutions such as "thank you for your service."[14] When this happens, soldiers' identity and character are at risk.

Basic training recruits are often told to "leave your brains in the footlocker." The opposite is true in combat, where circumstances can easily go from "zero to stupid."[15] During combat, soldiers must engage their brains in order to survive and win. General Stanley McChrystal encouraged his special operations soldiers to "get your brains out of your footlocker," in order to cognitively connect with their rapidly changing operational environ-

12. Sherman, *Fabric of Character*.

13. Wood, "Warrior's Moral Dilemma."

14. The following authors explain the lightning rod that this phrase engenders within morally injured soldiers due to the depth of issues associated with their service: Sherman, *After War*; and Finkel, *Thank You for Your Service*.

15. A phrase used by soldiers to express the jumbling of time and meaning during combat conditions. This jumbling includes moral and ethical considerations.

ments.[16] He also advocated that his soldiers needed to get their consciences out of their footlockers in order to morally function in these ethically gray environments. In response to a question about losing his humanity in making ethical decisions to target a high-profile terrorist, he responded with the obligation for soldiers to connect their moral voice with their agency. "Every soldier has to ask himself that [question]. The danger of the operators [soldiers] drawing the conclusion that anything is worth it to stop Zarqawi is a natural conclusion. But it is a dangerous conclusion, because once you step away from your humanity, then I'm not sure where you are."[17]

Keeping in step with humanity is a foundational counsel for mitigating and reconciling moral injuries. This is the first step in healing moral dissonance. Not everyone will agree with General McChrystal's decisions. However, his moral struggle to maintain his human identity with his military character is an effective example for all soldiers.

Moral injuries damage veterans' self-identity and significant relationships. The damage begins from within, from the soldiers' psyches. Thus, soldiers often do not realize the extent of their injuries until they return home from combat. Psychiatrists, doctors, chaplains, social workers and other health care professionals are beginning to connect these invisible injuries with a measurable rise of mental health issues among combat veterans.[18] Recent studies of Iraq and Afghanistan war veterans (serving between 2001–2007) reported that both deployed and non-deployed veterans had a significantly higher suicide risk compared to the US general population. However, other studies report that current deployed veterans showed a lower risk of suicide when compared to populations of non-deployed veterans.[19] One often-cited statistic is that an average of twenty-two veterans commit suicide every day. To be fair, this statistic doesn't directly correlate the combat experiences of these veterans with their deaths. So, it is improper to link these tragic deaths directly to MI, PTSD, or TBI.[20] From the quantitative perspective, there indeed are no data showing moral injuries as causal agents of suicides or any specific behavior. Furthermore, no study documents how moral injuries affect family members and communities. Investigated qualitatively, correlation and causation may be discerned by focusing keen attention to the war narratives of combat veterans.

16. McChrystal et al., *Team of Teams*, 155–71.
17. McChrystal, "Good, Bad, and Ugly."
18. American Psychological Association, "Critical Need."
19. US Department of Veterans Affairs, "Suicide Risk."
20. Lee, "Missing Context."

Multiple behaviors and expressions of moral pain are listed by veterans and family members in these narratives. These narratives form a recognizable pattern in the expressed moral dissonance that soldiers associate with their issues. Soldiers' narratives reveal their struggles for survival through combat and their searches for healing grace and peace as they return home. These are not abstract struggles. They are concrete experiences involving highly honored values embodied in flesh-and-blood events.

Combat can "recalibrate" soldiers' moral compasses and leave them with the task of reorienting the values that determine their self-identity. Army Ranger Nate Self describes the two wars he fought during his service. The first war was the disorienting trauma of combat and the second war was his inner battle to reorient his "bearings" after returning home. In making the transition between combat and home, Self's character as a soldier no longer fit with his identity as a husband and a father. Usually a man of professed religious faith, he experienced emotions that changed his character and his self-image. For Self, reconnecting his values with significant relationships in his daily life slowly helped him reconcile his emotional trauma. Experiencing this healing path is an active struggle. Special Forces Soldier Barry Beikirch, a Medal of Honor recipient, states that this experience is where "life feels like a never-ending game of fifty-two card pickup."[21] The disorienting emotions and cognitions of which Self and Beikirch speak signal the presence of moral dissonance and possible moral injuries.

Beikirch's never-ending game of scattered cards is a simile for the disconnected values and purposes that compose his self-identity. This disconnect is similar to the last scene of the movie *The Hurt Locker*. In this scene (titled "The Warriors' Dilemma") a veteran who recently returned from Iraq is losing his bearings between war and home and is caught in a widening gulf between himself and his family. His disorientation is an internal, emotional distance between what he values and what he experiences. At one point, this veteran tells his infant son that he will reach a point in life where "some of the things you loved might not seem so special anymore." In the movie's penultimate scene the veteran is portrayed as alone in a large grocery store, unable to decide what he needs, while isolated from his wife who is preparing dinner in their small kitchen. The film ends with the veteran returning to combat in Iraq. The viewer gets the impression that the soldier does this because combat is where he feels most connected. Sebastian Junger writes, "Maybe the ultimate wound is the one that makes you miss the war you got it in."[22]

21. Self, *Two Wars*, 357–58.
22. Junger, *War*, 268.

Soldiers operate with a moral voice that psychologists Eric Erickson and Carol Gilligan describe as an inner voice of "self-observation, self-guidance, and self-punishment."[23] Some describe this inner voice as a moral "conscience" or as an element of "soul." Soldiers' moral voices (their FRAME senses) express themselves in how they link their specific ethical duties with their broader moral obligations. Moral dissonance happens when soldiers cannot fulfill their duties and obligations. Moral injury occurs when this dissonance becomes irreconcilable and affects behavior. Thus, the specific values supporting soldiers' moral voice cannot be separated from their practice of moral agency. Their war narratives become the report card for their service, because these narratives reveal the specific causes and sources of their moral dissonance. Recognition of these origins is essential for healing moral injuries. It is not enough to identify soldiers' behaviors and their moral pain linked to morally injurious events. It is equally important to reconstruct the ethical and moral criteria they use to process their specific emotions and traumatic events. This reconstruction addresses the roots of moral dissonance so that genuine healing can begin.

The goal of the healing process is reconciliation of the tensively related images and the "space" between them that amplified the moral dissonance. The conditions for reconciliation can be emplaced before combat's almost necessary generation of moral dissonance. This is mitigation, and it is a matter of soldiers' training and combat leadership. However, reconciliation also needs to continue post-combat when soldiers begin to reengage with their lives. Mitigation is rarely one-hundred percent effective on "the front end. And reconciliation on the "back end" normally will take time. Some events in combat are irreconcilable due to time and proximity. So, some clinical distance is necessary in order to gain perspective, and the gain of a better perspective is naturally inhibited because soldiers suppress their perceptions of combat. At times suppression is an essential survival mechanism, but moral dissonance from these events remains active within a soldier's psyche or soul.

Moral dissonance and moral injuries occur outside of the military. But, military service in combat creates specific contributions to the formation of moral dissonance that are unique. Ideally, we are raised to know the difference between right and wrong, and we live by values that guide our conduct. These guides can differ between individuals and social groups. However, when individuals enter military service they become bound to a uniform ethical code that incorporates these individual and moral differences. This

---

23. This definition is developed from two foundational works: Chu and Gilligan, *When Boys Become Boys*, 36; Gilligan, *In a Different Voice*.

uniform code of values and expectations forms a level of vocational obligation to the moral requirements faced by a civilian. In peacetime, we live in a world of competing moral claims that complicate our choices. Conditions in war make these choices more complex. Combat places soldiers in life-and-death situations that stress their capability to do the right thing. These situations are not only about vulnerability to personal injury; they also include the capability to inflict personal injuries. The capability to inflict injury adds dimensions of moral voice and moral agency that are unique to soldiers.

It is not difficult to imagine the moral injury done to victims of an atrocity or a crime. In these cases some illegal or immoral act or actor has betrayed their basic values. This betrayal contributes to a change in their identity. However, these illegal acts haven't challenged the validity of their basic values. For example, a person may live by a code of fairness and trust that defines his/her personal character and social responsibility. If this person is the victim of an assault, the unfairness of the attack may violate that person's sense of fairness, and the resulting moral dissonance alters his/her character, *but it does not change the legitimacy of fairness and trust.* Just the opposite, the assault has validated the legitimacy of these values, even though the event itself generated moral dissonance within the victim, who has no responsibility for causing the event.

The attribution of moral agency constitutes the difference between moral victims and moral actors. Suppose that you are a passenger in a fatal two-car accident. This is a significant traumatic event. Now suppose that you were the driver of one of the vehicles involved. Regardless of your physical injuries, your role as a driver changes you from a victim to an actor by adding elements of control and responsibility to the incident. However, at this point there are many variables to what caused the accident, and these variables do not necessarily challenge your core values. Now suppose, that you are the driver after having one glass of wine. This one glass may or may not have placed you over a legal limit or impaired your driving ability, but it has added another dimension to assigning accountability for the incident. The glass of wine has introduced a moral element involving your values and your judgment. Suppose, further, that some of the fatalities in the crash are friends or family. There also may be additional moral layers placed upon you as the driver based upon your fidelity to a system of values, and your maturity level to process your conflicting emotions and values. It is logical to suppose that all these factors combined with your sense of efficacy would cause you to consider how you could or should have prevented the crash. Finally, suppose that you as the driver are obligated by a legitimate authority to get behind the wheel and drive, regardless of your physical or mental condition. This obligation places an additional requirement upon your capability to prevent the accident. This is how the moral senses of FRAME (fidelity, responsibility, accountability, maturity, and efficacy) introduce dimensions of moral agency that differentiate the effects upon moral actors and moral victims.

Perhaps this hypothetical scenario seems insensitive, because you have similar personal experiences. However, the scenario does express the differences separating moral actors from moral victims that are critical factors for understanding moral injuries. Different emotional responses may originate from a traumatic event. Whatever their differences, these emotions are associated with conflicting senses of FRAME generating the moral dissonance that inflicts moral injury in civilians and soldiers.

Civilians can and do experience moral injuries. Recently Sue Klebold, the mother of one of the Columbine High School shooters, wrote about her feelings of grief for her son and the moral pain his actions caused her and other families. "I would give my life to reverse what happened that day. In fact, I would gladly give my own in exchange for just one of the lives that was lost. Yet I know that such a trade is impossible. Nothing I will ever be able to do or say can possibly atone for the massacre."[24]

Mrs. Klebold is expressing moral pain in the form of grief as a mother, and empathy toward the families of the victims. Her pain resonates from moral dissonance caused by her responsibility as the mother of one of the shooters. Her responsibility is a testimony to the goodness she believes and longs for. It is also an expression of the moral voice and agency she voluntarily assumes as a loving mother. Her moral dissonance is real and understandable, but her sense of responsibility is not the same as the ethical responsibility defined by the vocational obligations of a professional.

Klebold's moral agency differs from the moral agency expressed by Merchant Marine Captain Glenn. He diverted his cargo ship from its scheduled route in order to rescue survivors from a sinking ship adrift on the ocean. Believing that he was put on this planet for such moments, Glenn reflects upon the effects of his moral responsibility: "What still bothers me to this day is the thought that when we picked up those two small heads in the water, what if there were four more heads further off who could see us because we had our lights on. They could see our ship and they would see us leave. That still bothers me."[25]

Now compare Sue Klebold's and Captain Glenn's moral agency with a statement made by Admiral David McDonald, who served as the Chief of Naval Operations at the beginning of the Vietnam War. In reconsidering

24. Klebold, *Mother's Reckoning*, Kindle loc. 205.
25. George, *Ninety Percent of Everything*, 218.

his leadership role in planning and conducting the Vietnam War, he stated, "Maybe we military men were all weak. Maybe we should have stood up and pounded the table [in protest]. . . . I was part of it and I'm sort of ashamed of myself too. At times I wonder why did I go along with this kind of stuff?"[26]

Admiral McDonald's words are less empathetic than Sue Klebold's or Captain Glenn's. All three people express moral dissonance, but the origins for their dissonance are different. Glen and McDonald convey a different sense of moral voice and agency that comes from their vocational obligation as sailors. Captain Glenn and Admiral McDonald share similar responsibilities as commanders of ships. However, Captain Glenn didn't put those victims in the ocean, and Sue Klebold didn't train and command her son to harm others. Admiral McDonald, out of a sense of duty, actively ordered the mobilization, training, and deployment of the men and women who executed the Vietnam War. His sense of responsibility is linked to the moral voice and agency these soldiers exercised in combat. He is a moral actor of a different sort precisely because of his vocation and agency. McDonald exemplifies the moral responsibility that separates soldiers from civilians.

All three of the above people carry a moral burden. All three experience moral dissonance from their burdens. However, they have different ethical obligations because of their vocation. These differences are significant in interpreting the origins and intensity of soldiers' moral dissonance. Soldiers are recruited, trained and deployed into environments where they *must* act as moral agents in making life or death decisions for which they are responsible. Soldiers' moral voice can be defined by the FRAME senses (fidelity, responsibility, accountability, maturity, and efficacy). Soldiers' moral voice expresses the unique vocational obligations that command their moral agency. They are bound by duty to obey orders, and in following their orders the must exercise their moral agency. Their agency operates up and down a chain of command that orders participation in combat and grants an ethical permission and an imperative to kill. However, this imperative may or may not resolve the moral responsibility for killing or injuring another. Thus, Admiral McDonald, at the strategic level of command, expresses his moral dissonance differently than a soldier, at the tactical level, who carried out his orders in combat. A Vietnam veteran summarizes his moral dissonance for the "stuff" he did in combat. Listen to the moral pain expressed within an excerpt of his narrative. "I became a fucking animal . . . they [his immediate chain of command] wanted a hero so I gave it to them . . . they wanted a

---

26. McMaster, *Dereliction of Duty*, 262.

fucking body count, so I gave them a body count. . . . I hope they're fucking happy. But, they don't have to live with it. I do."[27]

Soldiers are moral actors conducting war. Similar expressions of moral pain are directly related to the moral dissonance between the moral voice and agency of their vocation. Each one of these expressions can be defined by a soldier's senses of FRAME: (1) the level of fidelity to a set of voiced values, (2) the level of responsibility or ownership for agency, (3) the level of accountability they assign to an event, (4) the level of maturity that provides the capacity for their agency, and (5) the level of efficacy that is their capability to act.

Try to imagine moral dissonance from the perspective of a soldier who is obligated to act as a moral agent in combat after events go wrong. Consider the war narratives of Private Marshall Storeby and Private First Class Justin Watt.

During the Vietnam War, Private Storeby refused an illegal order from his sergeant to participate in the rape and murder of a Vietnamese woman. Storeby was correct in his refusal, but powerless to stop the actions of his fellow soldiers and prevent her murder. In spite of threats to his life, he later reported the crime and testified against his squad leader and fellow soldiers. During the court martial the sergeant's defense attorney asked Storeby why he made his decisions. His answer is a powerful testimony of his strong sense of his moral voice and agency. "We all figured we might be dead in the next minute, so what difference did it make what we did? But the longer I was over there [Vietnam], the more I became convinced that it was the other way around that counted—that because we might not be around much longer, we had to take extra care how we behaved . . . we had to answer to something, to someone—maybe just to ourselves."[28]

During Operation Iraqi Freedom a squad of soldiers murdered an Iraqi family after raping and murdering their fourteen-year-old daughter. Similar to Storeby, Private First Class Justin Watt did not participate in the murders, and he was powerless to prevent the crime. Later, he reported the murders and made statements against his fellow soldiers. His reasons for reporting the crime are different than Storeby's, but his narrative expresses a similar sense of obligation.

> If I kill someone in combat that is the risk that the other guy involved has agreed to take. And I stand just as much of a chance of getting my ticket punched as the guy I am trying to kill. But civilians are different. The guys who did this [committed the

27. Shay, *Achilles in Vietnam*, 83.
28. Lang, *Casualties of War*, 110.

rape and murder] had to pay. Not to say that if I never turned them in, they wouldn't be paying for it, in their own heads. Your own conscience is worse than any punishment that anyone else can lay on you. I think that's part of why Yribe [another soldier who knew about the crime] was saying he wouldn't turn them in. But that's not good enough. Not for that shit. Not after I, and all the rest of us busted our balls the entire time. I didn't get to go out on a kill spree because I was hurting. We all sucked up the same bullshit and we didn't get to wig out.[29]

These criminal events occurred during combat, but they were not ordered acts or intended conduct. Yet some combatants believed they were allowed to do such things while Storeby and Watt held themselves accountable for *preventing* such acts from happening. They did the best they could, and they tried to live up to the high standards of their profession. This is the essence of moral voice and agency that is a part of every soldier's character and ethos. However, notice that Storeby and Watt hurt because of their sense of moral agency, not because of their exposure to physical trauma. At some level, their core values were violated, and they hold themselves accountable through association, and failure to prevent these crimes. This violation forms the story line for their war narratives. In listening to their stories, one can hear the core values they use to judge their actions and the actions of others. These values are vital parts of their professional character and self-identity. Both Storeby and Watt continue to struggle with their moral dissonance long after they left combat.[30]

The military is a social ethos consisting of professional values and standards that determine the expected conduct of its members. But, in combat traumatic stresses and unimaginable conditions combine to override the harmony between soldiers' moral voice and agency. This complex relationship may be counterintuitive for those who want to believe that conscience is a matter of personal preference, and fighting well in a just war prevents moral dissonance. However, combat consists of complex situations where soldiers cannot always achieve their desired ideals (moral voice) or control the consequences of their perceived conduct (moral agency). The long-term effects from their moral dissonance can and do injure them. Thus, moral injury from combat is a vocational risk for those who volunteer to serve in the military. Yet, this risk does not have to become an occupational hazard.

29. Frederick, *Black Hearts*, 314.

30. This conclusion is taken from their accounts located in sources already cited.

Moral Injury as a Vocational Risk

MI is not a new risk to soldiers' health. Historical texts and clinical reports contain many war narratives about how war changes lives and results in difficulties after returning home. What is new is an emerging awareness of how ethical conduct and moral reasoning contribute to the complex emotions and behaviors that appear in veterans after they leave combat. These emotions and behaviors are the products of both their moral voice and agency. They are expressed in conscious reasoning and subconscious reflexive responses.

Diagnoses of PTSD and TBI have "unique components that make them separable consequences of war and other traumatic contexts."[31] Branch manuals are uneven, however, as to the relations between PTSD, TBI, and MI. The current Department of Defense and Air Force instructions for mental health and combat stress do not mention MI. The Army's stress control manual comments once about the moral effects of combat along with spiritual and ethical dilemmas as consequences of post-traumatic stress.[32] Only the Marine and Navy stress continuum model lists moral injury as a *contributor* to, not a cause of, combat stress and post-traumatic stress injuries.[33] The latest Mental Health Assessment Team surveys of returning veterans from Iraq and Afghanistan asked participants about experiencing moral or ethical issues. But these same surveys did not ask soldiers about how they judged their experiences, the standards they used in making their judgments, and how they felt about these experiences.[34]

This is a regrettable oversight. Soldiers are moral actors. Their actions have moral consequences that can outlast their time in service. Just ask them. In combat, they live by value systems they will use to judge conduct. These values and standards obligate them to participate as professional agents of our national policy. Without these standards they are mercenaries operating under their own authority for their own ends. This is what we mean in saying that "soldiers possess a moral voice that holds them accountable for their moral agency." Today in America, soldiers serve voluntarily, but in other times and places they have served through involuntary levy. Whether by choice or levy, soldiers in combat participate (directly or indirectly) in

---

31. US Department of Veteran's Affairs, "DSM-5 Criteria for PTSD."

32. See: US Air Force, *Disaster Mental Health Response*; US Army, *Combat and Operational Stress Control Manual*; US Navy, *Combat and Operational Stress Control*; Department of Defense, *Maintenance of Psychological Health.*

33. Nash, "U.S. Marine Corps and Navy Combat and Operational Stress," 107–20.

34. US Army, *Mental Health Advisory Team Study 1–9.* There were nine Mental Health Assessment Team studies conducted between 2003–2013. None of these studies mentions the subject of moral injury.

decisions to use armed violence. These decisions involve deeply rooted personal and social values that control professional competencies. Thus soldiers carry a moral weight and ethical responsibility in choosing how they will act. As a profession, the military is publicly accountable for its ethical standards. Thus, a wider society expects its military members to judge their conduct in combat using their professional standards.

Soldier, Warrior, or Pirate

Language is limited, and the historical use of the word "soldier" has become specifically linked with Army service as opposed to Marines, Sailors, Airmen or Coast Guardsmen. Throughout this text we will identify the specific services when used by quoted sources, and when referring to specific individuals and groups. The term "soldier," as we have used it and will continue to use the term here, connotes further the broad moral and ethical obligations of military service. It is possible to be inclusive by using terms such as "service member," or veteran to denote military service. Some use the term "warrior" for this inclusive purpose. However, "service member" and "veteran" do not convey senses of moral voice, and the use of "warrior" does not reflect the high standards that obligate professional conduct. We use the term "soldier" as a vocational term in order to make a three-tier moral distinction regarding the professional standards required from all military members. These standards are embodied within the values of the military ethos, and braided with the moral values of its individual members throughout their time in professional military service. The "tiers" are identified by "soldier," "warrior," and "pirate."

In the profession of arms, character controls competence. This is a qualitative distinction that separates the moral obligations of a "soldier" (character with competence), a "warrior" (competence alone), and a pirate (warrior competence without character). This distinction is critical for understanding the moral reasoning processes that control professional competence. The professional character of a "soldier" controls the lethal competence of a "warrior," and this separates both from the immoral character and lethal conduct of a "pirate." These reasoning processes are important for understanding the ideal standards and perceived conduct that generates the moral dissonance forming into moral injury. These reasoning processes are active within a veteran's war narrative.

The powerful draw of being a warrior is well established in literature. A current example is the moral dissonance of "not serving in combat" expressed by Marine Lieutenant Nathan Eckman: "As a Marine infantryman

I wanted to kill like I'd been trained to do. The fact that I haven't weighs on me. Its weight comes from the scars I don't have. . . . I feel less capable because of it, why I can't fully understand what it means to be a veteran, and why, despite the irony of which I'm very much aware, I believe I need to have killed a man to become a man."[35]

It is ironic that a person would feel a moral failure for not killing. But this feeling is understandable when professional service is defined by the warrior skill of "killing the enemy." However, this warrior skill must be controlled in combat. Army veteran Lieutenant Colonel Benjamin Sledge stresses the moral and legal boundaries of a soldier controlling his warrior competence. "According to the Rules of Engagement, we could shoot her [a young girl who was used to carry weapons for insurgents]. No one ever did. Not even when the First Sergeant morbidly reassured them on a rooftop in the middle of Iraq. Other soldiers didn't end up so lucky . . . I often wonder what would have happened if the Flower Girl pointed a rifle at me, but I'm afraid I already know. . . . How do you talk about the morally reprehensible things that have left a bruise upon your soul?"[36]

Sledge's moral connection between "being a soldier" and "acting like a warrior" reveal his moral dissonance. The unified boundary between ideals and conduct separates the moral voice and agency of soldiers from warriors and pirates. All three types can exist within the same unit, and mission. These impulses may also exist within the *same person*. Army Sergeant John Diem was a member of an infantry unit where some soldiers crossed these boundaries and brutally raped and murdered noncombatants. He didn't participate in the crime, but he testifies to the injuries effects of association with this pirate behavior in the war zone.

> In ways that are important to young men, like what you do, what you stand for, and what you are willing to put on the line, this [the rape and murder] was the defining moment in a lot of people's lives. And I don't think their [the guilty soldiers'] actions will withstand their own scrutiny. I know mine don't. But I know what kills soldiers now. I know what kills them. Not in the physical sense, but in the psychological sense: what causes soldiers to fail themselves, and what command can do to set them up for failure.[37]

Ethicist Michael Walzer argues that "soldiers may not be responsible for the overall justice of the wars they fight. However, they have clear

---

35. Eckman, "What It Means to Be a Veteran."
36. Sledge, "Conversation with Our Veterans."
37. Frederick, *Black Hearts*, 348–49.

obligations, and they bear responsibility for their conduct and the actions that result under the limits of their authority. They are moral agents because; 'at some stage have to decide, to choose, to make a moral decision.'"[38]

There is a moral difference between developing soldiers, training warriors, and breeding pirates.[39] The control of "warrior" competence has ethical and moral consequences that create moral dissonance. Some authors cited in this book will use the term "warrior" differently. Some authors will use warrior as a generic term. More importantly, some authors and military leaders will often use "warriors" to focus upon the tasks and skills that define competence while neglecting obligations of moral voice and agency. Warrior competence doesn't define military character or personal identity. When competence becomes the standard for military service, then character is removed from combat, and the results can lead to moral injury.

As stated earlier, a warrior's honor and purpose is to defeat and kill his/her enemy in combat. In doing so, the character of a warrior is defined by his/her ability to fight; not by the values and standards that control his/her fighting. The focus upon warrior competence creates a "slippery slope" weakening the vital link between moral voice and agency. Warriors can lose control on this slope and fall off a moral cliff as they begin to use their lethal skills for their own ends and become "pirates."

Not much needs to be written about the intentional conduct of pirates operating outside of legal and moral boundaries. However, it is vital to understand the ethical and moral distinctions between the character of soldiers, warriors, and pirates. Sometimes, the conditions of combat create situations where one tries to act like a soldier (operating with a sense of moral voice and agency) and ends up acting like a warrior (with lethal competence overriding moral voice and agency) or a pirate (lethal skills without moral voice and agency). The best of individuals can act the worst at times, and combat can bring out the worst in all participants. The particulars of these distinctions are where moral dissonance originates and moral injuries begin to form. To experience moral dissonance one must have a troubled conscience from trying to act according to some standard. Soldiers operating in the "gray zones" of combat can and do end up acting like warriors or pirates. It is even worse when these soldiers successfully act according to their highest ideals and end up perceiving themselves to be pirates. Storeby, Watt, Eckman, Sledge, and Diem are doing this because of something they

38. Walzer, *Just and Unjust Wars*, 304–6.

39. Couch, *Tactical Ethic*. The authors are borrowing from a statement made by Air Force Colonel Jay Aanrud, ethicist and retired Navy SEAL Dick Couch, and other military members. The use of "pirates" to describe the rogue, immoral, and illegal conduct by some unit members in combat.

did that was beyond their control, something they failed to do, or something that they were associated with. When the stakes are life and death, the resulting moral dissonance can easily develop into a moral injury. This risk is the consequence of their vocational choices as soldiers, not simply the result of a common humanity.

Moral injury in soldiers has real consequences. Peter Marin introduced the issue of soldiers' moral pain in an article documenting how Vietnam veterans experienced resentment and deep anger from: (1) bad consciences over inexplicable or inexcusable events, (2) internalized suffering absorbed from those around them, and (3) personal suffering caused by the inability to give back or contribute in a positive manner.[40]

It is probably easier to imagine pain arising from levels of moral dissonance as a moral victim than it is to identify with the pain caused from being a moral actor. Imagine that you had to act, regardless of the outcome and the consequences to yourself or to others, because you were *responsible* for achieving a specific outcome. Now imagine that this outcome was in violation of everything you valued, intended, or desired. Whether you directly participated in the outcome, failed to prevent the outcome, or were related in some way to the outcome—your perceptions are now in conflict with your ideals, and you are experiencing some level of moral dissonance. If the intensity of your dissonance is high enough, then you are probably expressing some type of moral pain and experiencing some level of moral injury. To understand this complex dynamic is the key to understanding the formation of moral injuries in soldiers.

Some moral injuries may result in an increased personal and social awareness that leads to a revision of life. This is a part of post-traumatic growth. But suppose there is something blocking the path to this type of growth. Suppose the source of the moral dissonance and pain is a traumatic event that leads to enduring, drastic changes in a person's physical, social, and spiritual identity. For "passive" moral injury victims who may not be military, their injuries will reflect the injustice of the traumatic event, and their involuntary participation in the injurious event may even witness to their core values and identity.

The situation is slightly different for those who assume the active vocation of a moral actor. Their very participation in traumatic events contradicts their core values and identity. Participation of moral actors in morally injurious events is not always voluntary, but their ideal values (their "moral voice") obligate them as responsible agents accountable for the consequences of their perceived conduct. The resulting dissonance morally

40. Marin, "Living in Moral Pain."

injures them. Thus, moral injury is the secondary, internal psychic hemorrhaging and subsequent infections coming from the wound of the presenting morally injurious situation.[41] As seen earlier, the original wound may originate from a single event or from the cumulative effects of many events. However, the enduring secondary effects generate moral dissonance, which then causes moral injury; and the greater amplitude of the dissonance, the greater the severity of the moral injury.

Various students of MI, of course, have their own accents in defining MI while they also share much common ground. Psychiatrist Michael Linden believes that high levels of dissonance stemming from issues of failed moral agency can lead to a prolonged embitterment that results in altered moods, attitudes, and behaviors.[42] This state of embitterment describes probable consequences from combat. Combat involves acts of cruelty where sanctioned violence becomes necessary, even desirable, for soldiers' success and survival. These acts of cruelty may or may not be intended, but they may be the unavoidable outcomes of actions set in motion. In 1864 General William Tecumseh Sherman wrote to the citizens of besieged Atlanta, "War is cruelty, and you cannot refine it."[43] His words were both a subjective justification for his actions and an objective description of the effects of total war upon populations of "noncombatants." It is interesting to note that his letter did not include a discussion of the effects upon the soldiers who carried out his orders.

Theologian Michael Trice links cruelty to the annihilation of well-being in both moral victims and actors. He believes that cruelty is an internal feature of humanity that makes us complicit in acts that simultaneously invite our allegiance while contradicting our core values. Thus we honor and justify the very conduct that destroys our character by violating what we value. Trice believes that cruelty places humanity in a "dark place" where the potential for reconciliation is questionable because it depends upon the very relationships that it destroys.[44]

Chaplain David Bachelor uses the metaphor of a "death shadow" to describe this contradictory state.[45] He borrows from the language of Psalm 23, where "the valley of the shadow death," describes the dark effects of embitterment and cruelty upon moral actors. Soldiers existing in a "death

---

41. This is a developing definition used by Jonathan Shay and others in a variety of sources. See Shay, *Odysseus in America*, 83–86, and Guntzel, "Invisible Injury."

42. Linden et al., *Posttraumatic Embitterment Disorder*.

43. Sherman, letter to the mayor and council of Atlanta.

44. Trice, *Encountering Cruelty*, 1–5.

45. Bachelor, "Death Shadow," 17–41.

shadow" isolate themselves in self-defeating behaviors that obstruct post-combat growth. The "death shadow" can be another powerful metaphor to describe the ongoing effects from invisible moral wounds.

As Childs and Jensen underscore, soldiers are moral actors and their moral agency has living consequences. Linden, Trice, and Bachelor describe in depth the continuing destructive processes that trap soldiers in injurious patterns of thought and behavior. Soldiers' war narratives describe their ongoing struggles to reconcile their moral dissonance. Studies from current operations indicate that "large numbers of troops clearly believe they did or witnessed something wrong downrange, perhaps terribly wrong, and what matters here is how the individuals judge their experiences, not what others say."[46] The spectrum of damage from these "something went wrong down range" events depends upon the levels of the soldiers' moral dissonance. Likewise, the potential for their post-traumatic growth depends upon how soldiers live with their moral dissonance. Moral injuries can and do heal, but this process is as complex as the injury itself. Marine Captain Timothy Kudo expresses the importance of moral voice and agency, as well as the holistic resources for healing his moral dissonance.

> I think about what happened over there [Iraq] and try to come to grips with the depth of it . . . the morality that we have experienced over there whether we deal with that through ethics or through religion is something that we shouldn't just get rid of, and we shouldn't ignore that these are real questions and war is evil and yet sometimes, it is necessary. . . . I haven't reconciled my experience. . . . The harm that was done, wasn't done to me; it was done to these other people. And I do believe that in some time, maybe after this life that there is a possibility for that [forgiveness and healing], and that is an essential nature of faith, to me. But that's the only real option for this. So you keep pushing in spite of what you've done, you're more than your worst action—it is an incredible part of moving forward and trying to create good in the world.[47]

Two War Narratives of Moral Injury

Combat requires warriors with lethal competence. Extreme conditions in combat require warriors attempting to "fight well" to make very tough decisions in using their violent skills. These warriors must decide whether to

46. Pryer, "Moral Injury," 34–36.
47. Martin, "For Many Returning Vets."

act like professional soldiers or like immoral pirates. This duress may "fade" ethical boundaries or tempt soldiers to "overreach" these same boundaries. The great temptation for soldiers to override their moral voice indeed can distort or even suspend their sense of responsible moral agency. This is the frightening character of contemporary close-up warfare.

In combat soldiers often find themselves fighting in a "three-second war" where they have: one second to figure out what is happening, another second to decide what to do about it, and a final second to act. This time component may refer to a literal three-second decision, or it may be a metaphor for a quick, unpredictable chain of events. In both cases, a soldier's maturity and efficacy become factors in controlling their responses under fire. When General James Mattis was asked how long it took to make a complex targeting decision, he replied, "three seconds, but I've been thinking about it for thirty years."[48] His experience, training, and education influenced his moral voice and agency. The same may not be true for a junior soldier with less than a year in service. Combat creates emotionally charged, timed reactions where maturity and efficacy may collide with moral voice and agency. Marine veteran and embedded reporter David Morris describes his immediate reaction after an improvised explosive device (IED) struck his vehicle. "And just like that I got pissed. Here I was, trapped in a Humvee [a military vehicle] full of buffoons who were practically begging to be murdered by a bunch of half-assed insurgents. Was there ever a bigger ship of fools?"[49]

Morris's perception reveals his emotional reactions to value judgments concerning the importance of his mission, the character of the Marines traveling with him, the purpose of the war, and the value of life itself. This is a perception of a traumatic event while under duress. But suppose this event left him with enduring anger from something he judged to be an immoral event? What if his emotional response was linked to these warriors forming a defensive perimeter around his damaged vehicle and indiscriminately providing "covering" fire into a crowded street? Could these perceptions affect the important relationships in his life after he returned home? This hypothetical question demonstrates how a conflict between values and perceptions can generate into a moral dissonance that inflicts a moral injury.

In combat, soldiers may be required to act as warriors, but they are not trained to be pirates. It is appropriate to assume that most soldiers will attempt to exercise their moral voice and agency to "fight well." However, ideal standards can become active components of MI when things go wrong in combat. This is where good soldiers are left believing that they are moral failures

---

48. Mattis, *Ethical Challenges in Contemporary Conflict.*
49. Morris, *Evil Hours,* 17.

in spite of their intentions. Their moral voice shapes the self-perceptions which then lead to self-condemnation. This needs to be considered when listening to soldiers' war narratives. These narratives transmit meanings that are highly dependent on context and the nuances of soldiers' character and ethos. The stories reveal the wrestling matches within a soldier's conscience and expressions of the pain that indicates the presence of damaging moral dissonance. These war narratives may also linger nascently, inarticulate, as silent and hidden memories that remind soldiers that something still isn't right long after they return home from combat.

Consider the following experiences of Sergeant First Class Robin Johnson and Major Jeff Hall, two Army soldiers deployed to Iraq in 2003 to 2005. The two men served in different units with different missions, and they conducted themselves differently in those missions. However, they experienced similar reactions to similar tragic events. Sergeant First Class Robin Johnson, a platoon sergeant in Iraq, describes his direct moral agency in an incident where he and his soldiers killed an Iraqi family who attempted to drive through their checkpoint. Johnson often relives his participation in this event. Here he has an angry, hypothetical conversation with the father who was driving the car.

> The window [of time] of signaling, shooting a warning shot, shooting to disable and then engaging can be milliseconds. You have to make that judgment call of "Is this a threat?" Once it was done . . . it was just a family. You know, a mother, father and infant, in the mother's lap, and then two little girls in the back seat . . . "why didn't you stop?" What was his logic? Was he trying to get down the next side street? Did we scare him? What was going on in his head at that moment? Now, this whole family is gone—they got up that morning and they ate breakfast together, they talked and they laughed and they planned their day, and now, they're gone.[50]

Major Jeff Hall was a Battery Commander in Iraq. He describes a similar moral dissonance generated from a similar event. However, while Johnson was responsible for exercising his moral agency in conducting a checkpoint, Hall was responsible for commanding a cleanup of an event where an Iraqi family was killed while trying to drive through a cordon and search operation. Neither Hall nor his soldiers were responsible for directly killing the family, but Hall held himself accountable for what happened next. Hall and his soldiers were required to take care of the bodies, and Hall received a tasking from his commander to deliver a condolence payment of

50. Kaplan, "Military Is Going Beyond PTSD."

$750 to surviving family members. Unlike Johnson and his soldiers, Hall and his soldiers did not fire a shot during this incident, yet they morally associate themselves with the consequences. Hall talks about his ongoing reactions to this incident.

> [Responding to the incident site] . . . the Iraqis wouldn't touch him [the dead driver]. So, I got a Soldier and I started to peel him [the father] out of the seat. . . . I still see his hands and how they were reaching out like he could stop what was happening to him and his wife and his son. I think the car took close to a thousand rounds. The car was torn to pieces. No one could recognize him . . . they [the crowd] were pretty pissed off at me . . . all I knew was this guy drove into an inner cordon of a raid on Saddam's relatives and he was there at the wrong time. I think I might have done the same thing if I was the shooter because you just don't know. . . . [Later] . . . I was told we would be paying them [the family] damages. By "we," my command meant "me." I asked why do I have to do it. I had done everything from securing the scene to being there to grieve with them [the family], to finding the bodies [removed from the scene to a US morgue and returned by Hall to the family]. Now I was being tasked to go pay 750 [deleted] dollars to them. . . . I had no idea how I was going to be able to look them in the eye.[51] I kept to myself knowing that I was representing America. I put another $100 in from my own pocket because that was all I had, and I took it to them. Still I feel bad about that. I realized that this is no kind of war I was ready for.[52]

Johnson's and Hall's words convey a range of moral dissonance where their emotions, values, and judgments churn while they try to reconcile what happened against what they thought should have happened. By definition, Hall and Johnson "fought well" according to traditional just war criteria. Both men acted with the ethics of professional soldiers. They did not violate the rules of engagement. They did not cause the deaths of civilians intentionally and did their best to care for the survivors. Both men still operate with a moral sense of fairness and a deep-seated belief that "soldiers do not kill civilians." They use these and other beliefs to judge what they perceived happened. Their narratives convey a common anguish between what they value, what they did, and what they could not prevent.

51. US Forces Afghanistan, *Money as a Weapon System in Afghanistan*. By 2012 the US was paying about $2500 per death with allies reporting similar amounts. This article is a critical examination of this policy: Boros et al., "A Few Thousand Dollars."

52. From the diary of Major Jeff Hall written during 2003–2004, used by permission.

Their ongoing moral dissonance affects their identity as human beings and their character as soldiers. They believe they are less than they are; more like pirates than soldiers. Believing they are so, they live with debilitating guilt and shame, about which we will reflect later in this book. They are experiencing moral injury.

After redeployment, Major Hall struggled with questions from his initial MI-inducing incident that blended with further incidents of marketplace bombings and injuries to his soldiers on missions. He struggled with all these experiences to find moral justification. As part of his healing process, he drew an image of a hand trapped by barbed wire trying to grab hold of a cross nailed to a post (see page vi). The sketch symbolized his desire to reconcile his values with his experience in Iraq. Hall saw reaching hands on many dead bodies. For him, they represent an effort to protect others. The barbed wire represents external constraints upon his sense of moral agency; both his responsibility for what he couldn't prevent, and his accountability for what he can't fix. The cross that is nailed to the post symbolizes the violated sacred values that Hall, his soldiers, and the civilians in their area of operations can no longer inhabit. Some may think that Hall is chasing ghosts by reliving the past. This isn't true. He is expressing his moral voice and the reality of his struggle to reconcile a moral dissonance that will not subside.

The above narratives differ from the other soldier narratives recounted in this book. Some may wonder why a combat arms officer and sergeant merely doing their duty would have a problem with unintended consequences that occurred in a combat zone. Both Johnson and Hall are expressing moral pain. To understand their reactions is to understand the subjective dynamic that grows moral dissonance into moral injury. These events became crystallizing moments for them because the values informing their moral voice also became the standards for judging their moral agency. The resulting dissonance between their values and their conduct inflicted a moral injury as their dissonance changed their character. Their moral pain from their injury is expressed in their anger, their shame, their guilt, their frustrations, their alienation, and their sense of betrayal. They express their pain in their personal war narratives.

Notice how Johnson and Hall are acting as warriors trying to operate with the ethics and moral responsibilities of professional soldiers instead of acting like pirates. They judge their participation in terms of injuries done to others in the course of their duties by using moral values as ethical standards that hold them personally responsible and accountable for choices they and others made. This level of accountability may not make sense in a modern courtroom where extenuating circumstances can dismiss a defendant from responsibility and guilt. However, moral dissonance is quite unlike a demo-cratic legal process because personal conscience simultaneously plays the roles of prosecutor, jury, and judge by making charges, deciding guilt, and pronouncing punishment. In extreme cases the conscience may also assume the roles of jailer and executioner, as the conviction is served in a variety of self-punishing, self-defeating, and even self-annihilating behaviors.

These behaviors are only the symptoms of the hidden, enduring moral injury. The primary traumatic events that happened in Iraq aren't as impor-tant to Johnson and Hall as the ongoing secondary wounds caused by their moral dissonance from these events. It is important to remember that the specific causes of a soldier's moral dissonance are important. Their moral dissonance is generated by the process of their moral voice judging their moral agency. This enduring process becomes the mechanism of injury and the source of soldiers' emotional pain. These cognitions, emotions, and behaviors are expressions of soldiers' moral pain shared in their narratives. These narratives often indicate the presence of the hidden moral injuries that drive the visible signs of distress such as isolation, depression, chemical dependencies, relationship difficulties, and violence. In telling their stories, soldiers—if not yet so self-consciously or articulately—intend to express the intensity of their moral pain and to reveal the degree of damage in their hidden, moral wounds.

War Narratives from Home

During combat, soldiers often compartmentalize their lives by putting their thoughts and emotions "on ice." This "icing" is an autonomic reaction in-fluenced by adrenaline. It is also a conscious survival mechanism. Later, in quieter and safer places, the ice melts, allowing memories and emotions to return. It is then that soldiers wrestle with their moral dissonance. The best way to expose the invisible wounds that gnaw at soldiers' existence is by listening to their war narratives and aiding them toward expression. It is a severe understatement to say that this work for both the injured and the accompanier is hard.

Aleksandr Solzhenitsyn asks an essential question that defines the di-mensions of moral dissonance. "If only there were evil people somewhere insidiously committing evil deeds, and it were necessary only to separate them from the rest of us and destroy them. But the line dividing good and evil cuts through the heart of every human being. And who is willing to destroy a piece of his own heart?"[53] The dividing line between good and evil

53. Solzhenitsyn, *Gulag Archipelago*.

residing within the human heart becomes a moral battleground for soldiers. Vietnam veteran Jim George summarizes his moral dissonance: "The worst thing about being in it [war] is killing. . . . The worst for me was that I got to like it. I got pretty good at it. I hated myself for a long time for getting that good, liking it that much."[54]

Moral dissonance exists on both sides of Solzhenitsyn's dividing line. It becomes an existential struggle for soldiers. For some, the struggle becomes a battle for survival. Soldiers trying to fight well are not trying to destroy themselves. However, when caught participating in systemic evil or particular events of cruelty, their conscience brings them to trial. The resulting moral dissonance becomes a storm where soldiers participate in the destruction of their own identity. Moral injury storms may leave different damage, but the generating storm cell that produces these injuries follows a similar process. It begins when soldiers' moral expectations for fighting well in war do not match the reality of combat. When this happens, their expectations do not always allow them to return home in peace to reconnect with their lives.

The psychological and spiritual cost of this duel in human identity may be expressed in terms similar to WWII German Soldier Guy Sajer's story of returning home: "People who hated me would pursue me with vindictiveness, seeing in my past only cupidity and culpable error. Others might someday understand that men can love the same virtues on both sides of a conflict, and that pain is international. . . . I took part in a huge parade in Paris, in '46. There was also a long silence of remembrance for the dead, to which I added these names . . . [names of his friends killed in action]. I refused to add Paula to that list, and I shall never forget the names of Hals, or Lindberg, or Pferham, or Wollers. Their memory lives within me. There is another man, whom I must forget. He was called Guy Sajer."[55]

Sajer won't forget those who mattered to him, but he will try to forget himself. This dissociation within the self is caused by moral dissonance. Its effects do not stop with the individual. They carry over to the soldier's family and community. Sajer's quiet storm had different internal effects than the storm experienced by Ranger Captain Nate Self after returning from Iraq.

> I want to die. I want to kill the man who has taken my place. But no one will let me. My family sees the brokenness and they've closed in around me, forming a tight perimeter. No one is going to get in. Or out. Julie [his wife] won't leave me. My parents won't abandon me. Still, I'm not sure if God is even here anymore. I've

54. Finkel, *Thank You for Your Service*, Kindle loc. 3371–73.
55. Sajer, *Forgotten Soldier*, 465.

rejected him, walked away, too many times. He has every right to let me burn. I can't function. My family is paralyzed by it. No one sleeps—and on top of this, Noah's [his son] still a baby, which makes it harder on Julie. She knows we need to find help, but she doesn't know who to call.[56]

Sajer wants to disappear. Self contemplated suicide. Sometimes MI leaves hidden damage and only reveals itself over the course of time. Former infantry commander and psychologist David Grossman relates the story of a soldier named Tim. While manning an outpost (OP) Tim loaned his watch to a new soldier, while he took his turn resting. The new soldier woke Tim when he noticed a significant enemy force was moving toward their unit's perimeter. Both men fired off warning shots and ran. After the battle Tim returned to the OP and found the soldier to whom he loaned his watch was wounded. Grossman continues Tim's story. Tim says,

> "He tried to give my watch back to me, but I said no buddy you keep it—to this very day I cannot wear a watch." [Tim's wife replied], "oh that's why . . ." [Tim] "Do you understand I abandoned those men . . . I left them . . ." [Grossman intercedes] "Tim listen to me, an OP is a sacrificial lamb staked out to bleat when the Tiger approaches—you provided a warning and cover fire and you came back and got out 25% of your men. You should have gotten a medal for what you did that night."[57]

But a medal isn't what Tim wanted. Years later, Tim was still trying to save his soldiers while his wife wondered why he never wore a watch. If the stakes were not so high, this story could become a comedy. Tim brought the effects from his moral dissonance home with him from Vietnam and he carried it for many years without his wife knowing his story. The moral injuries soldiers experience in combat and the time-delayed expressions of these injuries bring this hidden storm into soldiers' homes and communities.

The above war narratives express some of the damage caused by moral injury. Military spouses have war narratives of their own. Spouses and communities often feel the effects from these moral injuries and participate in moral dissonance of their soldiers without knowing its source or intensity. Staff Sergeant Stephen G. Martin hints at the importance of his wife's participation in his vocational choice as he wrote to her prior to his death in Iraq. "Thank you for enduring this time of separation in our lives. I guess when this first started, I did not fully grasp or understand that it was not me, but

---

56. Self, *Two Wars*, 309.

57. Grossman, *On Combat*, 306–11.

both of us that were and are bearing the burden of this war. I'm sorry for not understanding this sooner. I know that your sacrifice is greater than mine. I simply changed my uniform, and arenas. You sent me off to the unknown."[58]

Just as soldiers' levels of moral dissonance vary, so do the reactions of their spouses to their dissonance. Consider the words of Taya Kyle, wife of Navy SEAL and "American Sniper" Chris Kyle.

> It was hard for him [Chris] to pinpoint how he felt about any-thing. He was just wiped out and overwhelmed. I felt sad for everything he'd been through. And I felt terribly torn about needing him. I did need him, tremendously. But at the same time, I had to get along without him so much that I developed an attitude that I didn't need him, or at least that I shouldn't need him. I guess it may not make any sense to anyone else, but I felt this strange mixture of feelings, all across the spectrum. I was so mad at him for leaving the kids and me on our own. I wanted him home but I was mad, too. . . . Now finally he was back, and all of my emotions just exploded inside me, happiness and anger all mixed together.[59]

David Finkel includes Army spouse Saskia Schuman in his examina-tion of deployment and redeployment issues. Saskia's husband, Infantry Sergeant Adam Schuman, served in Iraq and struggled with the conse-quences of missions involving the deaths and wounding of his soldiers. In the following conversation with her counselor, Saskia expresses her frus-trations about the effects that her husband's treatment program had upon her and their family.

> "I'm pretty much tired of doing it myself," she tells the coun-selor as she sits in her living room, "My daughter cries every night. . . . His leave is pretty much gone. . . . I'm sorry. I'm not trying to be rude. . . ." Her voice is rising, enough for Zoe [her daughter] to come in from the pool and see if something is wrong, and Saskia goes to the front porch. She lights a ciga-rette as she keeps talking—her newest habit. "I'm sick of it. I really am. I did not have kids, I did not get married, to be on my own. . . . It doesn't matter. If I lose my house, if I lose my car. . . . What I'm getting really pissed at . . . my entire family is falling apart because of this. . . . There's only so much I can take. . . . I have not gotten any help. From anyone. . . . That isn't the point. I shouldn't have to be doing this twenty-four-seven

---

58. Sheldon, *Their Last Words*, 103.

59. Kyle et al., *American Sniper*, 304–5.

while he's out there having fun [Sergeant Schuman was in a resident treatment program]. . . . I can't . . . I can't. I can't afford it. . . . I'm so angry because he's not fucking taking care of what he's supposed to . . . I am done. I am done. I am fed up. I am sick of it. I am tired of being made to feel guilty. Poor Adam. It's always poor Adam. . . . I can't do it anymore. I cannot do it anymore. . . . Why is it fair? So when he comes home in two and a half months, I can't even leave for the weekend."[60]

These war narratives do not convey stories simply about marriage problems. The presenting problem is the marriage relationship, but the injuring force is the moral dissonance that links home to combat. This is an example of what Jonathan Shay identifies as complex, secondary wounding. These types of problems won't be resolved by simple couple's therapy, because the cause is moral injury, not the marriage itself. This does not mean that marital counseling is not a part of healing moral wounds; just the opposite. Because moral wounds are complex injuries, treating the presenting problem must be combined with recognizing and treating the hidden wound and the deeper dissonance. Great care must be taken to define the complex issues and address them as part of a holistic, healing plan. The common element linking these problems is the soldiers' moral dissonance. Psychologist Joseph Currier's research in the identification and treatment of MI believes that this linkage is necessary for successful care. "Another major implication of the preceding discussion is that comprehensive care for morally injured returning service members will include active collaboration with their social networks, as these communities are likely to play powerful roles in eliciting and framing moral emotions."[61]

The Importance of Healing War Narratives

Moral dissonance is not the same for all combat veterans. Specific correlation studies linking the violation of values to post-traumatic stress do not exist. But qualitative research shows a strong possibility of MI's link to PTS. Navy Psychologist William Nash states, "I would bet anything that if we had the wherewithal to do this kind of research, we'd find that moral injury underlies veteran homelessness, criminal behavior, and suicide."[62] The causes of these hidden injuries are highly contextual, and the effects from these injuries are very subjective. This makes soldier war narratives an important key

60. Finkel, *Thank You for Your Service*, Kindle loc. 3402.

61. Currier et al., "Role of Moral Emotions," 249–62.

62. Wood, "Warrior's Moral Dilemma."

for understanding and treating moral injuries. These war narratives are not nice or "politically correct." They bring out the "nasty" stuff of combat that psychiatrist Jonathan Shay believes is necessary for healing.[63] The temptation may be for the veteran to "put it all behind" and "move on." Therefore, this nasty stuff often remains hidden, and the reasons for veterans' behaviors remain a puzzle. Friends and family witness the damage, but they do not get to view the sources of the dissonance. As a result, we've tended to treat the symptoms without getting to the cause.

One unexpected place of healing has been the Vietnam Veterans Memorial in Washington DC. Here the nation can view some of the dissonance behind the injury. The black memorial wall was built as a reflective, accounting for all who gave their lives in Vietnam. In the dark stone, living Vietnam veterans, family members and others can see their reflections through the chronological listing of names of those who died. The effects of the monument didn't stop there. Later groups added two groups of statues: (1) three male soldiers standing together and looking toward the future through the pain of the past, and (2) one female nurse hopefully looking up for the arrival of a medical evacuation helicopter, while one kneels to hold a wounded soldier in her arms and another bows her head. Over the years many veterans and family members have deposited narratives and other memorials as tributes to the fallen. The National Park Service collects and catalogues these items, such as a note from a nurse, named Dusty.

> The first few times you cut someone's uniform off and the leg falls off, yes, your mind screams, but you stuff that down very, very quickly. You have to. If you lose control, they're going to die. It's as simple as that . . . the wounded kept coming, the war was getting worse and I was good at what I did . . . these people would have a future because of all of the s___ I was going through. Goodbye David—I'm the last person you will see, I'm the last person you will touch, I'm the last person who will love you. So, long David—my name is Dusty—David—who will give me something for my pain?[64]

Dusty participated in the war as a healer, not a warrior. Her note expresses a moral pain that goes beyond stress-based trauma. It expresses her identity as a human being, as well as her character as a nurse and soldier. Her moral voice and agency focused upon saving the injured. She did what she could, regrettably failed at times, and witnessed the trauma unfold. Perhaps.

---

63. Shay, *Odysseus in America*, 154.
64. Palmer, *Shrapnel in the Heart*, 124–26.

Her letter communicates that she wished to have done more. Her narrative indicates a level of moral dissonance that reveals her moral injury.

The narratives in this book are here because soldiers *told* their hidden stories! Psychiatrist Robert Lifton views these war narratives as vital sources for healing. These narrative accounts reveal the historical circumstances and the resulting emotions that separate veterans from their communities.[65] Thus his treatment goals involve reworking these narratives using the same specific personal, cultural and historical forces that formed their injuries. By working through their historical data, veterans can balance their unending struggles to reclaim the approximate "truth" of their service. One of Lifton's intense interviews involved a veteran of My Lai:

> The My Lai survivor, for instance, told me that [he] had learned a great deal, "just by talking about it because . . . it's something that I never talked about before. So I don't think I could have ever made sense of it . . . even to myself if I hadn't actually said it." What he was saying here and elsewhere in the interview was that our talks, in comparison to those with journalists and military investigators, had brought him closer to his own experience. He had still not achieved anything like comfortable mastery of this truth, as we know from his residual guilt, self-doubt, and confusion. But he had touched a certain level of truth, an interface of personal experience (self) and larger forces (world), around which he could build and grow. That level of truth became inseparable from personal integrity and wholeness.[66]

Summary

The two-mirror model (TMM) provides a way to hear and understand the causes and effects of moral injury present in war narratives. Listening, understanding, interpreting, are essential tasks in helping soldiers and family reconstructing healing narratives from the effects of combat. Without this reconstruction, moral dissonance will continue to inflict moral injuries upon soldiers and families. Sergeant First Class Robin Johnson and Major Jeff Hall returned home wrestling with their moral dissonance and living with the effects from their combat perceptions. Author Susan Kaplan reports: "Sergeant First Class Robin Johnson is now 34. He served three tours in Iraq and two in Afghanistan. He says events like the killing of the family in 2004 are chewed over and judged by a public that has no concept of the battlefield. So Johnson

65. Lifton, *Home from the War*, 15–21.
66. Ibid., 316.

talks only to a few people (mostly soldiers) about the worst of what he's seen and done. 'I don't think people can possibly understand,' he says. 'You keep fighting, but you know, it's hard to explain. We joke about it a lot. We kind of make jokes of it—that we're not human anymore. Like the humanity is dead in us.'"[67]

Is Johnson's humanity really dead, or does his joking reveal a struggle with all soldiers to reconcile their pasts in order to reclaim what really matters? Major Jeff Hall retired from the Army in August 2014 in front of a hometown gathering in Woodward, Oklahoma. The ceremony included Jeff's wife, Sheri, their daughters, parents, friends, and extended family. It also included former commanders, soldiers, and healers who worked with him. The highlight of the ceremony was Jeff and his family placing items from his combat service into a handcrafted wooden container, topped off with a carved wooden sword beaten into a plowshare. The Hall family wasn't locking away memories as much as performing a ceremony that signified his transformation of moral healing. Jeff wrote in the program, "Sheri was the one that held on when the world spun out of control. 'In sickness and in health' always meant something to her. I was not that strong. . . . Thanks is not enough."[68] Together they had endured much through his deployments, and reconciled the dissonance together. As part of the ceremony Major Hall placed his war journal and some of his artwork into the container. In his journal are the following words that express his ongoing struggle to maintain his moral voice and agency:

> I was unable to save anyone of them [a multitude of soldiers and Iraqi civilians] but I tried. . . . I will never forget this place where I spent my loneliest time on earth so far. Love is here in this hell we call Iraqi Freedom. I don't like the fraud I see here. . . . But I will always love those that gave up everything for a cause . . . they came to me with their sorrows, but I was the one who needed them. . . . Lots of my experience in Iraq was too little too late.[69]

War narratives continue long after soldiers leave the battlefield. They express the moral dissonance between soldiers' moral voice (what they value) and their moral agency (what they do). Soldiers express their dissonance in describing their professional senses of fidelity, responsibility, accountability, maturity, and efficacy (FRAME). These are not abstract concepts. They are specific expressions of moral voice grounded within the particular events

67. Kaplan, "Military Is Going Beyond PTSD."

68. From the retirement program of Major Jeff Hall held on August 1014 in Woodward, Oklahoma. Used with his permission.

69. From the Iraqi Freedom diary of Major Jeff Hall. Used with his permission.

where soldiers served. Soldiers' ownership of moral *agency* distinguishes moral injury from PTSD. The specific moral and ethical obligations placed upon soldiers distinguish their moral dissonance from the betrayal of values experienced by victims of violent trauma. Psychiatrist Jonathan Shay believes that moral injuries are a complex, secondary injury more akin to an internal hemorrhage or infection than a traumatic injury. Traumatic events may be a factor in moral injury, but they are not the cause of the injury. Unresolved moral dissonance is the causal factor for MI and it is the source for multiple consequential symptomatic behaviors and emotions.

On the eve of battle in Iraq, Lieutenant Colonel Tim Collins told his soldiers, "If you harm the regiment or its history by over-enthusiasm in killing or in cowardice, know it is your family who will suffer. You will be shunned unless your conduct is of the highest for your deeds will follow you down through history."[70] His words have a double effect. They present an ideal moral boundary for soldiers trying to fight well under duress, and they also present a resource for moral condemnation by soldiers who perceive that they have failed. This condemnation is the "Mark of Cain" that some soldiers bear, and their moral dissonance isolates their existence. Captain Nate Self didn't assume the "Mark of Cain." Nevertheless, moral dissonance from his combat experiences separated him from his family and brought him to the point of suicide. He regained his balance and identity through the care of family, clergy, and fellow soldiers. After metaphorically putting down his sword, he reconstructed his war narrative and regained his peace as he stayed with his family in places such as a mountain cabin.[71]

Johnson's and Hall's narratives reveal the moral challenges facing all who accept military service during combat and try to return home with their identity and character intact. Families and communities accompany their soldiers on these journeys. After Vietnam, an interviewer asked war correspondent Joe Galloway if he learned anything from reporting on the war. Joe responded, "Yes, I learned how to cry."[72] Crying can be an expression of moral pain. Our nation and military members empathize with hurting soldiers and family members. We need to transform this empathy into healing opportunities that address the kinds of deep moral wounds our soldiers and family members face today.[73] Healing must include the integration of moral reconciliation into the training, leadership and healing practices that

70. Collins, "Tim Collins' Iraq War Speech in Full."

71. Self, *Two Wars*, 353.

72. Moore and Galloway, *We Are Soldiers Still*, xix.

73. Kaplan, "Military Is Going Beyond PTSD."

develop soldiers' moral voice and agency. Jonathan Shay best summarizes the intent of this task:

> Military psychiatrists have been telling us at least since World War I that cohesion, leadership, and training can prevent some (not all) of the life-long symptoms that can follow combat. I believe that they can prevent—perhaps absolutely—the damage to good character that wrecks veterans' lives, that destroys their families, that disrupts their workplaces, and in the extreme, threatens democratic institutions. . . . The psychologically injured veterans I have worked with for more than a decade carry terrible wounds. They do not want other young kids to be to be wrecked the way they were. These veterans are proud Americans who want to see the armed forces attract the best young people in the country and for those young people to flourish. . . . The veterans I work for say, "Do it!"[74]

74. Shay, "Trust," 16.

CHAPTER 3

Current Practices for Healing Moral Injuries

Your soul is like your shadow. Sometimes it wanders off like a butterfly, and that is when you're sad and that's when you get sick, and if it comes back to you, that is when you are happy and well again.

—The Hmong belief of soul loss[1]

As a platoon leader, I feel responsible for everything my platoon does or fails to do. . . . I failed to keep Jesse Dietrich safe, and you know, it was just tough. . . . I keep thinking of other ways I would have done it, but it was a very tough mission and the enemy beat us that day. It was just a really bad night.

—Captain Alejandrao Villenueva, Army Ranger[2]

IN CHAPTER 2 WE introduced the TMM (two-mirror model) and FRAME (fidelity, responsibility, accountability, maturity, effectiveness) as means to understand and interpret soldiers' war narratives. Their narratives convey the meaning of soldiers' memories and events. Their narratives reveal the deep emotions indicating the intensity of the moral dissonance between their values and perceptions. At severe levels this dissonance can be disorienting and some soldiers believe that they have lost something of them-

---

1. Fadiman, *Spirit Catches You*, 100.
2. Fox, "Alejandro Villanueva's Long NFL Path."

selves; it seems to have "wandered off." They are painfully aware that they exist between two realities of: (1) who they desire to be (ideal self), and (2) who they experience themselves to be (perceived self). In the midst of their pain and coping behaviors, they come to recognize their moral injury. MI is not a simple "identity crisis." MI is harm done to identity and character when one's core values are essentially conflicted.

MI is a value-based injury, distinguished from a trauma-based injury such as PTSD. It begins within a person's conscience as that person is stressed beyond the capacity to guide one's conduct, control reactions, and achieve desired outcomes. A soldier's conscience involves the presence of a moral voice (a set of desired values) linked with their professional practice of moral agency (an obligation to practice that same set of values). Soldiers link their voice and agency through their habituated senses of fidelity, responsibility, accountability, maturity, and efficacy (FRAME). In combat, where the stakes are life and death, perceived failures in moral voice and agency affect a soldier's very being. These perceived failures generate moral dissonance between what is valued and what is done. Unaddressed and unreconciled moral dissonance creates moral injuries. Moral injuries can be the catalyst for future growth or ongoing pathologies. Either way, left unaddressed, these injuries compound and finally extend beyond the self to family members and communities.

This chapter presents a summary of current practices for healing MI. These practices are based upon research studies, clinical accounts, and healing theories intended to assist those who support morally injured soldiers and family members. These practitioners are the sources for our definition of moral injury. Together they provide an interdisciplinary approach to healing moral injuries.

Those who suffer moral injury, of course, do not all have the same background and do not share the same cultural traditions or moral and spiritual values. The fact of pluralism notwithstanding, values guide a person's conduct. They give a person a frame for meaning-construction. Values provide the frame for human beings to have internal conversations with themselves. "Is my life on the right track?" "Is this action the best possible one in accord with how I understand my purpose in life?" "Will I feel good about myself with this conduct?" "If I do not, how will I get 'okay' again?" These are the kinds of value questions that anybody with a conscience and sense of purpose asks; the questions are gravity laden when stirred by moral injury.

The work of reconciling moral dissonance involves a soldier having profound and genuine "conversations" with his/her self and with those who accompany them throughout their difficult, healing journey. For this conversation to happen, it is important for soldiers, family members, military

leaders, educators, chaplains, pastors, counselors, and other health professionals to have a model for analyzing and deconstructing the formation of
moral dissonance in order to build new practices that create moral reconciliation. The two-mirror model (TMM) introduced in the previous chapter
is intended to serve the same ends and is based upon the research, clinical
accounts, and theories presented in this chapter.

The Three Interactive Processes of Moral Injury

Here, again, is our definition of moral injury. *Moral injury is the complex
"soul" wound that results from a person's inability to resolve the difference
between their idealized values and their perceived experiences. This wound
produces a chain of emotions and maladaptive behaviors that corrode character and damage an individual's capacity for living.*

Any analytical model for MI needs to account for three interactive
processes that combine to form a moral injury: moral development, moral
judgment, and moral reconciliation. First, an analysis of MI begins by looking at the moral development of a soldier's moral voice and moral agency. In
the profession of arms, moral voice and moral agency braid human identity
with military character. This process occurs within an ethos whose objective
is to empower its soldiers to serve honorably under difficult conditions and
successfully return home. This desire forms an "ideal" standard of conduct
that is required in combat. However, under fire, soldiers' reasoned choices
give way to reflexive reactions. When this happens, their "idealized" voice
and agency do not guarantee acceptable outcomes and they must live with
the consequences of their *perceived* conduct.[3] Idealized moral voice is reflected in the first mirror of the TMM.

Second, MI grows from moral judgment. A soldier's moral voice both
guides and judges moral agency. A soldier's conduct is always judged according a set of standards defined by their values. These standards presuppose
that soldiers want to accomplish what they value. However, these standards
also imply the existence of a gap between intent and practice. Sometimes
this gap is a matter of simple disagreement; sometimes it is evidence of a
full-blown divorce. For soldiers the very nature of their work requires them
to live *in* the gap between what they believe should be right and what they

---

3. This follows either of the two patterns identified by Jonathan Shay, both of which
severely compromise character and the ability to trust. In Shay's "form 1," MI happens
when (a) there is a betrayal of what's right (b) by someone of legitimated authority in
(c) a high stakes situation. In "form 2" (b) is replaced by the MI subject; i.e., "I did it." In
either case, MI destroys a person's capacity for the flourishing of life. Shay, comments
during the MI Group Discussion at the American Academy of Religion, Nov 21, 2015.

perceive as wrong. This is their obligation to "fight well" while operating in volatile and ambiguous situations that disrupts their capability to achieve what they ultimately value. Moral judgment involves the reasoning processes between principles, utility, context, and virtue in which soldiers may justify doing the "wrong thing" by appealing to their intent to do the "right thing." In doing so, they accomplish what they later condemn. This inversion results in degrees of moral dissonance indicating conflicts between moral voice and moral agency. Perceived moral agency is reflected in the second mirror of the TMM.

Third, MI is healed through moral reconciliation. Soldiers' inability to reconcile their moral dissonance results in their moral injury. Soldiers live and work in a vocation where their moral agency requires them to personify their moral voice under extreme conditions. Soldiers not only expect this of themselves, they also require this from others. Perceived failures in moral agency become reality. When soldiers' condemn their conduct or the conduct of others, the severity of the resulting moral dissonance can grow into recognizable MI. Moral dissonance may manifest as negative moral emotions such as anger, guilt, shame, disgust, condemnation, alienation, betrayal, and distrust.[4] These emotions contribute to maladaptive behaviors such as loss of self-identity, isolation, abuse (self and others), dependencies, and other pathologies. Just as soldiers are expected to correct differences between their values and conduct, it is logical to anticipate that they will attempt to reconcile the differences that caused their moral dissonance. The specific forms and pathways for this reconciliation process will require soldiers to reexamine their moral development and moral judgment process. Soldiers habituate their values within an ethos, and they must reconcile their dissonance within a community. Moral dissonance happens within and from the comparative reflections between the two mirrors of the TMM.

The processes of moral development, moral judgment, and moral reconciliation are present throughout the current research, clinical accounts and theories describing the formation and healing of moral injury. Each of these approaches describes different aspects of these processes. Together, they provide an eclectic understanding of the influence that these processes have upon the formation and healing of moral injuries. However they do not deal with the specific formations of soldiers' identity. We will deal further with these formations in chapters 4 and 5. For now, it is best to begin with the research that allows us to differentiate between trauma-based and value-based injuries.

4. Currier et al., "Role of Moral Emotions," 249–62. Crystal Park et al. have documented soldiers' inability to accommodate or assimilate new meaning from trauma and links to dysfunctional behaviors. Park et al., *Trauma, Meaning and Spirituality*, 77–94.

Differentiating Moral Injury from Post-Traumatic Stress Disorder (PTSD)

PTSD is a threat-based injury diagnosed from soldiers' persistent reactions to combat stressors. MI is a valued-based injury from severe moral dissonance generated by soldiers processing what they *value, do, and experience*. Because of this, MI may not manifest itself in the same post-trauma patterns as PTSD.[5] This manifestation is due to the description of traumatic triggering events attributed as causes of PTSD. "Soldiers suffering from PTSD feel anxious or afraid. That fear can take over their lives. . . . Moral injuries occur less from fear and more from loss—specifically violent, traumatic loss. . . . Loss is a very important and [a] separate, potential harm for service members in war."[6]

The following graphic represents the relationship between the diagnostic criteria for PTSD and our working definition for MI.

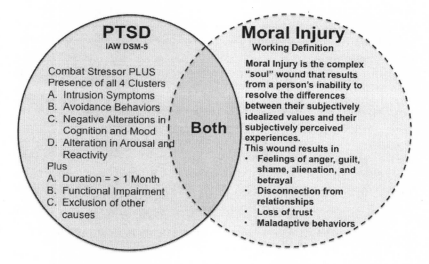

Figure 3.1 Differences between
PTSD and Moral Injury[7]

5. Litz et al., "Moral Injury and Moral Repair." This study found the presence of significant behavioral changes in soldiers that do not result in the hyper-arousal criteria needed for a PTSD diagnosis.

6. Litz as quoted in Kaplan, "Military Is Going Beyond PTSD."

7. Constructed from the US Department of Veterans Affairs, "DSM-5 Criteria for PTSD"; Shay, *Achilles in Vietnam*; Tick, *War and the Soul*; and Litz et al., "Moral Injury."

Current statistics indicate that approximately 18.6% of the soldiers deployed since 2001 exhibited symptoms of PTSD as defined by the current Diagnostic and Statistical Manual of Mental Disorders (DSM-5).[8] DSM-5 defines PTSD as the result from exposure to actual or threatened death that causes significant distress or impairment in the individual's social interactions through the persistent presence of four behavior clusters that are not the physiological result of another; medical condition, medication, drugs or alcohol.[9]

In working with groups of veterans, Jonathan Shay found that veterans' *perceptions* about their combat experiences led to their post-trauma symptoms; it was *not their direct exposure to a violent traumatic event itself* which caused MI symptoms.[10] For these soldiers, their subsequent awareness of their conduct and association with the conduct of others is what traumatized them. Second, this growing awareness is what subverted their character and fueled their self-defeating behaviors. This is where Shay derived his definition of complex moral wounds. In moral wounds the primary wound is linked, but decidedly separate from the secondary wound. The primary wound injures, but the secondary wound produces the ongoing damage that destroys soldiers.

The soldiers in the narratives presented in the previous chapters did not focus upon their personal vulnerability to trauma. Instead they focused upon the moral agency they exercised in injuries done to others in the course of their duties. Thus, these narratives reveal the relationship between moral development and moral judgment as soldiers hold themselves accountable for the choices they and others made. Their anguish is an expression of the contextual and nuanced moral dissonance that differentiates moral injury from PTSD.[11] Lieutenant Colonel Douglas Pryer describes this differentiation and its relationship to combat veterans:

> PTSD is physical in origin, while moral injury is a "dimensional" problem. Physically stressful experiences may cause PTSD, but nonthreatening events may still serve as a source of moral trauma. . . . Moral injury is real and any nation that desires to truly honor its warriors must place perceptions of "what is right" at the forefront of its deliberations on when and how to wage war. . . . Some leaders . . . can and do protest that moral injury cannot possibly apply to U.S. service-members. Despite

8. Tanielian, "Assessing Combat Exposure."

9. US Department of Veterans Affairs, "DSM-5 Criteria for PTSD."

10. Shay, *Odysseus in America*.

11. Kaplan, "Military Is Going Beyond PTSD."

their protests, large numbers of troops clearly believe they did or witnessed something wrong downrange, perhaps terribly wrong, and what matters here is how the individuals judge their experiences, not what other say.[12]

Currently we do not know the number of combat veterans experiencing MI. But we can estimate the proportion of the numbers by combining the above definitions with known PTSD data, then applying these numbers to the number of veterans who deployed into combat since September 2001. In the last decade of war, 85% of the deployed force experienced exposure to combat with about 18.6% of this group reporting post-traumatic stress symptoms. In raw numbers, this means that 2.2 million of the 2.6 million soldiers deployed in Iraq and Afghanistan have combat exposure with over 411,000 reporting PTSD symptoms. Currently, over 260,000 Iraq and Afghanistan veterans have been diagnosed with PTSD, with about 50% actively seeking treatment.[13] Navy psychologist William Nash believes that large portion of veterans diagnosed or undiagnosed post-traumatic problems that can be linked to moral injuries.[14]

If Nash and Shay are correct in asserting that: (1) many veterans exhibit debilitating effects from moral injury that either do not meet the full criteria of PTSD, and (2) they exhibit similar symptoms attributed to different causes, then (3) it is reasonable to infer that the number of veterans with some form of moral injury is at least equal to or greater than the number of soldiers diagnosed with PTSD. Furthermore, if the National Vietnam Veterans Readjustment Study (NVVRS) data is indicative of a potential future trend in the population of veterans experiencing some form of PTSD (about 35.8%), then we can assume that the number of veterans experiencing some type of moral injury is potentially similar to the current number of VA veterans diagnosed with PTSD.[15]

This theoretical calculation needs to be supported with hard data. However, clinical narratives and current research tell of soldiers expressing issues that can be attributed to moral dissonance. These numbers may be skewed by preexisting conditions that soldiers bring with them into the military. Some complex, trauma-related conditions, such as child abuse, predispose combat veterans to post-traumatic reactions.[16] In 2009 between

---

12. Pryer, "Moral Injury."

13. Veterans and PTSD, "Veterans Statistics."

14. Wood, "Warrior's Moral Dilemma."

15. Shay, *Achilles in Vietnam.*

16. Litz et al., *Adaptive Disclosure*, 154–59.

15%–20% of the new soldiers screened positive for some type of mental health issue.[17] These issues specifically included depression, attention-deficit/hyperactivity disorder, panic disorders, or trauma disorders.[18] Recent reports indicate that one in ten recruits qualified for a diagnosis of "intermittent explosive disorder" or impulsive anger: which is a catalyst for acting on other impulses. This rate is five times higher than the rate found in the general population.[19]

Such pre-deployment conditions may influence the way that soldiers morally develop and process their combat experiences. These factors need to be considered in interpreting the results from post-deployment assessments designed to measure soldiers' trauma levels. The recent data from the Mental Health Advisory Team (MHAT) studies are the most systematic and comprehensive look at issues Soldiers and Marines faced while on deployment. From 2003 to 2013 that military conducted nine surveys of redeploying troops to determine their responses to combat. In 2003 the initial MHAT study reported that

- 80% stated they participated in a continuum of events where lethal force was used.

- 65% reported they were responsible for the death of an enemy combatant.

- 28% stated they were responsible for the death of a noncombatant.[20]

Combine this data with subsequent MHAT studies where Soldiers and Marines reported the following ethical issues:

- 60% said they saw and were unable to help ill or wounded women and children.

- Less than 50% felt that noncombatants should be treated with dignity and respect.

- 41% percent of Soldiers and 44% of Marines believed torture is acceptable to save the life of a fellow warrior. (Note the morally and emotionally charged use of "warrior" in this question.)

- 36% percent of Soldiers and 39% percent of Marines believe that torture is acceptable to gain intelligence on the insurgents.

- More than 30% admitted insulting and swearing at Iraqis.

17. O'Connor, *Collateral Damage.*
18. Zarembo, "Nearly 1 in 5 Had Mental Illness."
19. Carey, "Study Finds Suicidal Tendencies."
20. Hoge et al., "Combat Duty in Iraq and Afghanistan," 13–22.

- Nearly 33% said their officers had not made it clear that maltreatment of civilians is unacceptable.

- 32% felt responsibility for killing an enemy combatant.

- 20% felt responsibility for the death of a noncombatant.

- 31% reported insulting and cursing at civilians.

- 25% reported they experienced ethical situations where they didn't know how to respond.

- 17% believed that noncombatants should be treated as insurgents.

- 10% admitted to damaging property unnecessarily.

- 5% admitted to mistreating civilians.

- 4% of Soldiers and 7% of Marines confessed to hitting or kicking noncombatants.[21]

The MHAT data reveal that a greater percentage of Soldiers and Marines report witnessing or taking part in acts of violence than the number of those who are treated for post-traumatic stress. Furthermore, a significantly higher number of Soldiers and Marines admit to witnessing what they perceive as immoral or unethical acts than actually committing them. The higher number is understandable, but the existence of this data supports the broad effect of value-based stressors within combat veterans. The specific MHAT questions describe what Linden and Trice define as acts of cruelty and embitterment. Therefore the data potentially links veterans' combat experiences with the psychological and spiritual effects of cruelty and embitterment documented by Linden and Trice.[22] This linkage raises the probability that an identifiable population of soldiers with some type of moral issue exists outside of the conventional DSM-5 diagnosis for PTSD.

Although, the MHAT data reveals a general picture of *what* Soldiers and Marines perceived about their combat experiences, the MHAT didn't ask Soldiers and Marines about *what* they valued, and *what* they specifically felt. More importantly, the MHAT didn't explore *how* veterans' emotional responses to combat and their combat perceptions affected their present behaviors and identity. Therefore we do not have any definitive data that directly tests any definition of moral injury against veteran experiences.

---

21. US Army, *Mental Health Advisory Team Study IV*. This trend can be found in all MHAT studies. See also Barrett, *Finding "the Right Way."*

22. Linden et al., *Posttraumatic Embitterment Disorder*; Trice, *Encountering Cruelty*.

However, the existing MHAT data allow us to estimate the levels of moral emotions and moral dissonance present within the force.[23] If we assume that each of the above categories includes some level of moral dissonance, then up to 80% participated in such events and up to 60% had some type of negative reaction. When we apply this percentage to the NVVRS and VA PTSD studies, the comparison suggests that although 18.6% of combat veterans experience PTSD, a larger number of veterans experience some type of combat stress reaction that is related to value-based perceptions. The following graphic represents the relationship between the numbers of soldiers diagnosed with PTSD and those who report some type of emotional response to a moral issue.

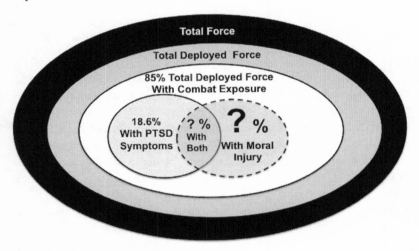

Figure 3.2 The Relationship between Soldiers with
PTSD and Potential Moral Injuries[24]

The exact number of soldiers experiencing some type of moral injury is unknown. This may be attributed to the noninclusion of moral injury within the DSM-5 PTSD criteria, and the current studies not collecting specific data on MI symptoms. However, the lack of data may also be attributed to the lack of a common model to build a definitive study. We believe we have learned enough from the existing data to build a testable model for analyzing MI. The TMM provides this type of model. We need such a model because moral injury and value-based reactions are not specifically a part

23. US Army, *Mental Health Advisory Team Study IV*. This trend can be found in all MHAT studies. See also Barrett, *Finding "the Right Way."*

24. Tanielian, "Assessing Combat Exposure."

of the existing PTSD criteria. Therefore, moral dissonance goes untreated as veterans experiencing both PTSD symptoms and value-based issues are treated only for their fear-based traumatic stress. Furthermore, veterans reporting moral issues without PTSD criteria are treated for presenting problems not necessarily related to the cause of their condition. We believe that more is needed to provide hurting veterans with appropriate care.

Current research, although incomplete, reveals that we know something about the causes and effects of moral injury. In addition, researchers, clinicians, and healers provide further compelling practices and theories for helping veterans' deal with the effects from moral injuries. Each of these interdisciplinary perspectives informs our definition of MI. Taken together these perspectives deepen our understanding of MI, and provide critical means for analyzing its effects. This analysis prevents a minimization of destructive moral dissonance and a mistreatment of moral injury. Navy psychiatrist William Nash concludes, "The more that is learned about the full nature of these injuries [PTSD and MI], the less room there remains for narrow, reductionist models to explain them. Multidimensional, integrated theories require testing with multidimensional research that seeks to uncover not only individual cause-effect relationships but the interplay between multiple causes and effects at the levels of brain, mind, and society."[25]

Four Perspectives for Understanding Moral Injury

Researchers, clinicians, healers, and soldiers contribute to multiple definitions for moral injury. In 1981 Peter Marin used the concept of moral pain to publish an article in *Psychology Today* to help the public understand the linkage of value-based effects from combat upon the well-being of returning Vietnam veterans. This was an attempt to identify moral injury and separate it from the developing theories for combat stress. Marin provides a foundation for what each of the four perspectives provide to an analytical model for MI.

> We seem as a society to have few useful ways to approach moral pain or guilt; it remains for us a form of neurosis or a pathological symptom, something to escape rather than something to learn from, a disease rather than—as it may well be for the vets—an appropriate if painful response to the past. . . . Of course, many vets have problems directly traceable to other sources, and no doubt there are vets who are not disturbed in any way by their participation in the war. Yet the fact remains

25. Figley and Nash, *Combat Stress Injury*, 89.

that in private conversations with many disturbed vets, one begins to sense beneath the surface of their resentment the deep and unacknowledged roots of their anger.[26]

The Researchers

Brett Litz and a large team of researchers have conducted a comprehensive literature study of the research data supporting a definition for moral injury. They define MI as "perpetrating, failing to prevent, bearing witness to, or learning about acts that transgress deeply held moral beliefs and expectations."[27] Their definition emphasizes the cognitive and affective relationships between commission, omission, and association for mental health. Veterans' specific acts of commission, omission, and association form the basis of viewing MI through moral voice and agency. Their work differentiates MI from PTSD, and it opens the door for exploring ways to incorporate MI research into the DSM-5 definitions of PTSD.[28] However, the inclusion of MI as a subcategory of PTSD may not be helpful for mitigating its risk or healing the injury.

William Nash, the author of the *Navy and Marine Operational Stress Model*, views the issue of moral responsibility as the critical element separating MI from PTSD. He writes, "What makes a warrior a warrior is taking personal responsibility. And when they [warriors] fail to live up to that enormously high ideal, that's moral injury."[29] Nash implies that fear-based stressors without moral responsibility may cause PTSD but are not sufficient for generating moral injuries. Some code for model conduct is necessary to guide responsibility. Litz et al. reported multiple studies linking aspects of moral agency to emotional and behavioral problems. These types of studies justify rethinking the distinctions between "fear-based" and "value-based" injuries. These differences have implications for the ways that moral injuries are mitigated, diagnosed, and treated. For Litz, the implications of his research led him to develop adaptive disclosure therapy (a type of cognitive behavior therapy) with the treatment goal of helping veterans examine their self-narratives to reclaim their goodness and self-worth.[30]

26. Marin, "Living in Moral Pain."
27. Litz et al., "Moral Injury and Moral Repair."
28. US Department of Veteran Affairs, "DSM-5 Criteria for PTSD."
29. Kaplan, "Military Is Going Beyond PTSD."
30. Litz, "Adaptive Disclosure Talk."

Adaptive disclosure therapy (ADT) distinguishes three types of harm-causing post-traumatic injuries: life-threat, loss, and moral injury. ADT provides a therapeutic agency separating PTSD from grief, and MI to help soldiers identify and change the issues that are consuming them. Litz et al. found that these injuries do not respond to the same healing strategies used for working with civilians because military members have been trained to operate under combat stress. ADT employs breakout sessions to specifically address issues of loss and moral injury, to begin clarifying and unfolding new meaning to destructive combat experiences. This new meaning includes self-forgiveness.[31] For this to happen, ADT requires all acts of moral injury to be examined within the stresses of war and the totality of the self.[32] This raises the importance of moral development and moral judgment within the specific military ethos for healing MI. Litz's work describes the causes of moral dissonance without naming its existence. ADT is based upon constructions of the "ideal/perceived" self and self-forgiveness without describing the specific aspects of moral voice and agency that contribute to soldiers' identity and character.

Psychologists Joseph Currier, Wesley McCormick, and Kent Drescher completed a small population study of Iraq and Afghanistan combat veterans and concluded that four distinct clusters of morally injurious events (MIEs) contribute to moral injuries in veterans. These clusters include: (a) organizational circumstances, (b) environmental circumstances, (c) cultural and relational circumstances, and (d) psychological circumstances. Soldiers express the effects from these events through their "moral emotions" that are visible and audible indicators of moral injures.[33] Moral emotions are both positive (compassion, elevation, gratitude, and pride) and negative (guilt, shame, anger, disgust, and contempt). These emotions are linked with how soldiers process their MIEs. Thus, the expression of these emotions is connected in some way to soldiers' core values. This connection demonstrates how context and conduct are essential factors for evaluating the formation and effects of moral injuries. However, they didn't deal with the specific constructions and content of the value systems that are active within the military. Currier, McCormick, and Drescher conclude their study with a general observation: "We found four broad categories of circumstances by which MIEs may occur, underscoring the potential organizational, environmental, cultural/relational, and/or psychological dimensions of these warzone experiences. Appreciating a fuller range of contextual factors that may

31. Litz et al., *Adaptive Disclosure*, 3–9.

32. Ibid., 119.

33. Currier et al., "Role of Moral Emotions," 249–62.

precipitate these potential traumas will increase the ability of researchers/ clinicians to more fully address the needs of morally injured veterans who served in modern guerrilla wars."[34]

The Clinicians

Military psychiatrist Colonel Charles Hoge believes that "the development of PTSD after combat experiences has very little (or nothing) to with the character, upbringing, or genetics of the warrior. What remains is that certain events are profoundly devastating and have a much stronger impact neurologically than others, a situation that the warrior has no control over. PTSD in these situations represents normal reactions to extremely abnormal (or extraordinary) events."[35]

Hoge focuses upon the intensity of the traumatic event and its neurological effects, and on the surface this collapses MI into a personal injury that is a subcategory of PTSD. Yet his work important for healing MI, because his work includes studies about mitigating the risks of PTSD conducted by the Walter Reed Army Institute of Research (WRAIR). Hoge believes that strong command leadership, unit cohesion, morale, and family support highly influence resiliency and recovery.[36] He views traumatic stress as autonomic nervous system reactions, but he views recovery as cognitive reprocessing of these responses. Hoge demonstrates the processes where primary emotional responses (such as hurt, fear, anger, powerlessness, or grief) to traumatic events develop into complex emotions (such as depression, despondence, guilt, and shame). These complex emotions, similar to Currier's moral emotions, have lingering effects upon the lives of soldiers.[37] Therefore, Hoge advocates for a holistic healing process similar to Park et al that includes: life skills, modulating responses, narrative formation, resiliency, coping, and accepting. The treatment goal for soldiers is the recovery of their vision, their voice, and their community. Hoge's work describes how combat perception can develop into the intense emotions that accompany moral dissonance.

Psychiatrist Jonathan Shay locates moral injury at the deep roots of veterans' anger. Shay describes MI as "Complex PTSD." This is similar to Hoge's explanation of complex emotions. Unlike Hoge and those who believe moral injuries are the result of PTSD, Shay believes that post-trauma

34. Currier et al., "How Do Morally Injurious Events Occur?"
35. Hoge, *Once a Warrior*, 28.
36. Ibid., 28–20.
37. Ibid., 227; Park et al., 77–94.

stress is the visible symptom of a more dangerous hidden wound that acts like an internal hemorrhage and post-trauma infection. This complex secondary injury causes "the destruction of the capacity for social trust, and loss of a flourishing human life."[38] This makes the causes of the moral injury the primary focus for treatment. These causes conceptually differ from "fear-based" trauma, and require different methods of prevention and treatment. Shay uses the classical works of the *Iliad* and the *Odyssey* to illustrate how emotional responses to traumatic events convey moral meanings that affect soldiers' in combat and when they return home. He uses the combat and homecoming experiences of Achilles and Ulysses to connect with the war narratives of veterans to help soldiers understand and interpret their own experiences.

For Shay, the concept of "honor" binds Greek soldiers' self-identity. When honor is violated, soldiers struggle. The same is true for modern soldiers. "The moral strength of an army is betrayed by every injustice."[39] For soldiers the betrayal of "what is right" (a moral judgment based upon voice and agency) becomes the trigger for emotions and behaviors that erode character and shrink soldiers' "social and moral horizons." This erosion and shrinking includes their ideals, attachments, and ambitions.[40] These behaviors cause what columnist David Brooks calls "moral exile."[41] This type of alienation requires mitigation practices integrating military ethics and leadership training.[42]

While Shay focuses upon personal responses and effects, Navy psychiatrist William Nash and Dr. Charles Figley categorize combat stress reactions into three categories: "traumatic stress, caused by the impacts of terror, horror, or helplessness; operations fatigue, caused by the wear and tear of accumulated stress, and grief, caused by the loss of someone or something that is highly valued."[43]

Nash and Figley believe that differentiating traumatic stressors will increase the likelihood that injuries not caused by terror will be recognized and treated. They find value in understanding *why* veterans feel the way they do, and they demonstrate how traumatic damage to core beliefs form "imprinted, dark" effects such as shame, guilt, and dissociation of the self. Thus,

---

38. This is a model used by Shay in a variety of sources. For examples, see Shay, *Odysseus in America*, 83–87; and Guntzel, "Invisible Injury: Beyond PTSD."

39. Shay, *Achilles in Vietnam*, 27.

40. Ibid.

41. Brooks, "Moral Injury."

42. Shay, "Trust: Touchstone for a Practical Military Ethos."

43. Figley and Nash, *Combat Stress Injury*, 50.

the initial causes (context) of the traumatic stress are less important than the cumulative effects of the stress, and the value of the losses. They advocate for treatments that extend beyond the analysis of the primary trauma in order to focus upon the damaged core values forming into post–traumatic effects that disrupt soldiers' identity. Their conclusions allow for a vital distinction between fear-based and value-based injuries based upon moral voice and agency. Their work opens the door for exploring the nature of soldiers' moral development and moral judgment. Their work also links the healing of moral injuries with issues of forgiveness and reconciliation. "Since warfighters train and prepare themselves to withstand the traumas of combat, it is much harder for them to forgive themselves for failing in any way to triumph over it. Recovering from traumatic shame and guilt requires the construction of a new set of beliefs about oneself and one's place in the world, beliefs that allow for very human weaknesses at sometimes crucial moments. Overcoming guilt and shame depends on forgiveness."[44]

Psychotherapist Edward Tick defines injuries to core beliefs in terms of spiritual values. He believes MI is a "shadow wound" created by judgments between good and evil.[45] While Shay focuses upon systemic causes of moral wounds in his treatment models, Tick focuses upon individual processing and communal healing. For Tick, good and evil are not diametrically opposed. They are parts of internal value systems that soldiers use to process the external events of combat. The resulting stresses cause moral wounds. The negative effects from these moral wounds form a shadow that darkens a soldier's future pathway. This dark shadow draws him/her into a post-traumatic injury that "is best understood as an identity disorder and soul wound, affecting the personality at the deepest levels."[46] Tick believes this wounding is best understood in terms of human conscience. Soldiers can strengthen their conscience through a psycho-spiritual "warriorhood" that provides resiliency against combat exposure and promotes healing for their wounded soul post-combat.[47] "Warriorhood" is a maturation process built around a community of mature warriors that empowers a moral healing process. In this process, returning warriors experience the healing of their "soul" wounds as they learn to "follow the dove" and become healers themselves.[48] Tick's work expands value-based injuries to include the spiritual beliefs and practices that support soldier's moral voice and agency.

44. Ibid.
45. Tick, *War and the Soul*, 22.
46. Ibid., 5.
47. Ibid., 177–98.
48. Ibid., 251.

He broadens practices of forgiveness to include issues of reconciliation essential for healing soul wounds. His focus upon healing warriors' conscientious wrestling with their contradicting values and conduct allows for further examination of moral dissonance as the cause for moral injury. It is important to notice Tick's specific use of "warrior" to convey moral meaning. Tick's theory relies upon the values that veterans use to morally judge their function as warriors without focusing upon the moral development of their obligations as soldiers. This distinction will become important when accounting for military ethos and moral development in naming and healing the causes of veterans' moral dissonance.

Similar to Tick's "soul wound," psychiatrist Larry Dewey describes MI as a "breaking of the Geneva Convention of the Soul." He believes that four areas of pain and horror produce effects worse than the killing of enemy soldiers. These areas are: (1) seeing and committing acts resulting in civilian causalities, (2) involvement in friendly fire incidents, (3) killing while filled with hate, rage or something like elation, and (4) incidents of battlefield justice (committing, failing to prevent, and/or condoning a retributive act against an helpless enemy or civilian).[49] These areas are similar to the survey questions used in the MHAT studies, where up to 60% of the Soldiers and Marines said that they were associated with specific events defined by these areas. Dewey demonstrates how issues of moral agency evoke deep emotional reactions within combatants. Under fire, one soldier may approach the edge of a moral cliff and safely turn away, while another trips and falls into the abyss, and another willingly jumps.[50] His work relies upon the foundations of moral voice and agency that differentiates between soldiers, warriors, and pirates. Dewey demonstrates how failed moral agency forms into moral injuries through a contradiction between values and conduct. His areas are similar to the categories of morally injurious events (MIEs) that Currier et al. associate with injurious moral emotions. Dewey believes the resulting moral wounds necessitate different treatments than those for "fear-based" injuries. Like the other researchers and clinicians, Dewey believes that healing must occur over time and in specific ways that allow veterans to process the sources for their wounds in order to reconnect with their lives.

49. Dewey, *War and Redemption*, 73–75.
50. Ibid., 77.

The Healers

Ethicist Nancy Sherman is a scholar who focuses upon the formation and healing of MI. For Sherman, MI is a philosophical and psychological anguish that grows out of soldiers' reactions to "doing wrong, being wronged, or witnessing wrongs."[51] Her work is similar to the other researchers and clinicians, and she focuses upon soldiers' moral reactions to MIEs. However, she demonstrates how these reactions form into moral judgments between conscience and obedience. Soldiers use criteria such as national justifications for going to war (*jus ad bellum*), and their personal conduct in war (*jus in bello*). These judgments carry considerable emotional weight defined by the values that determine soldiers' existence. Disconnections between soldiers' desired values and their experienced conduct results in their feelings of being tainted, suckered, disillusioned, and betrayed.[52] Like Shay, Sherman interprets individual soldier judgments thru the lens of classical philosophy to explore how MI forms within conflict and destroys identity and character. "Psyches fracture, and self-empathy with the warring parts is often in short supply. There is not only a sense of accountability for one's part in collective ends, but also a sense of being manipulated, beyond easy control, to carry out others' mistakes or deceptions."[53]

This destruction also provides the elements for healing. Sherman uses Stoic philosophy to peel away soldiers' false perceptions in order to find a renewing balance in the pursuit of virtues. Thus, moral wounding exposes soldiers' false limitations, and the resulting shame breaks down their barriers for growth. For Sherman, this growth is a matter of empathy and self-forgiveness that emerges from shattered myths of existence. Sherman voices the necessity for reconciliation within the healing process, and she understands that this is a difficult task. "Estimations of worth and goodness, of course, needn't have anything to do with estimates of a person's psychological capacities to overcome crippling and harsh guilt, or to accept the limits of agency and what is beyond one's control. But *admiring* another's goodness or capacity for hard work in the service of important and worthwhile ends *may* have such an influence."[54]

Shay, Tick, Dewey, and Sherman believe that healing comes within community. Brian Doorhies and the social impact group Theater of War use Greek dramas to help veterans and communities wrestle with the complex

51. Kime, "5 Questions."

52. Sherman, *Untold War*, Kindle loc. 650.

53. Ibid., loc. 1011.

54. Ibid., loc. 2650–52.

ethical and moral issues needed for recovering from combat.[55] Their program believes that healing begins with understanding the depth of soldiers'
specific anguish in order to generate genuine conversations between veterans and civilians. These conversations extend beyond the cheap grace of
"thank you for your service," by empowering veterans to create meaningful
reconnections with their lives.[56] For example, the group will use scenes from
the classical tragedy *Ajax* to address the issue of veteran suicide through
moral emotions such as betrayal, rage, and isolation. Ajax was a veteran of
the Trojan War who returns home with a sense of rage after betrayal from
his king and fellow leaders. His unresolved emotions lead to his suicide,
much to the pain of his family and comrades. Ajax had his reasons for these
emotions, and the drama group helps veterans and communities unpack
these reasons. Thus, Ajax's story connects with their war narratives. This
process is a way of helping veterans begin a healing process by reframing the
emotions accompanying their perceptions in a community experience. This
is much the same way that the Greek playwright Sophocles used tragedy and
community to train and heal future generations.

Theologians Rita Nakashima-Brock, and Gabriella Lettini view moral
injury as the violation of conscience. Like Tick and Dewey, they view conscience as the holistic, spiritual construction of "soul." They define MI as the
"reflection on memories of war or other extreme traumatic conditions . . .
[that] transgressed basic moral identity and violated core moral beliefs."[57]
Their intent is to repair soldiers' injured souls through a restoration of their
sacred values. This healing requires connecting soldiers' souls to the pain of
their victims through communal moral action and healing through experiences such as truth commissions. They believe that soldiers' moral pain
comes from their moral objections to war. In a similar manner, theologian
Robert Emmet Meagher believes that the healing of moral wounds begins
by uprooting the just war traditions that enable rationales for virtuous killing that morally injures soldiers.[58] Brock, Lettini, and Meagher approach MI
from the perspective of moral justice, and they want to label "war" for the
sin that they believe it is. The inevitable result of war sinks "warriors into
states of silent, solitary suffering . . . [and] torments to the soul can make
death a mercy."[59] Their use of "warriors" is descriptive of the moral function they believe that military service requires. This description supports

55. See Theater of War, http://theaterofwar.com/projects/theater-of-war/overview.

56. Brooks, "Moral Injury."

57. Brock and Lettini, *Soul Repair*, Kindle loc. 78.

58. Meagher, *Killing from the Inside Out*, Kindle loc. 282–95.

59. Brock and Lettini, *Soul Repair*, Kindle loc. 104–26.

elements of moral voice and agency within soldiers' narratives that decry the pain and the cruelty of war. Their work demonstrates the important roles that conscience, moral development, "ideal" values, spiritual connections, and perceptions have in the formation of MI. Like Tick, they work for the restoration of veterans to the "way of the dove," but they are less concerned with understanding the moral development of Tick's "warriorhood" that allows healing to occur. The moral development and moral judgment that differentiates soldiers, warriors, and pirates is necessary for healing the combat veterans who continue to serve in the military.

Military chaplains David Bachelor, Dean Bonura, Robert Hicks, and Tom Frame define MI similar to the other clinicians, researchers, and healers described in this chapter. Similar to Tick, Brock, and Lettini, they view MI as a soul wound and spiritual malady. However, they view "fighting well in a just war" as an obligation for conscientious, honorable service. They understand that this is not always possible, and soldiers experience moral wounds in combat. Navy Chaplain David Bachelor uses the metaphor of a "death-shadow" to describe the cumulative effects of war-zone exposure that threaten soldiers' identity. Similar to the work of Nash, Figley, Currier, and others he focuses upon the effects of MI in terms of traumatic death "imprint" experiences. These experiences permeate soldiers' thinking and defeat their attempts to socially reengage. Similar to Tick, Bachelor advocates for the creation of spiritual healing communities that empower soldiers to experience a "warrior wash," where they can name, renew, and cleanse their identities from their wartime experiences.[60]

Similar to Hoge and Litz, Army Chaplain Dean Bonura approaches MI as a sub-category of PTSD. He links the violation of soldiers' values with traumatic stress events similar to what others define as MIEs. Like Shay, Tick, Sherman, and other researchers, Bonura believes that soldiers' moral pain is expressed within their war narratives, and these narratives provide the key for healing their moral injuries. His pastoral approach focuses upon helping soldiers achieve post-traumatic growth by reframing and reconstructing their narratives. This process shares a similar treatment goal with Litz's ADT, to provide "a new perspective that helps sufferers discover meaning in their trauma by connecting their present experience to past experience in a way that delinks the painful memory of their trauma from their present experience."[61]

---

60. Bachelor, "Death Shadow." Bachelor specifically focuses on the biblical concept of *zalmot* (Death Shadow) found in Pss 23, 44, 107, and Isa 9:14 to describe the effects of moral injury in combat veterans.

61. Bonura, *Beyond Trauma*, Kindle loc. 2072–74.

Air Force Chaplain Robert Hicks provides two pieces of practical guidance for veterans and their healing communities: (1) a proposed assessment tool for post-traumatic stress, and (2) a proposed framework for processing trauma narratives. His assessment tool invites veterans and communities to assess the specific contexts of MIEs as well as their impacts. He believes that veterans form imperfect narratives from these MIEs, and these narratives become the means of deconstructing their identity. Therefore, the reconstruction of meaningful narratives is needed to restore spiritual health and relationships. This healing occurs when veterans work through four unhealthy assumptions they use to judge their MIEs: invulnerability (it can't happen to me), rationality (the world makes sense), morality (the universe is just), and identity (I know who I am).[62] Hick's model provides a way for veterans to process the existential questions that are a part of their core values and worldviews.

Finally, Australian Chaplain Dr. Frame has edited a collection of essays on the effects of MI from a multidiscipline group of ex-soldiers, scholars, clinicians, and chaplains. These essays parallel the above perspectives with the exception that they focus upon the systemic cultural and spiritual issues of war that underlie soldiers' hidden wounds. These essays are important for: (1) their direct exploration of MI within the Australian Defense Forces, (2) their focus upon moral issues as the cause of "alienation" as an emotional expression of MI, and (3) their realization that healing MI is an iterative process involving questions of ultimate meaning. Frame introduces this work. "Asking 'what was it all for?' is not a sign of mental illness, but of human maturity. To find the answers do not come all at once, or in an instant, does not signify that someone cannot cope with life. Rather, it is an affirmation that life is complex, insight is rare and wisdom is precious. Asking the best questions, challenging convenient answers and wondering whether the right words are being used to describe human emotions are welcome signs that individuality is being respected and the totality of experience is taken seriously."[63]

The contributions of healers raise questions about the morality of war that are foundational to the moral perceptions of the veterans who fight in these wars. They focus upon the "value-based" standards of judgment that soldiers are using to form their war narratives.

---

62. Hicks and Petersen, *Returning Home*, 148–54.

63. Frame, *Moral Injury*, 14–15.

The Soldiers

The work of these researchers, clinicians, and healers provides understanding of the "value-based" injuries that are separate from "fear-based" traumatic stress in both causes and effects. The resulting injuries are the product of conflicted values from traumatic events and emotional pain that affects soldiers' physical, psychological and spiritual health. The presence of this conflict requires a set of values that soldiers use in forming their perceptions. Soldiers' war narratives describe the pervasive reality of these causes and effects. These narratives link their moral voice with moral agency in acts they commit, acts they fail to prevent, and acts with which they associate themselves. These commissions, omissions, and associations should be considered as categories for interpreting moral injuries. The researchers, clinicians, and healers are not "discovering" a new phenomenon. They are trying to make sense of what is present in soldiers' visible symptoms and hidden in their invisible wounds. Together their multidiscipline approach provides a wide aperture to view MI.

Chapter 2 presented a model for interpreting MI from the perspective of a soldier. To empathize with the layers of meaning contained in their narratives, one must consider the perspectives and obligations that drive their moral conflicts. First, we'll examine the importance of perspective, and then we'll examine the importance of obligation.

Soldiers' perceptions of context are essential for treating moral injuries. In the first edition of his work, former infantryman and psychologist David Grossman proposed a scale to assess post-traumatic response. His work is useful in examining soldiers' perceptions of their levels of combat stress. He used Likert scales (scores of 1 to 10) for rating soldiers' perceptions of three distinct sources for traumatic stress: (1) individual vulnerability (defined as proximity to killing), multiplied by (2) degree of trauma (defined as duration and intensity), multiplied by (3) social support (defined by levels of individual and public condemnation). Grossman didn't confine his definition of traumatic stress to combat, but extended this to the home front. Grossman believed that higher scores from these scales would reveal greater levels of post-traumatic responses within the soldiers. Today these responses are labeled post-traumatic stresses or combat operational stress responses (COSR).

In 1997, Chaplain Zust used Grossman's scale as a counseling tool with Desert Storm veterans and pre-tested this scale with two veterans he knew. The results surprised him.[64] The first veteran was a World War

---

64. Veteran interviews conducted by Chaplain Jeff Zust in spring 1997.

II Army paratrooper who had three combat jumps and fought with the 101st Airborne from D-Day through Bastogne. His experiences included "liberating" a concentration camp. This veteran measured himself in the following manner.

1. On the vulnerability scale he scored himself an 8. This was based upon his estimate of 110+ days under intense fire. He reported "fear-based" traumatic stress responses.

2. On the trauma scale he scored himself a 10 based upon the fact that he killed in close-quarters combat.

3. On the support scale he scored himself a 1. He returned home a hero, and received overwhelming support. More importantly, he viewed himself an honorable soldier because he participated in events that he believed stopped a great evil. He also actively grieves lost comrades.

The second veteran was an Army truck driver during the Vietnam War. He performed long haul duties, and never saw what he considered front line combat. This veteran measured himself.

1. On the vulnerability scale he scored himself an 8. This was based upon eleven months of convoy operations that daily placed him under fire. Several times people riding in his vehicle were killed or wounded. Multiple times his base was under fire, and his "hootch" (quarters) was hit by mortar fire. He estimated about three hundred days under fire. He also reported "fear-based" traumatic responses.

2. On the trauma scale he scored himself a 2 because he seldom fired his weapon in combat, and never saw the enemy face to face. To his knowledge, he never killed or injured another person.

3. On the support scale he scored himself a 10 because several members of his small town, and family members were active in anti-war groups and used him personally as a subject for some of their protests. Because of this, he began questioning his own service. Thus, he reported "value-based" traumatic responses.

Using Grossman's scale, the World War II combat veteran scored a post-traumatic response number of 80, while the Vietnam service support veteran scored 160. Their scores demonstrate the profound differences in how veterans perceived their combat service, and perhaps themselves. In later editions of *On Killing*, Grossman changed his model to two scales: the degree of trauma and the amount of social support. His changes imply a movement away from focusing upon soldiers' "fear-based" vulnerability toward focusing upon the "value-based" perceptions of the trauma they inflict. Thus, Grossman's revised trauma response scale can be a subjective measurement for how soldiers perceive themselves as moral actors in combat. Using Grossman's revised scale, the WWII veteran scored himself a 10 and the Vietnam Veteran scored himself a 20.

Granted, these scores are based upon subjective perceptions. The scores can be explained in a variety of ways: different wars, different years, time removed from combat, combat circumstances, personalities, training, soldier maturity, social contexts, etc. However, these scores underline the importance of soldiers' perspectives about the specific details of their service and its effects upon their identity. Soldiers' narratives consist of their subjective perspectives, and these perspectives reveal their moral judgments. These judgments are based upon their sense of obligation.

Soldier narratives also reveal their obligations that are the product of their moral development measured by their perceptions of voice and agency. Soldiers' war narratives are contextual pixels of the larger picture that reveals their core values and what they accept as expected standards of conduct. The researchers, clinicians, and healers may differ on the cause and effects they assign to post-traumatic stress (PTS) and morally injurious events (MIE). They begin to agree on the importance of how soldiers employ their values while assessing their combat experiences.

In combat, autonomic responses and habituated reflexes can override the cognitive reasoning that is traditionally associated with ethical decision-making and moral agency. Soldiers joke, "In combat, things go from zero to stupid in a hurry." This statement is as much a description of the physical necessity for cognitive processing as it is with the speed of action under duress. In these unpredictable and demanding conditions, Navy SEAL and ethicist Dick Couch states that soldiers "can't wait until the eve of battle to talk about this stuff."[65] In combat, soldiers are obligated to control their responses and actions as they use their warrior skills. Their responses and reactions are both individual and social choices, governed by the character and ethos of their moral agency. The Law of War, the rules of engagement, mission orders, and their own moral voices define their standards for conduct. These standards obligate soldiers to operate in a spectrum of contexts from the best to the worst conditions.

One essential goal of military education and training is to develop soldiers' moral voice and empower moral agency. Both voice and agency define the moral obligations that separate the professional conduct of "soldiers" from the lethal reactions of "warriors" and the lethal recklessness of

65. Conversation between Chaplain Zust and Dick Couch in spring 2016.

"pirates."[66] Soldiers are expected to be master craftsmen in their profession, defined by the standards of conduct, the rules, and public trust that govern their service. Warrior skills do not cover the full spectrum of the ethical and moral character required by law, public trust, and the military ethos. Thus, young warriors require external control: at best they are novices and journeymen within a trade. They can accomplish their mission, but they may also use the wrong tool, at the wrong time, for the wrong result. All soldiers are warriors, but not all warriors are soldiers, and some warriors act as pirates. Combat leaders define "pirates" as groups of individuals co-opting unit integrity by using their combat skills for their own ends.[67]

Here is where it gets complicated. The conduct of soldiers, warriors, and pirates may be considered legal, but it may be judged immoral by both individuals and society. As Captain Mike Boock, a Navy Judge Advocate, explains, "the law is the floor, but we don't live on the floor: we live in the house above it."[68] This makes legal boundaries the minimum, instead of the maximum, boundary for professional service. Professional values and ethics obligate soldiers to a higher standard than that expected of warriors and pirates. The absence of these higher standards requires legal restraints. However, human core values may obligate soldiers to an even higher standard.

In the fog of war and the chaos of combat, the best intentions and the highest standards can still result in unintended consequences that inflict moral damage upon victims, perpetrators, and spectators. The moral danger is when a human being desires to act like a soldier, but reacts like a warrior, and then judges himself/herself to be a pirate. This is what Shay labels as the "undoing of character"; the nullification of the core values that soldiers are obligated to uphold.[69] Moral perceptions of failed obligations are the stuff that generates moral dissonance. These obligations determine what soldiers do, fail to do, or associate with as moral actors. The lines differentiating the moral judgments of "soldier, warrior, and pirate" character are not neatly drawn, and failure to stay within these boundaries affects the emotions and behaviors of veterans.

Lieutenant Barry Romo volunteered for service in Vietnam, and was honorably serving in a combat brigade. His nephew, Robert Romo, was drafted and assigned to the same brigade. Robert, a young private, asked

---

66. Fromm, "Warriors, the Army Ethos, and the Sacred Trust of Soldiers," 19–26.

67. This specific term was defined earlier. It is used among combat leaders to train values at the unit level. For a discussion on the "Pirate Factor," see Couch, *Tactical Ethic*, 5.

68. Chaplain Zust's conversation with Captain Boock, Naval Judge Advocate General Ethics Fellow at the National Defense University, 2014.

69. Shay, *Achilles in Vietnam*, 36, 210.

for Barry's help to get an assignment away from combat. Barry couldn't help him. Robert was killed while trying to help a wounded buddy, and Barry was chosen to escort Robert's body home to his family. Because of Robert's death, Barry didn't have to return to Vietnam. Years later he still has trouble with this experience. "I had white gloves on, and a uniform with my medals, but I felt dirty," Barry says. "You know, I thought I was gonna die in Vietnam. But I didn't have to go back there. I had my ticket punched by my nephew's blood. . . . I felt that I failed him, I failed my family, . . . I still feel guilty to this day."[70]

To honor Barry's narrative is to hear his moral dissonance and understand his moral injury. Some readers may think that Barry had nothing to do with Robert's death. Other readers may reason that a first lieutenant cannot obtain the transfer of a private (not under his direct command) away from combat duties during a war. Both statements may be true, but they are irrelevant. Barry's ultimate judge is his moral voice and agency as a human being and a soldier. To understand his narrative, the listener must account for: Barry's fidelity to his core values, his level of responsibility, his level of accountability, his level of maturity, and his empowerment to make a change. Barry uses these FRAME senses to voice the human and professional values he uses to judge his professional agency. The result is his moral dissonance.

Barry cannot, and he will not put these things aside; they are too much a part of him. He may not have actively committed Robert's death, but as an officer he failed to preserve his life. Therefore he believes that he is guilty of omission: failing to do what he believes is right. Instead, as a unit officer he participated in Robert's death by bringing his nephew home. Thus, he believes that he is also guilty by association with the events that led to Robert's death. Finally, he also believes that he is guilty by commission for leaving his soldiers in combat while he lived in safety.

Although grief is an expression of Barry's pain, this is not a simple grief reaction. Nor, can it be understood as survivor guilt. It is a complex emotional expression of Barry's conflicted values. Barry will not abandon his nephew or his fellow soldiers, so he is stuck with a hidden wound that is still festering. Barry is not a "pirate," but he feels less than a "soldier." He is conscientiously living between his ideals and perceptions. His narrative reveals his moral goodness and dissonance. This doesn't mean that he is hopelessly trapped between his ideal standards and perceived conduct. His moral voice may provide the way for his healing, because the same values he uses to condemn himself may also help him reclaim what is good and

70. Esty-Kendall, "Death That Ended His War."

essential within his identity and character. As a first lieutenant and a grieving family member, Barry may not have possessed the necessary maturity
and efficacy to prevent Robert's death. However, his capacity as a human
being and officer may equip him with the capability to reconcile his dissonance: but this is a question of healing for him to decide and his current
community to facilitate and support.

Summary

Barry's emotions and behaviors can be understood using the work of the
researchers, clinicians and healers cited in this chapter. When soldiers' continually "rethink" their experiences, and feel that a part of them has "wandered off" then they are experiencing some level of moral injury. When one
considers MI as the undoing of character, soul wounding, or the betrayal
of conscience, then MI becomes differentiated from PTSD. The presence of
soldiers' moral dissonance shifts focus away from the "fear-based" nature of
the traumatic events toward the "value-based" formation of the injury and
the resulting effects.

Soldiers wrestle with their moral dissonance within the arena of their
conscience by comparing their core values to their conduct. The two-mirror
model (TMM) explains how soldiers' moral voice and agency contribute
to the formation and healing of moral dissonance. Specifically the model
describes how processes of moral development, moral judgment, and moral
reconciliation affect soldiers' lives. Definitions of voice and agency depend
upon specific processes that describe soldiers' levels of FRAME; fidelity
(buy-in), responsibility (ownership), accountability (culpability), maturity
(capacity), and efficacy (capability). The ideal mirror and perceived mirror
continually reflect images of soldiers' intents and practices. Conflicts between these two images generate the moral dissonance that forms soldiers'
complex emotions and behaviors. These emotions and behaviors reveal
their moral injury.

The TMM provides a strategy for mitigating and healing moral
wounds. Military service in combat can be described in terms of human
agency (moral agency) as "the tragic plot of character in pursuit of goals,
and the reversals of fortune that take place trying to reach these goals . . .
and with it goes the recognition of the conflicts and impediments that
can frustrate otherwise successful action."[71] Those who lead, love, support, and heal morally injured veterans need to understand the processes
where soldiers morally question their service based upon their ideal core

---

71. Sherman, *Fabric of Character*, Kindle loc. 1199.

values. Morally injurious events (MIEs) present "crystalizing moments" when soldiers must make decisions that defines their human identity and their military character. Author David Wood captures the essence of these crystalizing moments when soldiers "sense that their fundamental understanding of right and wrong has been violated and the grief, numbness or guilt that often ensues."[72]

Human identity and military character combine to describe a soldier's braided sense of self that is composed from the self-images reflected in the ideal and perceived mirrors described in the TMM. Conflicts between soldiers' ideal and perceived self-images generate "value-based" moral dissonance that results in moral injury. The TMM provides the means to examine how moral development, moral judgment, and moral reconciliation form and mitigate moral dissonance within the military. Chapters 4 to 6 will examine how soldiers' develop and judge their identity and character. The subsequent chapters will examine how soldiers reconcile their identity and character, and provide some conclusions for healing soldiers' moral injuries.

72. Wood, "Warrior's Moral Dilemma."

CHAPTER 4

Sources of the Self

MARINE E. B. SLEDGE RELATES a horrid incident he experienced in the battle for Okinawa. He had come upon an old woman who wanted him to kill her because she had been in such agony with a gangrenous abdomen. He could not do it. He stepped away from her and went searching for a medical corpsman to help her. Having found one, on their return to the woman's hut they heard a gunshot and met a mild-mannered Marine leaving the hut. They asked him if he had found an enemy combatant. The Marine answered that he had just killed an old woman who wanted to be put out of her misery. Sledge blew up. "You son of a bitch," he yelled, further ripping into him with a slurry of curses. The executioner's face flushed. An NCO came up and asked what happened. Doc and Sledge told him. The NCO glared at the young Marine. "You dirty bastard," said the NCO.[1]

Sledge never knew if the young Marine was disciplined for his cold-blooded act. And Sledge never forgot the woman. Her image and his involvement in her death were burned into his memory and self-image. That event caused in him a moral dissonance that became moral injury. MI indicates its presence by its very character of contradiction between one's positive intentions and one's action in or witness of contrary conduct. Just as the pain of a bone fracture implies that strong healed bones are meant to be the norm for good osteopathic health, so also the pain of moral injury—what Augustine named "soul sorrow"—implies that what is traditionally called a *good conscience* is the norm for good moral health.

The task in this chapter is to consider a complicated question that theologians and philosophers have struggled with for millennia. What is the conscience? What is it that is injured when we speak of moral injury? A complete answer is quite beyond the scope of this book. We can only address the matter with some reference to psychology, philosophy, and religion as conveyed to us in the Western and Judeo-Christian tradition, though we also must interrogate

1. Sledge, *With the Old Breed*, 289–91.

the military's adapted teachings within that broad stream. There is significant overlap of the Judeo-Christian tradition with the Western military tradition. There is also significant contradiction between the two traditions. The cause for moral injury mostly involves a conflict between these two perspectives on human nature and the conscience. Both traditions indeed jockey for prime position in defining "the ideal" of the two mirrors.

We cannot fully understand all that goes into making us the humans and the individual persons we each are. But we can identify philosophies and practices that are most influential. We begin with a basic conviction from the Judeo-Christian tradition: that being human is good. The human person is fundamentally good. The Judeo-Christian tradition holds this as a given. God created human being. God even called and calls human being "very good" (Gens 1:31). All Christian denominations assert the fundamental dignity of human being. Judaism and Islam assert the same.[2]

Except for the Greeks before Plato, the whole course of Western philosophy and ethics, to which much of atheism also subscribes, is dominated by the notion that being human is good. The secular legal tradition, dating back to the Magna Carta, accords fundamental rights to every human person on the basis of a human being's inherent dignity. "We hold these truths to be self-evident, that all men are created equal, that they are endowed by their Creator with certain unalienable rights. . . ." These signature words in The Declaration of Independence were not arbitrarily chosen. They belong to the Enlightenment's own grand secular summation of the affirmation by Western philosophy and religion of the goodness and inherent dignity, deserving of basic rights, of the human person.

We need not cover fully Western civilization's understanding of human dignity. But it is important to ask what the "sources of the self"[3] are and to compare them with the specific tenets of Stoic philosophy which play a normative role in the training of military personnel, especially military leaders. We will also outline how Christianity's understanding of human being has points of convergence and conflict with the military's teaching and practice of Stoicism. After considering these issues, we will offer a more expansive definition of conscience, that moral center wounded by the conflict between one's deepest personal values and one's often necessary personal actions.

---

2. Judaism concurs with and antecedes the Christian interpretation of Gen 1:31. The Qur'an in its introduction confesses the same.

3. Taylor, *Sources of the Self*, 3.

Psychology and Conscience

"Subcultures of morality" are central to any account of a human life. People are raised in unique moral cultures that nevertheless share common features. A devoutly religious family that regularly reads its holy books will influence its children with memorized verses that support a particular ethical stance and practice. Another family may center its own "culture" on music and literature that instill values more indirectly, but the values of discipline and appreciation of beauty will be found to be most important. A family and school system that values pluralism will likely forge a common social bond by teaching and honoring its variant of the Golden Rule. A father may teach a son by close example on the hunting field or with a speech at the dinner table about the importance of discipline, respect, and "family first." The father even may imprint the point further on a young boy's mind with the gift of a Bible that may never be read, but still symbolizes powerfully the fatherly teaching. This was the case, for example, of Navy SEAL Chris Kyle, who begins his autobiography with a detailed examination of the impact his family's faith and strong values had upon his identity.[4] The fond memories that sons have of fathers playing catch while fathers dispense advice, or children have of a mother's care in a time of distress, or a daughter's conversations with parents at the kitchen table: these images are as powerful as, if not more powerful than, the content of the teaching itself.

In other words, increasingly "conscience" is thought to be developed more from "sense impressions" while young than from direct verbal teaching. Much psychological research supports this intuition of the noncognitive development of the conscience. Jonathan Haidt proposes that humans operate with a set of inborn foundational senses (care, fairness, liberty, loyalty, authority, and sanctity) that function similar to the inborn taste receptors that allow individuals to develop preferences for different types of cuisine.[5] Foundational senses help individuals identify and adapt new values and behaviors based upon relationships and practices in new environments.

This means that people develop their values through challenges to their senses of care, fairness, liberty, loyalty, authority, and sanctity. These

---

4. Kyle et al., *American Sniper*, 10–12.

5. Haidt, *Righteous Mind*, 179–88. "The righteous mind is like a tongue with six taste receptors." All analogies have their limits. We would not equate a "foundational sense" for fairness with a taste for Thai food. Haidt's point might be better made with the term "disposition"; that we are born with dispositions toward certain values that, when challenged by the "nurture" of external events, evolve into some approximation (or not) of that to which they were initially oriented. Put this way, this indeed is an attempted definition of "conscience," articulated with attention to a socio-biological evolutionary worldview.

challenges trigger reflexive, emotional responses that subsequently require people to incorporate new data and adopt changes in their thinking.[6] Studies show that children will use these foundational senses to extend their empathy for parents and siblings to the plight of strangers, and in doing so enlarge their social awareness and adapt their social behavior. This extension process continues into adulthood. Thus people adopt values by instinctively and purposefully incorporating the new with the familiar. This theory suggests that junior soldiers will adapt military values to their familiar foundational senses and personal values instead of simply adopting the new values without connecting them to their personal values.

Haidt's moral development theory challenges traditional ethical reasoning theory that believes cognitive reasoning drives moral action. This does not mean that human morality is a mindless activity. It does mean that human beings are prone to a condition that Haidt labels "homo duplex"—where individuals fluctuate between individual and group behaviors determined by both reflexive and reasoned alternatives.[7] This is especially true in adolescence and young adulthood when individuals will often interpret values and express significant interpersonal responsibility through their relationship to their peer groups. Foundational senses are biologically predetermined and then socially constructed, according to this theory of moral development. Later, young adults will develop cognitive processes that utilize individual approaches to define their values and social behavior.

This group process theory differs from Lawrence Kohlberg's individual cognitive stages of moral development that succeed one another over time as a part of classroom education. For Kohlberg, group/peer reasoning is a stage of moral development. For psychologist Carol Gilligan, this group or peer process is a necessary context and a means for adolescents to develop their individualized moral voices. Her research shows that both social and cognitive development happen in an iterative process from adolescence to young adulthood.[8] Educator Mary C. Gentile researched how individuals develop their sense of moral voice by repeatedly applying their values in multiple social contexts.[9] The development of moral voice occurs at different rates. Females mature morally at about the age of twenty-four, well ahead of males who generally do so between thirty and thirty-three, due to different dynamics within their socialization.[10] Recent research has discovered

6. Haidt, *Righteous Mind*, 179–88.

7. Ibid., 261–70.

8. Gilligan, *In a Different Voice*, xvii–xviii.

9. Gentile, *Giving Voice to Values*, Kindle loc. 203–432.

10. Gilligan, *In a Different Voice*, xvii–xviii, 5–8.

that psychosocial (group) maturity develops more slowly than individual cognitive ability. Consequently, young adults tend to be more impulsive in a group than when acting alone.[11] The development of the moral voice is not all due to socialization, however. This matter is clearly a case of nature *and* nurture, as comments below will show with regard to the development of the cerebellum differently in boys and girls.

Notwithstanding these varying rates of gender and group/individual moral development, psychologist Daniel Romer insists that adolescent group impulsivity and neuro-developmental deficiency can be overcome through training programs that reinforce behavioral control and persistence toward valued goals.[12] His argument about cognitive and social development makes sense if all the variables are subject to "healthy" environments.

But there is an additional concern caused by diverse mental health conditions that alter both cognitive and social development. Prior to 2001, 6% of all US Military service members received treatment for a mental health condition. In 2009 between 15% and 20% of soldiers screened positive for mental illness.[13] Recent reports indicate that one in ten volunteers qualified for a diagnosis of "intermittent explosive disorder" or impulsive anger, which is a catalyst for acting on other impulses. This rate is five times higher than the rate found in the general population.[14] We noted in the previous chapter that nearly one in five volunteers had a mental illness before enlisting in the military: conditions such as depression, attention-deficit/hyperactivity disorder, panic disorder, or prior PTSD.[15] These findings challenge Romer's argument and the way the military wishes to develop ethical behavior within its ranks.[16] Other military leaders suggest that military ethics cannot be inculcated in a training program that is taught as an idealized code easily applied as a social guide.[17]

What do these varied conclusions about moral development mean for moral dissonance, which, if not attended to in training before combat and in treatment after a morally injurious event, will erupt into MI? Even with their variations, the perspectives and data above finally agree that the moral self—the conscience—is the product of individual and social development combined with peer group influences. And these varied and multivalent

11. Steinberg, "Risk Taking in Adolescence," 55–57.

12. Romer, "Adolescent Risk Taking," 273–76.

13. O'Connor, *Collateral Damage*.

14. Carey, "Study Finds Suicidal Tendencies."

15. Zarembo, "Nearly 1 in 5 Had Mental Illness."

16. US Joint Forces Command, *Final Report*.

17. Chief of Defense Staff, *Duty with Honour*, 9.

influences on conscience cannot be separated. It is not correct even to assume that there is such a thing as an identifiable "core self." But a human being is not a center of "multiple selves," either.[18]

So argues pastoral psychologist Pamela Cooper-White. She argues for "an expanded view of the human subject—at both conscious and unconscious levels—as a web or network of self-states."[19] After all, as we look back on the course of our individual development, we can ascertain how differently at certain stages we understood ourselves. Further, we can reflect on how at certain times we were "under the influence" of some people and cultural factors more than others. In a certain respect, Picasso was right in his imaging of persons. Picasso's image was right if the observer could understand that a particular subject was the assembly of the components of that person from different eras and different influences in his/her life, all gathered into the present moment.

In other words, we are not a succession of selves, one person at time x and then another at time y. Instead, at any time one is both x and y. One's present identity always includes one's past identities. Even as I might understand how I am different now, I am different because I include in myself the ones from whom I am now different. As the saying has it, "wherever you go, there you are." And the makeup of you wherever and whenever you are includes all the history and personal relations you have had and have, now all assembled as the unique identity that is "you."

We are, of course, more coherent as identities than Picasso's imagery suggests. When healthy, we are neither a mere assemblage of multiple identities nor a series over time of different identities. When healthy, I sense myself as one and whole. But I also know that I am a whole of many well-blended influences from both individuals and groups. But as a blended one, I also do not have hidden down deep within a "core" or "true" self as an identity distinct, separate and more authentic than the blended person I am. I am singular. But I am also plural.

"Core self," "true self," "essential self," even "soul" and "self" are terms that have been used interchangeably over centuries to refer to the one he or she "really" is. This idea "permeates our Western understanding of what it means to be a human being."[20] The notion of "core-self" has proven helpful in some circumstances. It stands as a bulwark against the incessant violations and traumas of a self that we all experience. Were we subjected only to fragmentation in a dissipating endless flux of sociability, we could only self-

18. Cooper-White, "Reenactors," 141–62.

19. Ibid., 143.

20. Ibid., 149.

identify according to whatever affects and defines us at any given moment. So the notion of "core self" can give one some sense of stability.

But this social construction is finally unhelpful. "Core self" isolates a human identity and excludes from recognition all the other relationships that concomitantly influence, construct, and "make up" who a person is. As Cooper-White recognizes in the work of Lisa Cataldo, dependence on a "core self" finally only keeps one "self-contained," and this makes no sense whatsoever when one experiences any violation,[21] as with (we suggest) PTS or MI. We do better for ourselves *and* our society when we make space for a multiplicity of identities that constitute us simultaneously and as an integrated whole.

To be a healthy self, Cooper-White concludes, is more analogous to being a "braided self." There are many threads that weave together into "the fabric of our mental lives."[22] By "mental lives," Cooper-White does not mean to suggest that the braid is purely (or merely) intellectual or private. This is about our full perception of ourselves as unitary persons. The braids include our social/professional ethos and our professional experiences. The braids include, too, our ideals and desires, our conduct, our voice, our agency. We live our lives as a physical body constituted by many self-states. We are an amalgam of selves, but a centered and integrated amalgam. We live as selves of selves—obviously and sometimes not so obviously—in relationships that range from utter dependency to circumstantially full autonomy. Most significantly for our purposes here, we live our lives spiritually whether we are cognizant of our spirituality or not. Our life is a serial experience of finding coherence in and giving meaning to the multiple forces and relationships that make up our lives. James Fowler identifies in this experience the developmental stages of "faith." These stages are "a person's way of seeing him- or herself in relation to others against a background of shared meaning and purpose."[23]

Our lives are made up of unconscious behaviors and consciously moral practices influenced by both recognized and inscrutable forces. We negotiate our way with and within these forces. In doing so, at our best, we reach an integration and equilibrium as a self of selves that still depends on memory and hope for more positive meaning and further purpose. Our self-identity is never finalized, certain, or perfected. Otherwise we could never be remorseful or optimistic about our past or present situations. We could never really exercise the agency that comes from recognizing, braiding, and

21. Ibid., 152.
22. Ibid., 155.
23. Fowler, *Stages of Faith*, 4; quoted by Cooper-White, "Reenactors," 158.

then acting as best we can with what we can in order to be individual agents of dignity within the broad ecology of human being.

Not to be a fixed and "true" self may appear to be bad news for some. However, this self of selves is a more hopeful understanding of self, especially for those whose fixed views of themselves have been injured. It is also a more realistic outlook for those whose lives have long been unstable. We will find ourselves further on the road to renewed health if we can see ourselves as this interweaving of personal identities. After all, no personal narrative can be written fairly without a recognition of the many other persons in one's life. When construed morally, then, if the self is braided, conscience is communal.

A Philosophical View of the Self's Sources

Charles Taylor provides a still broader historical context for understanding the psychological and philosophical influences that have shaped the modern Western mind.[24] All Western society is influenced by certain ways of viewing reality and understanding one's human place in it. These ways of thinking are deeply important; they influence a person's sense of well-being; they help shape a peaceful conscience. Understood more philosophically, we see that our moral standards—our standards of conscience—that have been handed down through time through church, culture, subcultures, and families—are the enacted values which have been expressed in written religious and philosophical teachings. The particular values in their origin and content were sometimes quite varied. But since the earliest literate eras, when different cultures met each other, new written versions of what constituted "the good" emerged. Thereby conscience itself was also shaped.

Let's begin with Plato (ca. 429–347 BCE), as he, arguably, is one of the most influential of early philosophers for the synthesizing and focusing of the Western philosophical tradition. He recognized that human beings were composed of body and soul and theorized that the human soul was composed of three parts: natural appetites, spirit (*thumos*), and reason. Before Plato, *thumos* referred to many different components that aligned with human passion (e.g., spirit, desire, will, appetite, strength, et al.). Philosophers, especially Socrates, set out to parse better the meaning of *thumos*, and thus also set the terms more precisely for the development of the understanding of the conscience. Before Plato, one would do better to identify the warrior as acting according to his Id, with no concern of warring for a god or a

24. Taylor, *Sources of the Self*.

country, or even honor.[25] Military slogans of "for God and country" or "the few, the proud, the Marines" as branding phrases attributable to the earliest warriors would be historically inaccurate.

In the *Republic*, Plato sought to control spirit in the vocation of the warrior in his ideal state. Plato argued that virtue is the proper functioning of reason-spirit-desire. In the ideal state, a small class of "spirited" soldiers, living together without private property or family, are rendered by their education completely devoted to the protection of the state. The warriors carry out the reasoned decisions of the ruling philosophers. Plato also argued for the recognition of the material world as external to human being. This made the external world subject to the strategic and tactical uses of reason, as well as effectively divorced the warrior from his primal intimacy with spirited nature.

Later, Augustine (354–430 CE), one of the greatest and most influential Christian theologians, followed Plato with an affirmation of the reality and basic goodness of the external world. But Augustine also recognized an "internal" world of the human person that was more important than the external world of nature. Indeed, Augustine argued that while the external world maintained a coherence and order established by God, the ability to recognize that order as having a spiritual origin was only possible when one was tuned in to one's own God-enlightened soul. Unlike for the ancient Greeks, *for Augustine a person's identity was established well only when one attended primarily to one's own soul (psyche).* Inwardness, or interiority, became the standard of human consciousness after Augustine. The distinction between a person's external and inward life—that is, the very idea that one had both a private and a public life—became even more pronounced after the seventeenth century. With the age of the Enlightenment, the rational mind itself was asserted to be much more in control of the external world. The mind was a powerful player, the main actor on the universe's stage. Driven by and also discovering universal rational principles, the mind itself was like a god who designed and operated the individual's world like a machine. Or at least that was thought to be the mind's potential. Individual reason came to be understood as "technical" and manipulative. It could change

25. Much discussion could be had here concerning both Shay's and Tick's "reader-response hermeneutic" that flies against much of the facts and literary meaning, per classics scholars, in ancient Greek literature, philosophy, and civic life. For our purposes, we suggest that the earliest Greek warrior's disposition was "pre-conscience," more in accord with Freud's Id, than any other sense of conscience prior to Plato. For a most interesting contemporary suggestion about this, see Castner, "Still Fighting." "At its core, explosive ordnance disposal work is . . . not simply feral id, but rather id ennobled, harnessed in the interest of protecting others." The earliest warrior Greek may have been much more like the pirate soldier than Shay and Tick portray.

the natural order. The superiority of the human being was celebrated, and the Industrial Revolution was the proof of the mind's role in executive management. The individual human being was in all respects autonomous, a law unto oneself. And so even human relations were perceived to be matters of a social contract in accordance with reason's prudence.

For most Western people up into the twentieth century, the designer of human being and all the rest of the universe was understood to be the Judeo-Christian God. But the character of reason as technical led many to think that a personal god was unnecessary. God as the Designer Mind became ever less personal, separated from but "over" the external world, not a being with whom a relationship was possible or desired. Likewise, the idea of the human being as simply the rational image of Divine Reason gained value while any sense of human being as relational was devalued.

There was comfort in this view of how the world worked. If God was rational and designed human beings and the world, then they were rationally ordered, too. By means of good empirical investigation, many believed, reason could discern this order and could even adjust it toward the goals of human improvement and the attainment of peace. But reason could not discern the origin or purpose of *all* things. Nor could reason come to learn more about reason. What reason finally could conclude though, was that human sentiments themselves—like love, hate, compassion, joy—were among the "givens" established by God the Designer. Therefore a person led by these sentiments could evaluate and do the good in any given situation. In other words, a new synthesis and balancing of "reason," "spirit," and *desire* had been found that echoed similar attempts in the Greek classical era. *Reason* could conclude that the *desire* for the good was established by *spirit*. The Deists, those who professed a distant and inactive God-Designer, believed that the human inclination toward the good was both natural and God-given. So *how*, again, a person lived one's life was a matter of governing reasonably and spiritually the best of your desires.

This era of philosophy was called "the turn to the self." But its rebalancing of the three Platonic components then explicitly added a fourth component to human being: the will. Willpower came to rule the inward self as well as the external world. Less subject to the id (we hope) and more in control of our dispositions, we "modern" persons, however, are aware of ourselves and think of ourselves in a way that humans in previous stages of identity development did not. We do analyze ourselves; we second-guess. We even say of our divided minds, "Part of me wants to do such and such, and part of me wants to do something else." At such times we display the incoherence of our will, desire, spirit, and reason. We show no unity of conscience. This is a phenomenon that was expressed differently in former eras.

On another hand, we are not *so* different. After all, St. Paul exhibited the same sense of self-division with a keen sense of interiority later accented by Augustine, when St. Paul wrote, "I do not do what I want, but I do the very thing I hate" (Rom 7:15).

This stage of human being poses questions and challenges about identity. Our coming to self-awareness has morphed into a kind of self-idolization. We can think that we are more powerful than we really are, especially if we are men under the age of thirty, which just happens to be the prime time for recruits to enlist in the military. Brain science has shown that the male amygdala still "rules" young men up until between 24 and 30, at which time the cerebellum reaches maturation and begins to govern their emotions and behavior.[26] So concludes the current research from cognitive science on human development. But it has been purported for decades, if not centuries, that a practiced philosophical mindfulness can exert a "top-down" control of human behavior. If I eat a heavy meal for lunch, my biological processes from "the bottom-up" will tempt me to take a nap. But I can exercise "top-down" agency by willing myself mentally to get on with my day, maybe first by splashing cold water on my face if necessary. Intentionality—willpower—can redirect my primal forces. I can choose how to deal with external forces too, or at least I can inoculate myself against their power, when I turn to a practice of indifference to pain. This practice of "mind over mind" as well as "mind over matter" attains primacy in contemporary military culture's embrace of Stoicism. Now we think we know how to get "at one" with our selves and nature, even if the "knowing" implies a separation at the same time as our oneness.

This is our contemporary situation. We are more aware of the interplay between our will, our desire, our spirit, and our reason than ever before. The history of philosophy itself can be written as the ascendancy of any one or more of these human faculties over others in a given era. "Let desire and will defeat reason's reign of terror," says the will to power. Or "practice the marriage of reason and spirit," says the Stoic. Or "adopt a scientific materialism," as some evolutionary psychologists suggest, who consider that human being is little more than neuro-biochemical processes that can be adjusted better toward survival with the right drugs. To be divided or not divided at all: that has become the question for human identity today. We do not like the options. We intuit that these options are neither right nor just.

Our intuition is correct. A major part of this "turn to the self" is that it has only been about the solitary human being, and has failed to think about human being more contextually. We humans are not just what we eat,

26. Wallis, "What Is the New Cut Off for Adulthood?"

nor just what we do, as is so often assumed when we meet someone new: "Hi. What's your name? What do you do?" We humans are not islands. We belong within the doubled ecology of human beings and the natural world. This is also to say that we are *both* modern *and* ancient. The primary awareness of our "selves" in the modern age does not displace the human unity with nature that was primary in the consciousness of the earliest civilizations. There is an external world to which we belong over time and space as integrally as we belong to and govern ourselves.

Our values are not developed only inside and projected out onto the world; they come also from the outside in. Our expressions of our beliefs are needed by the external world, including each other, as much as we need the world's formative influences upon us. We are connected, we humans, with one another. We are not only connected, we are implicated in each other. There is no "me" without a "you" or "they" or "us." The implications are both positive and negative. We may dislike others, like them, even love them. The same goes for them about us. The human connection is "ecological." We are necessary to each other. The gain of another can be a gain or loss to me. We have learned that it goes better for everyone when our blessings and our burdens are shared. It is also bad for the other if I am not here or there at all.

There is much to be said for the truth of this, spiritually and scientifically. It is a profound and necessary truth for human health. Philosophy here affirms the psychology of the braided self. We are not merely individual beings who get along by a social contract, even though the idea of the social contract (and social contact) is the unspoken assumption in Western society today. We live with the understanding that we are individuals who "get along" as autonomous agents best when we "contract" with each other through a larger governmental matrix to meet our common needs in order to thrive. This may be true for building roads and bridges and arguing about the necessity of Social Security and Medicare. But it is just not so with regard to our moral standards. *Modern culture in East and West shares an agreement about moral standards that goes deeper than social contracting. We human beings persist, all of us, in "the demand for universal justice and beneficence . . . the claims of equality . . . freedom and self-rule . . . and . . . the avoidance of death and suffering."*[27]

We humans also disagree about the moral sources that support our agreement. We give different weight to each of Taylor's three primary sources for moral character: (1) theism, the belief in God; (2) "a naturalism of disengaged reason"; and (3) subjective expressivism, with its contemporary lobbyists of emotionalism. Note the similarities to the pattern

27. Taylor, *Sources of the Self,* 495.

of nature, reason, and spirit. Too often those who oppose reason against emotion forget the poetry necessary for their own lives to be fulfilling. Opponents of technology forget that reason led in forging the democratic experiment and the celebration of human dignity. Then again, the pure naturalists and expressive romanticists both have complained bitterly how "the highest spiritual ideals threaten to lay the most crushing burdens on mankind,"[28] as when unreflective religious fundamentalism succumbs to the temptation to power.

With Taylor, we assert that the theism of the Abrahamic religions stands against "partisan narrowness." Indeed, we believe that most religious traditions offer what the Abrahamic religions do, which is the "central promise of a divine affirmation of the human."[29] It is a central point of the Abrahamic religions that we are not left to ourselves to validate who we are. It is not up to humans alone to devise a contract that holds us together. Nor is it the responsibility of humans only to assign ourselves meanings and identities. We already *belong* to something larger. What is larger has already given human being purpose and value beyond our own rational calculations or poetic expressions. As all the Abrahamic faiths proclaim, we are made in the divine image and God called what God made "good." Emphasis must be laid upon the "good" and the "we."

A Spiritual View of "Self"

Having taken summary looks at the psychological and philosophical understandings of what it means to be a human person, we now turn to the spirituality of personhood. "Spiritual" is a tricky word. It has been used as a placeholder for millennia to point to aspects of human experience that are among the most difficult to pin down, repeat, or subject to empirical verification. Sometimes the word has been used to refer to anything that cannot be commonly explained. Its worst use has been its deployment as a ready cover-up for lazy intellect and sheer ignorance. Today it is used in opposition to "religious," as when a person describes herself as "spiritual, but not religious." Both terms when so used are quite inexact. "Spiritual" in such a case is just a cipher for one's freedom and autonomy in constructing a devotional life and affirming a transcendent quality or source for that life. We support that "spirituality," but also affirm that "religion" at its best is a strong foundation with rich traditional language. Religion can well affirm such personal aspiration and the sense of belonging to something so much

28. Ibid., 519.
29. Ibid., 521.

larger, more beautiful, and more purposeful than ourselves. With that more positive sensibility, we speak here in the terms of a more particular, but still broad, religious tradition—the Abrahamic tradition—whose terms can and do align with humane spirituality of almost any type.

Most people would agree that being a human person is a good thing and that this is the most common spiritual value. Whether we believe we are "on the way" through a series of different and progressive lives (like those who believe in reincarnation) or believe we humans are simply the present stage of a long series of materialistic evolutionary processes since the big bang (stardust come to self-awareness), the conviction that being human is "good" is the common affirmation. We hold this value whether the purpose for human being is established by a designing Mind or is simply the result of our having made a social contract. The Abrahamic religions take the middle ground: that all of us are made and given purpose by a transcendent creator we call Adonai-God-Allah.

Judaism and Christianity share the foundational conviction that human beings are made "in the image and likeness of God" (Gen 1:27) and that God appraised all that God had made as "very good" (Gen 1:31). The extraordinary value of all humankind to God is the conviction behind the Jewish and Christian narratives of God's concern to preserve and redeem humankind. The Qur'an, in the Islamic emphasis on the difference between Allah and all created beings, nevertheless grants humankind a special place in God's ordering. Created by the breathing of Allah's own spirit into the first humans (male and female together), human beings are established by Allah as his caliph or vice-regent, with the special capacity to "name things" (Qur'an 2:31). In unity with each other and God, humans are delegated the primary share of God's ordering and stewardship of the creation (39:6). This task includes the charge to create the conditions for life to be lived with dignity and moral purpose. This is a privileged status indeed for humans (95:4), which nevertheless, as *vice*-regents, underscores that humans are accountable for the choices we make. In sum, the terms "image" and "vice-regency" display a common conviction throughout the Abrahamic tradition that human beings possess a quality of moral agency that is both gift and task.

While the term "image of God" taken literally is anathema in Islam, Islam's naming of humans as caliphs or "vice-regents" shares an important part of the meaning of "image of God" in Judaism and Christianity. In neither Judaism nor Christianity is the phrase understood literally. God is not known by any image. Metaphors for God do abound, including feminine metaphors. But not even Moses got to see God face to face, as the glory of God's face would have killed him. It was a holy and comical grace that

Moses got to see God's backside.[30] God is so "Other" and transcendent that no one can handle a direct encounter with deity. Christianity considers Jesus Christ to be the image of God insofar as one who knows Christ knows the Father. But mortals, still on this side of eternity, can only see through a glass darkly. It will not be until we are on the "other side" that we will be able to see God face to face.

Islam stresses that no image of God is possible or allowed because God is so holy and "other." While both Judaism and Christianity claim that humans are created in God's image, they also insist that no direct image of God is possible for mortals to apprehend. So, "image of God" for Jews and Christians must be about a relationship, a "part-ness" of God, which then is rather like the belief in Islam of humankind's vice-regency.

What of God did God breathe into humans? There are several parts to the answer. Thomas Aquinas summarized the consensus.[31] While different theologians and varied Christian traditions since have accented different aspects of his answer, taken as a whole, these are still helpful for our own contemporary understanding of what makes up a human self.

First, an image is a copy, which implies that the image is an utterly different matter from the original and can in no way share the original's perfection. Second, "image" denotes a single entity, an inseparable unity of soul and body. One can never separate soul from body, although virtually the whole of Western popular theology, following the Greek philosophic tradition, has spoken of the soul and body as separable and opposed. The true relationship of the soul to the body, however, is analogous to the relationship of God to all of God's creation, including humans and their bodies. God is distinguishable from and greater than God's creation. But as its creator, God has chosen to be everlastingly and intimately related to it. Thus "image of God" in human being reminds us of God's omnipresence and faithfulness to what God made.

Third, "image" connotes the mind, or rationality, and so also the self-awareness of God. As God is pure mind in Greek philosophy, so also God's mind-fullness is included in Jewish and Christian understanding of the God of the Bible. Because humans are seen (perhaps occasionally) to display rationality and self-awareness, so then this characteristic, too, is part of what it means for humans to carry God's image.[32] This extends into the exercise of ethical and moral deliberation.

---

30. Exod 33:17–23.

31. Aquinas, *Summa Theologia*, Q93.

32. See ibid., Q93, A5.

Finally, "image" suggests a unity of a community, or a relationship of selves that is so close and intimate (like soul to body) that the several have become one. This is, admittedly, a more complicated part of the whole answer and requires some background explanation here. It is fascinating to note that the Hebrew word for God in the creation story of Genesis 1, from which we get the "image" term, is "Elohim." "Elohim" differs from the term used for God (Yahweh) in a second and different creation story in Genesis 2. "Yahweh" consistently refers to a single transcendent creator. While "Elohim" refers to one creator too, the term, interestingly, is plural. A plural word to denote "God" could indicate that God is a socially complex unity. Many Christian theologians, including Augustine, used this Old Testament expression of God to support the New Testament trajectory of identifying God as the Trinity (Tri-unity) of Father, Son, and Holy Spirit. It may be useful for us at this point, though, simply to suppose that God is no simpleton. God is richly related and relatable. Indeed, as God relates to so much, so intimately, as the Creator to the created, God should be understood as a complex or social unity, a unity of many relationships, a self "made-up" of many selves. And yet, God is one. No literal understanding of language can rationalize this conclusion. But by now, when it comes to religion, and especially the Hebrew terms here, maybe we understand better that religious language very rarely acts in a literal way.

If human selves carry the "image of God," we can at least temporarily conclude that this means human selves are rational, self-aware, coherent unities of body and soul, and focused unities of many relationships. We are created to be social. Sociality has been and is among the most basic aspects of being a human person. We cannot not be social. This is emphasized across many cultures. For example, the African concept of Ubuntu ("I am because we are") runs deeply and widely through sub-Saharan societies. Further, as individuals too, we are social. We are even communitarian: the many are one and the one is a reconciled many. I am a self of selves created in the social image of the one God. So are you.

Made with and for a Conscience

Caregivers, especially spiritual caregivers, of the morally injured may find it significant that the term "conscience" is not often used in written or spoken reflection on moral injury. Insofar as "postmodernity" argues that truth is only subjective, perhaps civilized Western caregiving culture has become more postmodern and has accepted social constructivism more than we realized. "Conscience" sounds a bit old-fashioned to our ears. It belongs to categories of natural law and human essentialism that can only cohere with worldviews that admit no shades of gray; or again, so it seems. We speak of ethical and moral formation, of cultural and moral relativism, and the virtue of respecting pluralism at the same time that we still, if quietly, insist that some things are just right, and some just wrong. Yet we recognize that the conscience of one person might be different from and as deserving of respect as the quite different conscience of another.

If we simply consider the semantic roots of the term "conscience," we may be surprised at how aligned the word is with our argument about the social construction of human personhood. Technically, "conscience" is the combination of the Latin "con," which means "with," and "science," from the Latin *scientia*, "knowledge." Already in classical Latin, *conscientia* meant "the act of being aware of something one has done or is responsible for; an inward perception of the rectitude or otherwise of one's actions, moral sense, conscience." With the "turn to the self" of modernity, "conscience" was used only to refer to one's private internal moral sensibility. Still, its plural form might function the same as its singular. People commonly and unreflectively subscribe to the notion that conscience varies little from person to person, as if the conscience, though most personal and private, were a matter of natural law, a common denominator among all human persons.

It is also interesting that the privatization of the term "conscience" accompanied as a matter of degree the rise of individualism in Western culture.[33] With some irony, perhaps, it would seem that the more conservative understanding of the term would align with the original social meaning; that a person's knowledge of self and moral conviction was always a "knowing with" the other selves of one's community. Many argue that until recently an unschooled person's conscience was more shaped by external authorities like the church or state. But as more people in society were educated, individuals became more self-knowing. It should be no surprise that larger powers like church and nation would try to affirm a keener knowing of oneself and simultaneously seek ways further to impress their views on individual consciences. Some also argue that individual conscience plays a role in Protestantism that is larger even than in Catholicism. In the latter, the tenets of natural law and the magisterium's infallible teaching about what constitutes venal and mortal sin can be appreciated as very effective shapers of the conscience. The lack of a magisterium and the privilege of an

33. See Stout, *Flight from Authority*. Stout says this, but other classics scholars question how he can support it. In classical Latin *conscientia* is personal. Cicero writes to Atticus: "praeclara conscientia sustentor," "I am sustained by a clear conscience." So we are informed by Dr. Kristine Wallace.

individual's interpretation of scripture in Protestantism generally has given conscience more autonomy.

Still, there was enough of a common denominator within the several understandings of conscience that it was considered its own special category. Luther and Calvin, in their own ways, agreed that conscience naturally expressed the common awareness in humans that we should worship God and love our neighbor. In other words, conscience was thought to be natural to human being and exercised a softly prescriptive role. But conscience never exercised agency apart from scripture, tradition, and the community of faith. It was also affected—as was the whole human being—by the original (i.e., natural, from a person's birth) state of sin. In this the Reformers were in agreement with the whole tradition since Aquinas.[34] Without the guidance of the faith community and tradition, and still affected by sin, conscience on its own was a risky resource for ethical and religious guidance. Roman Catholics and Protestants, of course, recognize that moral influence on conscience comes from other sources than faith communities. On this, diverse researchers like Haidt, Gilligan, and Gentile agree, as we noted above.

Most theologians since the Reformation understood that conscience was connected with one's internal and external life. Luther, with others, saw that the conscience exposes our life in a world that becomes too small for us; the world can afflict and drive us into anguish as much as the purportedly quieter voice of moral law. Therefore conscience attempts to build its own defenses against the world's threats. It proposes its own virtues, its own salvation systems, even its own substitute for what counts as authentic human being. The history of conscience underscores its fickleness. Conscience left unto itself is never (!) certain about its present situation, and memory surely brings past sins to haunt our present.

Nevertheless, philosophers since the Enlightenment have taken a more optimistic view of conscience, and this was sustained into the early twentieth century. They believed that conscience exercised a privileged authority over other motives. Conscience as deep-seated sentiment or the heart's instinct became even more authoritative and autonomous. This cheery philosophic understanding of conscience is linked, somewhat incongruously, with contemporary conservative Christian insistence on conscience as an essentialist given. But, perhaps again with irony, the contemporary postmodern recognition of conscience as more socially constructed looks much more like what both Aquinas and the Reformers described.

In sum, the assessment of the "conscience dynamic" for at least the last five hundred years affirms what many writers from different disciplines call

34. Aquinas, *ST*, 1a, 2ae, Q.19 arts. 5 and 6.

the social construction of conscience today. The role of conscience is even larger today than before. It is not so much the internal compass that guides the ship at sea as it is the whole moral disposition of a human being. My moral disposition is both something I was "given" at birth, at least as a potentiality, and it is shaped by the many relations I have had with the world. Like my self of selves, my conscience is individual and social. It belongs to me while it is also given and shaped by innumerable others. My conscience is braided. And it is vulnerable to fraying.

Good *and* Sinful

No one is an island. But neither is a person merely a cog in a collective. We are "both and" knowers of ourselves and knowers along with other selves. Philosophically we persons belong to an ecology and cannot not be so. Psychologically, we are each and together a braid, a rich tapestry in which we co-constitute each other as human persons. Spiritually speaking, we are the fully social centered selves of selves in whom divinely given self-rule also requires the shaping-correcting-orienting activity of the community that gives us a history longer than our memory and a future that fires our hope.

But we are not perfectly braided or balanced socially centered selves. Things go wrong. Our choices are not always right. Paradoxically, the best baseball players give us a language that moderates our self-image. The best fail on average 70% of the time at bat. Humankind as a whole does not "strike out" that often. But we violate our conscience more than we admit and certainly more than we would like. Our conscience is abused apart from our will, too. To say, as we often do, "we're only human" is to confess that we cannot and will not be perfect.

It might seem that we are trained in our vocations to acknowledge and uphold an ideal of perfect behavior, as if we could perform our obligations like conscience-less robots. For all the protocols, policies, safety nets, "perfect systems" and more that we design to get a job done, including when violence seems necessary, such designs at best serve only as the best articulated aspirations. We fail. Heroes will fail. This is the stuff of Greek tragedies. It is also what is later called the condition of sin.

Humans never can be perfect. But humans are foundationally good. How can these two assertions stand together? The authors' own tradition describes human beings as "both justified and sinful." God considers us basically good because that is how God created us. But we are unable to live fully righteously. We know enough about history and ourselves to know that we cannot escape being sinful. Nor can we "save" ourselves or make ourselves wholly good. Only God can do that. So God did and does. God justifies us. We do not justify ourselves. We try to obey the dictates of conscience. We try to follow orders, especially God's commandments of love and care for the neighbor. But we can only do so in acceptance that it is the work of God to justify us, to "make us holy," even as we are not able not to sin.

That's a major realization that is health-giving! We are not able not to sin. But we still are good because God says so. Since God will not break God's word, God calls us good even while condemning our sin. As Martin Luther so famously put it, we are *simul justus et peccator*; at the same time justified and sinner. Neither term cancels the other. It is God's work to sustain our goodness and redeem our sinfulness. In both actions God wants us to love ourselves, too. But it is *not* in our ability to do any of it without divine care and companionship. The human person is fundamentally good *and* not able not to sin. When sin happens by our own commission or by our omission, the suffering and guilt we experience is the first and most evident symptom of MI. There has been a violation against our own fundamental dignity and against others, including God.

This is a basic realistic statement about the human condition that needs to be brought "front and center" again. This theological anthropology brings us to an observation that can be woefully binding or wonderfully freeing. Though we are good, we cannot not sin. Therefore we cannot make ourselves righteous heroes in any final sense. The case is more critical, but no less hopeful, for the person who suffers MI. A person by oneself cannot cure one's own MI because the basic human condition is essentially as a "self of selves" *and* we suffer from a long-practiced egoistic and mistakenly imagined self above selves which we call sin, notwithstanding our deeper foundational goodness.

We are not required and we are not able to be perfect. Such a requirement would make any MI incurable. Instead, we are free and encouraged to entrust ourselves to the gracious care of others. Indeed, we must, if we are to achieve a sufficient sense of safety that will let us accept how others esteem us. We need a community of understanding, compassion, and loving action on our behalf if we are to receive forgiveness enough to finally accept ourselves as respected and purposeful. Then we are able to reconstruct hope enough to take new and healing steps.

The Military Stoic Self: Blessing and Bane

Such trusting steps within a caring community are not always possible for the soldier. Yes, the importance of the soldier's unit, "the band of brothers" and sisters is still a strengthening value. But modern practices of platooning, cross-training, and operant conditioning, both to obey and to shoot at the enemy without pause, focus more on the individual than on the importance of the unit. The soldier is inculcated with a fundamentally different way of construing the human person, too. This different construal competes with the understanding of being a human person articulated above. This competing philosophy is a kind of Stoicism.

When a person enters the grand hall of the National Defense University in Washington, DC, for the first time, she or he may need to take breath and pause. The first thing seen is a contemporary sculpture along the hall. Abstract combat scenes are rendered in black silhouette. Large splashes of red denote human blood spurting at the tip of a bayonet or in response to bullets or bombs. Planes fly and shoot and bomb. Warriors individually and in large numbers from different eras are thrown into every imaginable (and unimaginable) combat situation. The art strives to communicate the inevitability of suffering, violence, and self-sacrifice, all on the supposition that glory comes from devotion to the transcendent cause of sacrificing for the greater good of the neighbor and love of country. The sculpture also indicates that no human history is free from the necessity for such self-sacrifice, as key world leaders and every United States president from Wilson to Obama are included in the open-ended story.

Would one think by simply seeing these images that the cause is transcendent? Perhaps as compelling as the art is the attitude of those who work in these halls every day: passing by the violence could be construed as just business as usual. Or is passing by and through the violence a pious act of reverence and an appreciation of the soldier's vocation? During such walks does the soldier particularly recognize the cost of war he or she and others must absorb and so develop a sense of responsibility for ending war? Constant exposure to this sculpture could also inure one to war's inevitable suffering. The sculpture can also call to mind the responsibility for advising and carrying out national policy. Whatever interpretation one may choose, the art itself works as a Stoic tutor of many disciples.

Stoicism was never "the warrior's philosophy" in the classical age, though it has surely been co-opted as such since.[35] One might even theo-

---

35. Panaetius (ca. 185–109 BCE) adapted Stoicism (begun by Zeno ca. 300) to the needs of active statesmen and soldiers, especially at Rome. Philosophy was for educated men, who were in Greece as in Rome statesmen and soldiers. There is no known code however, that was taught to the ordinary legionary soldier. Stoicism taught that the virtuous man should avoid death, illness, pain if he can do so without acting unvirtuously. Those things are "indifferent," neither good nor evil; virtue is the only good. To be virtuous is to live in harmony with reason. The virtuous man is absolutely brave, since he knows that pain and death are no evils; absolutely continent, since he knows

rize that it was a necessary means to safeguard a soldier's self, exposed to the worst a human being in such a vocation must experience. Today this philosophy is honored and taught by a no less celebrated example within military culture than Medal of Honor recipient, and former prisoner of war, Admiral James Stockdale. In his published lectures and books he recounts his use of Stoicism to survive his ordeal. Most importantly, by his own sense of Stoic responsibility, Stockdale sustained the lives and hopes of the other prisoners with him at the "Hanoi Hilton."

Central to Stockdale's Stoic character was the last verse of Ernest Henley's famous poem *Invictus*.

> It matters not how strait the gate,
>
> How charged with punishments the scroll,
>
> I am the master of my fate:
>
> I am the captain of my soul.[36]

These words were on a small note written in rat dung and covertly delivered to [then] Commander Stockdale after he was returned to a "standard" North Vietnamese prison cell after another long solitary confinement marked, also again, by torture. As a prisoner Stockdale's practice of Stoic virtues (bravery, continence, justice) enabled him to control his own responses and to strengthen other prisoners under the duress of extreme tortures that were designed to break them. As he parachuted from his disabled plane into North Vietnam, he decided, "Five years down there, at least. I'm leaving the world of technology and entering the world of Epictetus."[37] Epictetus was a freed Greek slave and Stoic teacher who taught that we should not let our happiness depend on things which are not in our power. The only thing which is always in one's power is one's own self and one's will. This we must keep unblemished. We must be indifferent to death, pain, and illness, and even the loss of our dearest relatives must not touch us. For all this not only belongs to the external world, but also happens through Divine Providence, which is always good. Individuals are responsible for their actions and need to practice self-disciplined service to others regardless of their circumstances.[38] Stockdale explained his moral

---

that pleasure is not a good; and absolutely just, since he is not influenced by prejudice or favor. One might call the latter Stoic responsibility. We thank classics expert Dr. Kristine Wallace, professor emerita of Rice University, for this insight.

36. There is no reason to suppose that Henley was a Stoic. This is how Stockdale interpreted the verse for himself.

37. Stockdale, *Master of My Fate*, 6.

38. Ibid., 4–7.

reasoning in the midst of his hardship as a matter of focusing upon the essentials necessary for survival, not the peripherals.

For Stockdale, internal self-control defined by principles of virtue, honor and resiliency, not external conditions and raging emotions, should determine the individual's response to combat stress. He does not devalue ideal standards or the power of autonomic reactions, but he agrees with Haidt that emotion and instinct can both "bind and blind" human responses.[39] Therefore, he agrees with ethicists like Nancy Sherman that soldiers need the capability to control their responses through a deliberate and disciplined awareness of their identity and purpose not defined by their circumstances. "The circumstances may be beyond our control, but ultimately what affects us for good or ill are only our own judgments about them. We undermine our own autonomy and dignity if we make material and external things responsible for our happiness."[40]

Stoicism worked religiously, as well as philosophically, for Stockdale ever since he was introduced to it while a Navy pilot pursuing graduate studies at Stanford University. Stoicism for Stockdale became a daily practice and overall guide for how he would act in his daily relationships, including his relationship with himself, and his circumstances. The word "religion" comes from the Latin *religio*, which means "obligation," that is, what is binding (Latin *ligo*). *Re-ligio* is what is binding; what is left over, not binding, counts grammatically as *superstitio*. There is no question but that Admiral Stockdale felt bound to his essential convictions, and thereby he maintained his respect for himself and his Stoic God. At the same time, and no less important, Stoicism protected Stockdale from those forces that would, if they could, sever him from his convictions and values.

Stockdale became a proselytizer in the military for this Stoicism. His powerful teaching and example has given him wide influence still in a military establishment that seeks to do whatever it can to form resilience in its personnel.[41] The core message of Stoicism for Stockdale is to take seriously the freedom of one's will to do the best that one can in the conditions one is given. So writes Epictetus: "Remember, you are an actor in a drama of such sort as the Author chooses—if short, then in a short one; if long, then in a long one. If it be his pleasure that you should enact a poor man, or a cripple, or a ruler, see that you act it well. For this is your business—to act well the

---

39. Haidt, *Righteous Mind*, 301.

40. Sherman, *Stoic Warriors*, Kindle loc. 127–28.

41. Stockdale, *Courage Under Fire*; *Thoughts of a Philosophical Fighter Pilot*; *Master of My Fate*.

given part, but to choose it belongs to another. To do well what is within one's power to do is one cardinal Stoic maxim.

To do well, even excellently, is not to fall victim by one's own choice and act to guilt and shame. One cannot be a victim of another, Epictetus taught, according to Stockdale. One could only be one's own victim. Stockdale thus interprets Epictetus as follows: "Each individual brings about his own good and his own evil, his good fortune, his ill fortune, his happiness, and his wretchedness. It is unthinkable that one man's error could cause another's suffering; suffering, like everything else in Stoicism, was all internal-remorse at destroying yourself."[42]

Stockdale concedes that Stoicism requires much discipline and that it would appear to be an impossible ideal of perfectionism. "The Stoic demand for disciplined thought naturally won only a small minority to its standard, but those few were the strongest characters of that time. In theory a doctrine of pitiless perfectionism, Stoicism actually created men of courage, saintliness, and goodwill."[43] These great men inspired numerous subsequent leaders, including George Washington, who often quoted Cato in his speeches.[44] In short, no other philosophical disposition and practice has had more influence on the current ideal of the military hero as "the strong silent type," who without regard to his or her own vulnerability, does what one must in any given situation to serve and protect others.

Should Stockdale's famed practice and preaching of Stoicism be as central to the shaping of the "soldier" as is the case in the military culture of today? Make no mistake. We heartily affirm the exemplary importance of Stockdale's teaching and character. He is one of an inestimably long line of military/political leaders who demonstrated what still is universally recognized as "virtue": he lived up to his values and served his country with honor in the midst of the worst circumstances.

Stockdale did not concur in every detail with canonical Stoicism, however. It was central to his belief system, as well, that any soldier could be pushed into brokenness and that it was important for prisoners to restore their broken fellows. Forgiveness and resilience must be the duty-bound practices of the prisoner community. After the effort to resist one's torturers, one needs help from one's battle-buddies and shipmates for healing and

---

42. Stockdale, *Master of My Fate*, 2.

43. Ibid., 3.

44. There were actually two famous Romans named Cato. Washington's reference is probably to Cato the Younger who, though not a professional philosopher, was a Roman politician and general, whose constitutionalism was a mixture of Stoicism and old Roman principles. He committed suicide in 46 BCE. No surviving written works of his survive, but he was much written about and quoted by later writers.

restoration. In other words, Stockdale's Stoicism included the recognition that the Stoic physician could not heal himself! Stockdale recognized that Stoicism has its limits.

But evidently Stockdale's concession that "only a small minority" could meet the Stoic ideal is not respected by the military, since it still continues to inculcate Stoic principles in its resiliency programs. As PTSD and suicide rates began to rise, the Pentagon realized that resilience and mental hardiness in the face of compounding psychological stresses had to become a part of predeployment training. So the Army rolled out a $145 million "positive psychology" program in 2009. The USMC developed a similar "preventative" tactic "to teach everyone better to thrive." The program's emphasis on "the study of strength and virtue" was attractive to Army leadership. But the program did not plan or account for the results for soldiers in the field. Indeed, the program's emphasis on something like the Stoic ideal even exacerbated a returning soldier's sense that his or her MI or PTS was their own fault, having little to do with the external causes. Also overlooked was the incoherence between training for emotional resilience and the operant conditioning of recruits to neutralize moral compunctions against violence.

Moral philosopher and psychoanalyst Nancy Sherman, from ample "embedded" work with returning service members, agrees that the philosophical ideal of detachment does not cohere well with the reality of a soldier's seeing his buddy's skin left hanging in a tree or seeing a child's head explode from the grenade launched against an insurgent. The soldier is trained to have his buddy's back always. The reality is that the soldier then feels compelled, too, to remember his or her buddy. Yet, to remember a buddy's death is a decision, Sherman admits, to honor always that friend. The military's inculcation of both solidarity with the fellow soldier and of Stoicism creates a double bind. To honor the friend is a virtue far higher than Stoic apathy. This means that moral injury cannot be avoided. And it means that Stoicism has its limits.[45]

Augustine's Response

Augustine argued mightily against Stoicism back in the fourth century. Initially much attracted to it, Augustine in his mature years arrived at a much more conditioned opinion. Augustine's fully developed perspective regarding Stoicism did conclude that to practice the Stoic virtues was a healthy habit. They accorded well with a human being's purpose to pursue the true,

45. Sherman, *After War*, Kindle edition. Sherman more explicitly criticizes the ill-planned roll-out, with detail of the program, 11–14.

the good, and the beautiful, especially when added to the explicit Christian mandate to care for the neighbor.

Augustine's theology and psychology remained influenced by Stoicism. But important differences between his reception of Pauline Christianity and earlier Stoic influences became quite clear in his mature thought. Three points stand out.[46] First, while the young Augustine followed Stoicism's optimism about the perfection of personal virtue in the mortal life,[47] the mature Augustine renounced this, perhaps after sufficient pastoral experience as he cared for many would-be faithful who could not meet virtuous expectations no matter how hard they tried. Only in the next life, Augustine concluded, can we attain perfect virtue and that not by human being's own striving.[48] Second, Augustine agreed with the Stoics that virtue is a necessary condition for happiness, but denied that it is a sufficient condition. Happiness, for Augustine, ultimately requires immortality.[49] Third, Augustine agreed with the Stoics in their rational appraisal of the emotions as mistaken judgments of the mind rather than elements of the body.[50] But he rejected their notion of *apatheia*—a cultivated lack of feeling—in favor of moderation of the emotions. Augustine not only questioned the possibility of avoiding emotions. He also came to value some emotions, such as love, more positively.[51] The positive emotions, after all, were part of the human being that God called "good." The Stoic ideal of complete freedom from emotions ruled out love of God and the enjoyment of beauty, truth, and goodness!

These three points are clearly interrelated and point to Augustine's final rejection of Stoic moral autonomy. In sum, Augustine dismissed the Stoic claim that through the power of individual reason alone one may become completely virtuous, free, and happy. Augustine finally concluded that such a claim for reason alone was the height of arrogance and sharply contrasted with human dependence on God's grace for virtue and happiness.[52]

These considerations, for Augustine, were logically and, more importantly, *theologically*, compelling. But a more practical pastoral concern led him to his rejections of Stoicism, too. Augustine's preoccupation with war and his writing on the principles of "just war" were no mere exercise in theological abstraction. Nor were they initially a foray into policy-making

---

46. Augustine, *Against the Academics*, 1.2.5, and *Retractions*, 1.2; 1.6.8.

47. Cf. *Against the Academics*, 1.2.5.

48. *Retractions*, 1.2; 1.6.5.

49. Augustine, *On the Trinity*, 13.8.11.

50. Augustine, *On the Immortality of the Soul*, 5.7.

51. Augustine, *City of God*, 14.9.

52. Augustine, *Retractions*, 1.1.2; 1.8.4.

at the governmental level. Augustine struggled over the New Testament's (seeming) lack of any prohibition against military service. In a recapitulation of his grounded opposition to certain Stoic principles, Augustine underscored the horror of war. "Let everyone, then, who thinks with pain on all these great evils, so horrible, so ruthless, acknowledge that this is misery. And if any one either endures or thinks of them without mental pain, this is a more miserable plight still, for he thinks himself happy because he has lost human feeling."[53]

Augustine's *antipathy* to war may well have been lost on the many who have secularized just war theory and ripped it from its Augustinian foundation and subsequent elaboration by Aquinas's elaboration. For Augustine motivation and intention in his outlines of just war theory were for the pastoral care for those Christians concerned to practice virtue within the horror of compelled warfare. It makes a critical difference to interpret just war theory as pastoral care rather than theological justification for the exercise of power.[54] Support for this comes from a reading of Augustine's letters to a General Marcellinus, to whom Augustine dedicates his *City of God* and, particularly, to the African General Boniface.[55] Isaac Logan notes that this correspondence, along with correspondence with several other Christian soldiers, lies behind Augustine's strong statement of the misery of war quoted above. Indeed, the term "mental pain," Logan suggests, following an unpublished lecture by William Portier, should be translated as "sorrow of soul." Might not this recognition of "soul sorrow," which so motivates Augustine's Christian pastoral care, already be an observation of what we see as moral injury?

Augustine's correspondence with General Bonifacius, all of which predates *City of God* by a decade, reveals a general who had become Christian and was worried about his faith's "fit" with his vocation. How was Bonifacius to use his God-given bodily strength against those he was called to love? "Father Augustine, I know not what I do; help me understand who and what I am as a Christian soldier." Was Bonifacius thinking about becoming a "repentant pacifist?"[56] Over a decade later, Bonifacius inquired about becoming a monk, removing himself from the struggle that challenged his faith and soul. Augustine counselled Bonifacius not to do this, not because of his martial vows, but because of his marital vows. This demonstrated how

53. Augustine, *City of God*, 19.7.

54. On this see Bell, *Just War*, and Wynn, *Augustine on War*.

55. Isaac, "For What It's Worth." The following argument is indebted to Logan Isaac's illuminative essay in consideration of Robert Meaghum's seminal work, *Killing from the Inside Out*.

56. So asks Isaac, "For What It's Worth."

attentive Augustine had become to the details of his distant parishioner's life and that he perhaps sensed that an outright condemnation would be too severe an answer to Bonifacius's soul-sorrow. Further, relying on the high probability that Bonifacius was educated in the work of Cicero, who himself borrowed the idea of a just war from Aristotle, Augustine commended the just war principle to Bonifacius. Thus, it "might very well be that [Augustine] uses Cicero to establish trust with a wounded warrior in the same way" that we or contemporary non-theological writers might do today, by appealing both to "just war" theory, the Christian command to care for the neighbor, ameliorated by our dependence above all on God's mercy.[57]

Conclusion: A Mixed Bag

A pastoral-caregiver's interpretation of Augustine's just war theory, in alliance with his clear separation from critical facets of Stoicism, may for some appear still to be a work in progress. We see enough here to move ahead nevertheless with the supposition, per Dietrich Bonhoeffer, pastor and theologian martyred as a resister by the Nazis, that on its own "the sword of the Spirit will not allay the forces of darkness." Yet those who wield the sword find themselves like a Roman general trapped in circumstances now that guarantee or compound the misery of MI. A simple prescription of orthodox Stoicism for those so trapped only worsens the malady. The sword does not destroy the forces of darkness in humanity as portrayed in the NDU hall. Human being is not capable of such moral purity. Combat veterans know this.

We began this chapter with the confession that we cannot fully understand all that goes into making us humans and the individuals "who we are." But we can identify philosophies and practices that are most influential. The explicit affirmation in both the military and civilian society of certain Stoic virtues, for example, has a complex impact on the formation especially of the military psyche. The sources of the self as prescribed in military training are not the same as, and cannot supplant, the interconnected and braided identity of every individual self, created by God, nature, and culture. All human beings are created to be uniquely braided identities. The Western philosophical and religious traditions' accents on human beings as communal, of an ecology, support the psychological picture of humans as braided. Our consciences—our individuated value systems—are, as it were, the interweaving of communal influencers. This general formation of identity is part of the foundational "good" in humanity. But the very history of fraying

57. Ibid.

and imbalance, while not foundational to human identity, constitutes the virtually inevitable consequence in all human being which has been called "sin." There is the greatest joy and love in being human. But there is pain and suffering, too, which human beings cannot solve by themselves.

We can, however, better affirm how we all are in this together and that some steps toward overcoming disaster can be taken together. Not all the Stoic virtues have proven unhelpful. Admiral Stockdale's example is one to celebrate still, if not wholly to prescribe. Augustinian Christianity also advocates the virtues defined and aspired to by the pagan Stoic teachers. What we need today is a keener understanding of what "makes up" human persons so that we can translate that into the formation and teaching of human persons. We want to help each other retain our humanity, or certainly to retain the prospect of being restored after enduring the inhumanity which society calls upon us to experience. What we continue to need today is a more generously communal understanding of our essential humanity, not the false ideal of the individual hero who quietly suffers into the final night. We turn to a proposal toward that end in the next two chapters, where we address the need to revisit how soldiers can and should integrate their values with the ethos of their vocation.

CHAPTER 5

The Development of Military Character

Strive to be leaders of character, competence, and courage.

—Major Dick Winters, US Army[1]

[Soldiers] are not mere instruments. . . . It is precisely because they do (sometimes) choose to kill or not, and impose risks or accept them, that we require them to choose in a certain way. That requirement shapes the whole pattern of their rights and duties in combat.

—Ethicist Michael Walzer[2]

Introduction to Soldiers' Moral Development and Moral Judgment

IN THE LAST CHAPTER we focused upon the braided sources of the self that are reflected in both the ideal and perceived images of the TMM. In this chapter we will focus upon one source—military character. Soldiers develop their "military character" through the ideal standards they use to determine their vocational rights and duties. These standards govern the external relationships that define the military's collective identity as professional stewards of public trust, and as lethal defenders of national identity. These collective

1. Winters is considered to be an exceptional combat leader known for his care of soldiers and his ability to lead in extreme conditions. These three points are the central themes Winters develops in his talks with young officers. Kingseed, *Conversations with Major Dick Winters*.

2. Walzer, *Just and Unjust Wars*, 306.

standards also guide the individual moral voice, moral agency, and moral judgment of every military professional.[3] It is the exercise of moral voice and agency that differentiates the individual as: a professional soldier, a competent warrior, or a self-serving pirate. Each of these self-perceptions has a profound effect upon veterans' wellness. Therefore, it is also vital to consider military character in terms of soldiers' perceived identity formed from their moral judgments during the exercise of their rights and duties.

Marines will joke that they set their high standards by telling everybody how great they were, believing it themselves, and then trying to prove to the world that they were right.[4] This isn't humorous bravado. It is a habituated understanding where a leader can maintain discipline in combat by simply stating, "Marines don't do that."[5] Army Command Sergeant Major Mack Vereen states the intent of such standards are to: set the bar high enough to challenge soldiers' normal reach, humble them in their failures, and develop them thru their efforts.[6] Vereen refers to the specific training processes the military uses to develop both competence and character. These processes are active on the range and in the classroom from basic training to senior service schools.

Military character is the ethical and moral standard used for maintaining discipline. These standards entwine professional values with the vocational competency of controlling the lethal skills essential for national defense. Simply stated, the intent of discipline is to control conduct and prevent unwanted consequences. The military considers discipline as an active component in soldier resilience, defined as the ability to "bounce back" from adversity."[7] In terms of moral injury, it is logical to assume that: (1) the presence of discipline should mitigate the formation of moral injuries, and (2) conversely, the absence of discipline could increase moral injuries. However, combat is seldom a linear relationship between causes and effects. Its complex nature can invert this simple equation, and the discipline designed to preserve military character can also cause the moral dissonance that damages the self. Ironically, soldiers can be (and are) morally injured when the action that is ethically correct is also the conduct that is morally unacceptable. Thus, the uniting of soldiers' moral voice and agency forms a complex continuum for morally judging their successful and failed conduct.

3. Dempsey, *Mission Command*; Snider and Shine, *Soldier's Morality*.

4. Krulak, *First to Fight*, 1.

5. Krulak, "Commandant Message to the Marine Corps."

6. Personal interview with CSM (Retired) Vereen, fall 2002, United States Army Sergeants Major Academy, Fort Bliss, Texas. Vereen was the Division Chief of Training and Doctrine.

7. Jefferson, "Building Resilience across USARPAC."

This continuum is determined by the standards soldiers expect to achieve as individuals and as units. We cannot speak about soldiers' moral dissonance without examining the development of their moral standards and the moral judgment of their perceived conduct.

Soldiers' character is not solely the product of their professional training. It also includes their moral development as human beings. A six-word story for the military could read, "Professional soldiers required, human beings volunteered." In 1775 General George Washington wrote to the leaders of the New York Provincial Congress, "When we assumed the Soldier, we did not lay aside the Citizen." Washington's meaning was political, but it can easily apply to the values and standards that entwine human identity with military character. Braided together they shape soldiers' exercise of moral voice. In turn, their voice drives their moral agency in ways that empower their resilience or destroy their identity.

Soldiers' disciplined character controls their warrior competence in combat. They are moral agents, defined by their moral voice. This voice is the product of the traditions, beliefs, laws and orders that define the moral boundaries of their existence. These boundaries include a broad definition of spirituality as the discipline or root connection between beliefs and values practiced within and without all the aspects of organized religion. Spirituality has deep roots within the military that follow historical trends that change over time and context. Today these roots are within the "no-preference" and the non-denominational religious categories of the military and follow patterns of the emergent spiritual communities within society.[8] These beliefs, practices, and communities define "who a person is, what the person stands for, and serves as a guide for determining behavior—especially in ambiguous and chaotic situations . . . [and] also provides the courage and will to act in accordance with one's beliefs and values."[9]

It is a mistake to narrowly define soldiers' moral voices by a particular value, belief, decision, or act. Often their values, beliefs, and decisions are the product of a complex reasoning process that includes a blend of principles, utility, situations, and virtues. Their reasoning process is a habituated response incorporating all the ethical and moral standards that compose their character. Therefore, we need to understand soldiers' character by examining the development of their moral voice and agency. This examination will inform how we hear and understand their war narratives as expressions of the moral harmony or moral dissonance between their "ideal" and perceived self-images.

8. Jones, *Sacred Way*, 25–32, or Jones, *New Christians*.
9. Snider and Shine, *Soldier's Morality*, 1–3.

Human beings are "braids of identities" shaped through varied experiences where their "ideal" standards of right vs. wrong, good vs. evil, and grace vs. condemnation become their "perceived" reality. In the previous chapter we described how foundational senses shape a person's moral identity similar to the way taste buds shape a person's diet.[10] This chapter will describe how senses of fidelity, responsibility, accountability, maturity, and efficacy (FRAME) shape the moral development of soldiers' character. The FRAME senses function similar to Haidt's foundational senses of care, fairness, liberty, loyalty, authority, and sanctity.[11] These senses are reflected in the dual images of the TMM. The FRAME senses are not independent standards of a soldier's character. They are corporate sensors of the military ethos that shape how soldiers form and perceive their existence. The FRAME senses entwine military character with humanity informing how soldiers exercise their moral voice and moral agency.

It is often said that soldiers need to follow their "moral compass." We suggest that a soldier's moral voice and agency function more like synergistic components within a navigation problem than a single navigational instrument. Commander Michael Hallett argues similarly from his maritime perspective, with his proposal that an ethical fitness program be established, with "embedded coaching" at all ranks, so to meet the goal of "ethical competence that is both operationally effective in time-constrained, dynamic environments, including combat, and useful for sailors performing their daily tasks."[12] The FRAME model we propose helps us understand *how* soldiers' voice and agency are active within each of these components and *how* the dual images of the TMM reflect the harmony or dissonance within this reasoning process. Soldiers' war narratives embody the resulting harmony or dissonance that becomes a means for their resiliency or moral injury. Therefore, their narratives are essential windows into understanding the formation of the moral dissonance that causes MI. The FRAME senses within the TMM provide a vital tool for interpreting these war narratives.

Morally Navigating in Combat

Consider the following narratives from a Marine reconnaissance platoon ordered to conduct a hasty attack on an airfield during the march to Baghdad in 2003. As a sequel to their operation order, their company commander issued a warning order via radio that "all personnel on the airfield are

10. Haidt, *Righteous Mind*, 131.

11. Ibid.

12. Hallett, "Cultivating Sailor Ethical Fitness," 93.

declared hostile."[13] Platoon leader Lieutenant Nathaniel Fick describes his response to his commander's order.

> We normally operated within certain constraints. We could respond proportionally in self-defense—"fire if fired upon"—or we could shoot first at obvious military targets. Both categories depended on the target being a clear and present danger. "Declared hostile" meant there were no rules of engagement. It meant shoot first and ask questions later. At Quantico [the location of the Basic School for Marine officer training] we had learned about Vietnam's free-fire zones. They had been, it was acknowledged, immoral and counterproductive. Qalat Sukkar [the airfield] was being declared a free-fire zone.
>
> I clicked the radio handset to countermand the order. I wanted to tell the platoon to hold fast to our normal rules of engagement. But I stopped. I thought that maybe the battalion or the company had access to other information they had no time to share. I trusted that making the "declared hostile" call would save my Marines' lives when they ran into that unknown threat by shaving crucial nano-seconds from their response time. Let the order stand.[14]

Unknown to the platoon, enemy forces had abandoned the airfield. As a result, the platoon seriously wounded two Iraqi shepherd boys, who they perceived to be a threat. The Iraqi family brought the boys to the platoon to seek medical help and the Marines provided immediate first-aid. However, the battalion executive officer refused Fick's request for the immediate medical evacuation (MEDEVAC) needed to save the boys. His decision was based upon "mission" requirements.

This caused much concern throughout the platoon. The situation was not resolved until the battalion surgeon took charge of the boys and moved them to the battalion commander's location hoping to force the commander's approval for a MEDEVAC. The surgeon's plan worked, and the battalion commander approved the request in the face of a small-scale mutiny led by the doctor supported by Lieutenant Fick and his platoon.[15] Fick described his reasoning during this event as he struggled to help his Marines and the wounded boys by being "a psychiatrist, coach, and father, without anyone suspecting that I was anything but a platoon commander."[16] Fick describes

13. Fick, *One Bullet Away*, 237.

14. Ibid.

15. These events are recorded in Fick, *One Bullet Away*, 237; Wright, *Generation Kill*, 170–76.

16. Fick, *One Bullet Away*, 242–45.

his moral voice and agency when confronting his battalion executive officer, and addressing his platoon.

> [In reference to his battalion executive officer] Those cracks in my trust were getting wider, growing into chasms, filling with fear and rage, sorrow and regret. I felt impotent, but I wasn't powerless. I had an assault rifle in my hands. I could shoot the mother-fucker. I could hold him hostage until he called in the helicopter [the MEDEVAC]. There was just enough cool self-awareness left in my mind to stop me. This was one of those times I'd been told I'd face. After all that training, all the ego-inflating and power-tripping that went with being a Marine, this was it. My very own leadership challenge. I drove back to the platoon.[17]

> [To his platoon, after the wounded boys were evacuated] "Fella's today was fucked-up, completely insane. But we can't control the missions we get, only how we execute them. . . . I failed you this morning by allowing that 'declared hostile' call to stand. My failure put you in an impossible position."

> [To the readers, explaining his ethical and moral reasoning] Tragic as it was, shooting the two boys had been entirely within the rules of engagement as they had been given to us. There would be no command investigation into what had happened. Investigations exist in a narrow sense to assign blame, but they also serve to propagate lessons learned. I tried to draw out those lessons for the platoon. "First, we made a mistake this morning . . . we don't shoot kids. When we do, we acknowledge the tragedy and learn from it."[18]

The Marines directly responsible for the shooting explain their ethical and moral reasoning differently.

> [Gunnery Sergeant Mike Wynn, the platoon sergeant, tells the platoon] We're Americans. . . . We must be sure when we take a shot that we are threatened. You've got to see that these people are just like you. . . . [Then he adds] I'm not saying don't protect yourselves. If it's a case of losing one Marine versus one hundred civilians, I will save the Marine. You've just got to be careful.[19]

17. Ibid., 240.
18. Ibid., 242.
19. Wright, *Generation Kill*, 175–76.

[Sergeant Brad Colbert, the team leader, tells his Marine] "Trombley no matter what you might think or what anybody else might say, you did your job. You were following my orders."[20]

[Corporal Harold Trombley, the Marine who took the shot, tells Sergeant Colbert] "I don't care what happens, really. I'm out in a couple of years. I mean for you. This is your career."[21]

The above incident is an example of how these Marines used their moral voice and agency to implement the values and standards defined by their military character and humanity. Notice how they define "being a Marine" by standards that include their moral senses of: fidelity (buying-in to a set of values), responsibility (owning these values), accountability (culpability for living these values), maturity (capacity for expressing these values), and efficacy (capability to act according to these values). In combat their military senses of FRAME connected with their humanity. Their broader moral senses also acted within the reasoning processes that include the principles, utility, situation, and virtues that come with being a Marine serving in combat.

To understand the formation of any war narrative is to understand how military character binds with humanity to become an active voice in differentiating the moral agency of: soldiers (who fight under professional standards), warriors (who fight with lethal competence), and pirates (who fight by their own rules). Understanding this differentiation is vital for understanding veterans' attempts to reconcile the dissonance between their ideal identity and their perceived conduct. Soldiers are trained to act according to professional standards that control their warrior competence. For most soldiers, the greatest wrong is to disregard these standards and act in a manner that dishonors or endangers themselves and their unit. Their standards reflect both the intents of the entire branch of service and the localized interests of their peers. The broad and the specific nature of their standards is embodied within the differences between morally developing soldiers, training warriors, or breeding pirates.[22] This difference shows up within the moral voice and agency these individuals exercise in combat.

The Marines in the above story were constructing their war narratives by comparing their ideal values against their perceived conduct, and this comparison informs their moral judgments. Notice how the circumstances at the airfield pushed the limits of their character and control, both as a matter

20. Ibid.

21. Fick, *One Bullet Away*, 242–45.

22. This phrasing is adapted from the ethical code of Colonel Jay Aanrud (US Air Force fighter pilot) and Dick Couch (former Navy SEAL).

of cognitive reasoning and reflexive action. They are warriors, struggling to operate like soldiers in conditions where they could easily fight like pirates. Notice that their ideal standards, not their basest instincts or fears, drive their struggles. As a result, their war narratives contain living self-images of their ideal moral voice (what it means to be Marines), and their perceived moral agency (what it means to be Marines in combat). Their judgment over these living-images is the moral harmony or moral dissonance they express in their war narratives. Their narratives, like the narratives of all war veterans, are tangible accounts of real events with real consequences. Moral injury is one of these consequences. Therefore, understanding the moral development of military character is vital for interpreting the formation of moral injuries within war narratives. This understanding also provides the foundations for mitigating and healing these same injuries.

Ethical and Moral Navigation within Mission Command

In combat, ethical actions have moral consequences. By their very nature, soldiers are moral actors and cannot be considered as passive victims. In spite of being targeted and unable to guarantee mission success, soldiers are armed participants who are expected to exercise their moral voice and agency in combat. This expectation is a professional obligation not simply a voluntary choice. Therefore, *how* soldiers think is as important as *what* they think and *what* they do.

Inevitably, some commander or an instructor in a military ethics course will speak about a "moral compass." However, a moral compass is just one essential component needed for guiding soldiers' character. Haidt's moral development theory helps explain why ethical reasoning and moral development are more similar to orienting a navigation problem than simply following a moral compass. Soldiers operate in emotionally charged, ambiguous environments where levels of uncertainty test their professional character and warrior competence. These environments require soldiers to exercise their moral agency just like they navigate the physical terrain.

Successful land navigation requires soldiers to know their position, set their destination, and select an appropriate route for travel. They do this by aligning four elements: a compass / global positioning system, a desired destination / end point, terrain, visible terrain features, and a map. Each of these navigation elements function similarly to reasoning systems that abide within military ethos. In a digital age, we can also make the case that these navigational elements function like four positioning satellites to allow soldiers to locate their position and move within uncertain environments. Because these reasoning systems include ethical and moral requirements, as well as standards for professional competence, they form the means for building and employing military character.

Soldiers will use these four ethical reasoning systems to exercise their moral voice and agency. Principles, utility, situation, and virtue provide the specific contents and processes soldiers will use to define and perform their duties. Metaphorically, theses reasoning systems function similar to a compass, waypoints, terrain and maps. Principled reasoning functions like a north-seeking compass, by establishing a consistent relationship to a fixed point. Utility functions like a waypoint by setting a desired destination. Situation functions like terrain that varies with position and context. Virtue functions like a map showing the relationships between terrain features and personal position. Soldiers use these reasoning systems to orient and navigate in uncertain locations. When soldiers improperly use a compass, waypoints, terrain, or a map in a land navigation problem they choose poor routes, and become "lost in the woods." This can happen to the lowest junior enlisted or the most senior officer. The same is true in ethical and moral problems.

Military competence often includes ethical and moral dimensions. The Marines in the previous narrative were not "simply" seizing and holding an airfield. In carrying out their orders, they encountered value-based considerations that affected both the success of their mission as well as their personal identities. Soldiers will encounter ethical and moral consequences for practicing their vocation. When they improperly use principles, utility, situation, and virtue, they do so at their own peril. Worse yet, as they try to manipulate the consequences of their failure, they end up wandering lost.

Soldiers must be warriors. However, the lethal capabilities of being a warrior require controls that regulate reasoning, emotions, and conduct. This regulation comes in the form of a professional soldier. Without this control warriors are capable of being criminal pirates, or acting out of selfish concerns like a privateer. Historically, privateers were sanctioned to operate outside of the rules to do the "dirty work" that wouldn't be considered as legitimate acts of a nation-state. Some members of the military may be criminals and act with criminal intent. However, conditions in combat can degrade professional standards to the point that certain groups or individuals act by their own rules. They have the lethal skills of warriors, but they act like privateers. In doing so, they fail to uphold the ethical obligations of soldiers, but they are still under the moral obligations of their character.

Excluding criminal intent, combat conditions can push soldiers beyond the ethical guardrails emplaced to protect their character. They may ignore principles and values in favor of gaining a competitive advantage to achieve a military necessity. This is ethical overreach: where warriors deliberately operate beyond accepted boundaries to win. Or, soldiers may justify their conduct by misusing their principles and values. This is ethical fading; where warriors excuse their misconduct by redefining their standards. Ethical overreach and ethical fading blur the boundaries of moral voice and agency, and they generate the moral dissonance that causes moral injury in "good soldiers."[23] The source of this dissonance may be the result of group reasoning as well as an individual decision. At the airfield, mission orders from higher command as well as the ambiguous nature of combat contributed to the conduct of Lieutenant Fick's platoon.

Military command uses mission orders, commander intent, situational analysis, and professional competence to control combat operations.[24] Each element of mission command relies upon the use of the four ethical reasoning systems: principles, utility, situation, and virtue.[25]

Mission orders are based upon principled reasoning using laws, regulations, and doctrines. Mission orders function like a compass by guiding conduct in a fixed direction in accordance with the Law of the Sea, the Law of Land Warfare, International Humanitarian Law, National Laws, and the Uniform Code of Military Justice. Mission orders provide a "North Star" or magnetic north that require soldiers to conform and measure their conduct in accordance with a set standard.

Commander intents are based upon utilitarian reasoning systems using specified results and desired end states. Commander intents paint a picture of what "right" looks like. Intents function like end points by guiding soldiers' conduct to achieve mission goals and national interests. Commander intents allow for decentralized execution of mission orders, by allowing soldiers to exercise their judgment in changing environments.

Situational analysis is based upon contextual reasoning using circumstances, contexts, and environmental scans to maintain mission flexibility. Situational analysis functions like terrain by adapting soldiers' conduct with changing conditions, circumstances, and social/political climates. This flexibility and adaptability becomes a desired attribute for soldiers' survival and mission success.

23. Ludwig and Longnecker, "Bathsheba Syndrome." Balch and Armstrong, "Ethical Marginality," 291–303. Wong and Gerras, *Lying to Ourselves.*

24. US Joint Forces Command, *Joint Operations,* A-1–5; US Marine Corps, *Marine Corps Operational Doctrine,* 1–3; US Army, *Unified Land Operations,* 6–8; US Air Force, *Basic Doctrine,* vol. 1; US Navy, *Naval Warfare.*

25. Zust, "Ethical Land Navigation Model"; Zust, "It's All about Ethics."

Professional competence is based upon virtue-based reasoning using soldiers' values and standards. Professional competence functions like a map by guiding conduct in relation to character and ethos. Soldiers serve in units, and the complex relationships within their units connect the reasoning for their planning with the responsibility for their conduct.

Each of these four ethical systems is highly nuanced and conveys moral weight.[26] Each process rarely operates alone within mission command. Ideally, commanders align orders, intent, situation, and competence to lead soldiers in combat. Commanders are responsible for everything their soldiers do or fail to do. They not only bear responsibility for mission accomplishment, they also bear responsibility for the consequences upon the well-being and character of their soldiers. This is true from the Commander in Chief at the strategic level down to platoon leader and platoon sergeant at the tactical level. Commanders cannot lead their soldiers as a chess player moves chess pieces. Command responsibility cannot be legally delegated to others, but command authority for mission accomplishment can be legally designated to subordinate units and soldiers. Thus, centralized command responsibility in mission planning becomes decentralized authority in execution. This delegation results in a localized, moral responsibility accepted by soldiers at all levels of mission command.

Soldiers navigate this moral responsibility by balancing: (1) mission orders and military principles that function as an orienting "moral compass," (2) commander intents that define the ethical utility for achieving desired mission objectives, (3) situational awareness of the contexts and customs that are the "moral terrain" affecting operations, and (4) professional competence that locates military character within a specific environment. These four ethical systems combine with the four mission command elements to form the basis for soldiers exercising their moral voice and agency. Each ethical system raises critical questions that have moral impacts upon soldiers. Principle-based mission order systems ask, "What is required?" Utility-based commander intent systems ask, "What is necessary?" Situation-based analysis systems ask, "What is appropriate?" Virtue-based professional competence systems ask, "What is acceptable?" Soldiers use the answers from these questions to determine their ethical duties and moral responsibilities.

Unfortunately, there are competing answers to these questions, and this competition affects both military character and moral responsibility. Conflicts between competing ethical systems can result in situations where

26. Burtness, *Consequences*, 114–20.

soldiers "learn to talk of one world while living in another."[27] At times this has led soldiers to justify their violations of principle and character by claiming they were "good soldiers" as defined by the utility and military necessity for their conduct.[28] It is easy to understand how ideal expectations for professional conduct can fade as warriors overreach acceptable boundaries to succeed and survive in combat. Command authority can uphold the values and standards that support professional restraint and moral responsibility in combat. However, under duress, mission command can also grant permissions that remove soldiers' moral restraint of their warrior skills. The resulting misuse of violent force creates conditions for pirate conduct that creates moral injuries. This misuse includes both criminal and privateer conduct from the national to the small unit levels.[29]

The Moral Development of Soldiers

Developing soldiers for military service is not simply habituating a warrior code alongside of civilian values. The military is a vocation, defined by traditional and legal standards for public service. The profession of arms is a blending of values and competence that is analogous to a novice becoming a journeyman, and eventually a master craftsman. There is one important distinction. Unlike civilians, soldiers are resourced, trained, and tasked with the public trust for defending our nation. A master plumber may operate under legal contracts and public expectations to perform their skills. However, a soldier's mission carries the ethical moral responsibility and accountability for inflicting injury upon others on behalf of others. This ethical and moral weight is both a matter of personal integrity and social trust.

Our human identity is a braided construction from many sources, and being a soldier becomes a significant part of these braids. It is important to note that the character of a soldier is not an individual braid easily added to or removed from human identity. A soldier's character becomes an ingrained alloy habituated into the existing braids forming the whole person. Thus, the civilian cannot be easily separated from the soldier. To rephrase General Washington, "when we reassumed the role of civilian, we didn't cease to be soldiers." We are "soldiers for life," or, as the Marines proudly state, "Once a Marine, always a Marine."

27. Wong and Gerras, *Lying to Ourselves*, 20–22.
28. Montgomery, "Good Character Is No Longer a Defense," 2.
29. Grossman, *On Killing*, 188–90.

The military is not a profession because it "says it is."[30] The Constitution and national law establish the military as a public trust, and an elected civilian authority holds the military accountable for the accomplishment of its mission. When the military fails to maintain its discipline, accountability, and competency, it ceases to be a profession.[31] This is where soldiers and warriors can become privateers and pirates. Therefore, the character of a soldier is an essential, holistic habituation of the values and reasoning processes governing conduct with the military ethos. Being a soldier is not simply the accomplishment of a period of training, or measuring competence by the level of a specific skill set. The designation of a professional soldier implies that both personal and corporate character become matters of conscientious service for the common good. Thus military character is a lifelong pursuit developed through serving in many environments under challenging conditions.

The acronym FRAME (fidelity, responsibility, accountability, maturity, and efficacy) describes the moral senses that are active in the development of a soldier's professional character. These senses are not identical to the specific values that individual branches of the military use to describe their ethos. Instead, they provide the means the military uses to define and practice its values. Military ethicist Albert Pierce states that civilians habituate into the military through a deliberate, social process where they conscientiously join and identify with the professional ethos (fidelity), conduct themselves according to the standards and professional competencies of the ethos (responsibility and accountability), and view their conduct as a matter of public trust (maturity and efficacy). This process includes the developmental process where citizen/soldiers become competent practitioners of strategy and ethics.[32] The FRAME senses are the means that soldiers use to define, practice, and judge their professional conduct and individual character. These senses are active within the moral voice and agency that distinguish professional soldiers from competent warriors or rogue pirates.

Professional soldiers are known by their adherence to complex covenants where they voluntarily bind themselves to the values and standards of the profession of arms through an oath. Their oaths begin the process where they habituate into an ethos where *what* they believe and do is

30. Dempsey, *America's Military.*

31. US Department of Defense, *Armed Forces Officer.*

32. This is the foundation for professional military ethics taught at the National Defense University and other senior service schools. Dr. Pierce specifically makes this argument in the following three sources: Department of Defense, *Armed Forces Officer,* Department of Defense, *Noncommissioned Officer and Petty Officer,* Pierce, "Chairman's Conference on Military Professionalism," 8–10.

directly linked with *how* they think.[33] The military vocation is defined by individual and collective character. Therefore, it is important to understand the education and training processes where soldiers habituate the idealized values and standards that become their way of life and death. In this respect the professional military is both an ethical and a moral construction.

Ethical conduct is determined by established values practiced within a specific group. We speak of the military as an ethical construction because it follows established standards that govern its ethos and shape the expected conduct of its members. However, moral conduct has a wider definition. It is determined by broad, pluralistic value systems that are practiced within larger, less-defined communities. Consider the example, of a "good Samaritan" stopping on the roadside to help an injured traveler. Suppose that this person was a professional mechanic. We would not require him/her to respond with the professional competence of a physician. However, we would expect him/her to act out of a moral obligation to stop and help the injured traveler, and to a much lesser extent we might also expect the mechanic to stop and help a non-injured traveler repair a disabled vehicle. The situation of a disabled vehicle only requires a specific competency; the situation of an injured traveler requires a broader, moral obligation.

We wouldn't expect a physician to stop to assist a traveler with a disabled vehicle, but would require a physician to respond to an injured traveler. We would also expect her/him to provide a higher standard of care for the injured person. The physician's professional competency, ethical standards, and legal responsibilities create a higher expectation for conduct that extends across cultures. However, these competencies, standards, and responsibilities do not extend beyond vocational boundaries, and they do not supersede the basic, moral obligation to act. The moral responsibility to act has a broader obligation that extends across cultures and beyond the vocational boundaries imposed by more restrictive ethical and legal responsibilities. Thus, the physician and the mechanic have the same moral agency based upon a common moral sense that extends *into* their specific vocational identities.

This analogy is applicable to the profession of arms where military competency, professional ethics, and legal requirements grant specific

33. I, _____, do solemnly swear (or affirm) that I will support and defend the Constitution of the United States against all enemies, foreign and domestic; that I will bear true faith and allegiance to the same; and that I will obey the orders of the President of the United States and the orders of the officers appointed over me, according to regulations and the Uniform Code of Military Justice. So help me God." (Title 10, US Code; Act of 5 May 1960, replacing the wording first adopted in 1789, with amendment effective 5 October 1962).

permissions that do not apply to those outside of the vocation. These permissions increase the expectations and responsibilities placed upon soldiers, without superseding their basic sense of moral obligations applicable to all humanity.

In this sense, the military is a moral construction, because the moral obligations expected of civilians also extend *into* the professional responsibilities of soldiers. Ideally, the legal, ethical, and moral align; but even when they don't, the broader moral obligations remain active and maintain a wider-jurisdiction over ethical and legal boundaries. As a result, soldiers are held to higher standards of conduct *because* of the ethical and legal responsibilities associated with their profession, and their moral obligations as human beings.

The military's value-centric approach to defining character combines the foundational moral senses (care, fairness, liberty, loyalty, authority, and sanctity) common to all humanity with the military moral senses of FRAME (fidelity, responsibility, accountability, maturity, and efficacy) applicable within the vocation. The combination of these senses inform soldiers' moral voice, direct their agency, and become the standards they use in judging their participation in combat. These senses of moral obligation are active within the vocational values that equip individual soldiers to serve as collective members of units within the military ethos.[34] This dual service obligation defines the braided human/professional identity that is the foundation for the moral voice and agency of a citizen soldier's collective character.

At this point, we must begin to define soldiers' moral voice and agency in terms of conscience. Conscience is the arena where soldiers wrestle with the obligations and the consequences of their actions. This wrestling match is both individual and collective. It involves every aspect of moral reasoning, ethical decision-making, legal obedience, and professional competence. A healthy conscience may protect soldiers from ethical and moral failures by helping them maintain accountability to the values that define their existence. In this sense, conscience describes the values soldiers use to express their moral voice, prescribes the practices that shape moral agency, and thus sets in place the judgment processes that generate moral dissonance. Thus, it is appropriate to consider the practice of military character in terms of directed conscientious vocation (DCV).

---

34. Haidt, *Righteous Mind*, 261–63. Haidt applies Emile Durkheim's behavioral concept of *homo duplex* to describe how senses of care, fairness, liberty, loyalty, authority, and sanctity develop both group and individual morality.

Directed Conscientious Vocation (DCV)

The concept of a "directed conscience" is derived from the work of Christopher J. Eberle and Rick Rubel.[35] They write of directed conscientious action (DCA) as the holistic incorporation of personal convictions into communal reasoning and moral practice. The point is not the conversion of others, but the essential integrity and genuine conduct that allows for conscientious dissent and participation in the military. DCA conveys the social expectations and responsibilities that become the active moral voice and agency within the profession of arms. Therefore we propose the term directed conscientious vocation (DCV) as a derivative concept to convey the conscientious practice of character and competence soldiers use as the ethical and moral foundation for their service. We believe that DCV is the nexus for the mitigation and healing of the moral injuries also known as soul sorrow.

War creates conditions that morally injure soldiers by betraying the ultimate values that define their existence. War wounds are physical, psychological, social, and spiritual. They primarily affect the victims of war's violence, and secondarily they extend to the actors who inflict these wounds. The primary psychological, social and spiritual wounds include: direct harm to others, violations of human rights, lack of acknowledgment of the caused suffering, ignorance of the unjust consequences, and the standing victory of the wrongdoer's injustice. Primary wounds create secondary social and spiritual wounds within the actors manifesting as: memories, emotions, judgments, and actions that perpetuate the effects from inflicting primary wounds upon others.[36] Shay likens the damage from this type of secondary wounding to an internal hemorrhage that continues to injure long after the initial trauma.[37]

Primary and secondary wounds occur because soldiers are ordered by an authority to use violence for the sake of some purpose to achieve a desired goal. Authority, purpose and end states are the sources for the mission orders and command intents that shape soldiers' conduct in combat. An in-depth discussion about legitimate authority and "just cause" is beyond the scope of this book. However, it is vital to understand that the legitimacy of authority and the "justness" of cause influences *how* soldiers use their lethal skills in combat. Soldiers are moral actors. DCV is the stewardship of character that integrates soldiers' values (moral voice) with their conduct (moral agency).

---

35. Eberle and Rubel, "Religious Conviction," 171–85.
36. Philpott, *Just and Unjust Peace*, 4–29.
37. Shay, *Odysseus in America*, 83–86; Guntzel, "Invisible Injury."

Moral voice and agency are vital signs of an active conscience. The existence of moral injuries demonstrates that the violation of conscience has enduring personal and social effects. Any disassociation, nullification, or betrayal of conscience by an "illegitimate or localized" authority for "unjust or utilitarian" acts invalidates soldiers' moral voice and degrades their moral agency. Veteran Army Chaplain Herm Keizer believes the disregard of conscience is the equivalent of moral suicide from damaging guilt, shame, and exiling behaviors that corrode soldiers' existence.[38] Current research and veterans' war narratives support Keizer's claim. Therefore, professional soldiers must be trained as stewards of moral conscience with the capability and capacity to legitimately act in combat. DCV is soldiers' application of the moral voice and agency to legitimately correct the harmful conditions that corrupt warrior competence and breed pirate conduct.

DCV is practiced with reference to a continuum between the categorical poles of pacifism and militarism. Pacifism is the belief or conviction that rejects the use of armed force for resolving conflict. Pacifism morally reasons with rhetorical questions like "Who would Jesus kill?"[39] Pacifism is foundational for conscientious objection (CO), the legal status to not participate in military service. People who practice CO "know that 'collateral damage' is unacceptable to peacemakers," and that there are other means for establishing and maintaining peace.[40] At the other pole is militarism, the belief or conviction that armed force is a legitimate means of settling conflict. Militaristic moral reasoning asks such questions as "What would Jesus have the Good Samaritan do if he came upon a robbery in progress?"[41] Militarism is foundational for conscientious acceptance (CA), the legitimacy granted to those who serve in the military. People who practice CA believe that armed force is essential for the defense of society and the establishment of peace.

Between these poles is a continuum governed by the just war tradition. The just war tradition is not a checklist for participation in war. It is a legal and moral reasoning process that permits and prohibits the controlled use of military force in exceptional cases for the purpose of legitimate defense.[42] Christian theologians adapted the just war tradition from classical Greek and Roman philosophies to limit the use of war (*jus ad bellum*) and to control conduct in combat (*jus in bello*). Many cultures parallel the themes addressed by the just war tradition, and its specific criteria are formalized

38. Brock and Lettini, *Soul Repair*, Kindle loc. 29.

39. Allman, *Who Would Jesus Kill?*

40. Marty, *Anatomy of Grace*, 84.

41. Ramsey, *Essential Paul Ramsey*, 62.

42. Bell, *Just War as Christian Discipleship*, Kindle loc. 217–326.

within international law and the military's law of land warfare. These are embodied in the rules of engagement that soldiers follow in combat. The intent of this rule of law is to limit warfare as the means for legitimate authorities to defend sovereignty and restore broken peace. However, the criteria for "just war" are blurred in the uncertain, tangled web of international interests as they face constantly changing local environments. At the strategic levels of national command, soldiers experience this uncertainty and blurring as the "fog of war." Here, the moral conscience of a nation is exercised regarding questions of just cause, national defense and public policy. At the tactical levels of mission command, soldiers experience this uncertainty and blurring as the "chaos of combat." Here, the moral conscience of localized units and individuals is exercised within the retributive cycle of combat governed by contextualized rules of engagement. Therefore, from the strategic to the tactical levels, the very nature of war and combat necessitates the vocational consciences of men and women accepting or objecting to military service.

Categorical CA or CO for participation in war can enable evil while desiring to accomplish good.[43] However, the space between categorical acceptance and objection is fraught with morally "gray" challenges that stress the conscience of the men and women who volunteer for military service. In a democratic society, some have used these "gray" areas to create a hybrid category of selective conscientious objection (SCO). SCO is based upon the belief that a social contract exists between that state and its citizen-soldiers. In SCO soldiers have the right to expect legal and moral leadership from their leaders as a condition for their acceptance of military service. If this contract is broken, then they have the right and the moral duty to object to military service.[44] SCO exists within the moral reasoning where individuals can apply for CO status, and/or disobey unlawful or immoral orders. These alternatives may be simple to choose in peaceful environments, but these choices become difficult within combat conditions where soldiers' moral voice and moral agency become the focus of their moral judgments.

For professional soldiers, SCO is not an option. They are under oath and orders. They do not get to choose their war, nor conscientiously object or accept the situations where they must make emotionally charged, life-and-death decisions. In combat the enemy has an independent vote regarding timing and targeting, and this creates situations where soldiers may disregard the principles and virtues that define their professional character in order to achieve a desired end. In doing so, they act as warriors, or pirates, by fighting in ways that result in injuries to their character and

43. Biggar, *In Defense of War*, 3–9.
44. Foster, "One War at a Time."

humanity. Soldiers' loss of control over their situation does not mean their loss of conscience. Soldiers will continue to wrestle conscientiously with their decisions, and they will use their moral values to judge the rights and duties they exercise in combat. The very nature of their vocation requires them to operate between positions normally associated with conscientious acceptance and conscientious objection.

Major Jeff Hall summarizes the vocational stewardship of this duality, "Truly, I'm not a Conscientious Objector, but I was and am very conscious of my morality."[45] The vocational stewardship of conscientiously wrestling with moral voice and agency under fire is what separates the character and competence of professional soldiers from the character and competence of warriors or pirates. DCV unites the values of CA with critical elements of CO by merging the intents of DCA with the vocational requirements and moral obligations of being a professional soldier.[46] DCV requires soldiers to exercise their moral voice and agency thru mission command in combat. Failures in mission command (whether at the highest or lowest levels) separate soldiers' character from their competence and creates ethical and moral conditions where misuse of competence damages character.

In the appendix we will examine two unrelated cases (My Lai and drone warfare) in order to explore how moral dissonance forms within soldiers as they wrestle with incongruities in combat. Although the wars, the political contexts, the military branches, and the types of combat differ, both cases demonstrate the moral weight of DCV that military leaders command and subordinates control in combat. The common thread in these controversial cases is the depth of moral effects upon soldiers as they strive to perform the rights and duties of their vocation with character, competence, and courage.

DCV and the Sorrow of Valor

Soldiers do not have to participate in immoral acts to experience the lingering effects from moral dissonance. The military uses stories of heroes who performed the rights and duties of their profession with character and competence to habituate ethics and values within its ethos. These stories become ideal standards for DCV because they include stoic examples of heroism where professional soldiers went beyond the call of duty, at great personal cost, to perform noble deeds. Unlike the soldiers in the previous case studies, these heroes did not participate in controversial actions, and

45. Interview with Major Jeff Hall, 2014.
46. Eberle and Rubel, "Religious Conviction," 171–85.

their exploits are publicly celebrated by a grateful nation. However, their narratives also reveal the presence of ongoing moral dissonance from their service. We will briefly examine five Medal of Honor recipients from five different wars.

An iconic example of DCV is Joshua Chamberlain, a college professor who petitioned for a commission in the Union Army and served throughout the Civil War. He was promoted to major general for his courage and competence, and later served as the president of Bowdoin College and governor of Maine.[47] He was awarded the Medal of Honor for his actions in defense of Little Round that led to the Union victory at the Battle of Gettysburg. Throughout the war Chamberlain displayed incredible combat leadership and professional virtue that earned the respect of his soldiers, his leaders, and even his enemy. After the war, the stoic Chamberlain spoke and acted on the belief that the civilian/soldier serves with an ideal character that "can hold our spirits and our bodies so pure and so high . . . that we can determine and know what manner of men we will be whenever and wherever the hour strikes"[48]

"A successful public image can hide a hurting soul, and it may be that Chamberlain's struggles made him even more heroic than his celebrated accomplishments. He was, in other words, a human being."[49] There is a real man linked to Chamberlain's ideal, stoic character. During the war Chamberlain was wounded twice, and his war wounds never fully healed. He daily lived with debilitating pain in both his hips, and wore a catheter bag attached to an open fistula.[50] He became moody as he resumed his duties at Bowdoin, and became easily bored by academia and politics. His marriage struggled and nearly ended in divorce. In 1867 he wrote to his wife, "There is not much left in me to love. I feel that all too well."[51]

After his wife passed away, Chamberlain took an active role in reconciliation events held between Northern and Southern veterans, often emphasizing the reestablishment of the bond between veterans over the establishment of human rights for the freed slaves that he advocated prior to and during the war. He frequently attended funerals for his soldiers, and seemed to live with remorse, grief, and guilt.[52] Some considered him

47. Chamberlain is often used as a primary example of ethical and moral leadership for future junior and senior military officers. US Department of Defense, *Armed Forces Officer*, 3.

48. Debuse, *Citizen-Officer Ideal*, 61.

49. Longacre, *Joshua Chamberlain*, 293.

50. McAllister, "Lion of the Union," 713–16.

51. Longacre, *Joshua Chamberlain*, 259.

52. Ibid., 277–90.

egotistical. In spite of his reconciliation efforts with civil war veteran groups he actively opposed the efforts of the Alabama commander to construct a battle site memorial to the Confederate soldiers who fought against his unit at Gettysburg. He probably did so because the placement of the memorial potentially contradicted the contributions of his soldiers.[53] Many believe the Alabaman commander, William Oates, acted more nobly in this disagreement than Chamberlain.

Chamberlain displayed a stoic humility that conveyed his sad awareness of the dissonance between his highest ideals and the perceived cost for his military service. He would often speak at public ceremonies with a "martial masculinity" that emphasized the dual character of soldiers' sacrifice of all they held dear for a nobler cause and the reality they faced after returning home from combat.[54] In 1897 he delivered a Memorial Day speech that included the following appeal: "Because they have done these things, I reverence these men, whatever their calling. I had almost said, whatever their faults of conduct, which, if there be any, we who feel ourselves stronger should help them to correct."[55]

In 1909 the chairman of the Gettysburg National Park Commission rejected a request to erect a memorial statue of Chamberlain, writing, "If he [Chamberlain] has not interest enough in the matter why should be [we] push him. Let it go."[56] Chamberlain's motivation for not pushing the erection of his own monument may be found in the conclusion of the speech he delivered in 1889 at the dedication of unit's battle monument erected on the site of their heroic stand at Gettysburg. "Peace be to their spirits where they have gone. Honor and sacred remembrance to those who fought here with us and for us, and who fell elsewhere, or have died since, heart-broken at the harshness or injustice of a political government. Honor to you, who have wrought and endured so much and so well. And so, farewell."[57]

Chamberlain's humility and awareness of moral dissonance is echoed in Audie Murphy, a highly decorated WWII veteran. Murphy received a battlefield commission for his conduct, and was later awarded the Medal of Honor for his lone defense of his company's position against a superior

---

53. Oates was also the governor of Alabama. Although he shared much in common with Chamberlain, the two men never met to discuss their differences. Perry, *Conceived in Liberty*. See also Fifteenth Alabama, "One Last Battle."

54. Caswell, "Honor of Manhood"

55. Chamberlain, "Two Souls of Man."

56. Colonel John P. Nicholson, the Gettysburg National Park Commissioner correspondence with Major Henry S. Burrage in 1909 to finalize the matter of erecting a statue to Chamberlain at Gettysburg. Gwinn, "Joshua Chamberlain, Little Round Top."

57. Chamberlain, "Speech at the Dedication," October 3, 1889.

force. Yearly Army non-commissioned officers compete for selection to the Sergeant Audie Murphy Club recognizing their professionalism.[58] However, at the close of his autobiography Murphy wrote the following: "It was as though a fire had roared through this human house, leaving only the charred hulk of something that once was green. . . . When I was a child, I was told that men were branded by war. Has the brand been put on me? Have the years of blood and ruin stripped me of all decency? Of all belief? . . . Not all belief. . . . I will learn to look at life through uncynical eyes, to have faith, to know love. I will learn to work in peace as in war. And finally—finally, like countless others, I will learn to live again."[59]

Murphy was an iconic soldier whose courage and competence on the battlefield was beyond reproach. However, his life narrative reveals an honorable and very human character wrestling "to get over war."[60] His first wife described him as a man with a wonderful smile, who seldom smiled. Murphy slept with a pistol under his pillow and suffered from nightmares and insomnia. He also struggled with alcohol, painkillers, and a gambling addiction. He was charged with aggravated assault in 1970.[61]

During this time he courageously displayed wellness beyond his own struggles and used his public persona on behalf of fellow veterans suffering from hidden wounds. Currently there is a petition to posthumously award Murphy the Presidential Medal of Freedom for his efforts to promote PTSD awareness.[62] When he spoke about his combat experiences, he did so as one who was labeled as "shell-shocked." However, he also explained his struggles in terms that suggested he was mindful of the moral contradictions of his actions. When asked about the number of enemies he killed during his heroic stand, he answered, "I didn't keep count. I don't know how many. I don't want to know."[63] In 1967 he told an interviewer, "To become an executioner, somebody cold and analytical, to be trained to kill, and then to return to civilian life and be alone in the crowd—it takes an awful long time to get over it. Fear and depression come over you. It's been twenty-odd years already, and the doctors say the effect of all this on my generation won't reach its peak until 1970. So, I guess I got three years to go."[64]

58. US Army, "TRADOC Sergeant Audie Murphy Club."

59. Murphy, *To Hell and Back*, 273–74.

60. When asked, "How does a soldier get over war?" Murphy responded, "I don't think they ever do." Quoted in Phillips, "Audie Murphy Petition."

61. Gambrill, "Combat Veterans and Criminality."

62. Phillips, "Audie Murphy Petition."

63. The interview was given to Thomas Morgan of the *Chicago Times*, and related to Phillips, "Audie Murphy Petition."

64. Phillips, "Audie Murphy Petition."

From these statements, it is reasonable to conclude that Murphy's words reveal that he also struggled to reconcile an elusive moral dissonance that contributed to his post-traumatic stress reactions. Ranger David Grossman describes the difficulty commanders have in confronting their emotions involving soldiers who have died as a result of their command. He believes that these deep emotions remain hidden within the unspoken war narratives of conscientious leaders who maintain personal responsibility and accountability for the lives lost under their command. Grossman uses the heroic and tragic example of a battalion commander from World War I to demonstrate the damaging power of moral accountability.

> When I [Grossman] interview combatants, many tell of remorse and anguish that they have never told anyone of before. But I have not yet had any success at getting a leader to confront his emotions revolving around the soldiers who have died in combat as a result of his orders. . . . All the survivors [from the World War I Lost Battalion of the Argonne] gave full credit for their achievement to the incredible fortitude of their battalion commander, Major C. W. Whittlesey, who refused to surrender and constantly encouraged the dwindling survivors of his battalion to fight on. After five days their battalion was rescued. Major Whittlesey was given the Congressional Medal of Honor. Many people know this story. What they don't know is that Whittlesey committed suicide shortly after the war.[65]

What we really don't know is how and why Whittlesey died. After the war he was a lawyer, described as a sensitive and private man who was uncomfortable with public attention. He often praised his soldiers, but shared few details about his command and his actions in the Argonne. Like Joshua Chamberlain and Murphy, he cared deeply for his fellow soldiers, and dedicated his time to working with wounded veterans and grieving families. He regularly attended the funerals of his soldiers, and on one occasion he disregarded his own health to attend the funeral of a private that served in his command. His last public act was to attend the internment ceremony of the Unknown Soldier from World War I on November 11, 1921.[66] A closer examination of his death is contained in the following narrative.

> Later that month on November 24th, Whittlesey booked passage from New York to Havana aboard the USS Toloa, a steamship owned by the United Fruit Company. On November 26th, the first night out from New York, Whittlesey dined with the

65. Grossman, *On Killing*, 148.
66. Welker, "Tragedy of Heroism."

captain and then retired for the evening around 11:15 PM; it was noted that he was in high spirits. Whittlesey was never seen again. He was reported missing the next morning. It is presumed that he committed suicide by jumping overboard, although no one had seen him jump and his body was never recovered. His friends and family had no idea of his travel plans and were shocked when they received the news of his disappearance and that letters had been prepared to those close to him. None of the letters hinted to the reasons for his suicide and the recipients never made the letters public.[67]

Whittlesey's suicide is an assumption, not a fact. However, the descriptions of his disappearance and life after combat portray a veteran with a high moral sense of fidelity, responsibility, and accountability for the lives and well-being of their soldiers. Perhaps this high moral sense results in an ongoing moral dissonance that manifests itself as an ongoing moral burden. The presence of moral dissonance does not automatically result in debilitating moral injuries, but its presence can be a nuanced sign of veterans' ongoing struggles for post-traumatic growth and purpose. For Chamberlain, Murphy, and Whittlesey it led to a soul sorrow manifested in their efforts to help fellow veterans. For Charles Liteky it led to political dissent for national policies that he believed violated sacred principles of just war and just peace.

Liteky served as a Roman Catholic Army Chaplain during the Vietnam War. He was awarded the Medal of Honor for the personal risks he took to save the lives of wounded soldiers trapped in an ambush. Twenty years after Vietnam, Liteky returned his Medal of Honor to President Reagan in protest over what he believed were illegal and immoral acts being committed by the United States in Central America. He later served two federal prison terms for civil disobedience. Liteky reported the motivation for his controversial actions: "The reason I do what I do now is basically the same. . . . It's to save lives."[68] Liteky maintained his CO convictions during the current War on Terror, and explained his actions in terms of the same ideals that led to his participation in Vietnam. "I am in deep sympathy with all of those young men that are over there now doing what they think is their patriotic duty. . . . I think it is more of a patriotic duty of citizens of this country to stand up and say that this is wrong, that this is immoral."[69]

Liteky's bravery off the battlefield is linked to the moral voice and agency he displayed in combat. Chamberlain, Murphy, and Liteky are examples

67. Ibid.
68. Roberts, "Charles Liteky."
69. Ibid.

of how moral dissonance can also fuel ongoing convictions that are both a resource for healing and a drive for reconciliation of moral conflicts. Their legacy carries over to a recent Medal of Honor recipient, Sergeant Clint Romesha. Romesha received the Medal of Honor for his actions in defending Combat Outpost (COP) Keating against an overwhelming force that almost overran his unit.

Like Chamberlain, Murphy, and Liteky, Romesha served with a stoic courage entwined with a personal humility. After combat, he lives with a profound awareness of the moral costs he and his fellow soldiers incurred in battle. In Afghanistan, Romesha and his soldiers lived with the attitude that they could endure conditions that "sucked" beyond their control.[70] They dealt with their stress, including post-combat effects, like most soldiers; they bottled up their emotions and focused upon the work ahead of them in order to survive. Romesha describes the eventual outcome from this repression. "Then when you're back in the States you can unlock the door to the room where all that pain has been stored and try to take stock of what it all means. Or not."[71] For Romesha, one moment for unlocking the door came with the awarding of the Medal of Honor. As he listened to the reading of his award citation, he focused upon statements about his command's estimates of his contributions in defending the COP. Romesha reflected upon his perceptions of the event.

> Such estimates are notoriously inaccurate, but the real reason I place little stock in them is that official accounts tend to possess a cleanness, a sense of order, that could not be more at odds with the reality of what unfolds during combat. In the end, only one set of numbers means anything to me: the lives that were lost, and that might have been saved if we—if I—had acted differently. It's true that I did the best I could. What's also true is that I could have done more. In the space between those two facts reside eight graves, the memories of the men whose names are etched on the stones that mark those graves, and my own deeply mixed feelings about receiving the highest medal this country can bestow.[72]

Romesha regards himself as a "custodian or caretaker" of an award that he would "instantly trade" in order to bring back any of his fellow soldiers.[73] His mixed feelings are signs of an elusive moral dissonance generated by his

70. CBS, "Medal of Honor Recipient's Ongoing Burden."

71. Romesha, *Red Platoon*, Kindle loc. 364.

72. Ibid., loc. 367–68.

73. Romesha, *Red Platoon*, Kindle loc. 369.

comparison of his perceptions against his ideals. In making this comparison, he is making a judgment between moral voice and agency that is common among combat veterans. Veterans who can reconcile their moral dissonance experience a healthy conscience that aids their post-traumatic growth. For others, their moral judgments result in a growing dissonance that continues to damage their conscience and degrade their character. The intensity and severity of this moral dissonance determines the severity of their moral injury. This is where using the two-mirror framework becomes a useful model for interpreting veterans' combat narratives.

Conclusion

Soldiers go to war and veterans return home aware of the hypocrisy when their ideal and perceived self-images are different. The dichotomy between their ideals and perceptions, and the duality between their personal and social obligations results in moral dissonance. This dissonance challenges their self-image as professional soldiers, competent warriors, or self-serving pirates. It is vital to understand these self-images are not superficial "snapshots" frozen in time. They are existential "videos" that veterans continually replay to visualize the story line expressed in their war narratives. These narratives convey the moral judgment process where they assess their moral agency, characterize their service, and reconcile their moral dissonance.

Veterans do not often talk about their vocation or combat experiences by listing military values. Instead, they voice their character and competence through narratives using the moral senses they practice in performing their rights and duties.[74] These moral senses have a "double affect/effect." They affect moral voice and agency by shaping the high standards used to define military character and competence. These same moral senses also contribute to the effects from moral judgments resulting in self-affirmation or self-condemnation.

Moral senses can influence resilience, post-traumatic growth, and healing; or they can fuel their dissonance, post-traumatic disorders, moral injuries, and soul sorrow. Because of the duality, it is not helpful to consider moral senses as iconic and static standards. Standards are inflexible and easy to disregard under duress. They become unforgiving judges that fail soldiers in combat by causing damaging dichotomies that haunt veterans' existence. Instead, we should consider moral senses as living guides that help soldiers live with the dualities they experience in combat by conscientiously

74. A braiding of: (1) Haidt's foundational senses of care, fairness, liberty, loyalty, authority, sanctity, with (2) fidelity, responsibility, accountability, maturity, and efficacy.

practicing their vocation with character and competence. These senses guide moral agency and enable veterans to reclaim the "goodness" within their moral voice by providing pathways for healing and legitimate reconciliation of their moral dissonance.

War narratives tell the story of veterans' moral dissonance. Their narratives only begin to make sense when we examine them in terms of their fidelity, responsibility, accountability, maturity, and efficacy (FRAME). After combat, veterans will process the perceptions of faults and failings (whether their own or from others) that generate their moral dissonance. They experience their dissonance as a soul sorrow, and their inability to deal with their dissonance injures them and inhibits their healing and future growth. Moral senses provide the means for soldiers to deconstruct their injurious war narratives and construct healing narratives that recover their professional character and humanity. In the next chapter we will examine how the moral senses of FRAME shape soldiers' moral voice, agency, judgment, and reconciliation.

CHAPTER 6

The Role of Moral Senses in Directing and Judging Military Character

And this I know: all these things that now, while we are still in the war, sink down in us like a stone, after the war shall waken again, and then shall begin the disentanglement of life and death.

—WWI Veteran Erich Maria Remarque[1]

You are part of the world's most feared and trusted force. Engage your brain before you engage your weapon.

—Lieutenant General James Mattis[2]

Connecting the Moral Senses of FRAME with Moral Dissonance

VETERANS CANNOT "LOCK AWAY" or "block" their war experiences. Inevitably, they will process their emotions by constructing the stories of their experiences. This begins during and continues beyond combat. Each individual's narrative contains their subjective perceptions of issues that all veterans encounter in their journey from war to home. These narratives therefore also create a community storehouse of meaning among veterans themselves and become important resources for mitigating and healing

1. Remarque, *All Quiet*, 140.

2. From a letter LTG Mattis delivered to each of his Marines on March 19, 2003, prior to their engaging Iraqi forces. Quoted by Clark in *Task & Purpose*, June 24, 2016.

moral injuries. For example, the quotations above are from two veterans who in their different ways reflected on past combat experiences in order to better shape their futures and those of other combatants. Novelist Erich Remarque used his experiences in the German Army during World War I to write the classic novel *All Quiet on the Western Front*. It was for him a work to help fellow veterans and future generations recover from war. Lieutenant General James Mattis drew from his Vietnam experience to command Marines as they prepared to invade Iraq in 2003. Both Remarque and Mattis link their insights from their war experiences with soldiers' thinking about combat.

Soldiers begin constructing their war narratives when they identify all their intense war experiences and relate them to the standards by which they were trained. When "everything goes right" in combat, and soldiers believe that they have acted in accordance with their values and standards, then the construction of a war narrative is a simple process. However, something often goes wrong in combat, and just as often soldiers' perceptions of the resulting traumatic events lead to self-condemning judgments.

It is vital to understand that soldiers evaluate themselves according to the values of their braided foundational and professional moral senses, not according to the military's attempted infusion of a stoic morality with its defined set of virtues. Primarily, the military attempts to shape character with examples of personal virtue combined with some type of ethical decision-making to ensure professional competence. But these ideals often just accentuate the complex and real differences that exist between virtue, principle, situation, and utility in operational environments.

These differences create ethical and moral dilemmas that soldiers must reconcile with their own moral senses, or moral dispositions. As we noted before, moral senses are best considered as habituated instincts that inform soldiers' moral voice and agency. These senses do not exist in isolation, and they should not be confined to the practice of any particular value. For example, moral senses such as "care" or "fidelity" are not the desired outcome or reason for an action. Instead, the senses of "care" or "fidelity" will influence a person to act or think in a specific manner. Moral senses assist individuals in defining purpose, in acting, and in assigning meaning. They function in concert, and provide a variety of information that guides human behavior. Included are spiritual elements that contribute transcendent meanings to the concrete values soldiers use to practice their profession.

We propose that soldiers' moral senses are a combination of (1) Haidt's foundational senses of care, fairness, loyalty, liberty, authority, and sanctity with (2) the professional goals of fidelity, responsibility, accountability, maturity and efficacy (FRAME). This braiding of moral dispositions, better captures the reality of professional character by allowing for the virtually inevitable occasions of imperfect conduct, while retaining the essential values and standards of desired competence. In other words, a soldier's character is not the substitution of a warrior code for one's humanity. Instead, a soldier's character is an interactive interpretive process of integrating the foundational values of one's humanity with one's vocational standards in such a way as to reconcile the moral dissonance encountered in combat.

Soldiers' moral senses are at the heart of their directed conscientious vocation (DCV). They guide soldiers' conscientious practice of character and competence. Recall that in chapter 4 we defined "conscience" as the holistic summation of personal braided identity that acts in and for the world. Here we define conscience also as the composite of Haidt's foundational senses and FRAME in order to reveal what is distinctive to a soldier's conscience and, thus, what actually "directs" DCV.

Moral senses are active elements within the formation and understanding of soldiers' war narratives. It is important to realize that the same moral senses that guide soldiers' voice and agency also guide their judgments. Moral dissonance from perceived betrayals, faults and failures becomes the story line for some veterans' war narratives. Therefore, it is vital to understand moral dissonance in terms of its specific formation from active moral senses rather than simply interpreting it as a reaction to a single event.

In manageable amounts, moral dissonance denotes a healthy conscience at work, providing clarity and sounding warning alarms that shape soldiers' professional ethics. In unmanageable amounts, moral dissonance discovers a hurting conscience caught in a seemingly unending struggle to reconcile what "should have happened" and what "did happen." These struggles are the soul sorrow of a wounded veteran suffering from a moral injury. Soldiers cannot reconcile their moral dissonance without dealing with their specific experiences related to their moral voice and agency. Leaders cannot assess moral risk without accounting for moral dissonance caused by mission command. Healers cannot support soldiers and leaders in this process without understanding their struggles. The TMM allows us to identify soldiers' moral dissonance by revealing the hidden wrestling matches verbalized in their war narratives. These wrestling matches are often disguised by emotional outbursts linked with moral judgments over traumatic events and by subsequent coping behaviors. Thus injurious moral dissonance remains "hidden in plain sight," as veterans' emotional reactions to traumatic events become the wrong focus of healing efforts.

Instead of treating the emotional reactions, attention must be given primarily to the identification of the moral senses at play in the soldiers' stories. Veterans' war narratives need to be interpreted in terms of moral dissonance which has grown from moral judgments over failed moral agency. Specifically, soldiers' moral senses enable soldiers and healers to recognize, interpret, and reconcile the moral conflicts that develop into injurious effects. Only by identifying and honoring the real moral senses (dispositions) that compose one's conscience, and that encounter each other as combatants *within* one's conscience, can reconciliation of moral dissonance be achieved. And reconciliation of moral dissonance is essential to prevent and heal moral injuries. So, what moral senses compose war narratives? Are there themes or tropes that typify combatant story lines, particularly those regarding moral injury, themes that partners and caregivers to morally injured persons might more readily recognize in order to enhance healing? To answer this question, we return to the acronym of FRAME.

The Moral Senses in War Narratives

Fidelity: Ownership of Moral Voice and Professional Identity

Fidelity is the moral sense that orients warriors to fight as professional soldiers. It demonstrates soldiers' ownership of the values and the ethical reasoning that inform their conduct, as it also testifies to their devotion to their unit colleagues. When a veteran tells you his/her war narrative, ask yourself, "*Why* does he/she feel or think this way?" If you ask a direct question, chances are, he/she will begin to describe his/her commitment to the values and standards used for making moral judgments. David Grossman describes a soldier's sense of fidelity in terms of a sheepdog mentality. "Most citizens are kind, decent people who are not capable of hurting each other, except by accident or under extreme provocation. They are sheep. . . . Then, there are wolves . . . and wolves feed on sheep without mercy. . . . Then, there are sheepdogs, and I am a sheepdog. I live to protect the flock and confront the wolf."[3]

Notice how Grossman combines the intent "to protect" with the implied skills "to fight." In doing this he links the moral voice of a soldier with the competence of a warrior. Military values, standards, and skills not only tell soldiers how to fight, but also when and where. These values and standards are in place to preserve the humanity of the warrior and the professionalism of the solider.[4]

During Vietnam, SEAL team leader Dick Couch made a leadership decision not to send his SEAL team on a mission to guard a low-value

3. Grossman, *On Combat*, 177.
4. Palmer, *They Don't Receive Purple Hearts*, 97.

target. He declined an order that he believed placed his team in danger by taking an unnecessary risk for no military gain. His team was very capable of mitigating this risk, but he didn't believe that the gain outweighed the risk. Because of his decision, a less qualified unit was sent on the mission, and they suffered many casualties. Later in life, Couch reflects upon the consequences of his decision.

> I did not feel right about it. My men applauded the decision. . . .
> I debate the order to this day. There was no question in my mind
> that the order was stupid and ill-conceived, one that would have
> put my men at needless risk. The work we did was dangerous
> enough without inviting disasters, and getting caught at night
> in the mangrove swamp by a large VC [Viet Cong] force was
> just that. You either ran, fought, or died—sometimes all three.
> But I had sworn to obey the lawful order of "those appointed
> over me" and that day I refused . . . my men counted on me not
> to put them at risk unless it really counted. They had followed
> me into some hard situations that tour. I owed them a lot. . . . I
> don't really have a sure answer for this one. I didn't then, and I
> still don't. Had there been a Junior Officers Training Course for
> SEAL officers in my day, as there is now, I might have made a
> better decision. Or a more informed one.[5]

Couch's sense of fidelity keeps him reviewing a decision based upon conflicting values and complex moral reasoning in an ambiguous environment. As a SEAL team leader, he used his moral voice to guide his moral agency. Thirty years later as a veteran, he is making moral judgments over his decision by comparing his ideals with his perceptions. These ideals include both foundational and professional moral senses. So, Couch's professional sense of fidelity becomes linked with his foundational sense of loyalty, care, and fairness.[6] In reassessing his narrative, he fears that he might have acted like a pirate (out of self-interest) by refusing a lawful order. However, he also believes that he acted like a professional soldier by making a critical decision based upon the good of his team. Couch's sense of fidelity encompasses conflicting values that simultaneously form and reconcile his moral dissonance.

It is often said that soldiers fight for each other in combat, so it is not difficult to understand how a sense of fidelity to fellow soldiers within a

---

5. Couch and Doyle, *Navy SEALs*, 103–5.

6. We distinguish "fidelity" from "loyalty" here by emphasizing of the former that it includes an especially disciplined attention to command obedience *and* to the highest principles of military character, which may require disobedience in the face of the immoral.

unit forms a powerful bond in combat. This bond is forged through co-
hesive training and shared experiences. Soldiers train to fight this way,
and their sense of fidelity to fellow soldiers plays a significant role in developing their moral voice and agency. However, it is more difficult to
understand how their sense of fidelity to a set of values influences their
reasoning and judgment.

The goal of military training and education is for soldiers to "develop
the strength to face situations from which it would be normal to run away."[7]
In other words, the values and standards of the military prepare soldiers to
stand and fight as individuals and as a group. Their fighting, or not fighting,
has moral consequences.

Soldiers "want to be the good guys," and their values provide the
standards for their "good" character.[8] Each military service has a distinct
set of core values that shape the conduct of Soldiers, Sailors, Marines, Airmen, and Coast Guardsmen in times of war and peace.[9] These values focus
their sense of fidelity upon their battle buddy, shipmate, or wingman for the
"good" of the unit. Basic habituation of these senses into the chain of command formalizes command relationships. The shared experiences of unit
members under duress further deepens the values as a way of life. Soldiers
express the value of these senses in their war narratives.

Couch's war narrative demonstrates how difficult it is to interpret the
conflicting values placed upon these relationships in combat. Did he solely
act upon a particular value or code to protect his team? Probably not, because
he believes that he had both the duty to obey a lawful order and a conflicting
obligation to protect his team. He also believed that he had an obligation to
refuse a "stupid" command in order to fulfill his duty as team leader. These
obligations and duties are part of unwritten "honor" codes within mission
command that leaders are expected to uphold, and they influence how leaders evaluate the consequences of their decisions.

Couch didn't base his decision upon a single value or standard. Instead, he based his decision upon complex reasoning informed by his moral
senses. It is vital to note how his sense of fidelity combined with foundational senses such as care and loyalty to inform his reasoning. His moral sense
of fidelity allowed him to responsibly reject an unwise order, and simultaneously be accountable for a decision that led to the deaths of other soldiers. In
order to protect his team, Couch brought together all four ethical reasoning
systems within mission command (principles, utility, situation, and virtue),

7. US Department of Defense, *Armed Forces Officer Edition of 1950*, 13.

8. US Joint Forces Command, *Final Report*.

9. Dempsey, *Mission Command White Paper*.

but this didn't resolve the moral issue. In making his decision, Couch acted as both a professional soldier and fallible human being and lives with the ongoing moral dissonance caused by conflicting professional values and standards. However, nowhere in this process did he betray or violate his moral sense of "right."

Couch's situation is a variation of the moral dilemma that confronted Lieutenant Frick on the Iraqi airfield (described in the last chapter). The consequences of both Couch's and Frick's decisions are linked by their moral sense of ownership (fidelity) to a set of values they practice within their mission command. Later, they replay these events and make moral judgments over their reasoning and conduct. Like a pang of conscience, moral senses may be the primary indicator for soldiers that something isn't "right," or something important is missing. We speak of conflicting values and misaligned ethical reasoning. But what if soldiers are really experiencing moral dissonance caused by conflicting moral senses, senses that differ from values and ethics insofar as the senses are spiritually influenced? Furthermore, what happens to soldiers who separate their moral senses from their vocational practice?

Moral senses do not operate alone. Suppose foundational moral senses like "care," or "fairness" combine with "fidelity" and become factors in practicing the military value of duty. Here transcendent or spiritual values (such as life, family, and community) blend with military "core values" to form the bedrock of an individual's ideal moral voice. Thus military "duty" becomes "fidelity" to the "care and fair" treatment of others. As this blending happens, a soldier's sense of fidelity may be challenged by situations in which "duty" must either be obeyed or overridden. Nowhere is this more critical than in decisions to use lethal force in combat where human beings who are soldiers must act with lethal competence.

Combat is filled with traumatic, chaotic, and emotional conditions that affect ethical reasoning by opening gaps between desired values and necessary conduct. Requirements to win and survive as a unit create situations where soldiers disregard their personal character in favor of acting effectively with the team. This may be a tragic necessity, but it comes with a price. The military educates and instills values through Stoic philosophies and codes of conduct embodied in heroic soldiers who become role models. These heroes are often portrayed with all the ideal virtues but none of the real vulnerabilities that soldiers experience in combat. However, these vulnerabilities become evident when soldiers privately, or publicly, work through their war narratives.

As we noted earlier, a soldier's sense of fidelity is not achieved by simply laying a warrior code over his/her humanity. Consider the war narrative of Navy Corpsman John Bradley, one of the men photographed raising the first flag atop Mount Suribachi on Iwo Jima. Some claim that this photograph (actually based on another) captures the essence of professional service for all the military. However, there is a real man behind this ideal (and mythical) image. Following the battle of Iwo Jima, Bradley made ordered appearances to sell war bonds. After the war he returned home to Wisconsin, and became a small-town mortician. He honorably served his community, and raised a family. He seldom, if ever, spoke about his wartime experience. He didn't display any copies of the famous photograph and declined public appearances to honor his wartime service.

In 1964, his son took a copy of the famous photograph to school for Show and Tell, and his teacher told the class that the boy's father was a war hero. This was news to his son, and Bradley explained to him, "Your teacher said something about heroes. . . . The heroes of Iwo Jima are the guys who didn't come back."[10] His disavowal of heroism may be tied to the fact that he was misidentified in the famous second photograph.[11] However, in 1970 Corpsman Bradley finally told his son a part of the war narrative behind his reticence.

> I've tried hard to block this out . . . to forget it. We could choose a buddy to go in with [land on Iwo Jima]. My buddy was a guy from Milwaukee. We were pinned down in one area. Someone elsewhere fell injured and I ran to help out, and when I came back my buddy was gone. I couldn't figure out where he was. I could see all around, but he wasn't there, and nobody knew where he was. . . . A few days later someone yelled that they'd found him. They called me over because I was a corpsman. The Japanese had pulled him underground and tortured him. It was terrible. I've tried so hard to forget all this. . . . And then, I visited his parents after the war and just lied to them. He didn't suffer at all I told them. He didn't feel a thing, didn't know what hit him. I just lied to them.[12]

In combat you don't have to kill to hurt. Bradley told his war narrative twenty-five years after the battle for Iwo Jima, but the intensity of dissonance between his ideal fidelity to his battle buddy and his perceived failure of fidelity to others kept him replaying the event, and affected his own self-identity.

10. Bradley, *Flags of Our Fathers*, 194–98.
11. Michaels, "Marines Misidentified One Man."
12. Bradley, *Flags of Our Fathers*, 198.

Perceptions are real, but not all perceptions are accurate. Accurate perceptions (whether good or bad) are essential for healing moral dissonance. Understanding veterans' moral sense of fidelity helps differentiate healthy standards for moral agency from destructive perceptions of war experiences. Moral dissonance is cumulative and must be considered more than the violation of any single value. It is preferable to consider war narratives in terms of soldiers' moral sense of fidelity to a complex range of values. Soldiers get upset over violations and losses of what they value. Their sense of fidelity is their ownership of the values they use to guide their competence and judge their conduct. Thus, fidelity becomes the basis for understanding soldiers' moral senses of responsibility and accountability.

Responsibility and Accountability: Ownership of Consequences

Responsibility and accountability are necessary and complementary moral senses within mission command. Often, the military uses one sense to define the other. Thus, responsibility and accountability may be defined as: (1) command ownership for everything a unit does or fails to do, and (2) command acceptance of consequences for everything the unit does or fails to do. Responsibility defines ownership of moral agency, and accountability assigns moral judgment based upon this ownership. This applies from the most senior, strategic levels of mission command down to the most junior, tactical levels of "battle buddy." However, the moral senses of responsibility and accountability transcend these legal and hierarchal limits because they apply the obligation to "engage your brain before engaging your weapon" as the criterion for professional character and competence.

The military uses "warrior" as a generic term to describe the competence and purpose of its members. The term "warrior" becomes associated with the pathology of moral injury through the misuse of combat skills. Navy psychologist William Nash has written: "What makes a warrior a warrior is taking personal responsibility, and when they fail to live up to that enormously high ideal, that's moral injury."[13] We suggest otherwise. We believe that the moral senses of responsibility and accountability make a warrior a soldier, and prevent him/her from acting as a pirate. The military requires higher levels of professional conduct from its soldiers in order to maintain public trust. These requirements are intended to control warrior competence and mitigate the formation of injurious effects from combat.[14]

13. Captain William Nash, quoted in Kaplan, "Military Is Going Beyond PTSD."
14. Dempsey, *America's Military.*

The self-serving conduct of pirates reflects the absence of responsibility and accountability characteristic of narcissistic pathologies and nihilist philosophies, where individuals or groups become "laws unto themselves."[15] The military does not condone these types of behavior. However, combat presents conditions where warriors don't have to be criminals to act like pirates. All it takes to degrade soldiers' character is self-serving values combined with permissions from a localized peer group operating with a situational mentality. When this happens, an ethical or moral "fading or overreach" can occur that misuses warrior competence and degrades individual and unit character.

Some research supports the negative effects of moral fading in combat on soldiers' character. Between 2003 and 2013 the Army Medical Command conducted nine Mental Health Advisory Team (MHAT) studies of returning Army and Marine combat units. These studies found that large numbers of respondents reported some type of association with unethical situations, but few respondents reported any type of direct commission of a "crime." These questions asked about participants' perceptions of violations as well as about actual violations against noncombatants and civilians. About 25% of those surveyed reported that they didn't know how to respond to the ethical violations they witnessed.[16] A 2009 study conducted by Litz et al. documented how effects from multiple deployments combined with combat losses affected soldiers' future ethical reasoning and increased their guilt, shame, and demoralization. The study found that soldiers who perpetrated, witnessed, failed to prevent, or associated with groups who committed perceived atrocities had stronger correlations with re-experiencing the initial trauma, avoidance behaviors, and abusive behaviors than soldiers who reported only traumatic combat exposure. The study concluded that negative, post-combat behaviors are caused more by soldiers' perceptions of their conduct in combat than by their perceptions of personal injury or death.[17]

The above studies justify the association of injurious effects from combat with MI that occurs when "localized peer groups" within units weaken the values and standards by which they were trained.[18] Most of us would

15. Holmes, *Acts of War*, 50. Holmes is using a pathological definition provided by Erich Fromm applied to soldiers who self-justify atrocities using appeals to military virtues.

16. Barrett, "Finding the Right Way"; also US Army, *Mental Health Advisory Team*.

17. Litz et al., "Moral Injury and Moral Repair," 795–806. See also Hoge et al., "Combat Duty," 13–22.

18. These groups operate with processes that resemble Gentile and Gilligan's social development of moral voice and agency. Gentile, *Giving Voice to Values*. Also Chu and Gilligan, *When Boys Become Boys*.

like to believe that group thinking prohibits unethical and immoral decisions. However, research shows that peer groups can activate a situational "reward" mentality that diffuses responsibility and accountability for group conduct. This increases the potential for overriding personal ethical and moral boundaries because the individual is acting as a member of a team. Also, the incentive of immediate reward for risky decisions is more prevalent among young adults and adolescents.[19] This can make combat units more at risk to "localized authority," because a majority of its members are young adults, vulnerable to peer permissions that override the moral senses that connect an individual soldier with his/her humanity.

When "localized authority" is combined with the proximity of potential threats, it increases the risk that individuals will "switch off" the psychological and moral "safety catch" that controls their lethal skills.[20] In the chaos of combat, soldiers must not only operate with warrior competence, they must also operate with fidelity to the higher values and standards that preserve their humanity. Soldiers' moral senses do protect them from making morally injurious decisions. However, these same moral senses do not make them immune to the consequences of moral dissonance arising from their attempts to practice moral agency.

During the Korean War a company of Marines attempted to capture forty North Korean soldiers trapped in a culvert. When the North Koreans refused to surrender, the Marines killed them. Fifty years after the event, Marine First Sergeant Rocco Zullo describes his conflicted sense of moral responsibility and accountability. "I wanted to take them [the North Koreans] prisoner, but we had to annihilate them once they didn't come out. Otherwise, they would have hit us from the rear. Nice guys don't win wars."[21]

Zullo's narrative reveals that he is still troubled by the moral dissonance between his desired intent and his perceived conduct. Notice how he analyzes this event by affirming his ethical conduct while simultaneously questioning his moral character. Contrast Zullo's intent and conduct with the intent and conduct of Army Staff Sergeant Huntley and his soldiers after they captured an insurgent sniper who had killed a member of their unit. Huntley describes his platoon's reasoning for not killing or mistreating the sniper. "He [the sniper] had killed one of ours, and we should do the same

19. Steinberg and Levine, "You and Your Adolescent"; Parker-Pope, "Teenagers, Friends and Bad Decisions"; Chein et al., "Peers Increase Adolescent Risk Taking."

20. Grossman, On Killing, 323.

21. O'Donnell, Give Me Tomorrow, 62.

to him . . . but we did what we were trained to do, not by the seven Army Values but by being men and soldiers."[22]

These situations are not identical, but both Zullo and Huntley process the events using similar moral senses of responsibility and accountability. Huntley did act within the rules, but more importantly, he acted justly both as a human being and as a soldier. For Zullo, "good guys don't win wars," and he holds himself accountable for killing out of necessity in a bad situation. Zullo didn't act alone, or for his own selfish-reasons. As a member of a unit, he acted with a sense of responsibility and accountability for his fellow Marines. In vocational terms this makes him a professional soldier and a warrior; not a pirate. However, one can make the case that Zullo may perceive himself to be a "pirate" and a "bad guy" instead of the "nice" guy he wants to be. The "warrior" that was needed at the culvert is different from the soldier who needs to return home. Zullo's narrative reveals the way he realizes his moral dissonance, the perceptions of a veteran struggling with moral injury.

Soldiers want to be the "good guys," and they are trained to be the "good guys." Their professional ethos and moral senses create a personal and social expectation that will hold them morally responsible for the values they own. Michael Walzer believes that responsibility is the critical test for justice in war, and without responsible soldiers there can be no sense or talk of justice.[23] The close relationship between moral senses of responsibility and accountability links soldiers' deliberate responses with their instincts. In the heat of combat, autonomic reactions can override conscious reasoning, and combine with scrambled emotions and thoughts to override soldiers' moral senses.[24]

What guides a soldier's moral agency under these conditions? Some would say, it is the rules and principles that prohibit the intentional killing of innocent civilians. Others would say it is the mission requirements and situational contexts that allow for unintended consequences. Neither response is adequate for answering the moral questions that Zullo and Huntley ask. The senses of responsibility and accountability are required to answer the questions more adequately, even as these senses, like fidelity, might engage each other combatively. But to name them and to understand how they function within a war narrative is to begin to find a way toward healing.

22. Center for the Army Professional Ethic, *Integrity Case Exercise*.

23. Walzer, *Just and Unjust Wars*, 287.

24. Haidt, *Righteous Mind*, 102–65.

Maturity and Efficacy: The Capacity and Ability to Practice Moral Agency

In combat, moral character must control warrior competence, because combat creates severe conditions that divorce soldiers' moral voice from their agency. However, soldiers' moral senses of maturity and efficacy seek to marry their moral voice and agency for life. These moral senses are more than age and rank combined with experience. The military chain of command determines authority, and time in service results in promotions that provide increased freedoms and responsibilities to soldiers in accordance with their duties. Yet, it is also possible that with increased rank and professional experiences soldiers can learn the wrong lessons, repeat them, and then pass them on to others. Therefore, soldiers' moral senses of maturity and efficacy must be measured by their capability to learn the correct lessons and their capacity to apply them in future situations while under duress. Junior soldiers cannot do this without help from experienced mentors within the profession who help them "integrate often-brutal emotions and combat memories into their lives and histories."[25]

The military heavily invests in realistic training and education programs that use experienced civilians, veterans, officers and non-commissioned officers to develop warriors into professional soldiers who possess both the capability and the capacity to exercise their moral voice and moral agency. This lifelong approach to training and education provides a vocational identity that reinforces the moral senses throughout the chain of mission command. Thus the moral senses of maturity and efficacy should be considered in terms of personal growth and craftsmanship. Together these moral senses provide soldiers the emotional intelligence to integrate their character with their competence.[26] Without a moral sense of maturity soldiers may not have the capacity to process their trauma and grow through their experiences. This can be seen in the older veteran who cannot assimilate or accommodate his/her perceptions of combat trauma. Without efficacy soldiers may express fidelity, own responsibility, accept accountability, have maturity, and yet lack the capability to use any of it. This can be seen in a younger soldier trapped in perceptions of a situation that he/she couldn't prevent or control.

Soldiers are trained to believe that "one can carve out some domain of control even in the most constrained of circumstances."[27] This belief might

25. Kirkland, "Combat Psychological Trauma."

26. Emotional intelligence is defined and measured along two axes: (1) personal and social, (2) awareness and discipline. See Goleman et al., *Primal Leadership*.

27. Sherman, *Stoic Warriors*, Kindle loc. 2065–75.

be stoic in theory, but it is DCV within military practice. The military accustoms soldiers to believe this. The senses of maturity and efficacy, however, can positively qualify what otherwise might be a naïve and even destructive conviction. Consider the differing levels of maturity and efficacy in the following war narratives.

Army Infantryman Alex Horton shot an Iraqi civilian twice in the abdomen and watched him disappear out of sight. He does not know if the man lived or died. Horton's unit had taken up defensive positions to protect the extraction of wounded soldiers from a vehicle disabled by an improvised explosive device. Horton's unit began firing hundreds of rounds down a road to suppress "anything moving." When Horton saw the man running, he targeted him. Later, he began to doubt his instinctive decision, and now worries that the man he shot was a noncombatant civilian who posed no threat to him or his fellow soldiers. Now Horton blames himself and his warrior training that empowered him to instinctively target and shoot. He reasons, "That's not how good people act, but I did it, because I had to."[28]

Army Sergeant Kenneth Eastridge influenced his fellow soldiers to participate in a multitude of criminal acts including the indiscriminate shooting of noncombatants in Iraq and planting weapons on them, and the targeting and murdering of civilians in Colorado Springs. Eastridge grew up in a broken home. He pled guilty to reckless homicide at the age of twelve after he accidently killed his friend while playing with his father's shotgun. The court sentenced him to probation and he entered counseling. He later joined the Army, became an infantryman, and served in a unit where "they [the battalion soldiers] tend to be a little crazy, but a lot of times that is the mentality you are looking for. Those loose cannons sometimes are the guys who are gonna be good in a fight."[29] Eastridge blended this type of "warrior mentality" with his experiences of childhood trauma. This allowed him to operate as a "loose cannon" under a "dark self-revelation" that he was going to hell. He found this liberating: "he was already damned, so he could do what he wanted."[30] He did, and as a young NCO he committed murder both in and out of combat, and influenced others to follow his lead.

Finally, consider the contrasting narratives from two veterans. Army Specialist Nic DeNinno describes his moral alienation following the death of a fellow soldier. "That image still haunts me, it changed me. I don't know how many others saw that . . . but all I wanted was death and violence from

---

28. Taub, "Moral Injury."

29. Philipps, *Lethal Warriors*, 17–23.

30. Ibid., 23.

then on. To me, this is where I lost my old self."[31] DeNinno's response at a time of emotional pain reveals the divorce that occurs between moral voice and agency that soldiers will have to reconcile. Over time this reconciliation may happen as soldiers resolve the moral dissonance between their vocational conduct and personal humanity.[32]

An example of this type of reconciliation is the note Marine Sergeant Frederick Garten left with a wedding ring at the Vietnam Memorial Wall. His note read: "This wedding ring belonged to a young Viet Cong fighter. He was killed by a Marine unit in the Phu Hoc province of South Vietnam in May of 1968. I wish I knew more about this young man. I have carried this ring for 18 years and it's time for me to lay it down. This boy is not my enemy any longer."[33]

The moral senses of maturity and efficacy shape the way these veterans process their war narratives and judge their self-identity. Each one is a trained warrior expected to act like a soldier. They react differently over time to conditions that perhaps influenced them to respond like pirates. The consequences from their moral dissonance left them burdened. Horton and DeNinno still struggle with their decisions. Eastridge is left with a sociopathy that poorly distinguishes between a sense of right vs. wrong. Only Garten has been able to set down some of his moral burden. Psychiatrist Ed Tick believes that levels of maturity and empowerment must be factored into both diagnosis and treatment for post-traumatic stress. He uses the example of a young person surviving multiple car accidents in a short period of time to demonstrate the magnitude of healing challenges faced by veterans recovering from the adverse effects of traumatic combat stress.[34] We believe that maturity and efficacy are also essential factors for redressing MI and must be included as significant threshold markers in the shaping of a soldier's vocation. The above cases are negative and positive examples for this argument.

A common military expression states that junior soldiers do the fighting, non-commissioned officers direct the fighting, and officers manage the fighting.[35] This expression implies different levels of maturity and efficacy that may affect soldiers' ability to "accelerate" or "brake" the use of

31. Finkel, *Thank You*, 56, 66.

32. Tick, *Warrior's Return*, Kindle loc. 4910.

33. Palmer, *Shrapnel in the Heart*, 184–85.

34. Tick, *War and the Soul*, 101.

35. Chaplain Zust has witnessed some form of this reasoning in many military schools and training exercises throughout his career. The Marines have a very good description of the character and competence behind this reasoning in their basic leadership doctrine; see, US Marine Corps, *Leading Marines*, 27–52.

their warrior skills in combat. This difference also has serious consequences for how soldiers deal with their moral dissonance. The top 5 percent of the military's master craftsmen are in the highest ranks. They are also the recipients of the military's best education as measured by the quality of the schools they attend and the quantity of instruction and mentoring hours they receive. This level of instruction is not given to the 15 percent of its journeyman-level soldiers (mid-level officers and enlisted) who will lead in combat, or the 80 percent of the military's apprentice-level soldiers (junior officers and enlisted) who will conduct combat operations.[36] This exposes a vulnerability within the moral education of the military, where the members with the lowest levels of maturity and power to control their environment are the ones most likely to experience direct effects from the use of lethal force in combat.

The reflex to kill in combat is instinctually fast, and the operant conditioning of reflexive marksmanship increases the lethality of warriors in combat.[37] Similar training applies to pilots as well as members of crew-served weapon systems. The focus is upon increased survival by putting rounds on target. However, an improvement in aiming doesn't necessarily accompany an improvement in the reasoning used to integrate moral agency into targeting decisions. Operant conditioned marksmanship relies upon single-loop learning (focused upon cause and affect) where reflexive conduct can set soldiers up for moral failures in complex, chaotic situations.

Grossman has shown how operant conditioned marksmanship enables warriors to engage their enemy as targets without resolving the moral consequences of killing another human being. To correct this problem, he believes that it is necessary to combine reflective ethical training with operant reflexive training to develop soldiers who "understand where and what the psychological safety catch is [for targeting], how it works, and how to put it back on."[38] Grossman uses video gaming to illustrate the danger of operant reflexive training. In video games, players are rewarded for shooting and killing without having to make value-based targeting decisions or personally suffering any of the physical and psychological stresses of participating in actual combat.[39] Thus players can shoot, without engaging their brains. In this sense, video gaming may reflect what actually happens during combat.

36. These percentages are derived from US Dept. of Defense, *2012 Demographics Profile*.

37. Grossman, *On Killing*. In section 8 Grossman provides an extensive argument on the effects of operant conditioning upon young adults.

38. Ibid., 383.

39. Ibid.

Changes in soldiers' heart rates under duress reflect changes in *how* they reason and control their conduct. Physical exertion and complex mental stressors can raise heart rates up to 145 beats per minute (bpm). At these levels, soldiers still have cognitive control over their reflexive reactions. As soldiers encounter stressors that raise their heart rates above 175 bpm, they have limited capacity for cognitive reasoning, but can still exercise motor skills and experience intense emotions. This means that soldiers are still "taking in all the data" from their combat environment, but restricting their cognitive reasoning and relying upon operant conditioned responses.

The threats and risks soldiers encounter in combat can accelerate their heart rates well over 175 bpm. Research studies indicate that only trained individuals can operate at this level, for short periods of time, without overloading their capacity to function. During these short periods, individuals screen out peripheral stimuli and begin to lose their ability to analyze complicated situations. They compensate by making decisions based upon rigid performance standards to determine individual and group conduct.[40] During longer periods of time, cumulative fatigue produces similar effects. One measure of soldiers' cumulative fatigue is their lack of sleep. Army Surgeon General Lieutenant General Patricia Horoho summarizes the cognitive effects from lack of sleep. "If you have less than six hours of sleep for six days in a row you have a cognitive impairment of 20 percent—that is, you are as cognitively impaired as if you had a .08 percent alcohol level. . . . We never will allow a soldier in our formation with a .08 percent alcohol level, but we allow it every day to make those complex decisions."[41]

Within mission command, narrow thinking that fails to weigh alternatives can result in reflexive responses that allow for expedient decisions in urgent conditions.[42] When the cognitive reasoning essential for controlling the use of lethal force is absent, soldiers' narrow reasoning and fatigue can result in localized permissions that override laws, blur ethical boundaries, and violate moral character.[43]

Autonomic, operant-conditioned reactions will take control under fire unless there is a counterbalance that helps soldiers to control their reflexive responses. One such program is Close Quarters Drill (CQD) training that provides soldiers the capability and capacity for "dialing up and dialing down" their reflexive responses when fighting under duress. The "dial" is

40. Kavanagh, *Stress and Performance*. See also Grossman, *On Combat*, 8–20; Grossman, *On Killing*, 7–10, 314–20.

41. Jordan, "Army Surgeon General." For further information see the following studies: Miller et al., "Fatigue and Its Effect"; Krueger, "Sustained Military Performance."

42. Kahneman, *Thinking*, 12–13. Gompert and Kugler, "Lee's Mistake."

43. Grossman, *On Killing*, 188–94.

the product of a "double loop" reasoning process that trains soldiers to use a continuum of responses (similar to a rheostat) instead of reacting with an "all or nothing 'on/off' reflex."[44] Thus soldiers mature and develop their efficacy to control their marksmanship by engaging the logic centers in their brains during times of high stress.[45]

This training differs from the operant conditioning of reflexive firing by developing soldiers' "double loop" reasoning along with their marksmanship skills in order to: (1) *critically* process their past experiences and operations as a group, and (2) continually incorporate lessons learned from new experiences into their future mission command. In this type of training, mature soldiers serve more as mentors by asking reflective questions and by coaching soldiers through realistic training that stimulates peer group discussions among junior soldiers about their perceptions of acceptable and unacceptable reasoning and conduct in combat.[46]

These types of training are available throughout the military from small unit training to senior mission command exercises. The desired outcome is to develop soldiers' moral senses of maturity and efficacy that equip them to integrate their professional character, warrior competence, and mission command under fire. The popular book *American Sniper* contains an account of a disagreement between SEAL team members and Couch which involved the use of CQD in combat. Their disagreement was about practices of deliberate "dialed" targeting and the necessity for operant reflexive reactions in combat.[47] What's at stake in this disagreement is not warrior competence, but the differences that separate the moral senses of professional soldiers from the mentality of pirates. This is Couch's reason for advocating "double loop training" to empower soldiers' moral agency in conditions that tempt soldiers to immoral conduct.

> I contend that a warrior's [soldier's] performance on the battle-field is not only complemented, but also enhanced, by a firm moral foundation. Ethics and martial skills can and should be part of the same training package and the same deployment package. If our best and brightest are tempted to cover up wrong behavior in a school setting, what are we to expect of our soldiers and marines whose brotherhood is forged on the battlefield? . . . You must make honor and right conduct a part of your unit's branding: impress your men with the idea that wrong

---

44. Couch, *Tactical Ethic*, 90–111; Grossman, *On Combat*, 314–31.

45. Couch, *Tactical Ethic*, 90–111; Grossman, *On Combat*, 314–31.

46. Couch, *Tactical Ethic*, 90–111.

47. Kyle et al., *American Sniper*, Kindle loc. 317–18.

conduct tarnishes your brand and is a form of disloyalty to all warriors who fight for the brand. Train them, trust them, and hold them to standard. . . . Keep your honor on par with your marvelous professional skill. If some pirate in your unit tries to minimize you or tarnish your honor, take a stand, take action.[48]

Former Chairman of the Joint Chiefs of Staff Admiral Mike Mullen reminds all soldiers: "Nine years of close quarter combat has changed many aspects of what we do. It must not change who or what we are as a professional disciplined force."[49] When operant reflexes become disassociated from reasoned responses, fatigued, poorly led, and poorly trained warriors lack the capacity to control their lethal skills.[50] This is a recipe for generating moral dissonance. Warriors can retain the capability to engage their weapons, but lose the fidelity, maturity, and efficacy necessary to engage their brains. After combat, these veterans will be left with the responsibility and accountability for coping with what they did. Before combat, if all possible means for developing maturity and effectiveness are employed in other than only operant-conditioning training, the severity of moral injury later will be ameliorated, if not preempted. If all possible means for the realization of maturity and effectiveness are addressed post-combat, healing of MI is more likely to be achieved. Trainers and caregivers, in solidarity with the soldier the whole way, will seek to identify the levels of maturity and efficacy in that soldier and help that soldier finally to recognize them clearly, as with all the components of FRAME. *How* to do this will be the subject of our final chapters.

Conclusion

During World War II General George C. Marshall summarized the need for soldiers to control their warrior skills: "Once an army is involved in war, there is a beast in every fighting man which begins tugging at its chains. And a good officer must learn early on how to keep the beast under control, both in his men and himself."[51] Leaders must exercise this control because soldiers can still pay a physical, psychological, and spiritual price for doing

48. Couch, *Tactical Ethic*, 11, 81, 111.

49. Rondeau, "Identity in the Profession of Arms," 13. The original quote is from Chairman Joint Chiefs of 2011 staff guidance.

50. Armstrong, *Fields of Blood*, 8–10. Grossman uses the metaphor of a sheepdog, puppy, and wolf to describe these responses. See Grossman, *On Combat*, Kindle loc. 1207–11. See Haidt, *Righteous Mind*, Kindle loc. 102. Haidt uses the metaphor of a cognitive rider trying to control a rampaging, autonomic, and emotional elephant.

51. Barrett, *Finding "the Right Way*,*"* 42.

their duty according to their conscience. Indeed, one can pay a price for not obeying an order which violates conscience, or for carrying out an order in a crisis which action goes against conscience.[52]

Shay believes that soldiers are more likely to lose their humanity, their spiritual faith, in combat than to forge stronger connections in combat.[53] He points out that combat evokes emotions that can fuel immoral acts when soldiers "personally perceive a betrayal of 'what's right' in a high-stakes situation by someone who holds power."[54] This violation and betrayal happens within mission command when senior leaders issue orders that force soldiers to deny their moral voice, and it also happens in situations of localized authority where junior leaders and soldiers override their moral senses to commit acts that violate their conscience. Therefore, Shay believes the prevention of moral injury begins within a command climate where leaders train their soldiers to deal with the stressors they will encounter in combat in order to maintain their moral integrity.[55] At the conclusion of his foundational work Shay writes, "There can be no doubt that rigorous, realistic training does provide significant psychological protection to people who must fight, not to speak of enormously raising their chances of survival. The reader may have noticed that there are no accounts in this book of veterans attributing their psychological injuries to military training. In fact, many Vietnam combat veterans felt deeply betrayed by the irrelevance of their training to the actual conditions and enemy they had to face."[56]

Soldiers' resilience can be improved by reducing poor command climates where harmful stressors fatigue soldiers and violate the foundations of public trust which support military service.[57] General Stanley McChrystal believes that effective mission command allows soldiers to operate with shared media for communication and awareness that promote trust and empower execution at all levels of command.[58] These improvements are developed within training environments and command ethos where soldiers are taught to heed their moral senses and practice moral reasoning prior

---

52. Personal conversations with Marshall Storeby and Hugh Thompson at Fort Bragg in 1999; Marlantes, *What It Is Like to Go to War*, chs. 3–5.

53. Shay and Haynes, "Understanding Moral Injury and PTSD."

54. Shay, *Odysseus in America*, 240.

55. Shay, *Achilles in Vietnam*, 193–200.

56. Ibid.

57. Shay and Haynes, "Understanding Moral Injury and PTSD"; Covey, *Speed of Trust*. Ethicists such as Roger Wiler and Don Snider have written on the necessity for building and maintaining social trust as the foundation for ethical and moral practice.

58. McChrystal et al., *Team of Teams*, 214–18.

to "engaging their weapons," even in the changing and uncertain environments they will encounter in combat.

Moral injury is an occupational hazard organically related to military service. This is so because it is human beings who volunteer for a demanding vocation where soldiers encounter conditions that defy their professional competence and moral character.[59] Thus, the potential for moral injuries and soul sorrow resides within individual soldiers, unit members, the chain of command, and the national command authority that deploys soldiers into combat. FRAME provides the best means for helping soldiers and healers reconcile their moral dissonance.

Soldiers' moral senses are the means they use to assign meaning to their perceptions and conduct. They form the heart of directed conscientious vocation (DCV), and are also active in soldiers' forming and working through their war narratives. Moral senses may form the basis for soldiers' moral judgments that develop into ongoing moral dissonance that damages their self-identity. Or, these senses may serve as "reservoirs of strength that promote soldiers' hardiness, resiliency, and post-traumatic growth."[60] Moral senses have this deep impact because they include human and spiritual dimensions that extend beyond the legal and ethical boundaries of military vocation. In the next chapter we will explore how these spiritual dimensions are active within the guidelines soldiers use to practice their directed conscientious vocation.

59. Samet, *Soldier's Heart*, 128.
60. Marine Corps, *Leading Marines*, 2–8, and Bartone et al., "To Build Resilience."

CHAPTER 7

Spiritual Dimensions for Mitigating and Healing Soul Suffering

I enlisted imbued with a rather flamboyant concept of this country's destiny as the leader of a free world and the necessity of the use of armed force. I emerged a corporal three years later in a state of great turmoil, at the core of which was an angry awareness of war as the most vicious and fraudulent self-deception man had ever devised.

—Corporal Anton Myrer[1]

Those who in acting take on guilt—which is inescapable for any responsible person—place this guilt on themselves . . . they stand up for it and take responsibility for it.

—Dietrich Bonhoeffer[2]

THE MORAL SENSES THAT compose the braided character of a professional soldier include spiritual dimensions that support the two parts of a soldier's worldview. These two parts are (1) the beliefs and values that shape the meaning of his/her identity, and (2) the will to act in accordance with one's beliefs and values.[3] Spiritual dimensions influence soldiers' moral voice and

1. Gussow, "Anton Myrer."
2. Bonhoeffer, *Ethics*, 282.
3. Sweeney et al., "Domain of the Human Spirit."

agency. They also shape the interpretive processes that soldiers use to assign meaning to their war narratives. In this chapter we examine this specific influence using our own Christian construction of directed conscientious vocation (DCV). This construction will demonstrate *how* and *why* interactions between moral senses and worldviews are essential for mitigating and healing the moral dissonance that causes moral injuries and soul sorrow.

Soldiers' war narratives reveal spiritual dimensions that activate moral dissonance. On the surface these narratives seem easy to understand, because they express the traumatic events and intense emotions that convey meaning. These war narratives also express hidden subjective evaluations of one's own character, evaluations that are even opaque to the soldier herself, which moral judgments also influence self-identity and quality of life. Morally injurious events (MIEs) and moral pain are only visible indicators and symptoms of complex wounds caused by moral dissonance. Discerning the root meanings soldiers subconsciously attach to their moral dissonance is important for understanding *why* they think, feel, and act the way they do. Such discernment can set a basis for resolving moral dissonance and beginning the process of post-traumatic growth.

Soldiers and veterans represent a small percentage of our society. This distance itself increases the difficulty soldiers and veterans have in mitigating and healing their moral dissonance as they return home from war because they are not readily understood by civilian society outside the military. Amy Amidon, a Navy psychologist, describes the effects of this widening social gap. "Civilians are lucky that we still have a sense of naiveté about what the world is like. The average American means well, but what they need to know is that these [military] men and women are seeing incredible evil, and coming home with that weighing on them and not knowing how to fit back into society."[4]

"Evil" is a spiritual construction. Healing the consequences of "evil" includes taking into account the worldviews that define its existence. Soldiers wrestling with a concept of evil struggle with spiritual dimensions to gain a transformed meaning of their self-identity and purpose. All veterans make this spiritual journey in some form.

This chapter's opening quote from veteran Anton Myrer describes his moral dissonance from military service during the World War II Pacific campaigns. Myrer went on to write the classic novel *Once an Eagle*, describing the moral parameters of duty, honor, and country separating professional officers from self-serving, career militarists. His work is not religious in nature, but it includes many of the important spiritual

---

4. Sledge, "Conversation about War."

dimensions that transform the naïve self-perceptions of a morally injured war veteran into the wiser and healed moral agency of a professional soldier. Myrer observes that this maturation process comes through the shattering of delusionary misperceptions of vocation to create new interpretations of foundational beliefs and values.[5]

The second quote is from theologian Dietrich Bonhoeffer, who believed that this transformation process required the ownership, responsibility and accountability of ones' moral agency as the foundation for one's spiritual service. During World War II, Bonhoeffer viewed his participation in the war as an act of legitimate discipleship to oppose a greater evil. He worked with a group of German officers and political leaders who assumed guilt by association for the actions of their nation, and personal guilt by their participation in a plot to assassinate Adolf Hitler and other Nazi leaders. Bonhoeffer's practice of discipleship was similar in nature to Myrer's practice of vocation in so far as both men defined moral agency as the critical application of spiritual dimensions in their conscientious acceptance of national service. Both writers' conclusions serve as helpful lenses to see how good stewards of spiritual and vocational practices can still experience damaging moral dissonance.

The "critical application" of religion is essential for developing moral senses and worldviews where individuals

> learn to practice one's faith in ways that incline more toward peacefulness and legitimate, measured defense than brutality. . . . Yet if we delve more deeply into each religious tradition, we can arguably find at least one common thread between the mainstreams of these traditions: namely, that they profess a strong presumption against injustice and the accompanying understanding that, in some circumstance, action must be taken to defend human dignity. What constitutes injustice and how action should be taken are defined and understood differently, of course, yet these are common assumptions found across the traditions.[6]

Worldviews that connote justice support soldiers' identity and purpose. However, they are also sources for soldiers' guilt, anger, and betrayal in the context of their military service. Soldiers do great harm in war; therefore they require a foundation for moral agency that equips them to control their

---

5. Myrer's work is a prolonged narrative of public service that incorporates concepts of naiveté found in Ricoeur, *Symbolism of Evil*, 349. Ricoeur, "Hermeneutics of Symbols: II," 330; Wallace, *Second Naiveté*, 69.

6. Reichberg and Syse, *Religion, Ethics, and War*, 6–7.

lethal competence in combat and reconcile their moral dissonance as they return home. Religious communities are in a unique position to provide a spiritual basis for this foundation. Recently Pope Francis expressed his desire that the church operate as a field hospital after a battle to heal wounded hearts.[7] His message was intended to stimulate churches to become centers of healing for all humanity, but his words also convey a powerful metaphor for war veterans who seek healing within their communities of faith.

Soldiers with some type of wounded conscience "can no longer relate to their peers, friends, and family for fear of being viewed as some type of monster, or lauded as a hero when they feel the things they did were morally ambiguous or wrong given the nature of the situations they were involved in."[8] Spiritual communities must take into account "the moral inequality we're asking our soldiers to bear on their behalf."[9] As a member of a Christian congregation, veteran Benjamin Sledge wonders about his identity within his community. "What would have happened if the Flower Girl [an Iraqi girl] pointed a rifle at me? But I'm afraid I already know. The thought didn't matter anyway. There was enough baggage from tours in Afghanistan and Iraq that made coming home a place of uncertainty, anger, and confusion, not, as I had been led to believe, a warm celebration of safety."[10]

In AD 1526 a soldier named Asa Von Kram solicited spiritual advice from Martin Luther. We do not know the circumstances that led Von Kram to seek Luther's spiritual guidance. We do know that Von Kram probably served as a hired soldier in service to a prince during the bloody peasant wars that plagued Germany in the wake of the Reformation. Luther's advice followed traditional Christian teaching that equated faithful service to an established authority as spiritual service to God. However, Luther also included the following warning for Von Kram to practice his vocation with a clear conscience, because "foolish, confident, heedless people accomplish nothing in war, except to do harm. . . . It is therefore remarkable for a soldier who has a good cause to be confident and discouraged at the same time."[11] Luther captures a profound truth that good soldiers can be morally wounded in combat. Separations between faith and practice experienced by all who practice conscientious military service may include both significant moral dissonance and sources for moral reconciliation.

7. Spadaro, "Church Is a Field Hospital."

8. Sledge, "Conversation about War."

9. Ibid.

10. Ibid.

11. Luther, *Can a Soldier Too Be Saved?*, 124.

This both/and phenomenon can be found throughout the Bible in passages that allow for war and at other times temper participation.[12] After the conduct of war, ancient faith communities practiced purification rights and ceremonies that specifically addressed the political, social, and spiritual consequences for shedding blood and taking of life. The Bible describes such cleansing practices.[13] However, it is unclear how these ceremonies addressed the moral dissonance soldiers may have experienced as a consequence of their moral agency. The basic assumption was that all combatants acquired some form of bloodguilt and were in need of a cleansing that allowed them to return to their community. Given the perdurance of human guilt and anxiety in all cultures, we assume that these ancient veterans experienced forms of moral dissonance from combat that may not have been addressed by these ceremonies. For example, recent studies have found that the loss of a combat buddy was "comparable, more than 30 years later, to that of a bereaved spouse whose partner had died in the previous six months."[14] Could the effects from this type of event be worse, if the soldier believed that he/she was ethically or morally responsible for the death?

Consider, the biblical account of David celebrating a military victory over King Saul. Saul was David's enemy. He personally threatened David's life, and caused the current war that divided David's nation. So, David was justified in considering Saul's death as the conclusion of a "righteous war." But David's victory was bittersweet. David's friend and former combat buddy was Jonathan, Saul's son. Jonathan, who couldn't leave the service of his father, died with the rest of David's enemies in a battle that David commanded. Upon hearing of Jonathan's death, David tore his clothes and lamented. "I am distressed for you, my brother Jonathan; very pleasant have you been to me: your love to me was extraordinary, surpassing the love of women. How the mighty have fallen, and the weapons of war perished!"[15]

David's words in this passage illustrate the spiritual dimensions that soldiers use to try to understand their emotions, perceptions, and moral dissonance after combat. Perhaps David was processing his emotions and making a moral judgment when he considered that soldiers, like Jonathan, tragically ended up as perished weapons of war. It is debatable if the Old Testament purification ceremonies were intended to cleanse and heal soldiers of this intense dissonance. Yet, the Bible throughout affirms that

12. Eccl 3:8.

13. Numbers 19 and 31. See Wiener and Hirschmann, *Maps and Meaning*; Verkamp, *Moral Treatment of Returning Warriors*; and Bachelor, *The Sword and the Warrior Wash*.

14. Sledge, *With the Old Breed*.

15. 2 Sam 1: 26–27.

communities of faith are in unique positions to be "field hospitals" for soldiers as they seek healing from war by conscientiously applying their spirituality to their vocational practice.

The recovery and redirection of meaning and purpose is essential for mitigating and healing moral dissonance. Every war narrative conveys the meanings soldiers associate with their professional identity and combat perceptions. These narratives form over time as soldiers gain some distance from combat and can analyze their perceptions in light of the core narratives of their identity. Thus, reprocessing these war narratives become significant and powerful ways that soldiers can bring closure to traumatic episodes in their lives and heal from destructive emotional responses.[16]

We live in a global and pluralistic world composed of differing worldviews and limited language. However, God is not limited and there exists within these worldviews common experiences, meanings, and purpose that allow a dialogue about the spiritual dimensions within DCV. This dialogue must humbly begin with a critical examination of our own beliefs and practices in order to listen and dialogue with these soldiers. We begin this dialogue here by using the centurion texts found in Luke-Acts to connect our spirituality with the moral senses used by modern soldiers to practice DCV and to interpret their war narratives. These texts provide lenses for examining what Christian scriptures have to say concerning military service. More importantly, these texts offer the language, images, and patterns of human-divine experience that provide cross-cultural themes that soldiers and healers with can use to examine particular elements of DCV appropriate to their own beliefs and practices.

The Centurions: Vocation, Community, Conscience, and Sin in Military Service

The centurion texts in Luke and Acts convey a treasure trove of meaning for modern soldiers concerned with how most responsibly to steward their vocation.[17] These texts parlay vital biblical concepts into narratives that can illumine anew one's own situation and provide means for understanding the whole canon. Some interpreters may be tempted to use the centurions of Luke/Acts as character studies to provide ideal, prescriptive examples for conduct. These texts are much better understood, however, as

16. Wilson, *Redirect*, 54–59. Wilson provides a model for change and recovery of meaning through stories. His model provides a marked difference in healing from traumatic events over more established methods such a critical incident stress debriefing.

17. Luke 3, 7, 13, 23. Acts 10, 23, and 27.

narratives whereby the soldiers' moral senses and the Bible's transcending symbols become interactive partners that guide soldiers' moral reasoning and conscience.

The Bible includes many texts about war and those who make war. But it would be wrong merely to read and appropriate those stories for one's personal context without understanding the role these stories have within the biblical narrative. For Christians, the "rule and norm" by which to read the Bible in all its parts is God's redeeming activity in the incarnation, life, teaching, death, and resurrection of Jesus as interpreted in the New Testament. The Christ event cannot be separated from the redemptive history of God's people expressed in the laws, covenants, prophetic witness, and messianic hope for a redeemed creation expressed throughout the whole Old Testament. The fluctuating sine waves of this transforming history give voice to the faith and failings of God's people struggling with their purpose and identity. Luke and Acts describe this struggle in an orderly narrative wherein God's priorities of justice, righteousness, mercy, healing, forgiveness, and peace are actualized in Jesus' and the church's interactions with diverse people.[18] These interactions displayed new norms and relationships that created a "new culture capable of making life in Greco-Roman cities more tolerable."[19]

The centurions in Luke and Acts guarded the intersections of God's reign and human political authority where this new culture formed. Roman soldiers deployed for long periods from England to North Africa and daily interacted with local cultures while staffing the outposts and guarding the roads that maintained the political structure of *Pax Romana*. In Luke and Acts, the centurions' moral senses of vocation "come to life" in their dialogues with John the Baptist, Jesus, and the apostles. In a way, these dialogues are similar to modern religious leader engagements where soldiers meet with local religious leaders to gain cross-cultural understandings that advance human rights, resolve violent conflicts, and contribute to regional stability and security.[20] Ideally these engagements are planned dialogues that are conducted in formal settings. However, at the unit level these engagements often can be chance encounters between soldiers and local religious leaders that become important reference points for shaping operations within a particular context. These engagements are also significant events to which soldiers give meaning.

18. Luke 1:1–2.

19. Stark, *Rise of Christianity*, 161–62.

20. US Department of State, "Strategy on Religious Leader and Faith Community Engagement."

The five engagements recorded in Luke/Acts are mostly chance encounters often initiated by Roman soldiers, and must be interpreted in accord with the author's intent to explain Christ in a secular and pluralistic Roman culture. The Roman soldiers in these accounts provided a cross-cultural frame of reference for the people who lived in these political cultures. In Luke/Acts, each engagement with a Roman soldier provides a glimpse of the spiritual dimensions resonating between the kingdoms of this world and the kingdom of God. Each engagement also is a "snapshot" of the spiritual dimension of vocational military practice. In each of these engagements, Roman soldiers attempted to resolve dilemmas between requirements imposed by their mission command and the obligations imposed by their moral senses. In the performance of their normal duties these Roman soldiers interacted with the kingdom of God and became moral actors within the gospel narrative. They proactively influenced the meaning of the narrative, as opposed to being passive "moral patients" only receiving from their surroundings.[21] Thus, each engagement would have signaled "something "new"; especially when these dialogues challenged the religious, cultural, and political status quo in both Palestine and Rome. These Roman soldiers provide a transformative word to any modern soldier who seeks to understand stewardship of service to God and service to nation.

The question in the centurion texts is not *whether* religion influences government service, but *how*. Political theorist Andrew Preston borrows terminology from St. Paul to argue that religious dialogue in the public sphere acts as both a sword and a shield to shape human conscience and moral agency.[22] We can regret the militant imagery, while we accent the diplomatic intentions of the metaphors, exercised as they have been throughout history, no less used by Paul. Preston argues that the sword of religion adds spiritual inputs that critique and drive public moralities, while the shield of religion forms spiritual bulwarks and guardrails that set essential moral boundaries. At their worst, the sword and the shield have formed uncritical, religious permissions that justify any number of immoral practices in the name of God. At their best, the sword and the shield have formed critical tensions that create moral criteria that build and sustain justice and peace between pluralistic communities. These spiritual and political dynamics were present in the interactions between Roman soldiers, John, Jesus, and the apostles recorded in Luke and Acts. These dynamics are still present within current operational environments where modern soldiers serve in cultures foreign to them.

21. Winston, "Moral Patients."

22. Eph 6:10–17. Preston, *Sword or the Spirit*, 1–14.

Of course, the Roman soldiers in Luke/Acts are not identical to the modern American soldier. They served in a totalitarian political system that was based upon colonial conquest and not bound by international humanitarian laws. The Roman army in first-century Palestine was composed of freemen and citizens of Rome. These citizen-soldiers enlisted under oath into a specific unit at about the age of eighteen to twenty for long terms that made them loyal to the fellow soldiers and commanders in their unit. They trained and fought in basic units called centuries, consisting of eighty soldiers commanded by a centurion. Promotion came from within the ranks of the unit. It is important to underscore that centurion is a rank, not a generic term for a Roman soldier. In effect, the centurions in Luke/Acts were "home grown" within their units and probably reflected the localized authority of their immediate unit, operating under broader command guidance from Rome.

The Roman centurions, and their larger cohorts, were evaluated, ranked and rewarded for combat proficiency.

> The army provided little social mobility, and it took a very long time to complete your service; further, you would probably serve abroad, and whilst the pay was not bad, it was nothing special, and many deductions were made from it for food and clothing . . . and there were very harsh disciplinary orders. . . . The army provided a guaranteed supply of food, doctors, and pay, and it also provided stability. . . . The average centurion got 18 times the pay of the standard soldier, 13,500 denarii, and centurions of first cohort [a more elite unit] got 27,000.[23]

In spite of these differences, Roman soldiers also share some common values and characteristics with modern soldiers. Many of these values and characteristics inhere in the laws, regulations, warrior codes, and leadership styles that compose the military ethos. These commonalities can be explained in terms of the moral senses that braid soldiers' character into their practice of vocational conscience. This braiding forms the basis for deriving meanings from the Luke/Acts texts.

Conscience is the moral reasoning process wherein soldiers wrestle with dilemmas and judgments of their character using their moral senses of fidelity, responsibility, accountability, maturity, and efficacy. When soldiers include spiritual dimensions within these reasoning processes, then concepts such as conscience, moral dissonance, and vocation can be examined as matters of faith, sin, and stewardship. In extended arguments presented in letters to early Christians, the Apostle Paul described faith as

23. Lloyd, "Roman Army."

an active tension where faith relies upon a good conscience, and a pure conscience is symbiotic with faith.[24] In a similar manner, he considered sin as a violation or betrayal of personal conscience. The consequence of these human failures, faults, or sins resulted in a "seared" conscience or "shipwrecked" faith.[25] At this extreme, a damaged conscience can be considered as a pathology resulting from sin that recalibrates, damages, or betrays the moral distinctions between "right and wrong." One could argue that this damage could be corporate as well as individual. The role of moral conscience is not the major point of Paul's writings. But he used the language of conscience to express the spiritual tension between moral voice and agency, when human beings were neither capable of living up to their highest ideals, nor capable of reconciling their perceived failures. It is reasonable to assume that this tension applies to the stewardship of vocation found in other New Testament texts.

Jesus often presented the role of faith within the kingdom of God in the form of conscientious dilemmas. When Jesus responded to a question involving the righteousness of paying taxes to Rome, he did not resolve for his audience the evident tension posed in the question between faith and conscience. "Then render to Caesar the things that are Caesar's and to God the things that are God's."[26] His words invited all hearers to enter a moral reasoning process of spiritual dimensions that apply to all who seek responsibly to practice their faith in the public sphere. It is not clear what things belong to Caesar and to God. But Jesus' statement itself invites a reasoning process that forms a foundational understanding for every person's spiritual stewardship. Jesus' statement echoes in each Luke/Acts interaction where Roman soldiers encounter the kingdom of God in the course of their duty and newly experience a spiritual quality in their vocation.

Some characterize General George C. Marshall as the epitome of a professional soldier practicing conscientious duty to the nation. Marshall was also a practicing Episcopalian. In June of 1941, he uncharacteristically blended faith and vocation in a speech he gave to students at Trinity College on the eve of our nation's involvement in World War II.[27] Marshall used the words "soul" and "spirit" to describe soldiers' capacity and capability for military service. "The soldier's heart, the soldier's spirit, the soldier's soul, are

---

24. Rom 2:15; Rom 7–8; 2 Tim 1:3.

25. 1 Cor 8:9–12; Rom 14:23; 1 Tim 1:19; 1 Tim 3:9.

26. Luke 20:22.

27. Marshall, "Nobel Peace Prize 1953."

everything. Unless the soldier's soul sustains him he cannot be relied on and will fail himself and his commander and his country in the end."[28]

The military often uses this quote to support the recognition of spiritual dimensions in soldiers' vocations. Marshall never defined what he meant when he applied "soul" and "spirit" to soldiers' performance of duty. But, perhaps like Jesus, Marshall did place vocation in that tensive relationship between service to God and service to nation. This tension was as true for Roman soldiers in the *Pax Romana* as it is for soldiers today. The Roman soldiers in Luke/Acts did not resolve this tension. The engagements in Luke and Acts portray these ancient soldiers as unique participants in a transforming spiritual narrative that still conveys meaning to us. Their engagements with the kingdom of God provide us a fresh look at stewardship within military service by suggesting spiritual criteria that act as parameters for conscientious service rendered to God and service rendered to Caesar. The moral reasoning of these ancient soldiers may help future generations of soldiers grow in their own faith in ways that also nurture their DCV and mitigate and heal their moral dissonance.

Parameter One: Conscientious Military Service Combines Emotional Self-Discipline with Physical Control of Lethal Violence (Luke 3:14 and 13:1–4)

In Luke 3:14 John the Baptist targets the heart of military vocation when he tells a group of Roman soldiers, "Rob no one by violence, or false accusation, and be content with your wages."[29] This is the only place in the Bible where soldiers ask an existential, question about vocation, "What does God require from us?" and receive a direct answer from God's messenger. It is the outcome of a brief encounter in the line of duty between soldiers and a prophet of God. The soldiers ask a question from the perspective of moral agents, and John answers them from the perspective of moral victims. The simplicity of the soldiers' question and John's answer provide further protocols for discipline and care for soldiers' moral voice and agency, from tactical to strategic levels.

In this short passage Luke specifically identifies these soldiers as serving under oath in contrast to hired mercenaries, temple guards, or local police.[30] Some commentaries disagree with this interpretation; they

28. Marshall, "Speech at Trinity College."

29. Luke 3:14 RSV. Other versions translated the verb διασείσητε (meaning to "oppress or shake violently") as "extortion."

30. Kittell, *TDNT*, "στρατευομενοι," 1092.

focus interpretations of this passage upon lesser crimes of extortion by representatives of local authority.[31] However, it is more compelling and logical to conclude that these soldiers were Roman given (1) the open address of Luke and Acts to people experiencing life under Roman rule; (2) that John's dialogue with the crowd included the politically and religiously charged issue of tax collection; (3) that an oath was a distinctive entry for serving in the Roman army; and (4) the inclusion of centurions throughout Luke/Acts. The identification of these soldiers as Roman also allows consideration of the wide spectrum of tensions caused by the use of military force in occupied lands.

The presence of Roman soldiers in the crowd parallels the presence of modern soldiers conducting crowd control and religious monitoring missions during stability and support operations. But there is one important difference. Roman soldiers considered foreign civilians as subjects under absolute Roman rule. In contrast, modern soldiers must consider foreign civilians in terms of national sovereignty and basic human rights defined by the rules of engagement in accordance with international humanitarian law. Both considerations directly impact the permissions and accountability soldiers use to determine specific applications of lethal force.

We cannot isolate the conversation between John and the Roman soldiers from the transforming narrative contained in Luke-Acts. Therefore, we need to be careful in interpreting this passage to derive permissions for military service and resolve questions of just war. This conversation applies to both issues, but it is more important to understand that this short dialogue only introduces the enduring moral tension between self-discipline and the use of force.

John's answer implies that soldiers are neither accepted nor rejected in God's kingdom because of their vocation. His answer communicates a covenantal understanding of military vocation in relation to the emerging and transforming kingdom of God and uses of military force by the political authorities of this world. He makes soldiers' rights and duties to use military force subject to God's transforming, reconciling, and visible kingdom. This subjection includes how soldiers view themselves and how they practice their craft.

We will deal with the positive side of this transformation in the following examinations of the Luke-Acts centurion texts. Here in Luke 3 we must deal with the dark side of warriors' lethal competence that necessitates the arrival of God's transforming kingdom. The backdrop to this dark side is found in Luke 13:1–4, where a crowd questions Jesus about assigning

---

31. See Luke 3:14 at http://biblehub.com/commentaries/luke/3-14.htm.

responsibility and accountability for a moral atrocity committed by soldiers murdering worshippers making sacrifices at the altar.

The soldiers were probably Roman because they were described as acting under oath and they acted under direct orders of Governor Pontius Pilate. Historical accounts record how Pilate periodically sent troops into Jerusalem, causing violent riots resulting in additional acts of brutal suppression.[32] We do not know what caused this particular attack, but the resulting deaths caused public outrage and theological speculation. Was the murder a sign of God's judgment upon the dead? *Somebody* had to be held accountable for this tragedy. The potential for the skewed moral reasoning behind this kind of retributive cycle of violence exists in any political or social environment where blame for past unjust acts is used to justify future acts worthy of blame.

Luke 13:1–4 implies that a crowd sought to explain the "why" of this tragedy by assigning blame to the victims instead of the moral agents. The victims were Galilean and the crowd invited Jesus, a Galilean, to assign blame for the injurious event. They didn't speculate if Pilate was an immoral actor, nor did they debate if the Roman soldiers were failed moral agents. Maybe they assumed this conclusion, or they wanted Jesus to draw this conclusion for them. Jesus' answer didn't resolve the crowd's false moral dilemma. Instead, he rejected moral judgments linking their suffering with punishments for their sin. Jesus compared the suffering caused by the Romans to the suffering experienced by the victims killed by a collapsed tower. Jesus' answer implies that assignment of sin cannot be based on the mere perception of apparent cause and consequence. The murdered victims at the altar were no more morally accountable for their deaths than the people killed by a falling tower.

In a way, Jesus' addresses the immoral agency of the Roman soldiers indirectly by breaking the darkest side of retributive cycles of violence whereby warriors justify their killing by claiming that their victims deserved the suffering the warriors inflicted. This "false moral victory" destroys future pathways of reconciliation by robbing victims of their story and agents of their responsibility and accountability.[33] The crowd in Luke 3 was familiar with the type of violence caused by Roman soldiers, and so were the soldiers who approached John with the question of "what shall we do?"[34]

John's response to this question challenges the rules of engagement these soldiers used to operate as an outside conquering force living as

32. "Pontius Pilate," *biblicaltraining.org*.

33. Philpott, *Just and Unjust Peace*, 4–29.

34. Luke 3:14.

neighbors with the people of the covenant. There is a temptation to interpret this text by focusing on the specific crime of extortion. However, it is possible to interpret John's words as targeting the soldiers' misuse of force. Roman soldiers were responsible for their own provision, and in a hostile environment they were always responsible for their own protection.[35] John extends this responsibility to include the protection of the civilian population. John's words are grounded in the Old Testament warfare texts involving permissions for killing, conquest, and the taking of tribute in war.

Probably the most familiar story of a biblical figure participating in righteous combat is David killing Goliath in battle.[36] However, the Pentateuch and books of the Prophets record a range of positions between obligations to use armed force for building and defending the nation and prohibitions against the use of armed force for unjust political purposes. Rabbinic teachings of the Pentateuch texts divide warfare into two categories: obligatory war commanded by God, and permitted wars mandated by kings.[37] Obligatory war was a matter of national survival conducted under specific guidance and waged against seven specific nations and Amalek.[38] Only this type of war, directly commanded by God, could be considered a "holy war" requiring mandatory service under specific conditions. However, these nations were no longer traceable, so all other wars recorded in the Old Testament were relegated to the category of permitted wars.

Permitted wars were considered as optional and preventable.[39] These wars were not viewed as a religious duty and both scripture and theological practice set limits on the use of military force, including: the taking of prisoners and property, limited targeting, and accountability for all who fought.[40] However limited, some of these wars also included instances of

35. Davies, *Service in the Roman Army*, 56–65.

36. 1 Sam 17. See also Moses killing an Egyptian soldier (Exod 2), or the call of Joshua (Josh 1), or Gideon and the 300 (Judg 6–7).

37. Afterman and Afterman, "Judaism," in Reichberg and Syse, *Religion, War, and Ethics*, 12–19.

38. Hittites, Girgashites, Amorites, Canaanites, Perizzites, Hivites, and the Jebusites (Deut 7 and Exod 17). The category of obligatory war was also applied to Joshua's war of conquest.

39. See Deut 20. Afterman and Afterman, "Judaism," in Reichberg and Syse, *Religion, War, and Ethics*, 14–15.

40. These scriptures focus on the role of self-defense. Examples include: Abraham defending Lot (Gen 14), Moses killing an Egyptian guard (Exod 3), David killing Goliath (1 Sam 17), and Nehemiah defending the rebuilt walls of Jerusalem (Neh 4). Amid passages permitting the covenant people to conquer, scripture also includes specific prohibitions and restrictive rules of engagement for the people of Israel. Passages such as Numbers 19 and 31, Deuteronomy 20, and Joshua 7 allow conquest in fulfillment of

total/siege warfare that amounted to the annihilation or enslavement of noncombatant populations.[41] The purpose of these wars was the defense of the covenanted community by motivated warriors who could pray, "Blessed be the Lord, my rock, who trains my hands for war, and my fingers for battle: he is my steadfast love and my fortress, my stronghold and my deliverer, my shield and he in who I take refuge, who subdues peoples under me."[42]

These permissions included exhortations for soldiers to "be strong and courageous."[43] However, these permissions were tempered by passages that reminded soldiers not to trust in "human weapons, and passages that lamented soldiers' fear of abandonment when "you do not go forth, O God, with our armies."[44] All of these passages contain theological beliefs and moral dialogues that are foundational for Jesus' discipleship analogy of a king deliberating the costs prior to committing his nation to war.[45]

The cost for soldiers in these permitted (and preventable) wars was not only physical injury, but also an impurity or "blood guilt" that required a time of cleansing during and after combat.[46] Some current healers and chaplains have used these passages as the basis for establishing ritual healing worship and practices.[47] Later, the kingdoms of Judea and Israel entered times where God forbid permissive wars, as the people of God became the victims of wars waged by Gentile kingdoms. During these times, prophetic scriptures forbade war, and viewed the tragedy of war thru prophetic promises where God will restore and cleanse the people of the covenant.[48]

> And they shall beat their swords into plowshares and their spears into pruning hooks; nation shall not lift up sword against nation, and neither shall they learn war anymore.[49]

---

the covenant, but also set limits on combat behavior.

41. Gen 18–19; Exod 23; Deut 3–4; Josh 8–9; and Num 33.

42. Ps 144:1–2.

43. Josh 1:9.

44. Ps 76 and Ps 60:10.

45. Luke 14:28.

46. Num 31; Deut 23; and Josh 24.

47. Among these practitioners are chaplains like Father Opara who created a combined post-deployment counseling and training program that includes a liturgy of cleansing. See also Bachelor, *The Sword and the Warrior Wash*; Wiener and Hirschmann, *Maps and Meaning*; Tick, *War and the Soul*, and Tick, *Warrior's Return*.

48. Mic 4–6; Ezek 37; Hab 1; and Jer 21.

49. Isa 2:4.

> For every boot of the tramping warrior in battle tumult and every garment rolled in blood will be burned as fuel for the fire.[50]

In these prophetic texts, the people of Israel are discouraged from putting their trust in weapons of war or warriors.[51] Later Old Testament prophets invite the people to act upon the belief of a messianic and apocalyptic restoration where they will "beat their plowshares into swords," and oppose their oppressors.[52] These religious justifications for "liberation wars" can be found in the intertestamental period in the book of Maccabees and the Dead Sea Scrolls.[53] It is important to note that none of these texts grant categorical permission for Israel or any other nation to conduct war. Instead these texts express conditional permissions, tempered by visions and hopes for ultimate peace where God ends the wars that plague people of the covenant and restores God's kingdom. Some contemporaries of John the Baptist used these texts to support insurgency against the Rome, and these zealots were a part of the politically charged environment where he interacted with Roman soldiers.

On the other hand, none of these sacred texts applied to Roman soldiers serving the *Pax Romana*. War was the prerogative of Caesar and the Roman soldiers were his agents. The Roman historian Tacitus characterized the hubris and violence of Rome: "To plunder, butcher, and steal, these things they misname empire: they make a desolation and they call it peace."[54] This type of political climate raises the possibility of soldiers committing extortion by threats of physical and other psychological harms against a defenseless population.

The previously quoted scriptures assume some sense of "righteous killing" that was probably shared by the Romans. However, the preceding texts were also balanced by a personal, moral responsibility for "blood guilt" on the part of participants that may not have been shared by the Romans, as it is not shared by some modern soldiers. Modern theologians like John Howard Yoder or Stanley Hauerwas use restrictive interpretations for these scriptural passages to advocate strongly for high thresholds to justify any use of lethal force. On the other hand, military professionals like David Grossman combine these religious texts with legal distinctions between murder and

---

50. Isa 9:5.

51. Isa 31; Ps 20:7.

52. Joel 3:10; Zech 9:10; Ezek 34:10.

53. Afterman and Afterman, "Judaism," in Reichberg and Syse, *Religion, War, and Ethics*, 22–25.

54. Tacitus, *Agricola and Germania*, 21.

killing to lower the thresholds used to justify permissions for soldiers' use of lethal force while fighting under legitimate authority.[55]

Roman soldiers probably did not make such distinctions in their use of military force. And John's answer to these Roman soldiers didn't build upon any of these distinctions. "Rob no one by violence," he said.[56] John's answer to the Roman soldiers honors the restrictive interpretations by transforming these legal interpretations into a moral argument. He extends the prohibitions against violence to include murder, stealing, false witness, and coveting.[57] He then prohibits soldiers' misuse of violence for unjust gain by restricting any of the benefits they could gain from their illegitimate use of force. Thus, John sought to dissuade their use of violence by widening their consideration of the costs they inflict upon their targeted victims. This is a different type of cost-benefit analysis than the traditional military risk assessments used by soldiers. For John, military necessity, proportionality, and discrimination are unspoken considerations, in favor of civilian safety and security. Thus he focuses his answer upon soldiers' moral agency and implies an assumed personal risk as a condition for military vocation.

Nothing robs a person more than the effects of physical violence, regardless of its justification, cause, or circumstances. Terrorists, insurgents, and criminals can extort, injure or murder innocent victims; so can soldiers, warriors and pirates. John extends the definition of "violence" to include "rogue" conduct that is historically caused by soldiers' use of "localized authority" to target victims. In doing this, John makes soldiers' self-awareness and discipline a matter of professional moral agency. By adding, "be content with your wages," John places the control of violence at the tactical level where soldiers make lethal decisions.[58] John's answer doesn't resolve all the moral dilemmas of war, such as rules for combatants killing other combatants in battle. But he does set spiritual parameters for self-control in a soldier's vocational practice to include foundational moral senses such as care and fairness. To first abide within these parameters begins a spiritual formation that integrates soldiers' self-control with their lethal skills in the course of their duties. Research demonstrates how this self-control is a primary condition for mental health in combat.

Many biblical verses speak about soldiers' contentment under duress, assurance of God's presence and care, God's deliverance, and the

---

55. Grossman, *On Killing*, Kindle loc. 3196.

56. Luke 3:14 RSV.

57. Exod 20:13–17.

58. Luke 3:14 RSV.

spiritual toll of war.[59] The point of Luke 3, though, is not the establishment of soldierly contentment, but to reveal how a lack of contentment affects their conduct. If "contentment" can be interpreted as an emotional and cognitive state where soldiers can control their conduct, then variables such as fatigue, stress, adrenaline, anger, fear, and insecurity are conditions that negatively affect soldiers' moral agency. Thus, Grossman's "reflective firing" and Couch's "dialed responses" taught in CQD training (chapter 6) become elements of soldiers' spiritual contentment. The lack of this contentment manifests itself in combat when individual soldiers must make quick decisions to deal with a perceived threat. The following account from an Army medic includes his assessment of his contentment in making a decision to not use violent force against civilians on a motorcycle who posed a threat to his unit.

> Instead, without thinking, I raised my rifle, flipped the selector lever from "safe" to "semi," and started walking toward the motorcycle. It all happened within seconds. I remember yelling, Wodiraga!—the Pashto word for "do not move"—again and again. I remember the pressure of my finger on the trigger. I remember being scared that I'd miss. And I remember the incredible relief I felt when the bike skidded sideways across the dirt road and stopped in a cloud of yellow dust about 30 meters away. . . . I could've killed those men on that bike. And had we not found a single weapon on their bodies, or bombs under their shirts, that would've been perfectly fine. I know because after the motorcycle came to a halt, everyone in my platoon let out a collective sigh and guys patted me on the back. I know because a few months later, one of our sister platoons, which had also been the target of a devastating suicide attack, was approached by a motorcycle on that same road. This time, despite desperate pleas from both American and Afghan soldiers, the driver didn't stop. Someone shot him in the chest. The guy turned out to be

59. Porter, *If I Make My Bed in Hell.* Army Chaplain John Porter used the phrase, "If, I make my bed in Hell, behold, thou art there," to reassure his soldiers that even in combat God was with them (Ps 139:8 KJV). This assurance is found throughout the Psalms and these scriptures capture the spectrum of soldiers' struggle for contentment in the midst of combat. Psalm 27:3 celebrates God's protection in battle, "Though an Army encamp against me, my heart shall not fear; though war arise against me, yet will I be confident" (ESV). These assurances are tempered by the disintegration of a warrior's contentment found in words of Ps 142:2–5: "I pour out my complaint before him [God]. When my spirit faints within me, you know my way! In the path where I walk they have hidden a trap for me. Look to the right and see: there is none who takes notice of me: no refuge remains to me: no one cares for my soul. I cry to you, O Lord; I say, 'You are my refuge, my portion in the land of the living.'"

a local shopkeeper. His death, we all agreed, was justified. Even
the Afghan soldiers said so. Nobody was punished. It was just
another day in Kandahar.[60]

In some respects the moral dilemmas faced by soldiers serving in a
modern counter-insurgency operation (COIN) in Kandahar are not far removed from the dilemmas faced by Roman soldiers serving in first-century
Palestine. Luke 3 captures the religiously charged and political environment
where Roman soldiers clashed with insurgent zealots. Here a small number
of soldiers dialogued with John the Baptist's covenantal understanding of
violence within the emerging kingdom of God. These ancient soldiers simply ask John a question and they receive a complex answer that still applies
to actively deployed soldiers.

These Roman soldiers engaged their brains and asked a critical question that sought to unify the task and purpose of their vocation. Johns'
answer to their question continues to bind conscientious military service
with service to God. To understand the implications of his answer is to understand the spiritual foundations of justice, righteousness, mercy, healing,
and peace that underlie the remainder of the centurion texts in Luke-Acts.
John's message to all soldiers is that their control of violence begins with
their acts of self-discipline. The spiritual parameter for this control is a line
that cannot be crossed without negative personal and moral consequences.
Outside the line, soldiers will experience moral dissonance that inflicts significant soul wounds. But there is more to this narrative. So we turn to an
engagement between a Roman centurion and Jesus that reveals the spiritual
parameters of public trust and mission command.

Parameter Two: Conscientious Military Service Combines Strong Mission Command with Compassionate Public Trust (Luke 7:1–10)

The Roman centurion in Luke 7 is one of the few people recorded in the New
Testament who positively astonishes Jesus. Like John's discourse with soldiers, the centurion's engagement with Jesus occurs in the normal course of
military duties. But their subsequent dialogue communicates a transforming
message of a covenantal relationship that exists between neighbors within
a conflicted environment. Jesus' astonishment stems from the centurion's
understanding and practice of his vocation. The centurion's mission was
to maintain the *Pax Romana*; Jesus' mission was to proclaim the emerging

---

60. Linehan, "Why I Think Lt Clint Lorenz Is a Murderer."

kingdom of God, and he uses the centurion's compassion and strength as a transforming lesson of faith for future believers. However, the details of their engagement also reveal spiritual parameters of public trust based upon strength and compassion that define DCV for modern soldiers.

The centurion's encounter with Jesus in Luke 3: 1–7 must be interpreted in the light of Jesus' discussion with a lawyer over the dual relationship merging the love of God with the imperative to love "your neighbor as yourself."[61] The central question addressed by these texts is the transforming narrative of God's coming reign localized in interactions between neighbors. Like John, Jesus expands the definitions used to interpret the coming kingdom by widening the restrictive, legal definitions used to justify a person's moral obligations. Jesus, tells the parable of the Samaritan to answer the lawyer's restrictive question, "Who is my neighbor?"[62] The parable of the Samaritan (an unlikely neighbor) acting with compassion to help a wounded victim connects a transcending relationship with God with simple practices of restorative mercy between human beings who might otherwise have no connection. This mercy includes elements of justice, righteousness, mercy, and healing that results in restoring a wholeness, or peace that defines the coming kingdom of God. This *shalom*, or wholeness, contrasts with outward expressions of military peace defined by the Roman military. However, in these texts the centurion acts like the Samaritan, an unlikely actor on behalf of God's emerging kingdom.

At the beginning of his public ministry Jesus chose a passage from Isaiah to define his purpose of "proclaiming good news to the poor, liberty to captives, recovering of sight to the blind, to set at liberty those who are oppressed, and to proclaim the year of the Lord's favor."[63] Throughout Luke, this purpose unfolds in public encounters between unlikely neighbors when Roman soldiers act as moral agents in the emerging kingdom of God.

The centurions in Luke represented the lowest level of Roman authority in contact with the people of Palestine and messengers of God. A centurion is a rank of command responsible for a unit of eighty Roman soldiers and twenty military servants (*calones*). The emperor of Rome approved his election, not commission, from the unit where he enlisted, trained, and served. This makes a centurion the hybrid of a modern enlisted First Sergeant/and commissioned Company Commander.[64] Centurions were about thirty to

61. Luke 10: 25–37 and Luke 10:27. This text is based upon the rabbinic She'ma that combines Deut 6:4 with Lev 19:18.

62. Luke 10:29.

63. Luke 4:18–19 and Isa 61:1–2.

64. Barclay, *Gospel of Luke*, 84.

forty years old, and literate members of the lower to middle classes of Roman
citizens. Thus they represented maturity as well as authority in leading their
soldiers from the front of the formation in combat. Centurions were responsible for training, discipline, and command of their units, and they could be
executed for failing in their duties. They were known for their tough character and competence, and at times this included brutal means of discipline.[65]
Proficient centurions were assigned as town commandants.[66] This probably
explains the connection between the centurion (a town commandant), his
servant (a *calones*), and the townspeople recorded in Luke 7.

In Luke's Gospel, a centurion needs healing for his sick servant, and
makes a request through local Jewish leaders, who agree to approach Jesus
because the centurion has been good to their community and built their
synagogue. Today, we might consider this a religious leader engagement
that occurs as part of a *quid pro quo* relationship that develops during phase
IV operations within counter-insurgency missions as small units execute
public works projects in cooperation with local communities. The purpose
of these projects is to "win hearts and minds" and nonviolently deal with local insurgency. However, the engagement between Jesus and the centurion
challenges this transactional understanding.

The centurion has a demonstrated concern for others—both Jewish
civilians and his soldiers. His concern for his calones may not be a stretch
for a commander who values his soldiers, and who will give his life for
them. General Martin Dempsey, the former Chairman of the Joint Chiefs
of Staff, keeps a box on his desk containing the names of the service members who died under his command. On the lid of this box is inscribed
"Make it Matter." Dempsey believes that "a military leader should always
understand, of all human endeavors . . . the one that's the most unpredictable and the most costly is warfare."[67] In saying this he demonstrates

---

65. Historium, "How to Become a Roman Centurion": "Tacitus tells us of the centurion Lucilius who was nicknamed 'Fetch Another' by his soldiers because he would
break a staff over an unruly soldier's back and then call for a replacement. . . . Vegetius,
writing from the 4th Century CE, lists these requirements: 'The centurion in the infantry is chosen for his size, strength and dexterity in throwing his missile weapons and for
his skill in the use of his sword and shield; in short for his expertness in all the exercises.
He is to be vigilant, temperate, active and readier to execute the orders he receives
than to talk; Strict in exercising and keeping up proper discipline among his soldiers,
in obliging them to appear clean and well-dressed and to have their arms constantly
rubbed and bright.' . . . It is certainly within the realm of feasibility that the Emperor
could have had a hand in their selection. This tradition was a survival of one of Julius
Caesar's customs; he was fond of promoting centurions on the spot after a battle as a
reward for bravery."

66. Cartwright, "Centurion."

67. Stracqualursi, "Outgoing Joint Chiefs Chairman."

a commander's profound fidelity, responsibility, and accountability for his soldiers that transcends legal and ethical boundaries used to historically define command responsibility. From Luke's description it is reasonable to assume that the centurion led his unit by using similar moral senses that he extended to people of his town.

The townspeople want Jesus to do this favor for the Roman because the centurion is "worthy" on the account of the way he administrates their town. The centurion takes a risk when he steps out of his culture to engage Jesus on behalf of a member of his unit, but he stops short of meeting Jesus when he sends word that he is unworthy to be in the presence of Jesus. The centurion's action represents a public humility that should not be equated with religious piety, because his reasoning is based upon a trusting relationship that defines military chain of command as a commander's responsibility for everything that their command does or fails to do. First, a subordinate doesn't command the actions of a superior; instead the subordinate requests and advises the superior. Second, the subordinate understands that the commands of a superior create action. Thus, the centurion's engagement with Jesus (a local religious figure) to heal the calones can either be considered a command for Jesus to heal or a request for Jesus as a superior to heal. The answer may be found in the humble message he sends to Jesus that he is unworthy to have a superior come to him because: "I am a man set under authority, I tell one soldier to go, and he goes, another to come, and he comes, and to my servant do this, and he does it."[68]

Superiors issue command orders, and a commander's intent becomes action. Psychiatrist Jonathan Shay considers this type of principled leadership necessary for preserving soldiers' moral character.[69] This type of leadership also conveys public trust, and confidence in the character and competence of the commander. The centurion treats Jesus as a superior and expects him to act through a chain of command with God, as he himself is acting. This may not be an act of faith as much as it is his stewardship of vocation.

Jesus marvels at the centurion's actions and tells his followers, "I tell you, not even in Israel have I found such faith."[70] In this religious engagement, the centurion displays the professional competence and character required of a military leader through his command responsibility for others' welfare. Jesus uses the centurion's strength and compassion as a leader to instruct future believers about the use of authority and faith within the kingdom of God.

---

68. Luke 7:8.

69. Jonathan Shay, as quoted in Phillips, *None of Us*, Kindle loc. 117.

70. Luke 7:9.

This transforming word transcends cultural and political boundaries, as well as provides additional parameters of DCV for modern soldiers.

The central issue in this interaction is the centurion's vocational identity displayed in the values he practices. Goleman, Boyatzis, and McKee believe that a leader's moral agency is manifested in the level of a leader's emotional intelligence. One's emotional intelligence is defined by his/her mindful awareness of the personal and social dynamics present in a given context and the appropriateness of his/her personal and social conduct to said context.[71] Mission command relies upon moral agency that includes a strong sense of empathy, respect, and obedience to build the public trust necessary for daily operations and mission success. This understanding of public trust contradicts narcissistic and toxic command structures that fail to consider the effects of mission orders and command authority upon public trust. The centurion was a combat leader, similar to today's successful combat leaders who communicate clear values and create bonds of trust in the midst of crises that sift both emotional and reasoning capability.[72] Both strength and compassion convey clear values and relationships that are vital for healing from war. The centurion's engagement with Jesus embodies these qualities in a relationship with others and with God.

Scripture speaks volumes about the depths of human suffering and the compassion required for healing. The centurion's appeal to Jesus displays empathy for those who suffer and a longing for their healing that transcends culture and localized religious practices. Psalm 121 captures the depth and transcendence of this relationship:

> I lift up my eyes to the mountains, from where does my help come from? My help comes from Lord, who made heaven and earth.[73]

Command responsibility is defined by care for the force as much as accomplishment of mission. Jesus commends the centurion's appeal and confidence in a superior to accomplish for his unit what he could not by his own rank or position. Recent suicide rates of soldiers attributed to deployment issues have led junior and senior commanders to emphasize empathetic leadership and public trust between the military, military families and community services. Examples of this type of emotional intelligence and compassion can be seen in senior leaders such as: (1) General Peter Chiarelli, who energized the Army's risk reduction and suicide

---

71. Goleman et al., *Primal Leadership*, 27–31.

72. Klann, *Crisis Leadership*, 6–26.

73. Ps 121:1–2 ESV.

prevention programs through unit level, hands-on leadership programs, and (2) Major General Mark Graham, who empowered community-wide crisis programs at Fort Carson to respond to the crisis needs of junior soldiers and family members.[74]

One of these soldiers is Army Specialist Daniel Keller. His war narrative tells how his participation in combat contributed to his ongoing moral dissonance at home.

> There's a lot of stuff that you're not supposed to do, that you do over there, and . . . of course it raises the morality issues. . . . That's when you really start thinking about it, you're there alone at night in bed, staring at the ceiling, and you're thinking about all the bad stuff you did. And that's kind of how it hits you. . . . It's [torture's] always shown as a bad thing; the bad guy's doing it, and the bad guy is always portrayed as this ugly person, so, you're seeing how in effect everybody else sees you, and eventually you just can't escape that. And you start seeing yourself that way.[75]

Mission command ordered Keller into a position where he experienced this dissonance. Now he considers himself an ugly human and illegitimate soldier. Army Colonel James Lacey believes the lack of command responsibility robs soldiers of the maturity and efficacy to mitigate and reconcile their moral dissonance. "Sad to think all this [Abu Ghraib and similar incidents] could have been avoided by one strong captain who had a basic education in the difference between right and wrong."[76]

The centurion in Luke 7 was a strong captain who engaged his heart and followed his moral senses when he acted with compassion by inviting Jesus to heal his ill servant. The townspeople affirmed the strength of his character, competence, and conduct. In addition to the FRAME senses, he also acted with senses of care, fairness, loyalty, authority, and sanctity. Jesus used the centurion's moral agency as a lesson in faith for future believers, and his actions provide modern soldiers with spiritual parameters for building and maintaining public trust within mission command. In the following passage, the centurion at the cross will add candor and moral judgment to this list of spiritual parameters for soldiers practicing DCV in a combat environment.

---

74. Finkel, *Thank You for Your Service*, and Dreazen, *Invisible War*.
75. Phillips, *None of Us*, 136.
76. White and Ricks, "Top Brass Won't be Charged."

Parameter Three: Conscientious Military Service
Combines Candor with Self-Reflection (Luke 23:46)

Truth can be the first casualty of war, but this is not so at the cross. The centurion at the cross was literally responsible for executing Governor Pilate's execution order to torture Jesus to death. At the lowest level of unit command, he issued orders to his soldiers to physically punished and kill Jesus. If he was a good commander he probably led from the front and did some of the dirty work himself. Like Keller, he was acting under orders, but was Jesus' execution the justifiable killing of an enemy or the unjust murder of an innocent, noncombatant? The centurion answered his dilemma by making a public statement he was not authorized to make. When he stated, "Certainly this man was innocent," he was also making a moral judgment that he was "robbing by violence."[77] In other words, his victim was right and the cause for which he killed him was wrong. The centurion's orders denied him the moral agency and efficacy to change the outcome of the execution, but he retained the use of his moral voice. Thus, Luke records the generation of moral dissonance as a soldier forms his war narrative.

In the *Pax Romana*, people reading Luke would understand the political significance of this comment through its incongruences. Centurions were known for their fidelity to Rome and were obligated to speak the truth in accordance with Roman law and policy. Unlike today, these leaders could be physically executed for making disloyal statements. So who would believe that a Roman commander would say such a thing? Would the remark itself discredit the centurion's integrity, and therefore be useless in transmitting the gospel? Or might the candor of a professional soldier executing (pun intended) his duty be an unexpected proclaimer of a greater truth? Could the centurion's comment be noticed and resonate within the *Pax Romana* because it was an anomaly?

We consider this a remarkable statement because it is first a self-judgment of the centurion's conscientious service, rather than a profession of faith. Surely Luke intended the reader to see the confession of faith here, too; indeed, it was an occasion of both the soldier's confession of law as well as a "coincidental" profession of gospel. However, the statement has merit because the soldier was not a believer, and its credibility rests upon his identity as a centurion and his command of the execution detail. Regardless of his motivation for making this statement, his words demonstrate that soldiers' moral voice cannot be separated from their moral agency. Even in the modern military ethos, the centurion's candor is unique. Candor states

77. Luke 23: 42.

perceptions of what could go unspoken. In the military the things that often go unspoken are often interpreted as weakness or failure because they are contrary to the ideal standards of the profession.

The centurion's words express the ethical dilemma of a whistle-blower—whether or not to publicly tell the truth when you can't physically change the public wrong. In a moral sense, the centurion blows the whistle on himself by declaring himself a failed moral actor. He may be following orders as a good soldier, but his statement implies that he committed a wrong and held himself responsible and accountable for his actions. He and his soldiers robbed an innocent man by violence (Luke 3), and he possibly recognizes Jesus' execution as a violation of public trust with the local population (Luke 7). His remarks also break trust with his superiors and subordinates. So, is he trying to retain some type of moral integrity by stating what others at the cross are thinking, but cannot say?

His statement can be equated with critical prophetic texts where God condemns the injustice of those who oppress, rob, and kill the vulnerable. "Their works are the works of evil, and they are swift to shed innocent blood, their thoughts are thoughts of iniquity."[78] Candor "tells it like it is." The centurion does not explain the reasons for acquitting his victim, and he doesn't excuse his role in the crucifixion. Therefore, he can be categorized with all soldiers who measure their "bloody hands" against the ideal standards that require them to make moral choices that produce unwanted results.

Soldiers should not go to war by thinking that they are agents of a righteous policy, "because being a knight in shining armor only results in our [soldiers'] unrecognized dark side roaring out of control."[79] Instead, they need to approach combat knowing the great harm they can commit in the name of a cause. During operations, orders and rules of engagement may not settle all their moral dilemmas and may leave them to question their moral agency. At such times soldiers' candor is an expression of their moral voice that allows them to conscientiously wrestle with their questions, instead of silently suffering with their inadequate answers. Candor is an essential part of soldiers taking their brains and hearts out of their footlockers.

Shay found that veterans' perceptions about combat reflect their moral judgments of their personal choices and group behavior. The consequences from these choices are what traumatize them, subvert their character, and contribute to their self-defeating behaviors.[80] In this sense, the centurion's

78. Isa 59:7.

79. Marlantes, *What It Is Like to Go to War*, 58–59.

80. Shay, *Achilles in Vietnam*, 168.

statement of Jesus' innocence is the candor of a modern soldier living with the outcome of his moral agency because "they [his chain of command] don't have to live with it. I do."[81]

Candor is more than an outspoken perception. It is soldiers' genuine expression of their moral voice and their moral judgment of their conduct. In the case of the centurion at the cross, his candor is a statement of *failed* moral agency. Specialist Tony Lagouranis, an Army interrogator at Abu Ghraib and Mosul, candidly reflects back on his combat participation. "I was totally disgusted by the insurgents, by the behavior of my comrades, by the actions of my government, and by myself. I hadn't fully connected these still-compartmentalized and unfocused bits of disgust, but they were coming together. I was moving rapidly to a global sense of shame described by World War II veteran Glenn Gray: 'I am ashamed not only of my own deeds, not only of my nation's deeds, but of human deeds as well. I am ashamed to be a man.'"[82]

Psychiatrist Tim Wilson believes that this type of candor and moral judgment provides the necessary perspective and personal distance from traumatic events that allows veterans to recover meaning, hope, and purpose to begin building a healing narrative from their combat experiences.[83] In speaking candidly soldiers express their dissonance and attempt to reclaim their moral integrity. Sometimes their expression takes place in an organized forum, such as the Winter Soldier statements before Congress in 1971. Here a group of Vietnam Veterans played on Thomas Paine's phrase of "Sunshine Patriots" to express their moral judgments over their service in Vietnam. "We who have come here to Washington have come here because we feel we have to be winter soldiers now. . . . The country doesn't know it yet, but it has created a monster, a monster in the form of millions of men who have been taught to deal and to trade in violence, and who are given the chance to die for the biggest nothing in history; men who have returned with a sense of anger and a sense of betrayal which no one has yet grasped."[84]

Philpott believes this expression of this moral voice is a genuine acknowledgment where "the wronged can grant reconciliation and those convinced of their guilt or association with the guilty will seek it [reconciliation]."[85] Shay believes that candid, unvarnished acknowledgments

---

81. Ibid., 83.

82. Lagouranis and Mikaelian, *Fear Up Harsh*, 152.

83. Wilson, *Redirect*, 50–59.

84. Bolt, "Vietnam Veteran John Kerry's Testimony."

85. Philpott, *Just and Unjust Peace*, 264–65, 286–88.

are the "real stuff" of confession that cuts through false perceptions, and makes all types of reconciliation or forgiveness possible.[86]

It is debatable whether the centurion's candor amounts to a religious confession in the sense of biblical texts used to define confession.[87] He does not express a litany of guilt or emotions, and he does not make a theological statement. Literally, his comments are a candid expression of a soldier taking ownership for the effects of his actions. He executed a political threat who he came to believe was innocent. This is one of the first steps in confession, and it is also a necessary moral judgment that refuses to deny uncomfortable events by participating in the myths and delusions used to justify immoral, harmful acts. In this sense, the centurion expresses the prophetic condemnation of injustices where the poor are trampled and neglected by those in power, and where political leaders have misled and destroyed the physical and spiritual health of God's people.[88]

When the centurion claims Jesus' innocence, he implies that his superiors (and subsequently himself) are guilty, and he places his integrity above his rank and profession. This conscientious wrestling with the moral senses of FRAME, care, fairness, liberty, loyalty, authority, and sanctity isn't coming from the religious community; it is coming from a Roman outsider.

It is vital to understand that the centurion's words are expressed in the context of his participation in what he considers an unjust act, and a candid expression of his conscience sorting out the conflict between his values and the performance of his duty—*from the point of view of his victim*. The centurion neither justifies nor resolves this his moral dilemma—he simply owns his role and focuses attention upon Jesus and the cross. In the Gospels, the centurion is one of the few people who get away with proclaiming a candid truth about Jesus without getting silenced or corrected. For Christians, the cross is where the mercy, healing and peace of God are combined with the justice and righteousness of God. Together these elements intersect with the injustices of this world, as God does for the world what the world cannot do for itself. The centurion commands the guard and serves as a moral actor at this intersection. Dietrich Bonhoeffer wrote, "Because Jesus took upon himself the guilt of all people, everyone who acts responsibly becomes guilty. Those who want to extract themselves from the responsibility for this guilt, also remove themselves from the ultimate reality of human existence. Moreover, they also remove themselves from the redeeming mystery of the

---

86. Shay, *Odysseus in America*, 153–54.

87. 1 John 1:9; Rom 3:20–21; or Ps 51.

88. Amos 5:10–24 and Ezek 33–34.

sinless guilt bearing of Jesus Christ . . . and they are blind to the unhealed guilt that they load on themselves in this very way."[89]

The centurion doesn't extract himself from this event. This aligns him with God's "odd" preference to reveal God's presence just where a self-righteous humanity would think God, and an "unjust soldier," not to be. This principle is known as the "theology of the cross." It will be discussed more in the next chapter. We note it here because with all attempts of moral conduct is a spiritual horizon. Often these attempts happen in uninvited moments and God's presence goes unnoticed. In all the Luke/Acts soldier texts, God becomes "thick" in engagements where moral senses of care, fairness, loyalty, liberty, authority, and sanctity empower moral voice when moral agency is the thinnest. In this engagement, the centurion's candor, like God's presence on the cross, is exceptional.

Lieutenant General H. R. McMaster has documented how a lack of candor and moral judgment in senior military leaders led to serious mission failures and political miscalculations during the Vietnam War.[90] Their failed moral agency influenced the generation of soldiers who fought the war. In contrast, the centurion's candor at the cross invites future generations of soldiers to consider how they morally judge their conduct, and how their moral voice maintains their integrity when they are unable to control circumstances in their environment. This passage builds upon the moral failures spoken of in Luke 3 and Luke 13, and it also builds upon the moral agency demonstrated in Luke 7. At the cross, the centurion engaged his brain and heart to maintain his moral voice in an attempt to reconciling a moral failure. His candor expresses the power that moral senses of fidelity, responsibility, accountability, maturity and efficacy have to define a soldier's character and competence. His words suggest to modern soldiers that service acceptable to God is built upon a commitment to the truth, as a practical integrity that refuses to falsely disassociate moral voice from moral agency. The centurion did not express his perception of a wrong committed by others; he expressed his moral judgment over his own conduct in front of his victim, his fellow soldiers, and the crowd. In doing so, he expressed his moral voice to all modern readers as a moral actor. His candor and moral judgment exhibits another parameter integrating soldiers' moral senses with their practice of DCV. This practice is not just a personal standard, it extends to the families and communities where soldiers draw their support. We will address this matter in a final observation about a famous centurion in chapter 8.

---

89. Bonhoeffer, *God Is in the Manger*, 38.

90. McMaster, *Dereliction of Duty*.

Parameter Four: Conscientious Military Service Combines Acceptance of Personal Risk with the Purpose of Saving Lives (Acts 23:16–35; 27:1–43)

There are two final engagements with centurions recorded in Acts that on the surface appear to have little to do with any spirituality. However, in both incidents Roman officers display character and competence as they align their moral senses with their conduct.

The first engagement is almost comedic. A Roman tribune named Claudius Lysias competently minimized personal risk to his career by taking credit for information to protect the Apostle Paul from an assassination threat.[91] It is worth noting because here Romans are portrayed as moral agents who accepted risk as part of their duty to protect a foreign national. In this religiously charged foreign environment, they quite easily could have ignored this threat, as it was not directed at them. The point of this comic interaction is that the tribune, his centurions, and their soldiers served as moral agents of justice, and competently did their jobs *regardless* of whether their motivations were "perfect." They didn't allow the violent robbing of another life when they could have turned away. Those exemplary soldiers were in the same position as all soldiers today who assume personal risks by guarding civilian lives on foreign fronts.

The second engagement involves a centurion named Julius. He assumed great personal and professional risk in escorting the Apostle Paul to Rome. In a way, it is fitting that this Luke/Acts passage concludes with a message similar to John's message to Roman soldiers at Luke/Acts' beginning; that a soldier's professional maturity and efficacy matter in the kingdom of God.

In the first century CE, the gospel traveled over Roman pathways supervised by Roman soldiers. When Paul was arrested and appealed to Caesar, his case was passed on to Rome and Julius had escort duty. During the voyage to Rome, his ship ran aground in a storm and the soldiers planned to kill all the prisoners in order to prevent their escape. Julius prevented the killing and ordered everyone to swim together to shore.[92] In Julius' actions, one can almost hear the modern soldier's creed to "leave no one behind." His actions reflect what soldiers do; they accept risk and find a way to succeed under duress in the midst of chaos. This success includes the protection of noncombatant lives. It is the goal for soldiers to win against all odds. Julius' exercise of moral agency contrasts with the centurion at the foot of the cross who could only

---

91. Acts 23:16–35. A tribune is equivalent of a brigade level commander.

92. Acts 27:42–44.

voice moral objection to what he couldn't influence. It is no small matter that Julius influenced the outcome at personal risk to himself.

Paul was God's messenger for the gospel, but he is not the moral actor in Luke's account of the shipwreck. Julius is the moral agent. He aligns character, competence, and conduct in his own iteration of DCV. By his own authority, and with both his authority and personal life at risk, he changed his soldiers' situational intent to kill their prisoners to a principled intent to save everyone. This text's context suggests to the reader that killing the prisoners would probably have been a defensible decision within the Roman rules of engagement. But Julius chose the higher and tougher objective. Julius' mission command of his threatened and malcontent soldiers prevented the killing of their prisoners. He accepted command responsibility for the lives both of his soldiers and prisoners, and personal risk if his orders led to mission failure. Because of Julius' actions, Paul arrived safely in Rome. The rest is church history.

Expressions of fidelity, responsibility, accountability, maturity, and efficacy allow soldiers to align their character with their competence and conduct under duress. These moral senses have been foundational in the profession of arms from the times of the Romans to today. Major General Antonio Taguba, who was responsible for investigating the allegations of prisoner abuse by soldiers at Abu Ghraib, states: "We [the military] are an institution of values, rules, regulations, doctrine, and military laws that are regimented and inculcated throughout our training and education, field exercise, and combat experiences . . . these are not bumper stickers hung around on walls of offices and headquarters. They have meaning in our thoughts, and they are engrained in each of our services from privates and seamen to generals and admirals. . . . It's all about responsibility and accountability."[93]

Claudius and Julius are the last Roman soldiers recorded in Luke and Acts. Like all the Roman soldiers recorded in Luke-Acts, they were simply performing their duty, and by doing their duty they served in some capacity as moral actors within the transforming kingdom of God. Claudius and Julius may or may not have had the "best" intentions, but they demonstrate parameters for accepting risk and protecting innocent lives that can help direct DCV in modern soldiers. The acceptance of these risks includes moral decisions that go beyond political or military necessity.

93. Tagubu, *Ethical Leadership*, 7–8.

Conclusion

War exacts a terrible cost upon the character of those who choose to serve. One price of this service is moral injury. Soldiers assign meaning to their perceptions based upon their worldviews and moral senses that braid their human and military character. This is what makes them moral actors and what provides a basis for examining how they reason and why they feel the way that they do. Herein lies the means for mitigating and healing their moral injures.

The Roman centurions and soldiers in Luke/Acts are relevant reminders of what faithful military service can and should be. These texts provide us with basic spiritual parameters that invite dialogue with other religious cultures with the hope of preventing and healing moral injuries. The previous chapters explained the ethical and moral elements within military culture that mitigate and form these moral injuries. They set the stage for us to deconstruct harmful war narratives and explore soldiers' healing journeys. In the remaining chapters, we will examine reconstructing narratives for reconciling and healing veterans' soul sorrow. Marine Captain Timothy Kudo explains the complexity of his healing journey.

> I think about what happened over there and try to come to grips with the depth of it . . . the morality that we have experienced over there whether we deal with that through ethics or through religion is something that we shouldn't just get rid of, and we shouldn't ignore that these are real questions and war is evil and yet sometimes, it is necessary. . . . I haven't reconciled my experience. . . . The harm that was done, wasn't done to me, it was done to these other people. And I do believe that in some time, maybe after this life that there is a possibility for that [forgiveness and healing], and that is an essential nature of faith, to me. But that's the only real option for this. So you keep pushing in spite of what you've done, you're more than your worst action—it is an incredible part of moving forward and trying to create good in the world.[94]

The Luke-Acts texts provide spiritual parameters for military service that challenge the legitimacy of damaging war narratives. They do so by communicating the transforming presence of God's kingdom that reunites soldiers' moral voice with their moral agency. Further, these texts commend elements that could and should shape and infuse the narratives of morally injured soldiers today with the following recognitions, which

---

94. Martin, "For Many Returning Vets."

will be elaborated in the following chapter. (1) There is no just war or just warrior. (2) Soldiers are at the same time both saints striving to do the right thing and sinners searching for post-traumatic reconciliation. (3) Moral injury's roots are in sin that requires forgiveness. (4) The centurion at the cross affords the suffering soul a spiritual opening so to confess and heal the harmful effects from war. In the Western Christian tradition, this opening has been called the theology of the cross. These further four observations can support the Captain Kudos of the world as they "move forward" and "do good in the world" by assimilating and accommodating new life meanings from their war narratives.

CHAPTER 8

God's Solidarity with the Morally Injured

*Those who have killed needlessly will have the mark
of Cain upon them . . . an unspoken agreement was
formed to get us through this madness in a certain
way. Elements of another platoon had other ideas and
went about surviving in another way. Maybe theirs
was more effective. But I'm not sure which required
more courage.*

—Second Lieutenant Patrick Bury[1]

FROM OUR DISCUSSION IN the previous chapter, we learned that the books
of Luke and Acts were attentive to soldiers whose vocations placed them
in morally vulnerable situations. We saw no New Testament "either/or" in
counsel to soldiers; no direction to either "stay a centurion or be a Christian."
This, of course, directly contravenes that early, but not earliest, period of
Christianity wherein one could not both serve Caesar with the sword and
maintain that one was a Christian. Rather, earliest Christianity discerned
in vulnerable human beings an ethical dilemma that was not so simple as
advising soldiers that they simply obey the command structure or give up
their vocation. We saw this counsel extended to and through, for example,
both Augustine to Bonifacius and Luther to Von Kram. On the other hand,
notwithstanding some erroneous chaplaincy advice today, the soldier of a
Christian disposition in the depths of a moral tragedy is not simply to be
told that both his faith and vocation mean only to obey immediate commands in all circumstances.

Jesus, of course, went further with regard to the "general principles" of
Christian discipleship. In teaching that those who lived by the sword would

1. Bury, *Call Sign Hades*, 90–91.

die by the sword, he condemned those who too readily resort to or idolize violence. Such would be the fate of the military "pirate." Jesus' commitment was to life in the kingdom of God. Those whose ultimate trust is in their sword are subject to judgment for the way they wield their sword. In the kingdom of God it is also idolatry to employ the "sword" as the means to uphold ultimate values that maintain position, empire, and privilege at the expense of weaker neighbors. This unrighteous use of the sword is the same as robbing neighbors by violence. Those who intentionally commit such violence are subject to God's judgment. Such idolatry and misuse of violence, whether by personal choice or by orders from higher up the chain of command, including the state, leave soldiers with Bury's "mark of Cain."

Still, the ground is level at the foot of the cross. Jesus exemplified the pure love and service that God intends as care for imperfect neighbors when he bore the violent weight of all humanity's idolatries in his crucifixion. Jesus was executed as a political threat, no question. Soldiers wielded the state's sword for this act of violence. However, with Jesus' resurrection we see that his political and spiritual appraisal of the human situation is fully validated by God. The resurrection of Jesus by the Father constitutes for those who follow him God's seal of approval on Jesus' way of nonviolent care and uplifting of the vulnerable and the failed. This is the distinction of the Christian lifestyle; a "foretaste" of the great feast to come that we are to practice now in "realized anticipation" of the fullness of God's eternal rule.

To be sure, in this life, we try sincerely to perform our duties as we should, we meet our limits, and we have the scars to prove it. Yet, we are also claimed by God as good and secured by Christ for eternity with God. This is our dual identity. On one hand, we are empowered to live with the moral agency of grateful discipleship until the new day of lasting joy. On the other hand we live with the consequences of our transgressions. We are not perfect and we cannot be perfect. This is even more true with groups of selves—families, communities, and nations. The collective histories and unintended consequences of covert machinations and human foibles pit people against people and nation against nation. Soldiers live by the sword in this intersection, and their dual identity is marked also by the scars from what they did, failed to do, and associated with in combat.

Just as history is filled with examples of nations celebrating the heroic deeds of soldiers in war, there have also been occasions in history when whole societies have acknowledged the sin of waging war, accepted the accountability for their participation, and conducted communal exercises of purification/cleansing. These exercises included worship liturgies and dramas. They were cherished and even mandated exercises meant to rebalance the society, reconcile past sins, and restore practices of mutual care. These exercises empowered societies to move ahead in their lives together. There are examples in ancient Greek and Jewish cultures of this exercise of forgiveness and reconciliation that we will discuss below.

The foundations and means for the exercise of forgiveness and reconciliation relative to moral injury depend upon the holistic processes outlined in the previous chapters. Our analysis of the causes and consequences of moral injury uses FRAME (fidelity, responsibility, accountability, maturity, and efficacy) as the means to (1) develop moral agency and resiliency *prior* to combat, (2) mitigate the formation of moral dissonance *during* combat, and (3) recognize and heal MI *after* combat. We do not expect that all MI is abated hereby. War is complicated and MI is a complex injury. However, we do believe that the appropriate prevenient development of character, as suggested in FRAME, facilitates soldiers' healing process and return to health after MI. For the post-moral trauma stage, the reconstruction of a morally injured person's sense of self rests primarily on that person, with the present caregiver(s), reconstruction and rehearsal of his/her personal narrative, with attention to the elements of FRAME and the spiritual/theological fundaments we summarize in this chapter.

This has been our argument throughout the book. Healing requires that we understand questions of "why," as much as formulate answers to questions of "what." Now our task is to correlate FRAME with key religious principles that are central for the responsible spiritual care of MI. As has been generally the case, we write from a classically Christian (and Abrahamic religious) perspective and invite readers to integrate these elements into their own traditions and resources where possible. Similar themes and resources abound in other religious traditions.

Because MI Involves Sin, It Requires Confession, Forgiveness, and Reconciliation

We've already touched on the recognition that forgiveness is a necessary practice for reconciling the moral dissonance that develops into MI. To broach the matter of forgiveness begins to provide an answer to Karl Menninger's question posed over four decades ago in our age of secularization of "whatever became of sin?" Whatever sin is, it can and does result in MI. This simply means, though it is not so simple to redress, that MI is a consequence of sin, because MI grows out of a soldier's sense of moral agency. Even a secularized or at least a practically areligious consciousness understands it this way.[2] It may not be that the sin resulting in MI requires repentance in

2. Cf. Meagher, *Killing from the Inside Out.*

the traditional understanding of the term. But it does require the language of confession, in the sense that confession explicitly recognizes the causal agency of that event which the MI victim heretofore preferred to leave to her/his internal darkness. All the elements of FRAME work in a soldier's conscience so to evoke the need and act of confession.

What is confession? In our popular culture the word "confession" often may be taken as an artifact from an ancient religious system. If taken this way, the more secularized imagination will dismiss out of hand the prospect of "confessing" as irrelevant. This option is even more likely if the term "God" and everything associated with the term has been rejected by the morally injured soldier who sees no fairness, no justice, no goodness, anywhere. "Confession" in our popular culture has abused the word to refer to scandal, sex, betrayal, and all the behaviors that appeal to our baser inclinations and that most agree are private matters. Therefore confession in this popular vein refers to those things we all do, but by which to publicly trap "famous people." And so the term is trivialized. It is also legalized in the sense that public pronouncement is also an admission of guilt. Therefore, it is best to remain silently innocent and let somebody else publicly prove accountability and culpability. There are "things" about us that need to remain private; or so we are misled to believe.

Popular stereotypes of confession include a small interrogation room with a table, where a confession becomes public, or a strange looking divided closet with two doors where confession remains hidden. The first is the matter of legal process, perhaps like a truth commission. The second is matter of private faith. Let's view this as a matter of faith. On one side of the divided closet sits an anonymous priest/confessor and on the other side is the one who confesses. They converse through a small screen that can be slid shut. What counts as normal in such a conversation are the words exchanged, with some prompting as to fulsomeness and sincerity from the priest, and then a prescription order given by the priest so to send the sinner back to better behavior. This stereotyped version generally ends in some manner of saying, "Don't do that again."

There are elements in this familiar scenario that are true and necessary to the process of confession and forgiveness. But the overall effect has proven to undervalue the importance of the process. This is recognized by the Roman Catholic Church's (and other denominations') encouragement of face-to-face conversation that requires ample time for both parties truly to understand and to vocalize what must be confessed and forgiven. Priests, pastors, chaplains, or counselors may find themselves in need of much patience and self-awareness, in addition to other skills, in order to ask the right questions. The patient likely needs intentional direction to sort through conflicting memories, perceptions, thoughts, and emotions.

We've seen the unfortunate scenario play out with the chaplain or counselor who is quick to dismiss a soldier concerned about MI or PTSD. Maybe the chaplain is dismissive because the matter is not theological, the soldier is considered immature, or the chaplain perceives the soldier simply to be going after some easy money by seeking government benefits.[3] Other counselors may rationalize that a quick and rote word of absolution or a prescription could be given and the patient sent on her way. However, the ailment is not this simple, and the needed remedy is far more complex. Most military spiritual caregivers recognize the dangerous pragmatism caused by case overload that results in an analogy to "take two aspirin and call me in the morning."

Phil Klay, on the other hand, writes of how difficult a real encounter of spiritual conversation can happen between the field chaplain and a soldier agonizing over his entrapment in an evil situation. The soldier feels complicit in having put his buddy in harm's way, blames himself for the evil he has had to perpetrate on others, including children, and realizes he is trapped in a no-man's-land where he only wants to frag Iraqis. He resists confession. He simply exists with evil, feeling compelled to contribute to it, yet is fully conscious of his conscience, that he is a good man victimized into an evil time. This soldier also believes that chaplains have no real acquaintance with this awful reality because they do not share in the lethal moments. The chaplain himself is deeply troubled as to how he can be effective. He writes a mentor. The mentor answers the chaplain with the following words.

> Your attempts to bring transgressions to command attention are salutary. But as for your religious duties, remember these suspected transgressions, if real, are but the eruptions of sin. Not sin itself. Never forget that, lest you be inclined to lose your pity for human weakness. Sin is a lonely thing, a worm wrapped around the soul, shielding it from love, from joy, from communion with fellow men and from God. The sense that I am alone, that none can hear me, none can understand, that no one answers my cries, it is a sickness over which, to borrow from Bernanos, "the vast tide of divine love, that sea of living, roaring flame which gave birth to all things, passes vainly." Your job, it seems, would be to find a crack through which some sort of communication can be made, one soul to another.[4]

3. See an extended report of how the psychiatric department at Fort Carson triaged soldiers away from mental health consults in Dreazen, *Invisible War*, 223–36.

4. Klay, *Redeployment*, ch. 2.

Clearly addressing MI, this type of conversation must have no limits in order for healing to begin. It must take its time. The extension of this time of conversation will often give rise to new issues and provide a deep, authentic foundation for confession which forgiveness can address. This intentional process challenges a quickly dispensed aspirin confession, where the sheer open-endedness also can cause further damage to both patient and healer.

The examples of real chaplains and counselors occasionally may contrast with Klay's fictional characters (drawn from his real experiences). Still, both highlight by negation what is central in a process of confession and forgiveness. They also show what is lost when no structure for the process is sustained at all. In the chaplains' and counselors' circumstances, an unbearable caseload is imposed in a system that forces healers to spend as little time as possible in caregiving, with little time for personal reflection and awareness of their biases.[5] In Klay's story, the self-aware chaplain personally struggles with the growing angry cynicism of the soldier, and finds in the soldier his own self-doubt.

These are the types of conversations that unit chaplains and mental health teams encounter as they walk among soldiers. The soldiers will never officially seek the caregivers' help, but will stop them by asking, "Do you have a minute?" The lack of structure in these conversations can challenge healers and patients, and demonstrate what must rightly be in place for a viable process of confession and forgiveness to happen. Ad hoc happens all the time, but these familiar instances can only be preludes to carefully practiced confession and forgiveness. Furthermore, these elements must include a wider faith community, which was not rightly in place in the above examples. In sum, the process of effective confession and forgiveness attends to the subjective, objective, and communal dynamics that must imbue both confession and forgiveness.

Confession is a profound occasion and process of honesty. As we learned from the centurion at the cross, truth-telling is a central and necessary moment toward healing. Truth-telling is also an essential practice of the theology of the cross. The centurion at the cross stands as an example for all ages of a soldier who embraces both FRAME and faith. Confession recovers reality from tangled perceptions and distorting myths so that one may appropriately act and effectively live. Confession is as powerful as courage. It is as meaningful as liberation. Confession is as powerful and as meaningful as all these things because it *is* all these things and more. Confession

---

5. In an ironic twist with the particular evangelical chaplain I have in mind, his following the medieval Roman mode of dispensing grace was as if it were an *opus operato*, the medieval theological equivalent of a placebo, but also thought to be "magically" efficacious merely on the basis of uttering the right formulaic words.

is truth recognition and telling. The truth sets people free indeed to address reality and really live.

But confession needs help to get at the "really" real. Some readers may remember the final episode of *MASH* when Hawkeye was traumatized to such a degree he could neither effectively function as an Army doctor nor as an emotionally healthy man.[6] A psychiatrist friend, Dr. Sydney Friedman, was called in to consult with Hawkeye. Hawkeye told the doctor about a bus he had taken with members of his unit and locals. The conversation took a long while (much longer than the script for a television show). The bus had stopped and its passengers were hiding from a North Korean patrol. All had to remain quiet to not be detected. Hawkeye remembered being so angry that a Korean woman could not keep her chicken quiet. In his fear, he yelled at the woman to silence the bird, and so she dutifully smothered her chicken. In the course of the conversation, Hawkeye remembered that the chicken was in fact a young infant, and that the mother had smothered her child to death so that the rest of the travelers would live. At that point of remembering, Hawkeye collapsed in tears because he realized that he ordered a mother to kill her own child. The therapist "midwifed" the truth; his insistent and patient midwifery exemplified his own ingrained fidelity, responsibility, and accountability. Though it did take the expected amount of time for Hawkeye to fully heal, this painful truth freed Hawkeye to accept reality and take first steps through moral injury to be effective in his vocation and as a human being, again to live with maturity and efficacy.

This *MASH* episode demonstrated FRAME in the healing process of confession. Confession itself includes these processes: (1) compassionately guided reflection, (2) articulation to the point of acknowledging reality, (3) accepting reality, and (4) using reality to redefine and reclaim one's life purpose. This example of confession and forgiveness was not a part of any religious ritual, but it is based upon the foundational spiritual dimension of human being. Therefore, confession as a religious rite needs to be conducted in as wise and effective a manner as this dramatized example.

What were the primary components for this process of confession? First, the injured person (Hawkeye) was encouraged to begin the hard process of telling in his or her own way the story of "what happened." This is, of course, a "subjective" exercise that requires no accuracy at the outset. It is a midwifed "owning" of a shattering event or complex of events that must have the subject's own perspective on it. Often this perspective will come from the subject's moral voice as a perspective seeking perspective. As

6. The 256th and final episode of the television series *MASH*, entitled "Goodbye, Farewell and Amen."

Nancy Sherman writes, the outset of a conception of oneself is a narrative sense of self, as if one sees oneself as another, "And *this creates an evaluative and epistemic gap essential to reappraisal and reevaluation*" (emphasis ours).[7] In this sense, confession begins with naming one's moral dissonance which is the prerequisite for achieving an integrated unity again that marks the healing of MI.

This first telling will be and must be retold often. It will gain precision and clarity, and self-understanding in the retellings. At the beginning of the telling, though, as well as later but to perhaps lesser degrees, the story will be raw, emotive, and even visceral. This is as it must be. This is how the fracture between memory and self-respect will be healed. This subjectively-centered start is the beginning of what we here call "confession." This is the "real stuff" of confession that Shay advocates to bring healing to hurting veterans.[8] Confession may require the risky, re-breaking of mental bones that have fused wrongly, if fused at all before, so that the right alignment of healing can be realized.

The next primary component in the confessional process is the "objective" presence of a skilled caregiver (Dr. Friedman) to help draw out the story, challenge where necessary, and so "midwife" the truth. Acknowledgment of subjectivity and objectivity—at least as *relative* perspectives, notwithstanding the postmodern consensus that no viewpoint is unbiased—constitutes a truly confessional process. It takes "two" to confess, two for truth to emerge into view; two for both parties to speak and to hear.

The writers of that particular *MASH* episode had brilliant and compassionate intuition those three decades ago about how MI could and must be healed. Of course, the length of the screenplay could only symbolize what takes so much longer to achieve in reality. But the writers and actors had the components right, and they understood that it takes a community for the healing power of truth to overcome our physical, emotional, and spiritual pain. No story can be told without an audience that understands, provides the language, supports, and enables the patient to bring suffering into healing speech. It takes a larger group of fellow sufferers and friends to ensure that the morally injured person is not figuratively or physically isolated. In other words, it actually takes "three" to confess and forgive; the sufferer, the caregiver, and a larger spiritual community that embraces and connects all to each other. The injured and the healer both need a keen sense of belonging to something larger and deeper than themselves.

7. Nancy Sherman, *After War*, 96.

8. Shay, *Odysseus in America*, Kindle loc. 3080.

The sense of something larger in which we all are connected is also, surely, present in the most personal encounter even with just one other person. That is, with just one other, many others are implicated. Another story, this one from real life as compared to the *MASH* episode, underscores the necessity both of forgiveness as a declaration and that it must first come from "another" before the morally injured subject can work on his or her own process of self-forgiving. It may be that the "other" was on the receiving end of an injurious action from us, which also was a morally injurious event against ourselves. Or it may be that the other was not injured by our acts, but that the forgiving other represents the transcendent "Other" voice of forgiveness available to all people. Or, finally, the "other" who forgives may have been injured by our actions *and* represents the liberating forgiveness of the divine "Other." The following example can represent any and all of these options.

Over twenty-five years ago (now) retired Army Col. David Taylor commanded a tank battalion in Iraq. He led a maneuver in 1991, one of the final battles of the Gulf War. Tragically, a tank in that battalion fired rounds at a group of vehicles mistaken as the enemy. Thirty-five American soldiers were killed in that friendly fire. Among them was army specialist Andy Alaniz. Less than twenty-four hours later, President George H. W. Bush declared victory.

Before the battle, Col. Taylor recalls the brigade commander asking if anyone had concerns. Taylor's soldiers had been fighting for three and a half days with no sleep, and the weather was awful. Taylor knew there was potential for friendly fire. But he raised no concern to the brigade commander.

Recently, twenty-five years later, Taylor met Spc. Alaniz's widow, Catherine Alaniz-Simonds, at a reunion at Fort Stewart, Georgia. At the time of Alaniz's death, she was nineteen, and six months pregnant with their first child. The baby was named Andee, after her father. Taylor and Simonds had only met for the first time the day before the reunion. In their conversation, forgiveness took the initiative before confession. Alaniz-Simonds was the one who first sought out Taylor. She told him that she did not hold him responsible for her husband's death. "You know, mistakes were made, things happen, but I've never blamed you," she said to Taylor. "I don't think it's your place to carry that burden any longer. Andy would not want that, that's not how he was."

Taylor says he gained the most from them finally meeting and speaking. "Now that I met you, I feel whole," he told Alaniz-Simonds. "I can live my life now. And without doing this there would still be an emptiness in me."

Alaniz-Simonds said that for the last twenty-five years all she wanted to do was to keep Alaniz's memory alive. Now that forgiveness was given and gratefully received, two people were freed with the promise that Alaniz would not be forgotten. Two people—and who knows how many more because of them?—were able to move forward.[9]

Forgiveness and Healing of the Soul Sufferer Requires Community

There is such a thing and necessity as self-forgiveness. But it does not happen all on its own.[10] There is always and must be always the "other" of the primary hearer, like Alaniz-Simonds, like a counselor, like a confessor, who midwifes the suffering soul's words into an adequate and true enough narrative. There also must be the larger community that provides both the tradition and a hopeful future in which the speaker and the hearer—the injured and the healer—are steeped, for no one comes into a confessing and forgiving situation without having had one's identity "braided" in some kind of community. One may begin to write and teach of an MI soldier's "self-acceptance" after that. One may even equate that to "self-forgiveness." But self-forgiveness on its own is a non sequitur. Forgiveness does not and cannot happen in solitude. It is an exchange. It is a blessed and blessing transaction that by definition requires others, which is to require community. Even the most advanced Stoic must take comfort from the resources of her Stoic tradition and fellow community of Stoic priest-philosophers so to keep her subjectivity rightly calibrated to a caring reality.[11]

It used to be a required routine in ancient Greece that a play would be performed for all the local population upon the return from war of its combatants. The philosopher Nancy Sherman reminds us that the audience of 15,000 would include in its front rows all the generals and admirals. The foot soldiers would be in the upper rows. As with the plays of Sophocles that would be performed—himself a Greek general—the themes would include

---

9. White and Cooper, "For Decades He Carried Guilt."

10. Indeed, any professional or would-be philosopher recognizes that there can be no such thing as solipsism within a community of discourse. Even to talk about it is to deny its possibility. And the tragic figure who would be utterly, totally privatized, like the most extreme form of "the man in the iron mask" or the astronaut lost in space, could never confirm his solipsism. The only possibility for "communicating *to* oneself" the declaration of forgiveness is to be in a state of complete damnation, fully removed from any prospect of being *with* or *for* or *from* anyone and anything, which renders self-forgiveness both moot and mute.

11. This is in contrast with the use of forgiveness as a component of adaptive disclosure therapy and cognitive behavior therapy. For a further understanding of these therapies, see Litz et al., "Moral Injury and Moral Repair."

betrayals by command, the agony of family separation, "abandonments due to war-incurred disfigurements, and psychological maladaptions . . . [and] the theme of repair through trust and hope."[12] A chorus consisting of junior military leaders spoke pronouncements of condemnation and reconciliation to include the audience in the flow of the play.[13] Thus the theater also became the public venue for training future soldiers and healing veterans. Jonathan Shay emphasizes how such publicly performed rituals were required for all a city's population so that reconciliation of soul and memory in the individual combatant were triply enacted between the soldier and fellow combatants, between combatants and their fellow citizens, and between the whole community and its deities.

Edward Tick also testifies to the post-war process of how a society's citizens and soldiers must return to the mystic elements that define the vocation of our individual and collective lives in order to pursue peace, rather than perpetuate the pursuit of values that tragically mislead us into the primeval sector of our psyches.[14] This latter definition of warrior pursues the idolatry and abuse of power in living by the sword. Tick powerfully concludes. "We must return our charges—our children and our veterans, our deeds and our dreams, our soldiers and our adversaries—to the path of the mystic warrior. And we must do so in the name of healing, reconciliation, and restoration. We must make the pursuit of peace as mythic as the pursuit of war has been. The fate of our world depends upon how successfully we undertake and carry through this great task."[15]

We have used the word "soldier" instead of "warrior" to describe this ultimate and mystic sense of values and the spiritual dimensions of directed conscientious vocation, all of which are subservient to God. Substitute the terms "spirituality" and "spiritual" for Tick's "myth" and "mythic" respectively and one gets the correct import of most all MI writers' emphasis on truth-telling. Soldiers are communitarian (braided) beings who need a sense of a transcending spiritual agency that brings them into community with those they serve for personal purpose and fulfillment. Just as

12. Sherman, *Afterwar*, 115.

13. Conversations with leaders of Outside the Wire, http://www.outsidethewirellc.com/projects/theater-of-war/overview.

14. Tick, *War and the Soul*, 288–89. Tick underscores how it is that the myth of the mystic warrior attracts both the younger individual and societies at large into the mistaken belief that a soldier can and will do only justice, and that all soldierly actions are not to be questioned. The veteran, however, knows too deeply how wrong the myth is. Therefore "turkey dinners and beers"—and, we'd add, fighter jet flybys at sports events and patriotic country music rallies—are insufficient acknowledgment of the soldiers' experience. Indeed, they may exacerbate the soldier's soul suffering.

15. Ibid.

Sophocles produced plays to enact forgiveness, healing, and reconciliation for individuals and societies after the individual-collective traumas of war, so also modern rituals that bring together *all* the parties of war—soldiers, political leaders, and common civilians—offer the potential for forgiveness and healing to occur.

Forgiveness ritualized within community is the final stage of what begins with individual suffering, soul sharing, and confession between a morally injured person and a compassionate hearer. Shay and Tick underscore that spiritual communities that offer ritual and collective compassion often are more effective than private counselling alone or protocols ordered by the military.[16] A review of one more text from Luke/Acts about a centurion also posits the necessity of a community of diversity surrounding the suffering soul.

Conscientious Military Servants Inspire and Are Healed in Communities of Diversity (Acts 10)

There is one exemplary centurion story in Luke-Acts about which we have withheld comment until now. While the centurion stories we did review provided us examples of the positive moral values that inspire and guide a soldier in one's DCV, a certain Cornelius exemplified both the role of individual character and of the spiritual community for addressing and ameliorating MI. Acts 10 tells of an engagement that begins when a centurion named Cornelius invites the Apostle Peter to his home with a sense of wellness that helps change the composition of God's people. From the start Cornelius is a moral actor, but this centurion example differs from the previous ones because his morality transforms the early church. The earliest church was ethnocentric, but it grew pluralistically when outsiders like Cornelius, his family, and community became members in God's transforming kingdom. We don't know if the other Roman soldiers or the centurions in Luke 3, 7, or 23 joined the community of believers. We do know the outcome of Cornelius's story.

As the disciples traveled beyond Palestine, they traveled throughout the empire over Roman roads to towns guarded by Roman soldiers. One of the prominent engagements between this growing church and Roman culture occurred when the Apostle Peter met with a Roman centurion named Cornelius in the town of Caesarea. Both men had a bias. In the town of Joppa, Peter was convinced that God was moving him to proclaim the gospel within Jewish communities.[17] In the town of Caesarea,

16. Shay, *Odysseus in America*, Kindle loc. 2333–35.

17. Acts 10:9–16.

Cornelius thought faith was personal piety practiced in the privacy of his home. Both men were praying and God convinced Cornelius to invite a stranger named Peter into his home. At the same time God convinced Peter to reconsider his vision for mission and accept Cornelius's invitation. So, Cornelius sent a devout soldier and two servants with an invitation, and Peter went with them to Caesarea. Upon Peter's arrival, Cornelius gathered his family and friends to hear what Peter had to say. The result of the encounter was the birth of a "Jewish-Gentile" church in a "pagan" Roman centurion's home in a Roman town.

Cornelius's arguably most significant action was that "he prayed continually to God." Here is a soldier in touch with his spirituality. Thereby he discerned that he was called to be open to and provide great hospitality to an "other" in whose occupied land Cornelius kept order. Peter's engagement with Cornelius is the story of a pluralistic community coming together where the moral actor is a Roman soldier. In his meeting with Peter, Cornelius introduces his family and friends into a widening community that crosses cultural, gender, and class boundaries. Cornelius's actions demonstrate how the practice of prayer is not separate from practical conduct. The result was a widening definition of neighbor for the people of God. Peter's engagement with Cornelius influenced a growing church from North Africa to Southern Europe through a meeting with the apostles in Jerusalem.[18]

The interaction between Cornelius and Peter says much about the way modern soldiers interact with cultures and serve as moral agents in a globalized environment. Today's missions and outcomes may be more complex and violent than the encounter between Peter and Cornelius, but the intent and conduct of the interaction can still be influenced by the same spiritual connection between conscience and practice that brought a Roman centurion and a Galilean fisherman together.

Soldiers' professional service can be conceptualized as a braiding of three streams: (1) profession military service, (2) their humanity, and (3) their family and community. They also carry with them the relationships, memories, and practices they experienced during their service in other cultures. Likewise, soldiers leave behind their "footprint" which influences the cultures where they served. Many of these experiences are positive. Many are not. If the intent of military service is to defend the peace, then these interactions need to be positive. The engagement of the centurion with Jesus in Luke 7, and Cornelius's engagement with Peter demonstrate how DCV extends community through concrete expressions of trust, justice, righteousness, mercy, healing, and peace in relationships. Cornelius is simply

18. Acts 15:8–12.

acting like the unnamed centurion in Luke 7 by displaying his emotional intelligence, his strength of command authority, and his moral senses to build community. We don't witness his competence as a soldier; we only see his self-discipline and how he influences others, beginning in his own home and extending to the wider community.

We could imagine that the diverse community of faith which Cornelius helped bring to life played a significant role in caring for him in return, though, of course, we have no exegetical certainty about that. It is historically the case that communities of mercy, healing and peace are noted often, from covenantal instruction in Deuteronomy, to ritual purifications in Numbers 19 and 31, to the intentional communal eucharistic practices of the church exhorted in 1 Corinthians 11–13. These types of religious ceremonies and practices decrease isolation and provide catharsis for soldiers.[19] In his work *The Sacred Way*, theologian Tony Jones describes the common elements of these practices to include reflection, meditation, mindfulness, confession, and absolution. People from different spiritual orientations, both traditional religions and nontraditional spiritual practices, use these common elements in group settings to connect transcendent values with their lives.[20] This is similar to the spiritual approaches that healers like Edward Tick, John Sippola, Rita Nakashima Brock, and Gabriella Lettini have advocated.[21] Tony Jones, Bernard Verkamp, Nancy Wiener, Jo Hirschman and many others have explored methods of spiritual healing through reintegration processes using Judeo-Christian theologies and practices.[22] Together these pastors, rabbis and theologians describe community spiritual practices that are integral to the healing of soul wounds; including communal rituals and prayer.

Some healers have sought to restore broken community among veterans from opposing armies. Tick explains these trips are efforts to "achieve the mature warrior's vision of reconciliation by traveling to the places where they fought, visiting distant war cemeteries of their comrades, and providing charitable services to those they have hurt.[23] Lieutenant General Hal Moore describes the difficulty and the potential for this reconciling community when he brought some of his soldiers back to the Vietnam battlefield where they met with members of the Vietnamese Army they fought. "[While standing at the position of a machine gun emplacement on the battlefield, a former

<hr />

19. Verkamp, *Moral Treatment of Returning Warriors*, 1–9.

20. Jones, *Sacred Way*, 25–33.

21. Tick, *Warrior's Return*; Brock and Lettini, *Soul Repair*; and Sippola et al., *Welcome them Home*.

22. Verkamp, *Moral Treatment of Returning Warriors*; Wiener and Hirschmann, *Maps and Meaning*; and Jones, *Sacred Way*.

23. Tick, *War and the Soul*, 265.

Vietnamese officer tells the American machine-gunner Bill Beck] 'You killed my battalion, you killed my best friend. I am a godfather of his daughter and only last month I married her off. This is not very easy for me.' Beck, whose memory of those terrible hours alone on that machine gun mowing down waves of attacking North Vietnamese is photographic and whose nightmares linger to this day replays his hours alone on that machine gun, responded simply and quietly, 'It isn't very easy for me, either.'"[24]

Candor within community can empower healing by providing conditions for post-traumatic growth and reconciliation. Combat localizes moral authority to focus only upon the good of the immediate group. Soldiers will defend and fight for whom they love, and may digress to become warriors and pirates during the battle. After the battle they may adopt behaviors that destroys the families and communities where they might heal. Cornelius's DCV resulted in a pluralistic community where relationships and interactions between cultures integrate professional practice and personal spiritual growth. His moral senses of FRAME and human foundational senses are present throughout his engagement with Peter. They could have chosen to remain distant and operate within separate, monolithic communities that were adversarial. However, they chose to meet. The type of spiritual community that grew out of their meeting instructs that soldiers today should practice a moral agency that extends from their families to a widening community that includes other nations and possibly their former enemies.

Combat ceases at some point and some type of political peace becomes the new normal. A peace that allows soldiers to reconcile their moral dissonance and judgments from specific combat events is harder to achieve. This type of healing and peace can only occur within families and pluralistic communities that include soldiers in the ongoing acceptance of new neighbors in an exchange of mercy. Thus, community and family provide another parameter for DCV within a globalized operating environment. "What a returning Soldier needs most when leaving war is not a mental health professional but a living community to whom his experience matters. . . . If both mental health professionals and chaplains made authentic communalization of Soldiers' grief their goal, they would do more good than the best individual counseling. And such advice on communalization will be welcomed by commanders in wartime only if prior training and role modeling have prepared them to be receptive."[25]

This may not be happening in our land today. Most communal expressions of our national culture "thank soldiers for their service" without

24. Moore and Galloway, *We Are Soldiers Still*, 49.
25. Shay, *Achilles in Vietnam*, 198–99.

acknowledging the reality, pain, and sin of what they endured. Too many religious congregations today are in fact isolated entirely from military culture and can seem quite alien themselves to the occasional military person and family who might visit them for worship. Contemporary Corneliuses can't shape communities today in the way their prototype did unless they are welcomed and actively understood by extant congregations. On the other hand, too many congregations appear to take too many cues from military culture and do not identify as the essential and healing distinction that Peter brought in the good news to Cornelius and his family. About these we will comment further in the concluding chapter.

As for a communal sense of ritual at the national level, confession of a national character would be a rather sensible thing if we were really a religious country, as many voices claim we are. If such were true, we'd follow King Josiah's example and dictate national days of mourning and repentance. But we are not such a country. We are pluralistic, not only as a large aggregation of different religions, but also as a smaller, but still potent, aggregation of different Christian theologies competing for legitimacy. We do not rue this pluralism. Rather, the existence of moral injury argues for the practice and experience of any and all forms of confession-forgiveness-reconciliation that have proven and will prove to be effective.[26] We are not interested here in making claims about doctrinal correctness, as it appears also that neither Cornelius nor Peter were given over to an absolute doctrinal correctness when they met God's extensive grace and healing in and through each other, no matter their clear differences. We are confident that the values that drive confession and forgiveness exist in multiple traditions. We can recognize in other traditions the personal and communal practices that will mean healing for the wounded souls in our midst.

The Subjective and Objective Nature of Forgiveness

Allow us to summarize thus far. The common denominators that empower confession-forgiveness-reconciliation found in every long-standing religious tradition are the first spiritual requirement in our list of five caregiver principles to heal moral injury. In more formal and technical terms, in the religious realm, we speak then of the "objective presence" of God in and with the actions of "others" who are present in care for the distressed. Certain forms and structures (rituals and spaces) are commended through the ages as traditions, as nonidentical repetitions, so to commend the holy

---

26. In the authors' own Lutheran Christian tradition, this point is made in excellent, exhaustive, and postmodern detail in Lange, *Trauma Recalled*.

"otherness" of God over and against the injured self who is captive to his or her own subjectivity. The extended (and extensive) community of the similarly faithful is a necessary component of this.[27] The forms and structures are *not* sacrosanct in themselves. Rather, they mediate something otherwise elusive by definition. They bear the breakthrough, the surprising entrance of "the Other" (God traumatized in God's own self!), a major theme to which we will soon turn. The forgiveness the "Other" brings appears as nonidentical repetitions that evoke from the injured the blessings of faith and hope. At the same time, this forgiveness begins to provide words and images that realign the morally injured soldier's life toward faith and hope. The Other *gives* what the patient can only *receive*. Only after the patient receives can the patient then with that gift of forgiveness begin to *reconstruct/re-author* one's purpose and goals in life. And only after the patient receives the objective gift of forgiveness can the patient begin to forgive herself.

The elements of subjectivity and objectivity within a community of faith are necessary to construct-deconstruct-and-reconstruct the personal narrative. Confession begins the process whereby the wounded soul is assisted in reappraising what is "really real." Confession is the hard process of recognizing the truth of a situation along with the truth of one's own personal history and then expressing it. Forgiveness is the assurance that s/he is part of a larger healing story. This objective side is represented in both the caregiver(s) and the larger community of belonging. Further, forgiveness is the first-order antidote to confession. It is utterly necessary and must be objectively pronounced by a trusted other on behalf of the forgiving transcendent Other, God, the "Higher Power." Forgiveness thus also differs from the subsequent necessity of reconciliation, which itself might require much time to be worked out.

Thus, it is self-defeating that the military heavily invests in positive psychology and resiliency programs that formally recognize soldiers' need for forgiveness, without appreciating the substance and meaning of the confession/forgiveness process. This can be seen in the Army and Marine mandatory resiliency programs of 2015. This is further underscored by the fact that higher-ranking military chaplains were not asked to contribute to the construction of these resiliency programs, notwithstanding the important research and writing about forgiveness now happening in strategic academic

---

27. It is of interest to note that the foundational documents of Christian denominations, like the Augsburg Confession of Lutheranism (1530) and the Heidelberg Catechism of the early Reformed movement (1563) systematically order forgiveness or justification always after the identification of sin in humankind. And "God" is always first and primary in such ordering, rather than inferred. This ordering is based as much on empirical observation as it is theo-logical.

centers with chaplains at the middle of the work.[28] To exclude the spiritual dimension indeed not only denies healing to the suffering, it gives warrant to those who argue against any religious care within the military. It goes against Jonathan Shay's own "secularly" proven wisdom that religious traditions have within them more effective and realistic means to achieve that to which the secular guild of therapists can only aspire.[29] This also unwittingly supports a secular psychological conceptualization of forgiveness as *only* a subjective exercise always threatened by human fickleness. As we explored in chapter 3, the Augustinian strain within Christianity explicitly names this threat as the false promise of works righteousness and is as impossible to achieve as a full self-regulating life in the mode of Stoicism.

The Comfort That We Are Simultaneously Saints and Sinners

Recently the Garrison Chaplain of an army base hosted a prayer breakfast for the wider community. The service was designed to be interreligious. It was well attended by local religious leaders and by higher-ranking military staff. The usual coordination of patriotism with religious faith was present, to be sure. Representatives from the local major faith traditions (except mainline Protestantism) earnestly prayed in the vernacular and syntax of their own traditions. One pastor prayed that God would enable each and every person in the room and all citizens of this great country to obey God's commands and therefore attain righteousness. Immediately following him, a local imam with equal earnestness—but with a marked gentleness of spirit—prayed that God would be merciful to all us sinners.

There could not have been a better and more ironic example in this interreligious duet of opposite, sometimes even conflicting, understandings of God, human being, and the meaning of "righteousness" or holiness. The central Islamic theme of obedience would have led one to presume the imam would pray in that vein and the Christian pastor more in terms of mercy. Indeed, the zeal and content of the pastor's prayer, if decontextualized and heard without any knowledge of who was praying, could have led one to suppose that he was Muslim. And the imam's prayer could have

28. E.g., Rita Nakashima Brock's Center for Soul Care at Texas Christian University; the National Defense University at Fort Leslie J. McNair, and in some VA hospitals (e.g., St. Cloud, MN; Palo Alto, CA).

29. Shay, *Odysseus in America*, Kindle loc. 3055–57: "[Medical-psychological therapies . . .] often help manage guilt, but they are not, and should not be, the only therapies available for moral pain. Religious and cultural therapies are not only possible, but may well be superior to what mental health professionals conventionally offer."

been scripted straight out of anyone in the Christian tradition from St. Augustine to Pope Francis.

We make this point not to criticize or judge, but to illumine the more popular common and erroneous sentiment in America that God is one "afar off" who must be appeased by obedience, and that human beings have the quality within ourselves to do just that, even apart from God's help. This theme of obedience is not the central matter of Christian conviction, however, though it is "a" part of the tradition. The imam's prayer, on the other hand, was in language that is central to Christianity, and also a key theme in Islam, though the most central theme in Islam is obedience to Allah's will for peace. Muslims believe and confess that Allah is merciful. Christians also classically have taught that the first emphasis is God's mercy (or grace) and that human obedience follows as the inspired response to God. The reverse ordering evident at that prayer service could not be more telling for our concern here.

Sin is ineluctably at the core of human being and we cannot "obey our own way" to God. To our surprise and joy, God is gracious and we are not. We humans are not rotten to the core, to be sure. We are created, as said in chapter 4, in God's image and are declared by God as "good," even wonderful and precious to God, with all the dignity and rights to be accorded such dignity. But we are also descriptively, as any history shows, sinners. We cannot not sin. Even our best intentions and wisest acts are set within a history and horizon marked by sin, the influence of which no one can escape. We cannot "obey" ourselves into a state of righteousness, no matter how earnestly we might pray so. We cannot avoid the fact that we are born into a tidal wave of history compounded by intentional and unintentional abuse and mistakes, the evil and sinful wash of which foams over and into every moral good we do as well. The better angels of our God-given nature are, well, better. But they must dance on our shoulders with the less gracious partners of humanity's own making. So there it is. We are at the same time both saints claimed and "in-the-making" by God and sinners virtually inevitably but not necessarily unmaking ourselves along the way.[30] Or, as the central Christian tradition has put it for all its years, humans are at the same time justified and sinful, *simul justus et peccator*.

---

30. This theological assertion is integral to every orthodox Christian doctrinal system since its beginnings unto the present day. The classic Western *non posse non peccare* ("not able not to sin") is not cancelled by the Eastern Christian accent on "original blessing" and humans bearing the "image of God" (*imago Dei*). They are complementary recognitions about human being that have been expressed in every age of religious reflection, and have their cognates in every major religion, as well.

We are at the same time justified by God and sinners. *We* sin; God justifies. That means that God makes us righteous, counts us righteous. God does this because God's justice is God's mercy, and vice versa. Righteousness is not something human beings achieve on our own, even though we do have wonderful examples of heroic humans whom we've called saints. The emphasis here is on God's taking of initiative and God's promise that we humans caught in the throes of sin are protected and secured in and by God. We *are* sinners, the popular translation for this being that "we are only human, after all." And being so, we do not have it in ourselves to make ourselves perfect. But we are asked to strive toward perfection precisely on the assumption that love, which is the love of God within and for us, impels us to care for others. Obedience, then, is *only* for that purpose: to love God and others as best we can, inspired by God's own spiritedness, and not selfishly "on our own" so to secure our own futures.

Part of the meaning of "forgiving" and the act of so doing includes the comforting reality statement that we are simultaneously saints and sinners. It is a teaching that could be better effected long before the adult human journey as well as during and after our inevitable meetings with moral tragedy and injury. We've seen that the more common "American" sentiment about righteousness, its achievability, even its expectation from certain religious and military quarters, nevertheless is unreflectively loud in our culture and among our soldiers.

There are also those in military chaplaincy, notwithstanding the military regulation to preserve and protect the free exercise of religion, who believe and proclaim that categorical acceptance of all commands is to obey God. So if one has a "problem" with an order or what one has done in following orders, the call to obey is supreme and forgiveness is quickly dispensed if it enables soldiers to perform their duty. This is puzzling. This does not fit with Christianity, its Abrahamic kin, or even with other religions, almost all of which—except for Stoicism—to some degree have a place for the self-recognizing sinner and the requirement for divine mercy. For obedience-centered chaplains, or for the soldier who is left to his or her own devices and defaults to familiar and mistaken mix of civil religion and pietism, the righteousness of obedience is the way to salvation beyond this life. This falsely assumes that the choice and the ability for the righteousness of obedience is within any person's grasp. There is really no fullness of joy possible in this life, then, when a person is caught in such a catch-22. Such dominant misunderstandings and promulgations of righteousness have revealed themselves as setups to guarantee even more dire moral injury. The veteran who confesses that "God will never forgive me for what I did" tragically doesn't grasp the truths both of an intimately merciful God and sin's insistent presence in all human thought and act. Those who have heard and received such a reality state-ment of good news have a better chance of resilience and moving ahead with response-able and purpose-filled lives.

It makes a huge and consequential difference if every soldier could hear loud and clear from the outset that everyone is simultaneously sinner and saint; that there is no getting away from this fact; and, therefore, this *move toward realism* has the potential of enabling the healing of a fractured soul and according it the quality of resilience before any event of injury. There is no purely righteous soldier. There can be no purely righteous sol-dier. This is also to state in theological terms that there can be no such thing as a just warrior, just as there is no such thing solely as a just human being other than Jesus Christ. Even when an order is followed to the nth degree, pure obedience does not make one righteous, just as no cause is entirely righteous, while also not entirely sinful. And even when, especially when, failure happens and accuses a soldier's morality, God's care and promise abide. The point then for the soldier is not to "settle," but to be encouraged even more to act on behalf of what is good, true, and beautiful.[31]

This theological analysis (necessarily brief as it is) aligns very well with our proposal of FRAME as a way to form resilience before trauma and more effectively to restore resilience post trauma. The "responsibility" (R) and "maturity" (M) components of FRAME can become maladaptive if one does not appreciate, understand, and accept the nature of reality, including the realities of human character and the external world. With this spiritual assay we are returned to basic real elements of real life that have mostly been lost to the public's consciousness, just as the need for a public ritual after war so well practiced in ancient culture is lost to contemporary society. There are many reasons for this, which are outside the present task, most having to do with this culture's practice of artificial joy and denial of death and suffering. The shorthand of FRAME, however, is the practical "secular" ana-log to the spiritual condition of humanity we are exploring here. More will

31. Among many implications of this *simultaneously justified and sinner* theme is the necessarily dual *objective and subjective character* both of sin and the sinner. The "simultaneity" negates any ability to take a spiritual surgery knife to dissect the subjec-tive element from the objective element. There are, of course, clear instances where a public deed are judged "wholly" good or evil. This is a popular convention that has necessary legal and philosophical practical effect for societal health. But insofar as a *spiritual* analysis can only read enmeshment and ambiguity, a claim such as Nancy Sherman makes that only "objective" sins require an enunciated act of forgiveness just does not wash. Just as the line between objectivity and subjectivity can never be clearly discerned, so also the distinction between objective and subjective sin cannot be identi-fied clearly. God—as we so identify in this text—has a preferential option for mercy, which then by a "transcendental" analysis requires the enunciation of forgiveness in the most morally subjective of circumstances, too. See Sherman, *Afterwar*.

be considered shortly. Before doing so, we must turn to consider the very character of the God to whom we have referred here. And this character is not unique to the Christian description only. For just as society has come to misconstrue what it means to be human and what human being can achieve on righteousness's behalf, so too we far too often misconstrue, even speak erroneously of, the God our own scriptures and tradition reveal.

A God Who Will Be GOD Exercises Power in Suffering Love

The default understanding of God or of an ultimate god above gods throughout history has been of "all-powerful, all-knowing, unchanging, and non-suffering." Human beings typically have considered God as "far away," if not altogether absent from a world marked indeed by processing time and recurring suffering. If God is eternal, many think, then God is allergic to time. But if time and eternity are opposites, then so also God and history are opposite, maybe even combative. Miracles are "intrusions" into time, then; any act of God would be extraordinary; supernatural. Any prayer, consequently, any desire, any pleading, would have to be filled with enough urgency and "faith" to reach the Big Guy Upstairs and convince him (!) to change his heart and act on the petitioner's behalf with atypical mercy. Most of this description of divinity, at least in Western culture, is the trickle-down remains of the Greek philosophy of God (particularly what was known as Neoplatonism). It can and does often induce human beings into treating the divine as an absent, capricious magician with a capital M. Ironically, the god whom we make so distant is merely our own self-imaging, and so we have demeaned this god instead of giving respect. This is the god in which atheists appropriately do not believe. Unfortunately, this is also the unmoved and unmoving god that many think looks at our battlefields and the battle-weary only with judgment from a distant courtroom.

Too much of this unreflective "popular" idea of God infects even Christian language and thought. Orthodox (not the same as "conservative") Christianity could not be further from this tragic notion. For that matter, there is no recognized major religion in the world which does not have a personal aspect of relationship, and so, what we will call "intimacy," to a lesser or greater degree between God and the believer. A holy solidarity between God and the human creature is expressed in the varied vernaculars of the other major faith traditions, as in Thich Nhat Hanh's social Buddhism, Rabbi Abraham Heschel's suffering God, and the Muslim mystic Rumi's poetically compassionate universe. Whoever the unmerciful and distant "all mighty—all-knowing—and unchanging" god is before whom the passionate prayer-maker pleads for our self-justifying obedience, this is not the God of Western religions. It is also not the God of Christianity. In simpler terms, God is not the frozen and regal image of the Stoic ideal. God is not Virtue instantiated in an eternal stone image. God is the suffering power of love spoken and done in suffering human flesh, as with Jesus of Nazareth.

Come to think of it, would not a God who can and does choose to be incarnately associated with all changing history be more "powerful" than a god whose utter freedom actually means eternal separation from all history? A real god who creates (and destroys) could no more be "above it all" and still "relate" than parents who abandon their children. In the Judeo-Christian tradition, God not only creates and sustains, God also warns of judgment. God guides and warns and loves deeply with God's people from within their midst as prophet, angel, burning bush, tower of guiding smoke and flame, in and with written words (likewise with Islam), and profoundly, in the Christian witness. God does this by going the distance through birth, celebration and healing of life, crucifixion, and resurrection. Fundamental to Christian faith is that God reveals who and what God is really about on the cross of Jesus Christ. God suffers the death in himself of Jesus. And yet God will not let the human proclivity toward hate and violence (the manifest and regular expression of historical sin) be the last or "most realistic" word. God will raise. God will make new life. Just as God created and creates from nothing, so from the no-thingness of suffering and death God creates again. God raises us from suffering and death into lives again of enduring hope and purpose, that purpose being the fully manifest celebration of consummate justice: full love and full peace.

Only a suffering God could and would coordinate with human beings who are duplicitous in our faith and our freedom. Only the God who suffers can and would know the justice that must and will be achieved for saints who cannot avoid our sin. Only an intimately compassionate God who shares all our human condition without compromise of God's own intention to love and loving intention can and does stick with all who suffer. This is no general abstract principle. A loving, suffering, compassionate God loves particularly in the particular ways adequate and necessary to any suffering situation and person. This means that any persons, forced or freely, who enter into situations of moral injury are not alone. God is with them and God shares fully in the injured. God does not leave the morally injured on the battlefield. God will not. Only some "above it all" god would do that. But that would not be God. And such a god could not be also the all-powerful and creative God without just such compassionate solidarity.

A compassionate suffering loving God is not the one of whom our culture or its highest officials usually speak. That is, in sum, tragically ironic. It is also ironic to try to "teach" here of what has been called the theology of the cross; especially ironic insofar as we authors do not have a personal relationship of trust with you, the readers. About that irony we are aware and we confess. But we confess so in the hopes that others in a community of trust might then "do" and "show" this theology of the cross with their morally injured neighbors. The God of a theology of the cross may have tried to "teach" it, even from a "distance," before; but could only make the matter clear when God showed up personally in the life of Jesus and does so now in lives utterly inspired by and dedicated to amplifying such vulnerable holy love.

The promise for all who suffer, including the morally injured, is this: the God whom we authors identify as the God of Jesus Christ is with sufferers wherever suffering happens and wherever sufferers might know God by another name. Where there is suffering, there is the cross. Where there is the cross, there is the redemptive and future-giving creative God. This God is not keen about human glory-seeking. That common activity is usually so ego-centered that it loses sight of God and the suffering ones who need God's compassionate re-creative presence. Those who want to build their religion from "the ground-up" to God can achieve no more than any builders of Babel could. No human-made foundations could support the height and breadth necessary to reach righteousness. But God, not just from "top-down," but inside-out, is present to and in all conditions to recondition what human ambition has so disfigured. God will have what God intended from the beginning, which is our most well-being. History shows that sometimes suffering—particularly suffering on behalf of others—may be the only, un-preferred, modality by which new and holier life will come. But God is and will be there, nonetheless. The pain of moral injury is not borne in loneliness. Redemption of moral injury will be borne by the oft unseen Partner who is "God with us" all the way through.

Christian faith must speak in these real terms. But the speech must also take non-Christian terms, for the theology of the cross points also to the interreligious world we all inhabit. God abides with all of the awfully real. If we must do war, then we do so confessing that we have no alternative and we'd rather not, but do so as soldiers individually trusting in God's mercy rather than under misleading and idolatry-laden rationales. Caregivers, particularly chaplains, are the touchstones of the suffering, compassionate God. Chaplain Glenn Palmer knows this well, and why.

"The voice of the Lord is over the waters" Psalm 29:1. One day in Iraq, on our 2d tour, in the Triangle of Death, when we were being hit hard, a Soldier asked me, "Chaplain, how do you go outside the wire with us every day unarmed?" I shared with him that when I wake up I cross myself and I remember my Baptism. I remember that because I am Baptized into the Body of Christ, into the life, death and resurrection of Jesus, that I know who I am and whose I am, that nothing, not even death, can separate me from the love of God in Jesus the Christ and that as a Baptized child of God I cling, as I pray we all do, to the promises of God, that LIFE wins and that I can survive any "what" . . . because I have a "why."[32]

Quoting Nietzsche's famous line that "whoever fights monsters should see to it that in the process he does not become a monster," Palmer also went on to show how quiet and confident presence entices a more peaceful response to perceived aggressors. "July 16th 2003, Iraq 105 degrees. After giving 'last rites' to SPC Ramon Reyes Torres of Cleba, Puerto Rico, killed by an IED while driving through our sector, a crowd gathers as we recover his remains. The crowd starts cheering, Al-Jazeera starts filming. A Soldier next to me raises his M-4, I hear the safety 'click' off. I place my hand on the M-4, gently push it toward the ground and share, 'I understand where the anger and rage come from but you can't become what you hate.' THAT is why I serve as a Chaplain."[33]

Take careful note. This God does not always accord well with the chain of command. This God does not accord with national lines. This God does not serve as succor only for those on the "right" side. Indeed, the theology of the cross necessarily means that God is on the side of those who do not get to choose sides. God is always on the side of the suffering, the oppressed, the victim. But who is not suffering, not oppressed, not a victim? We do not argue we should be whiny, self-identified victims passively aggressing and manipulating others to serve our selfish desires. We do argue that were each and all of us honest about our desires, our offenses, our weaknesses, and our suffering, we would discover that God's power works through our weakness. Thereby true healing happens. And real relationships with God and each other are strengthened.

In this respect, the theology of the cross is the only truly democratic religious principle beyond the equally democratic principles of God's love for all and the effect of sin in all. Practicing *this* love and solidarity of God

---

32. Army Chaplain Sgt. Glenn Palmer, in an undated Facebook post.
33. Ibid.

in the vortex of war means also that wherever possible, soldiers and chaplains will never condone unjust killing and, certainly, any form of torture. To put it in the most fatefully tragic terms, a scenario in which a chaplain who heard screaming from a prisoner regularly in the next Quonset hut over and knew that the screams were from a torture victim, would be denying his Lord. There God was being crucified again. Such a chaplain could and should have done something about it.[34] To put this in a larger and even more provocative claim, the theology of the cross as the guiding Rule of Engagement can better protect and restore one from moral injury. Typically human theologies of glory (which describes self-justifying theologies) will only condone and even "set up" the solider for moral injury. They will deny the injured of any possible healing; they also will lead the injured and other watchers to sheer unfaith. We insist, with joy, on the faithfulness of God nevertheless.

Unjust War and Justified Soldiers

We have commented about the nature of human being, the nature of sin, the need for confession and forgiveness, the dual status of humans as both righteous and sinful, and God's choice to align with and be revealed in solidarity with all and each who suffer. Now it is time to apply our theological commitments to a central ethical issue that deepens the tragedy of MI. This issue is the question and purported practice of "just war."

The criteria for the just declaration of war and the conduct of war are meant to guide the government's deliberation and formulation for use of force. We will not enter into a fulsome reflection on just war doctrine here. But we will remind ourselves of the foundational criteria for entering into and conducting war.

The justification to enter into war (*jus ad bellum*) includes: (1) a just cause for armed action, (2) good intentions governing the use of arms, (3) the last resort after exhausting all reasonable attempts to avoid hostilities, (4) a legitimate authority to the decision, (5) an intent to restore a just peace, (5) the reasonable chance of success, and (6) that the proportional good achieved in the end state will be greater than the destruction caused by the means used in the conflict. One may quickly surmise that this ethical framework is rather flexible and open to much interpretation. This is because the stated principles, having been removed from their stricter Christian (Jewish and Islamic origins), blend the European philosophical traditions of deontic and utilitarian (intrinsicist and consequentialist) ethics. A keen devotion to

---

34. A hypothetical, yet very plausible, scenario.

originalist intentions, as of Augustine and Aquinas, would be necessary, for example, so to agree that "just cause" is normally associated with defending oneself or one's neighbor against explicit acts of aggression. "Right intention," for further example, would be also coherent with a desire to maximize peace as well as to maintain coherence with just cause, rather than, say, use war as a pretext for other colonial or imperial ambitions.

Criteria for the actual conduct of war—*jus in bello*—of course, remain coherent with the first stage rules. In addition, the criteria include what have not always proven evident in the fog and heat of war. These are: (1) minimize "collateral damage"; that is, do not indiscriminately engage and harm noncombatants; (2) keep offensive action proportional to the desired objectives; "scorched earth" and mass slaughter, in other words, are rarely, if ever, justifiable; (3) and we add, finally, that individual agents of war are responsible for their actions. This latter criterion attempts to ensure that individual conduct correlates with all prior more "general" criteria. General criteria have no force without force of ethical and moral behavior in each of the parts.

Jus ad bellum and *Jus in bello* are the foundations for the International Humanitarian Law, the Law of Land Warfare, and Rules of Engagement. There is a third set of just war criteria—*jus post bellum*—often overlooked but as integral as the former two sets. (1) As with the principle of discrimination in *jus in bello*, innocents and noncombatants should not be subject to retribution; (2) the rights and traditions of all the defeated should be respected; (3) claims to victory should have their own proper proportionality to how war had been waged; (4) compensation too should be tied to the principles of discrimination and proportionality. Finally (5) some argue controversially that the losing aggressor should be reeducated or rehabilitated.[35]

The room for interpretation and even false application of these principles in all three sets is massive. It is a simple matter even today for anyone introduced to just war doctrine to point to historical examples of the doctrine's having been transgressed. Indeed, the just war tradition has been manipulated by national policy and military necessity to protect self-interests at all costs. But there are examples enough of just war throughout history to provoke the question not of whether just war is possible, but whether the spirit of just war has really imbued its proponents. So Daniel Bell writes:

---

35. There are many fine introductions to and reflections on the criteria for just war. In addition to the longer reflections cited throughout this book, an excellent introductory resource is located in the *Internet Encyclopedia of Philosophy*, s.v. "Just War Theory," http://www.iep.utm.edu/justwar, to which this brief outline of criteria is indebted.

> War is not something that is imposed on humanity by forces outside itself, nor is war simply an outburst of an irrational and impulsive primordial beast that lurks just below the surface in the breast of humanity, always threatening to burst forth in an uncontrollable spasm of rage and violence. War is not simply a relapse into an extramoral prehuman state. Rather, it is a thoroughly human practice, subject to human control. Therefore, given the flexibility of warfare as a human practice, if war is waged in ways that are not disciplined by the tradition then one has to ask if those who wage war are indeed seriously committed to just war. Are they truly a just war people?[36]

Dan Bell has rightly identified the correct character of just war doctrine and its attendant morality as one of human spirituality. Banal human beings, following unawares their dispositions into the heat of anger at My Lai or Abu Ghraib, do not see their spiritual illness. Or they do not until they subsequently suffer MI and recognize something that had always been there inside them from which they or others had anesthetized. Likewise with the administrator who merely consults just war criteria as a calculus. As we have asserted, however, such an ill-ended secular employment of the just war tradition has forgotten its religious roots and its initial strategic aim as a modus of spiritual and emotional care for the mindful soldier.

Just war doctrine originated in specifically religious reflection. In the Christian tradition, it found a compelling articulation with Augustine, having had its roots recognized in ethical conventions of warfare in the Old Testament. It was then interpreted, reformulated, and refined by major theologians from Aquinas onward through the centuries, as also occurred with many Arabic theologians from the ninth through twelfth centuries. It carried forward as an identifying marker of a valid Christian military vocation in unity with all the church at the birth of Protestantism in the sixteenth century.[37] Our critical concern, though, is that just war doctrine has transmuted from pastoral care to general secular political principles today. And just as initiates in the just war tradition can identify innumerable

---

36. Bell, *Just War*, 66.

37. So article 16 of the Augsburg Confession concerning civic affairs: "Concerning civic affairs they [the Reformers] teach that lawful civil ordinances are good works of God and that Christians are permitted to hold civil office, to work in law courts, to decide matters by imperial and other existing laws, to impose just punishments, to wage just war, to serve as soldiers, to make legal contracts, to hold property, to take an oath when required by magistrates, to take a wife, to be given in marriage." Kolb and Wengert, *Book of Concord*, 49. We provide the full quote of article 16 so to underscore Daniel Bell's recognition that just war relates first to human civic and spiritual life in all its quotidian character.

transgressions against it, one does not need to read far in near and current history to discover that claims made by political and military leaders as to the "justness" of a particular war are almost routinely disputed by religious leaders, particularly of the Roman Catholic and mainline Protestant denominations. This fact, at the least, should lead one to infer that those most practically responsible for the administration of the just war tradition at the national policy level have become blind to its original and essential religious pastoral care nature. Thus, fractures between moral conscience and practical behavior begin with strategic planning.

So the question may not be so much as to whether just war is possible, but whether it is possible to follow the just war criteria successfully and consistently as generalized secular policy. An idealist advocates for such policies. A realist would answer that these are different days. Our national means to safeguard national and individual citizenry interests are based on expensive instruments designed for maximal destruction, not the discrimination of combatants from noncombatants. Threats to this country's or neighbor countries' security are presented by bad actor collectives that do not represent states, nor even tribes; yet to defend against them may mean aggression against non-warring states, too. In the face of such threats, just war doctrine can be disregarded by national leaders and the general public as an abstraction or obstruction to national security. This distorts and negates the protective intent that is the foundation of the just war tradition.

Therefore, we must speak then not of just war, but justified soldiers faithfully caring for the neighbor. We are compelled by arguments such as those of Robert Meagher, that there is no such thing as just war anymore. Yet we would qualify. We would say that there can be no such thing as *real* just war. But that should not vacate our responsibility and accountability to think and teach just practices in war, whether we prefer pacifism or militarism. And that fact should teach and *form* individuals in the spiritual and ethical dimensions of just-war thinking and conduct.

Is it possible for an individual combatant to conduct just war, as required in *jus in bello*? We cannot answer this with a univocal "yes" or "no," though we have provided the components for what we think make a better nuanced answer. We know the training, the resources, the policies, and on the ground exigencies make it virtually impossible to answer with an unqualified yes. In answer to these challenges comes the alliance of the religious principles we have just explored.

The very possibility of "just war people" who cannot escape an unjust world where we all are simultaneously saint and sinner, with a God alongside who suffers and promises, whose justice is mercy and vice versa: all these (and more) put then the accent we need on a combatant's *intent* more than actual behavior. When an individual is more realistic about her individual identity as braided by sin and more by a positive spiritual presence; when that individual better understands the ambiguous character of a world yet created for good; when an individual is trained to be more mindful than visceral, and so practices a directed conscientious vocation for the good of others; and, finally, when her or his intent is to do right even if evil results—as with Bonhoeffer's participation in the plot to assassinate Hitler—then the prospects of healing MI are amplified.

In the previous chapter we suggested a process of directed conscientious vocation as the tactical means to achieve the strategic end of mitigating and healing MI. This aligns with FRAME in all three sets of just war doctrine. There can be no such thing as a wholly just war. But there can and must be the individual aspiration toward being a just soldier whose vocation is for the defense of the neighbor. This said, it must be our ultimate spiritual conviction that war finally can and must be transcended and that warfare's imprint on typical humanity is a tattoo that will wear away. "Justified Soldiers" must be possible, but temporary, identities. If the identities are permanent, then we are fated to an even darker night, for acquiescence to war's finality means surrender to the idol of the worst in humanity.

Another way to see the challenge is to understand that the most idealistic of moralists will have as impossible a task of being truly moral as the most cynical and even sociopathic. Walter Wink—no militarist he!—writes, following the keen insights of Reinhold Niebuhr.

> Dreams of perfection are fatal to social change movements. As Michael Lerner points out, despite their vision of a better society, such movements are made up of idealists who are far from perfect. They are trying to change a society that has already conditioned them to believe themselves unworthy of love, and the system to be incapable of change. Consequently, they tend to act in ways that engender despair, causing them to use tactics that alienate the very people they need to affect. Driven by their ideals, they denigrate their own accomplishments as inadequate, as if they should have been able to do more. . . . Rather than recognizing that we are all racist or sexist or undemocratic as a result of our social upbringing [another way of speaking of how we cannot not sin] and developing ways to assist people gently in the needed transformation, the movement declares that anyone with these attitudes is a traitor or a deviant. When they can no longer stand their own hypocrisy or that of others, many drop out to enter psychotherapy, meditate, or earn money.[38]

38. Wink, *Engaging the Powers*, 71.

Summary

Of course, Wink writes of something that could not be more opposite to the waging of war. His own career was built on radical peacemaking and the rejection of all violence. His insight as to the impossibility of pure righteousness, still, is as pertinent to the responsible conduct of war as it is to the responsible conduct of peacemaking. We are multiply braided by the best and the worst of our society as society is of all its parts. We are even codependently both just and unjust. Purity and utter idealism cannot survive in this real mutually-implicative world. Just as ideology *always* self-destructs after eating its young, so also the temptation to believe in the full justness of one's own conduct in war labors to deliver moral injury. It is almost severely ironic to put it so, but the more spiritually and emotionally "righteous" conduct of war on the individual's part is to do so with selfless dedication to the good of one's neighbor (whether of same nationality or not) *and* with a concomitant spirit of repentance. A nation may need its heroes for its own unidentified mythic rites of continuity. But is this need helpful to healing the real heroes who performed the "dirty work" and took the risks on behalf of a grateful nation?

These real heroes require grace, space and time for restoration of their spirit. Apology for the necessity of having had to send the heroes into travail would be healthy for the nation, too. All of this could, indeed must, be done without rationalizations of just war, and without repressing or idolizing the human costs of such a war.

Meagher's *tour de force* on the history of just war theory as an historical sin against the essence of Christianity is compelling.[39] This is why Dan Bell calls for a refocus of just war doctrine as a matter of individual Christian discipleship. This work is a dire task that must be understood as a necessity to bring us to the final and proper rule of peace. Our position here is to exhort that such a reframing of just war doctrine, re-wedded to traditional and radically new concepts of sin-confession-repentance-forgiveness-vocation, is vital for the staving and healing of moral injury.

Recognizing that at least the terms of *jus in bello* in just war theory are practically irrelevant (even if ideally prescribed) is to recognize the ineluctable sin of war in the first place. One then must think more in Niebuhrian,

---

39. We have not reflected here on how just war conduct in this day is also virtually impossible and virtually suicidal, given the horrific modes of warfare that so many other bad actors practice in conscious rebellion against just war conduct. How not to become the mirror monster in such combat also is a major cause of PTSD and MI, and casts much theorizing about just war doctrine further into the stratosphere. Along such lines of reflection, even a Vatican Conference on just war doctrine, conducted on April 15, 2016, concluded that the doctrine is no longer employable.

or better, Bonhoefferian, terms that strive for the least evil while yet protecting the innocent. Sin would be recognized as a necessary action when there is no good action available at all. Such a "reality statement" would strip the veneer of righteousness and godliness from the mere invocation of just war. The reality statement would refuse the naming of a wrongful act as good and thereby place the naming where it "really" belongs at the point of the spear. This lessens the delusional blinding that contributes to moral injury, and empowers a moral agency that is necessary for healing moral wounds. The soldier who would be just should know there will never be a morally "good" shot to take. But for the sake of the protection of the neighbor it might be a necessary sin; one goes into such awful reality for the sake of neighbor and country with a *humbly heroic* dependence on forgiveness.

To accept that we humans are both righteous and sinful, to understand that on this human side there can be no such thing and there is no such thing as a purely sin-free act, but yet to aspire and act on behalf of the good and true and beautiful nevertheless: this is the liberated lifestyle in which God takes intimate joy. This peculiar and holy intimacy resonates with vulnerability and self-disclosure on both the human and divine side. This relationship acknowledges that suffering is a—even the most—profound and effective predicate of God whose vulnerable image is placed in human being. By such self-honesty, with real words and authentic utterances, we show who we are and meant to be: children of a greater Origin braided into humble service and relationship with each other, keeping faith, bearing mutual responsibility and accountability, showing forth maturity in our self-acceptance and divine-dependence, effecting the things that make for peace in all its dimensions. These are the marks of any person of well-shaped conscience, not only the soldier under the spiritual guidance of FRAME.

CHAPTER 9

Expressing and Healing Moral Injury

We are not meant to stay wounded. We are supposed to move through our tragedies and challenges and to help each other move through the many painful episodes of our lives. By remaining stuck in the power of our wounds, we block our own transformation. We overlook the greater gifts inherent in our wounds—the strength to overcome them and the lessons that we are meant to receive through them. Wounds are the means through which we enter the hearts of other people. They are meant to teach us to become compassionate and wise.

—Caroline Myss

ON THE LARGEST STAGE that is daily life itself, we've come to understand that life may be summed either as tragedy or comedy. These are, of course, the two dominant forms of narrative that took their footings, as it were, on the stages of Sophocles and Shakespeare. Tragedy dominates the story when the central figure all too late comes to understand his motivations and who he really is, if understanding is reached at all. As Jonathan Shay astutely observes, the conquering hero Odysseus is left in the end with his wife, family, and home. But he has lost much in himself, perhaps even suffers from MI, having so unreflectively thrown so many of his troops "under the bus" along the way for his narcissistic ambition. King Lear, at least, achieved insight and repentance after having lost all but perhaps some integrity, so dramatically confessed in his self-blinding.

Comedy, on the other hand, is the celebration of temporal redemption. It occurs precisely where and after the central figure learns quickly enough her common share in the human condition and so does not take herself too seriously, but responsibly, in the daily mix of other characters. The self-involved men in Aristophanes' *Lysistrata* achieve peace when their wives restrain and reveal to the men their real priorities, achieving peace with the return to self-acceptance and surrender of their warrior pride and ambition. "Perchance to dream" on a midsummer's night of fairies and multi-entangled love interests may help us accept that we can never succeed in grandiosity, but in the thick of life with its humbling absurdities we may accept ourselves and find redemption in things like love and laughter. Self and social awareness in comedy lead to emotional intelligence, self-compassion, and so also to redemption and reconciliation.

The contemporary postmodern philosopher Slavoj Zizek quite agrees. He writes, "Comedy does not rely on the undermining of our dignity with reminders of the ridiculous contingencies of our terrestrial existence. On the contrary, comedy is the full assertion of universality, the immediate coincidence of universality with the character's/actor's singularity. Or to put it another way, what effectively happens when all universal features of dignity are mocked and subverted? The negative force that undermines them is that of the individual, of the hero with his attitude of disrespect toward all elevated universal values, and this negativity itself is the only true remaining universal force."[1]

In other words, comedy reveals the universals of human life, the common condition. A component of the revelatory process is that the actor recognizes the universal attributes and values like imperfection, sin, righteousness, etc., and gives them their due. But the comedic "hero" has both insight and the courage of human freedom. She recognizes that none of the attributes or values of the common condition can be isolated and idolized, and that vulnerability and transparency are the only avenues toward healthy human being. The exercise of human freedom conjoined with insight, then, is the stuff of "comedy," a redeemed and healthy life.

This is where the best of making a story for one's self-understanding of life—the construction of narrative—is essential for the healing of moral injury. This is to say, too, that the promise of self-understanding *can* prevail over despair; insight *can* change tragedy to comedy. Recognition of reality for what it really offers, often recognized through authentic religious symbols where literalism or primal utterances cannot go, *can* lead to healing, new purpose, redemption. From the book of Lamentations to the book of Revelation in the Christian scriptures, the prehistory of Genesis to Malachi's vision of the most gracious God in the Hebrew witness, from the Suras of human obedience to those of Allah's overwhelming justice and mercy in the

1. Zizek, "Christian-Hegelian Comedy," 218.

Qur'an, in sacred scriptures everywhere *stories* that invite readers both to become part of them *and* to incorporate them into our own autobiographies are a human being's primary vehicle for the soul's healing. It is not just that stories of ancient soldiers wrestling with faith are "examples" of what soldiers today might do and become. Better and more effective than examples, these narratives can and should serve as guiding chapters of soldiers' own self-understanding, parts of their own narrative that includes tragedy becoming comedy, and fracture becoming new healed life with purpose. We believe that similar stories are involved in everyone's religious tradition. All mean more to heal and inspire personal life than merely (!) to provide a worldview to rationalize, justify, and sustain current and ego-serving power structures.

Narrative Form and Function

Should such personal stories of tragedy becoming comedy (stories with happy endings), as with the survivors of moral injury, have a similar language and form? Of course not. The pattern or structure of a compelling religious story—say, of a centurion's empathetic care for his dependent, wherein the healing includes the centurion's own life of deeper trust in the community of God—may well be the same while the story's terminology is quite otherwise

For example, in July of 2015, the seventieth anniversary of the torpedoing and sinking of the USS Indianapolis was remembered. This remembering was and is never a celebration. As some will recall, the USS Indianapolis was the ship that secretly delivered a fateful bomb to a base near Japan, soon after delivery to be dropped on Hiroshima. She then was ordered to proceed alone through dangerous waters. Being secret, communication with command in Hawaii was more than minimal. When a Japanese submarine found the Indianapolis during its return from the bomb delivery in the warm waters of the Pacific and then sunk it, no transmission went out from the ship and its crew of almost twelve hundred. No one knew of their destruction, their absence at port, and no one embarked on a rescue mission. Nine hundred survived the initial sinking that only took twelve minutes on the night of July 30. But the worst was yet to come. Some of the nine hundred had found their way to lifeboats, rafts, or floating debris. Many could not and worked hard to swim and float in the warm waters. When daybreak came, the sharks found them. Only some three hundred survived after a reconnaissance plane on routine patrol luckily saw them and reported their location four days later.

The story continues. We can easily understand how multiply traumatized the three hundred survivors were. Symptoms abounded of both MI and PTSD. But no help yet was forthcoming. The compounding of initial secrecy and all its privatizing dynamics atop such trauma gave the survivors no way of telling all the horror of the story until, surprisingly, the debut of the scary motion picture *Jaws* in 1975. In that film Steven Spielberg made definitively public the awful event of the USS Indianapolis, which, in turn, gave the remaining survivors the implicit permission to begin to speak aloud of the horror and to begin to reconstruct from tragedy the meaning of their own lives.[2]

Any form of storytelling from rap to high literature, from ancient ballad to a country music song, from a stage production to many occasions of truth-telling over beers with a shipmate or battle buddy at the VFW can aid the MI client in healing. More formally, there are always and must be always the family member, friend, caregivers, or "pro," who "midwife" the conversations. They are the ones who help to provide the patients' own words where necessary. They are the dedicated compassionate community sticking with the survivor into the full expression of his or her narrative. They are the ones who know when and how to deliver "objectively" as representatives of the divine Other the important announcement of forgiveness.

John Sippola is a retired chaplain now dedicated to redressing MI and PTSD by training faith communities how to understand and support their members who have been morally injured. He tells of how youthfully, even, the objective annunciation of absolution can happen. An early adolescent boy had been one of those in Sippola's church confirmation program whom the pastor and assistants had figured would probably not "get" it. He was a young boy, after all, interested more in sports and action of any sort than learning church stuff. They had been teaching about confession and forgiveness, including repeated practice of how to recognize the need for forgiveness and proclaim it rightly when needed. One day his thirteen-year-old boy was in the back seat of the family car with his younger sister. Dad was driving and mom was in the front passenger seat. They came to an intersection where Dad became unusually and visibly moved. Dad mentioned that every time he came to this intersection he would be upset. The son immediately took notice, moved his head forward to between his parents and asked, "Why is that, dad?" Dad answered, haltingly, "Many years ago here I missed the signal and crashed into another car, and killed the family in the car." The son responded, "So you still feel really awful about that?" "Yes, always," said Dad. At that point the son responded with urgent sincerity,

2. See Adams, "Cost of War."

"Dad, in the name of Jesus Christ I announce to you the forgiveness of all your sins." It might have taken some more time for the father to heal, but surely the son got the point of how "objectively" grace and forgiveness must be communicated, as every caregiver must learn.

Paratrooper Private Sonny Sisk belonged to the 506th Parachute Infantry. He was a combat veteran of Normandy, Holland, and Bastogne. During a unit reunion decades later, he displayed his active senses of FRAME, even as he evinced still the psychic scars of his MI. His reconciliation with himself and the circumstances that occasioned his MI had been taking time. Forgiveness had been pronounced before, but held no long-term effect. Such announcements would be necessary even long after his military service. "My career after the war was trying to drink away the truckload of Krauts that I stopped in Holland and the diehard Nazi that I went up into the Bavarian Alps and killed . . . all the killings that I did was going to jump into the bed with me one these days and they surely did. . . . I had a lot of flashbacks after the war and I started drinking. . . . Then my little sister's daughter, four years old, came into my bedroom and she told me that Jesus loved me and . . . if I would repent God would forgive me for all the men I kept trying to kill all over again . . . that little girl got to me."[3]

Both men received exactly what they needed to hear. The important transaction of confession and forgiveness was made between two agents in an objectively discernible situation. The pattern is clear. In each case, a story, however brief, was told that indicated the morally injured person's self-understanding and sense of responsibility. Another person, in these cases both young, both on behalf of transcendence, responsibly fulfilled their roles as peacemakers. Either occasion may well, indeed quite likely, need to be repeated, with different players. But the articulation of the narrative and the achievement of forgiveness would be practiced, thereby nurturing the morally injured toward healing. A reconciliation of a traumatized self into a new self would be made. This includes reconciliation with the victims of the presenting tragedy, with their and one's own family and extended associations, and reconciliation with God.

Storytelling, narrative construction, is a restorative therapy. Other restorative therapies, as with those for PTSD, focus on "automatic" physical behaviors that may accompany the resistance and denial mechanisms in the psyche in the attempt to reconstruct narrative. Stabilization of eye movement is one such tactic. Another, particularly with the lesser traumatized, is to reconstruct and "encounter" the traumatizing event as repeatedly as possible. This may help to overcome agoraphobia, for example, but

---

3. Brotherton, *We Who Are Alive and Remain*, 188.

the dynamics of moral injury are more opaque and require much more patient and lengthy coaching, most often in a combination of group work and one-on-one patient/therapist sessions. With the inclusion of narrative reconstruction in therapies, the goal is to realign the cognitive left brain with the emotive right hemisphere, thus helping soldiers rethink their perceptions of the injuring event(s). Narratives do this. We emphasize that MI is implicitly a spiritual issue. It involves matters of conscience and transcendence and questions of human destiny that by definition are beyond the usual clinical psychiatric expertise.

And, so also by definition, MI requires a compassionate community accompaniment that is at ease with the MI survivor's own language. The dynamics of Alcoholics Anonymous are a fine example. Members of AA recognize, as with the theology of the cross, that for the "higher power" to be "God" means that God always is in intimate solidarity with the survivor in the most base and coarse of an injured veteran's emerging narrative language. The emotive subjective confession of the phrase "Fuck them, fuck war, I'm fucked" and the objective forgiving pronouncement of "God is with you" are comfortable—and truly compatible!—grammars.

If God is in the tragic places into which we send our soldiers, then God also knows and speaks their language and can be spoken into their stories. We need the kind of language that Bonhoeffer sought, a non-churchy language, a real language that stops not at traditional pieties but names the personal experienced realities. We need a language that coheres with the daily behavior "as if God is not there." Yet our consciousness and our stories should be over-filled both with a sense of accountability to God and deepening dependence on the grace of God. The healing of MI will include the victim's story-making and storytelling. Caregivers, *especially* pastoral caregivers, need to be with, listen to, and honor the experience and the stories exactly as they are felt and told.[4]

In narrative we move from the alpha point of confession and forgiveness to the Omega point of reconciliation, which is also always itself a new beginning. The reader may remember Major Jeffrey Hall's story in chapter 2 and the picture he drew that provided the first "chapters" of his story of MI. Major Jeff Hall retired from the Army in August 2014 in front of a hometown gathering in Woodward, Oklahoma. The ceremony included Jeff's wife, Sheri, their daughters, parents, friends, and extended family. It also included former commanders, soldiers, and healers who worked with him. The highlight of the ceremony was Jeff and his family placing items

---

4. The postmodern therapy of narrative is already well-tested. See Tick, *War and the Soul*; Haidt, *Righteous Mind*; Jones, *Trauma and Grace*; Lange, *Trauma Recalled*.

from his combat service into a handcrafted wooden container, topped off with a carved wooden sword beaten into a plowshare. They weren't locking away memories as much a performing a ceremony that signified his transformation of moral healing into a new chapter of reconciliation. Jeff wrote in the program, "Sheri was the one that held on when the world spun out of control. In sickness and in health always meant something to her. I was not that strong. . . . Thanks is not enough."[5] As part of the ceremony Hall placed his war diary in the container. In it are these words. "I was unable to save anyone of them [a multitude of soldiers and Iraqi civilians] but I tried. . . . I will never forget this place where I spent my loneliest time on earth so far. Love is here in this hell we call Iraqi Freedom. I don't like the fraud I see here. . . . I hate the ones who have used this opportunity to advance their [deleted] careers. But I will always love those that gave up everything for a cause . . . they came to me with their sorrows, but I was the one who needed them. . . . Lots of my experience in Iraq was too little too late."[6] At his retirement celebration, he put into that box his precious symbolic objects of war and trauma. The terms of the narrative and his sense of forgiveness, including his realization of self-compassion, had been achieved. Reconciliation was marked and now would be the growing horizon of his new life.

Language Limits

When one's narrative of MI necessarily goes through many drafts during the long journey of a plot change from tragedy to hoped-for comedy, language itself poses many challenges. Too much language, or language for its own sake as in the form of logorrhea can hide the excess of cruelty and pain that the morally injured person has so suffered. It is a natural behavior to want to bury or anesthetize the pain with words. Words are ready tools for the usual first recourse of denial. Those who aid in the soul sufferer's work must therefore listen and watch well enough to encourage precision in language. Truth-telling as accurately as possible is the exact, if unwelcome, first step toward healing.

Yet, too literal a language incompetently addresses the wounds that are too deep for words. As Elaine Scarry so bravely documents in her exhaustive work on torture, mental and moral pain itself resists literal language.[7] Pain, both physical and mental, has no objects to which it can attach. There is nothing but the chaotic immediacy of the pain, and so both cause and the

5. From the Iraqi Freedom diary of Major Jeff Hall, used with his permission.
6. Ibid.
7. Scarry, *Body in Pain*, 4.

category of time are exiled by the immediacy of pain and suffering. On the other hand, imagination rests virtually in its imagined object. That object can be a flying horse, Pegasus, fully removed from reality but indeed conceivable. Or it can be a friend, based on reality, but on closer inspection hollow in comparison with the real thing.[8] Symbolism—not just any symbolism, but the self-evidently "naturally risen" symbolism—is of crucial importance as an aid to healing here.[9] The movie *Jaws* unintentionally commended itself as such a symbol to catalyze language for the long-traumatized survivors of the USS Indianapolis. Major Jeffrey Hall found for himself the right symbols and consequent words to illustrate both his experience of and recovery from MI. Art and symbols and stories still and must abound for individual and corporate moral injury from endless war—which is why, of course, Shay still mines the "classics" of Homer—and from ongoing cruelty and injustice wreaked by the political state upon all and any people of "difference," including women, people of color, people of differing sexual orientation and gender identity, and those who must live in poverty. Moral injury is tragically poignant with those who serve in the military. But its metastasis is unbounded. And the right symbols with their attendant thousands upon thousands of words must be recognized and respected.

All the more important, then, is the presence, solidarity, and skilled ear of "the divine Other" in the presence, ears, and words of a respected spiritual other. Veteran Lee Thweat, who served as a Judge Advocate General in the United States Marines, tells of such a respected chaplain. During his officer training, Thweat came to know well CDR Dennis Rocheford. Rocheford had fought as an enlisted Marine in Vietnam. Asked what it was like to fight there, Rocheford answered that it was terrible, that when he was in it, he thought it was hell on earth, even "a place with no God . . . or so it seemed to me and everyone I knew." He recounted in the battle of Hue City, he'd seen his best friend cut in half by a rocket-propelled grenade. Later, his platoon was rewarded for its lethality in combat with a hot meal when other platoons received cold food. For some reason, although he was hungry from the fighting he'd done, he refused to eat the hot meal. He said it took himself a while to realize that the refusal of this hot meal—such a simple thing—meant that he still had some shred of humanity, and that it

8. Ibid., 162–64.

9. Recall Paul Tillich's important and cautionary observation about symbols. They arise, as from a deep communal psyche, pointing beyond themselves to a transcendence so transcending that it is also immanent. It cannot be positivistically correlated with an object or a concrete experience, as does a "sign." It cannot be arbitrarily constructed. But the symbol does commend itself and work as an icon, a portal, to stand for a constellation of experience and meaning.

came from God. That God was still with him. It was the moment that he recalled his faith, and it overwhelmed him. He asked God for forgiveness in the particulars of his Catholic faith, and he was able to forgive himself, too. He used that personal revelation to become a priest, and he was extraordinary at ministering in the context of military service. Thweat continued, "We thought Father Rocheford was almost superhuman. He was 20+ years older than us, combat tested & combat wounded (physically and morally), and he marched every march with us in a full pack during our training. He was one of the most remarkable people I have ever encountered. He emphasized to all of us, privately and in group settings, that fear of death was ok, that we had a morality to our efforts, that such morality could be lost without proper attention and maintenance (as it was for so many in Vietnam), that we could prevent the My Lai massacres etc. Sadly, I learned in recalling him and googling him . . . that he took his own life in 2010."[10]

Rocheford practiced a ministry of authentic presence with his charges that infused and sustained in them a spiritual resiliency that, were we to more closely examine, would fit well with FRAME, DCV, and help ameliorate MI in his troops. That his own life ended by suicide is an awful tragedy. We do not know whether Rocheford himself suffered from MI, even long after his experience of transcendence and forgiveness so many years before. The importance of a true and personal narrative, rehearsed in the context of a continually sustaining and embracing faith community, cannot be overstated, especially because the prison bars of one's subjective critical self-judgment seem to close in on one again and again. Moral injury is insidious that way. In presenting our material to chaplain and other caregiver conferences, we authors have come to expect that chaplains in our groups will be surprised to discover and be compelled to acknowledge their own experiences with MI.

Rocheford stands as a cherished example of the listener who brought wisdom with grace to soldiers who learned gladly to trust him. He brought forgiveness to them and they accepted it. To this day they know how they need repeatedly to be assured of grace from one who understands, who's been there, and clearly represents the "Other" of God. Caregivers, too, cannot only re-present the grace of God. They need the grace of a faith community, of "others re-presenting the Other" to be sustained in the objective truth of grace and forgiveness. Faith communities themselves need to be trained better to be such re-presenters of God's goodness.

10. See "Died of Wounds," US Naval Institute blog, November 19, 2010, https://blog.usni.org/2010/11/19/died-of-wounds.

The Difference between Forgiveness and Reconciliation

There is a preference among many healers and caregivers remediating MI to replace the language of forgiveness with the language of reconciliation. We can imagine no worse a tactic for the culture and audience we want to address here, just as we can imagine no worse a theological confusion. Forgiveness and reconciliation are, of course, related. But the primary term of forgiveness (and its partner of confession) is distinct from reconciliation in very substantive and important ways.[11] Forgiveness is more precisely about the human need of and desire for forgiveness/affirmation from whom the client has violated, if at all possible, and above all from the One whom the client understands as the author of his or her life. Reconciliation is distinct, but not separated from that "subjective-objective" transaction and includes the broader range of restoring harmony and/or complementarity oneself, one's human relations, and one's world. Indeed, reconciliation is not even possible without forgiveness as the prevenient act. Forgiveness, again, is a much more specific and necessary, if even oft repeated, matter, while the latter denotes the longer process of reconnecting, even healthily "re-braiding," with the people and communities in which a person's moral identity is vested. The catalyst for all this is forgiveness; the word that says "Go in peace" before the subsequent instruction now made possible, "serve the Lord, love your neighbor."

The primacy of forgiveness, the self-forgiving and self-compassion side of which is realized only after the subjective-objective transaction of confession/forgiveness has happened, surely also means that the giving of forgiving cannot happen too quickly, but for the direst of situations (as with last rites). An objective word given lazily or in haste when the "client" has so much more yet to process is, again, no less than cheap grace (aspirin ministry). It also teaches cynicism. A would-be repentant soldier could justly conclude, "If that is all there is to it, Chappie doesn't have much to go on and God is pretty lame."[12] This also would be the god who "could never forgive me," because a "god" who responds too readily is not one who grieves the weight on the stricken soldier's own conscience. Such a god could not be a god at all. God, who insists on solidarity with the suffering, whose justice is mercy, with and from whom forgiveness first happens, can be the only true God. Because *this* God is true and the font of forgiveness, we therefore also locate

11. For the theologically sophisticated, a reminder of Barth's and Rahner's distinctions should suffice and put to rest any attempt to synonymize the terms.

12. Phil Klay comically and ruefully explores this repeated reality in his *Redeployment* stories.

the priority of forgiveness with God. This does not negate reconciliation. It is the reclamation of the priority of forgiveness we here accent.

Finally, again, it should be clear now that talk of "self-forgiveness," aided and abetted by the otherwise helpful storehouse of Stoic impassivity, is simply impotent when faced with transcendence, with what the morally injured survivor intuits as God. Self-forgiveness is a real possibility. It aligns with self-compassion and may even befit the one who is trained well in FRAME with a directed conscientious vocation. But the personal capacity for self-forgiveness without a sense for the Infinite simply does not exist. Post-traumatic maturity (M) and efficacy (E) of FRAME are impossible without the healing power of forgiveness and reconciliation.

Accompaniment

God chooses solidarity with the morally injured. This means also that God will "take" whatever time is required to achieve God's purposes. On our human side, then, we too will need to be gracious with time and language to care for the morally injured. This practice will include guidance from the above suggested prescriptions, even if we'd prefer that no Christian practice violence. We can't walk away. No one called to minister among the morally injured can walk away from violence and its effects. Nor can we utter a shallow word of "just obey" or supply a mere gesture of forgiveness and go on with our other business. If we believe that God in Jesus Christ redeems the world, and that those in military service have as much claim to that redemption as anyone else outside the military, then we must supply the enfleshed ministerial wherewithal to accompany them. If God abides *in* this awful reality, there is both hope and forgiveness available to the soldier stricken with MI. By this we mean that grace can overcome trauma through a narrative of solidarity and compassion. Indeed, since the standard procedure of military training employs consistent operant conditioning of the recruit notwithstanding the likely collateral damage of bypassing any internal moral compass, a narrative structure of solidarity and compassion could and perhaps should already be provided by wise chaplaincy at the outset of a soldier's career.[13]

---

13. After WWI it was discovered that only a very small percentage, 15%, of those soldiers on the front line pulled the trigger. Thanks to operant conditioning, that number now is almost a perfect 100%. Violent video-gaming has helped reach that number. This same training applies to personnel who operate drones from a cubicle in a steel office. They experience the breakdown of PTSD and MI too.

This narrative—which in the most formal grammatical sense is a liturgy—will comfort and promise with the terms of God and the church's real presence. It will also help us better to see and be healing help for the so many other morally injured whose numbers are on the rise. This goes against all the sacralized justifications of soldiers in American (and Israeli and Russian and any empire-oriented) culture. It goes against much of what has passed for Christianity too. And so it should. But this description "of reality" would cohere once again with the moral depth that most once knew and called conscience. It might be that to re-point out God is with us *in* the immoral depths, too, would bring healing to any soldiers who otherwise regard and carry their Scriptures as a talisman. God's word is not so much protection against physical injury as a testimony to the healing power of God.[14]

One soldier commends the healing power of a veteran's new narrative, and underscores how necessary the construction of narrative is for one's own well-being.

> It is not that something different is seen, but that one sees differently" [wrote] Carl Jung. 3 years ago at this time I had my final "flashback" while driving through a sandstorm in El Paso. For a moment I was back in Iraq during the invasion, during a sandstorm when the sky literally turned an eerie blood red and rained mud. I pulled over and practiced deep breathing and prayerful mindfulness until the moment passed. I shared the story with a doctor friend who offered a prescription. I said "Dude, just listen to my story." I pray that 2016 will find combat veterans and trauma survivors able to integrate the "event" into their story and lives, free of "prescriptions" and practicing good self-care through prayer, diet, healthy relationships, Yoga, exercise, etc. Remember that which happens to you does NOT own nor define you.[15]

This soldier implies that he knows, rehearses, and continues to edit the narrative that he has come rightly and healthily to know as his very own. We have touched upon theological principles all along in this book. While rooted in certain Christian traditions, these religious principles have analogs in and are practiced in many major religions. Just as we have reclaimed

---

14. Chaplain Jeff Zust tells the story of a metallic Bible with a bullet in it recovered from a wounded soldier. A chaplain in the aid station proclaimed that the Bible protected the soldier, only to be told by the wounded soldier that the bullet was from his exit wound. The story then was adopted more appropriately as a narrative of the faithful and healing grace of God in solidarity with the wounded.

15. Palmer, a quote from his diary.

"soul" in the opening chapter, we also reclaimed the name of the challenge to the combatant's vocation as what it is, "sin."

But that is not the all of it. God also sticks with human beings in all our trials, sins, and sorrows. By God's infinitely gracious sticking with us, we are restored and justified. This happens only by God's free decision of grace and love that does not lessen the severity of our sin. Rather, God's judgment and love call us to a deeper, more urgent, and smarter responsibility to do our best in care for the neighbor. Often that means we must sin so to prevent greater sin. This means we have no purity whatsoever, no reason whatsoever, proudly to celebrate our sinful acts. When there is no alternative, we endorse "sinning boldly," but never triumphantly, as with end zone dancing. The core of all the major religions is about compassion and humility. And compassion and humility are fueled by the intimate presence of the divine with any and all those who suffer.

The intimate presence of the divine is exceptionally important to realize for us humans, who by nature are essentially relational. Far too often "typical" religion—especially that kind of religion shaped to preserve the privileges of its leaders—leads us to believe and act as if God is distant and severe. But the divine is not far off to be appeased or obeyed, as if God is a distant commander whose only appreciation of soldiers is through a series of reports (positive and negative) that crawl up the chain of command. The divine is not one to whom the soldier must justify himself or herself. Rather, God is immeasurably close to all who suffer in the direst of circumstances and is deeply invested in the complicated and growing stories in which soldiers are co-authors.

This most certainly does not mean that everything the soldier does has divine approval. God still stands by what God has meant for human being and for what God values as holy. All humans are now embedded in a fulsome reality that does not and cannot separate the good from the bad and the holy from evil. We are not on our own. God loves all that God created. Like a parent's love even for the most wayward child, God does not abandon the child to all the consequences of his or her bad decisions. God may have to exercise tough love. But God does not and will not leave God's fallen creation "on the field." Though we sin, God does not and will not break up with us. God stays intimately close. And this means that God will suffer our bad decisions and consequences. This is the only way, the new beginning, by which God will redeem those who suffer in any manner, including the suffering of soul sorrow, moral injury.

In a certain sense, this spiritual view of directed conscientious vocation puts even more responsibility on our shoulders, heads, and hearts. But it also bestows a unique freedom—even a "postmodern" freedom—on the soldier to know that God is coauthoring and co-hurting. This is a God who is "solid" with the sufferer, who "has been there" and can "take" the horror, even while never justifying it. The soldier who knows and trusts this is a soldier with a 24/7 active conscience at work on behalf of the neighbor, without the false obligations and delusions that destroy soldierly character.

Such duty and freedom mark the soldier who carries all the elements of FRAME. Fidelity, responsibility, accountability, maturity, and efficacy all summarize the one who, having come to know forgiveness, has accepted oneself. This is the one who then moves forward into the denouement of reconciliation in his or her own narrative. Consider again the edit to his own narrative of moral injury that Marine Sergeant Frederick Garten made when he placed his enemy's wedding band at the Vietnam Memorial wall. "This wedding ring belonged to a young Viet Cong fighter. He was killed by a Marine unit in the Phu Loc province of South Vietnam in May of 1968. I wish I knew more about this young man. I have carried this ring for 18 years and it's time for me to lay it down. This boy is not my enemy any longer."[16]

Forgiveness and reconciliation, of course, are not only about the personal relationships of two people or two parties. It may be even that forgiveness is primarily a serious matter for individual persons and that reconciliation is the necessarily social and communal counterpart. After all, war is a community practice. Thus so also is peacemaking. Reconciliation, then, is highly charged by political and spiritual dimensions. Political scientist Daniel Philpott, for example, addresses how the spiritual domain contributes to a reconciliation process that is essential for restorative justice. Justice, righteousness, and mercy each have a political and spiritual history that inform every culture. Between and among different societies there are "zones of possible agreements" wherein processes of reconciliation can take root. An elaborate and deliberate reconciliation process will use mutual respect, disciplined listening to different communal narrative constructions, mutual acknowledgment, confession, and forgiveness—all as communal forms of what happens among individuals in midwifed narrative construction—so to heal the personal and social wounds of war.[17] The primary wounds to be addressed include violations of human rights, personal harm, ignorance of the circumstances of injustice, lack of acknowledgment of the suffering, and the standing victory of the wrongdoer's injustice. Secondary

---

16. Palmer, *Shrapnel in the Heart*, 184.

17. Philpott, *Just and Unjust Peace*, 4–29. The noted pages provide a summary of Philpott's extended argument

wounds include the memories, emotions, judgments, and actions that perpetuate the effects of the primary wounds.[18]

Philpott's concept of cross-cultural resonance with a shared spiritual dimension underscores how another practice of reconciliation, so-called reconciliation trips, are in fact important to both personal and communal wellness. Some theologians count these efforts as disingenuous.[19] However imperfect such trips may be, they are a first step in truthful confession and building of a reconciling community by giving the opportunity to retrieve the "hard data" and hold the substantive conversations that help resolve the dissonance that creates MI.

One of the most famous reconciliation trips occurred at Gettysburg, where the Grand Army of the Potomac veterans met with the Army of Northern Virginia veterans. The original event occurred in 1888 as a reunion for Union veterans. In 1913 the Union participants widened the event by inviting Confederate veterans. This resulted in a larger event where over 50,000 survivors of the battle attended (the actual battle had approximately 157,289 soldiers serving in both armies). Both sides camped together on the battlefield, and even reenacted a critical part of the battle without weapons. They exchanged handshakes and stories at the location of Pickett's charge, where many of their comrades had died. In 1938, 2400 survivors met again for the last time.[20]

The conveners of the Gettysburg reunion simply empowered the reconnection; the soldiers forged their own reconciliation on their terms. This type of reconciliation is also happening among Vietnam veterans. Edward Tick explains the reasoning behind these trips. "Veterans themselves sometimes strive to achieve the mature warrior's vision of reconciliation by traveling to the places where they fought, visiting distant war cemeteries of their comrades, and providing charitable services to those they have hurt, such as many do today."[21] Precisely because the matter is about reconciliation, those who were the direct objects of violation, rather than only the morally injured, find that they themselves may also be the agents of forgiveness so needed for the violator's own restored lives. On a reconciliation trip to My Lai, a

18. Ibid. We point also to the famous example of the South Africa Truth and Reconciliation Commission as a successful means of attending to these stated primary and secondary injuries. We note also that precisely the absence of such address in the stalemated dialogues between Israel and Palestine, as Rabbi Michael Lerner also notes, suggests state/corporate forms of PTSD and, we would add, moral injury. See Lerner, *Embracing Israel and Palestine*.

19. E.g., Brock, *Soul Repair*, 106–7.

20. Allen, "Gettysburg at 50."

21. Tick, *War and the Soul*, 265.

Vietnamese woman who survived the massacre told an American veteran who had been at My Lai, "It is important you have come here. . . . I have come to understand that the purpose of my survival was so I could live into this distant time when I could meet American veterans, take their hands, look into their eyes, forgive them, and help them forgive themselves."[22]

Some critics may perceive that the Vietnamese woman above falls into the misogynist category that simply advises women to forgive male abusers. We condemn misogyny and would never counsel, as we wrote earlier, that forgiveness be offered insincerely and so prematurely without the hard work of confession and repentance before. Others condemn such reconciliation trips as justifications of imperialism—"to the victor go the spoils of self-righteousness and purification!" However, sincerity and disingenuousness, like being simultaneously just and sinful, abide in soldiers and commentators alike. Surely we would not deny the prospect of an utter, even holy, sincerity, on the Vietnamese woman's part. These trips do not have perfect endings, but they are not cheap grace. They demonstrate that forgiveness and reconciliation happen at great cost over time as soldiers reconnect and work out their own healing.

Reconciliation trips empower soldiers to: name the "nasty" stuff of their dissonance, reconnect the distance between their values and their actions, and restore their sense of purpose. Soldiers who do not have this opportunity to reconcile the past with the present likely have more challenges in making their transitions to home and health. Of course, it is not always possible that a fulsome reconciliation can be achieved in real time with those we've hurt. We cannot always return to the fields in Vietnam or the Middle East, or the halls of justice where injustice had a louder voice for a time. We cannot always return to the home where domestic violence held sway or to the streets where our own racism ran riot. We cannot always perform the rites of reconciliation in the manner that a truth commission would prescribe. But we can write again the story with uncompromising memory. We can own the tragedy in many and various ways so finally to claim the redemptive healing intended in comedy. This is the stuff of healthy mythic and healthy religious care for the injured. As Jonathan Shay, too, agrees, "If the Church's ideas on sin, penitence, forgiveness of sin, and redemption are about anything, they're about the real stuff. What the Church offers is about cruelty, violence, murder—not just the sins you confessed in parochial school."[23]

22. Tick, *Warrior's Return*, 257.
23. Shay, *Odysseus in* America, 153–54.

Conclusion

The church, indeed, as well as most long-traditioned faith communities, takes the "real stuff," the really human stuff, seriously, which is why grace, forgiveness, hope, and love are lived more seriously still. The real stuff is communicated through the stories that we must help to be told, to which we must listen, and which we must understand better. Each suffering soul's story, with every painful and new iteration, reveals the struggle to reconcile moral dissonance and to reclaim the goodness that God intends for human being beyond sin and suffering. Individual caregivers and faith-communities do well when they claim their own reasons-for-being and employ all the proven practices (e.g., ritual, confession, absolution, reconciliation, teaching the analogical import of faith's narratives) of their traditions to accompany the injured in their recovery.

For better understanding, TMM and FRAME can provide useful models for future moral injury research. Future moral injury research needs to observe and correlate more closely to the worldviews of soldiers with their post-combat perceptions and behaviors in order to understand how they process and reconcile their war experiences. MI research needs also to invite and incorporate more clinical pastoral insight from the major religious traditions, while also teaching religious thought leaders the hard-won wisdom from military culture that could benefit wider society. Such intentional collaboration has the added benefit of bringing back together military and civilian cultures that otherwise have regularly proven a failure to communicate.

We have also emphasized that it is not enough to reconcile or heal moral injuries after the fact. The reality of MI as a combat injury challenges the military to evaluate how it morally develops its ranks. It is a moral failure to train soldiers to engage their weapon systems only using model examples and abstract principles for ethical decision-making. Instead, the military needs to consider ways to develop embedded moral reasoning that empowers soldiers at all levels to be moral agents and to practice directed conscientious vocation. Michael Hallett's exhortation to embed trained combat veterans as moral coaches within the ranks is consonant with our urgent concern.[24] It follows the priority to train our youngest to *practice* moral principles, as when an otherwise usually innocuous adolescent boy knows when to bring a clear pronouncement of absolution to the suffering soul of a father. In other words, embedding exemplars and coaches of moral character has proven to be a failure of the church as well as the

24. Hallett, "Cultivating Sailor Ethical Fitness," 103.

military. The point not only is better to mitigate potential moral injuries, but also to provide the means for resiliency by providing the morally injured anywhere themselves the means to resolve moral dissonance.

Finally, storied people—all of us—have our histories and our aspirations. That they do not match and that their dissonance does erupt even into moral injury speaks more to our healthiness than to our depravity. Most of us know indeed that we are not perfect. Most of us know indeed that we must speak truthfully, if sometimes in some places with nuance and discretion, if our lives are to be more blessing than bane. Most of us know the joy of personal freedom and the freedom of shared joy when we accept each other and ourselves with all our warts, woes, and wonders. When we live with more honesty than not, with a clearer story than not, we do better when we meet trauma and recover better after trauma, and we are at least a bit more saint than sinner. But to suppress the honesty, not to seek to tell or listen to our own stories, not to confess and not even to desire acceptance on the basis of our honest presentations to self and others: this is the truly tragic life. Such lives have no humor, no health, and no hope. We thank God that God will insist on curing us of our souls' suffering nevertheless, which means that health—the root meaning of the word "salvation"—is ever our real possibility.

In honest and explicated memory there is future, and the Infinitely Merciful One embraces both.

My Lai and Drone Warfare as Cases for FRAME

THESE FOLLOWING CASES ARE from two unrelated events from two different wars. The murder of civilians at My Lai during the Vietnam War involves a war crime. The use of drones to selectively kill the enemy involves current attempts to make legal decisions in a complex operating environment. However, both events involve similar patterns of moral reasoning within mission command affecting the moral agency of both commanders and soldiers. We include these cases to focus attention upon the formation of moral dissonance through soldiers' moral senses of FRAME. The reader is invited to consider how these cases may be different were FRAME employed at all levels, concomitant with the availability of a spiritual community that could encourage spiritual-ethical discourse.

My Lai

During the Vietnam War guerilla tactics contributed to a utility-oriented command intent that directly corrupted warrior competence and resulted in the deliberate targeting and murder of civilians at My Lai.[1] The killings at My Lai occurred in the wake of North Vietnam's Tet Offensive, when Task Force Barker entered a series of small villages with the mission to destroy a suspected Vietcong battalion. Senior commanders looked upon the area as a "free fire zone," and their lack of enforcing command policy and rules of engagement in issuing mission orders led to subordinate officers operating under their own "localized authority." The orders from junior leaders subsequently caused moral failures in junior warriors who committed mass murder. Lieutenant General William Peers led the official investigation. He summarized the panel's conclusions in terms of moral senses that should

---

1. Rielly, "Inclination for War Crimes," 52–58.

have influenced the conduct of soldiers at My Lai. "An officer's highest loyalty is to the Army and the nation. On those rare occasions when people around him engage in activities clearly wrong and immoral, he is required by virtue of his being an officer to take whatever remedial action is required, regardless of the personal consequences."[2]

The inquiry cited twenty-eight individuals for their conduct. These failures included the issuing of mission orders and command intents that directly led to the murder and the "suppression of a war crime of far greater magnitude."[3] The investigation primarily focused upon the orders and intents of the battalion commander, the company commander, and two platoon leaders. The battalion commander, Lieutenant Colonel Frank Barker, was later killed in action, and the panel was not able to fully investigate his orders and intents. The next officer in the chain of command was the company commander Captain Ernest Medina.

Prior to the operation, anti-personnel mines located in the general area of My Lai caused twenty casualties that contributed to feelings of anger and revenge within the company. Medina's orders and intent created a "localized" permission for his soldiers to act upon their emotions, evidence indicated. "Medina told his company they were to burn the houses, kill the livestock, and destroy the crops and foodstuffs. There is less unanimity about what he told them concerning noncombatants. However, by telling them that no civilians would be in the hamlet . . . and not issuing any instructions as to how to deal with civilians, he created the impression in the minds of many men in the company that they were to kill or destroy everything in the area. He also reminded them that they had lost several men to enemy mines and booby traps and this operation was their chance to get even: it was to be a revenge or grudge battle."[4]

Medina explained the reasoning behind his intent to target civilians: "The entire area was heavily infested with mines and booby traps. When infantrymen approach an area, the women and children will place these things out."[5] Two platoon leaders executed Medina's intent, if not his direct orders. Second Lieutenant William Calley did not question Medina's implied intent or orders. When he was later convicted of premeditated murder, he defended his actions, "If I have committed a crime, the only crime I have

2. Peers, *My Lai Inquiry*, 249, 287–88.

3. Army, *Investigations into the My Lai Incident*, 2–13.

4. Peers, *My Lai Inquiry*, 170.

5. Thompson, *Moral Courage in Combat*, 8.

committed is in judgment of my values. Apparently I valued my troops' lives more than I did those of the enemy."[6]

The other lieutenant, Steven Brooks, was later killed in Vietnam, and it was not possible to investigate fully his orders and intents. However, the circumstances of his death validate Calley's rationale for protecting his troops. In an incident unrelated to My Lai, Brooks and his platoon sergeant were killed while recovering the bodies of two soldiers killed in an anti-personnel mine explosion. One of his surviving soldiers wrote this epitaph. "Officers and NCOs who later led our infantry company probably would have ordered their men to do the grim work of retrieving a blown apart body. But Brooks and O'Hara weren't like that and so they ended up paying the ultimate price so that a scared, new guy could live to tell their story. God Bless You Both."[7]

Calley's and Brook's actions reveal the complex and sometimes contradictory senses of fidelity, responsibility, accountability, maturity, and efficacy upon junior soldiers. At a minimum the orders, intents, and actions of Medina, Calley, and Brooks established a localized authority that set the conditions for their troops to murder noncombatant civilians at My Lai. These leaders also violated and betrayed the professional values that govern soldiers' conduct and guard their character. Thus, they increased the potential for moral injuries in everyone associated with Task Force Barker.

One of the junior soldiers who participated in the My Lai killings, Private Paul Meadlo, explained his actions that day. "Why did I do it? Because I felt like I was ordered to do it."[8] Meadlo didn't act alone. Private Greg Olson wrote home, "These are all seemingly normal guys; some were friends of mine. For a while they were like wild animals. It was murder, and I'm ashamed of myself for not trying to do anything about it. This isn't the first time, Dad."[9]

Much is written about the public outcry in response to My Lai, contributing to a growing public protests against the Vietnam War. But not much is written about the personal consequences for the soldiers who participated in that debacle. Failures in mission command and personal emotions denied those soldiers the capacity and capability to "do the right thing." In "following orders" like professional soldiers, these warriors acted as pirates and participated in criminal acts. How then did these individuals deal with the moral dissonance?

6. McDaniel, "William Calley Apologizes."

7. Tom Chilcote as quoted in a memorial web page located at https://www.findagrave.com/cgi-bin/fg.cgi?page=gr&GRid=2933293.

8. Thompson, *Moral Courage in Combat*, 8.

9. Lindsay, "Something Dark and Bloody."

Shortly after My Lai, Meadlo was wounded and reportedly screamed at Calley, "God will punish you for what you made me do."[10] Meadlo returned home to his wife and family and tried to suppress his perceptions and self-appraisal. However, they eventually came out and affected his home life. When a reporter came for an interview, Meadlo's mother told him, "I sent them a good boy and they made him a murderer."[11]

"Localized authority" can result in a degraded group moral agency that has far-reaching consequences for both national policy and personal wellness. Morally injurious events inflicted upon a primary victim secondarily injure those who do not initiate the MIE but yet must obey the command to carry out the MIE and/or must witness its execution.[12] Once a moral boundary is crossed, it is difficult to heal the moral consequences.

Long after the war, one My Lai veteran, Kenneth Shiel, returned to My Lai in order to offer an emotional (and quite possibly, sincere) apology to the survivors of My Lai. In doing so, he stated that he shot until he realized that he was wrong. Of course, once the round leaves the weapon, the power of forgiveness resides with the victim, not the moral agent. One My Lai survivor, Pham Thanh Cong, was skeptical of Shiel's apology. Pham Thanh Cong had "no interest in easing the pain of a My Lai veteran who refused to own up fully to what he had done."[13] Shiel's and Cong's reactions demonstrate the profound obstacles confronting both moral victims and agents who seek reconciliation to heal their moral wounds. This difficulty extends up the chain of command.

Recently Calley spoke at a local civic group and offered the following explanation for his actions. "There is not a day that goes by that I do not feel remorse for what happened that day in My Lai. . . . I feel remorse for the Vietnamese who were killed, for their families, for the American soldiers involved and their families. I am very sorry. . . . If you are asking why I did not stand up to them [his chain of command] when I was given the orders, I will have to say that I was a second lieutenant getting orders from my

10. Hersh, "Scene of the Crime."

11. Ibid. Hersh provides a detailed account of Meadlo's narrative and how the killings at My Lai altered his life.

12. Philpott, *Just and Unjust Peace*, 48–49.

13. Hersh, "Scene of the Crime." Hersh reports that this event occurred as part of an Al Jazeera documentary commemorating the fortieth anniversary of the My Lai killings, which opens the reporting of this account to political intents. However, the authors included it because the account demonstrates the depth of human emotions that influence attempts at reconciliation.

commander and I followed them—foolishly, I guess . . . this is not an excuse; it was just what happened."[14]

Tran Van Duc, a My Lai survivor whose mother and brothers who were among the villagers killed and photographed, responded to Calley's statement in an interview where he summarized his pain and anger. "People that we respected and paid reverence to, you spat in their faces. You raped teenage girls and young women. Before committing your evil deeds, your units slowly encircled us, preventing any chance of escape. Maybe you do not care, in which case, an apology is useless."[15]

The Peers Inquiry noted that many soldiers did not participate in the killings. They were powerless to stop the killing or overturn the group agency permitted by their chain of command. During My Lai one private intentionally, or accidently, shot himself, in the foot to avoid participation.[16] Among these soldiers was one they nicknamed the "Chicken Farmer," who decided that surviving combat was his main mission after he witnessed his leaders go uncorrected after mistreating Vietnamese civilians. The panel described the Chicken Farmer's behavior at My Lai. "He knew that they were wrong, but refused to become involved, because of his earlier experiences and his lack of faith in his leaders. Thus the basic humanitarian instincts of this soldier . . . were suppressed, leaving him confused and frustrated."[17]

This suppression of conscience was temporary for some. After leaving Vietnam, some participants reported the killings, among those were Army photographer Ron Haeberle. He released his official photographs to the press. Door Gunner Ron Ridenhour released to the public his own letters to congress and Pentagon leaders. First Lieutenant Tran Ngoc Tran, Army Republic of South Vietnam, was one of the few officers to immediately report the incident to his direct superior. In his My Lai report he stated, "Only one American was killed by the VC, however the allies killed near 500 civilians in retaliation. Really an atrocious incident if it cannot be called an act of insane violence. Request that you intervene on behalf of the people."[18]

One junior leader, Warrant Officer Hugh Thompson, directly intervened to stop the killing. While flying support for the My Lai mission, Thompson observed groups of dead civilians on the ground, and on two separate occasions landed his helicopter to directly intervene to protect

14. McDaniel, "William Calley Apologizes."

15. King, "Reunion at Site of My Lai Massacre."

16. Peers, *My Lai Inquiry*, 178. However, there is also evidence that this private willfully participated in the killings as part of a larger group. See Lindsay, "Something Dark and Bloody."

17. Peers, *My Lai Inquiry*, 159.

18. Ibid., 279.

lives. Thompson confronted two officers (probably Calley and Brooks). He used his small helicopter to remove a limited number of wounded civilians from the village, and he called for additional helicopters to transport villagers to safety. Thompson also ordered his crew to fire upon troops if they witnessed soldiers killing villagers. Like Lieutenant Tran, he reported the killings to his chain of command. Thompson's reports and actions became key testimony during the inquiry and later trial of Medina and Calley.

Thompson was a pilot and not subject to all the risks of ground combat. But his moral reasoning reveals the moral senses that controlled his competence under fire. Like Medina, he had heard the same reports of civilians injuring and killing soldiers. Unlike Medina, when asked about how to respond to this type of insurgency, he said, "My answer to stop something like that from happening is not to kill every three year old in the country. There has got to be a better way."[19] Along with his crew, Thompson was later awarded the Soldiers' Medal for actions in saving civilian lives at My Lai.[20]

In spite of his honorable conduct, Thompson continued to live with moral dissonance. At first, some of his fellow soldiers considered him a traitor, and he changed his first name to "Buck" in order to avoid public association with his participation at My Lai. After the war, he served as a career soldier while struggling with alcohol and marriage issues linked to his involvement at My Lai.[21] Over time, Thompson began sharing his experience with groups of young soldiers, believing, "If I can go somewhere to a group like this or even younger and impress just one person to make the right decision, it'll be worth it."[22]

In 1998 Thompson returned to My Lai with one member of his crew to meet with survivors from the village. He received a different response than Private Shiel. Some villagers thanked him for his actions, but one woman wanted to know why the Americans killed the villagers and why Thompson was different?[23] He answered, "I saved the people because I wasn't taught to murder and kill. I can't answer for the people who took

---

19. This quote can be found in two sources: Thompson, *Moral Courage in Combat*, 8; Anderson and Kohn, "Return to Vietnam."

20. The Soldier's Medal is awarded to any person of the Armed Forces of the United States or of a friendly foreign nation who, while serving in any capacity with the United States distinguishes him/her self by heroism not involving actual conflict with an enemy.

21. Bilton, "Hugh Thompson."

22. Anderson and Kohn, "Return to My Lai."

23. A third crew member, Glenn Andreotta, was killed shortly after My Lai. At My Lai Andreotta left the aircraft and entered a ditch filled with bodies to rescue a child. In 1998 he was posthumously awarded the Soldiers Medal along with Thompson and Colburn for their actions in saving the lives of some villagers.

part in it. I apologize for the ones that did. I just wished we could have helped more people that day."[24]

Thompson's response demonstrates moral dissonance between what he wished would have happened and his perceptions of what did happen. Throughout his life, he maintained a high sense of fidelity to the values and standards he displayed at My Lai. After My Lai, he continued to own a moral sense of responsibility and accountability for the criminal suffering caused by his command. His apology to the villagers conveyed the personal burden that made his intent sincere, but incomplete. His rank probably allowed him to exercise greater maturity and efficacy than the junior troops trapped within a chain of command, yet he continued to suffer moral dissonance from what he couldn't prevent. At one of his last public presentations before a class of young Marine officers, he described the brutal injuries troops inflicted upon villagers, and told the group, "I personally wish I was a big enough man to say I forgive them [the troops at My Lai], but I swear to God I can't."[25]

My Lai is a good example of bad moral agency and failed directed conscientious vocation. Direct mission orders and commander intents granted permissions for troops to disregard the known rules of engagement and the general orders that applied to all soldiers deployed in Vietnam.[26] In doing so, they created a rogue mentality that stifled moral senses and removed any restraints upon the lethal skills their troops use to commit cumulative carnage. Without these orders, most of these warriors probably wouldn't have killed, and they might have been empowered to control any individual criminal behavior. My Lai is a horrific tragedy because soldiers doing the "right thing" could have prevented what happened. It is not difficult to understand how the criminal conduct at My Lai would lead to the betrayal and violation of soldiers' character and a corruption of their vocational competence. However, can this same betrayal and violation happen within a chain of command where great care is taken to follow public law and ethical practice in issuing mission orders? Perhaps yes, if these orders occur in morally "gray" contexts where professional soldiers cannot ignore their moral senses and do not get to selectively choose their participation.

24. Anderson and Kohn, "Return to My Lai."

25. Ibid.

26. All soldiers serving in Vietnam received training on following these rules and orders. They also carried pocket cards containing these rules and orders. To see the contents of these cards, see Peers, *My Lai Inquiry*, 260–67. For a comparison with a current rules of engagement card, see "Rules of Engagement for US Military Forces in Iraq," https://www.hrw.org/reports/2003/usa1203/11.htm.

Drone Warfare

The use of unmanned aerial vehicles (UAVs or drones) to target and kill enemy combatants presents many challenges for the military that result in ethical and moral dilemmas for soldiers. Some people categorize these targeting practices as extrajudicial assassinations. Others categorize them as proportional responses against legitimate combatants. A recent movie, *Eye in the Sky*, captures many of these dilemmas as the actors present the cross-cultural story of a targeting decision from four perspectives: (1) the political/strategic national command authority, (2) the operational mission command center, (3) the tactical team who executes the mission, and (4) the targeted people.[27] The storyline moves beyond political policy and technology to present the ethical and moral wrestling that happens within individuals and groups as they struggle with the principles, utility, situation, and virtues that influence their mission decisions, command relationships, and self-perceptions. Each of these wrestling matches is caused by moral senses informing soldiers' perceptions, judgments, and conduct.

Drone warfare does not have the clean or sterile effects that some believe, and these effects place soldiers at moral risk. The use of drones for targeted killing presents political and legal issues that are beyond the scope of this book. However, these political and legal issues occur within the morally gray areas in the operational environment. This ambiguity does not constrain national command authority from making its mission decisions. Each strategic level command to deploy a drone to make a kill presents the tactical level soldier-operators with unique ethical and moral dilemmas that affect their character and competence. These moral dilemmas are linked with operational limits. First, technology contributes to a false sense of security whereby leaders believe that they can see everything, hear everything, and know everything.[28] Second, drone technology includes guidance systems and optics that provide extremely accurate targeting, while creating a false sense of control where leaders believe the intended outcome will be the achieved outcome. Third, this false sense of security and control is contested within the space where the enemy and noncombatant civilians have a "real-time" vote, the effects of which can rapidly alter the situation and the nature of targeting decisions. Fourth, drones deploy ordinance that has a blast radius that can injure unintended noncombatants, notwithstanding accurate targeting. The combination of these factors creates a "false positive" targeting decision with which, even if the command decision seems

---

27. Hood, *Eye in the Sky*.

28. Major General James Poss, quoted in Chatterjee, "American Drone Operators."

legitimate and clear, operators cannot guarantee avoidance of unintended consequences. These complex situations place unique moral risks upon soldiers that are different from traditional combat.

Traditionally, proximity to a targeted person places a higher psychological and moral risk upon infantry versus pilots or artillerymen who kill quickly from a distance.[29] Infantry see their victims and dwell within the kill zones of their operations, so they make decisions to kill at the personal and tactical level. The decision to kill a target from a UAV is often made from a distance at strategic command levels. The execution of these orders occurs at the tactical level where drone pilots and sensor operators experience the psychological and moral effects from close combat. They relay data, but they do not make the decision to kill, they only execute the order. However, they are not immune from the effects from their decisions. Drone crews are snipers who linger over their targets to watch them prior to killing them. They watch them die, and then continue to watch over them in order to assess the damage. They are agents in every moral sense of the word.

At the strategic level, retired Air Force General and former director of the Central Intelligence Agency Michael V. Hayden describes the moral tension that exists in a targeting decision to kill a high-value enemy based upon strong intelligence and the assessment of unintended, noncombatant casualties due to unforeseen circumstances.

> Knowing what we know, there will be no explaining our inaction after the next attack. We tried to get better. Carefully reviewing video of one successful strike, we could discern—as a GBU [a type of ordnance] was already hurtling toward an arms cache—a frightened woman responding to another weapon that had just detonated. She was running with young children square into the path of the incoming bomb, and they were killed. We realized, once our after-action review was done, that we needed to put even more eyes on targets as they were being struck to try to avoid any future civilian casualties. And unmanned aerial vehicles carrying precision weapons and guided by powerful intelligence offer a proportional and discriminating response when response is necessary. Civilians have died, but in my firm opinion, the death toll from terrorist attacks would have been much higher if we had not taken action. What we need here is a "dial, not a switch."[30]

29. Grossman, *On Killing*, Kindle loc. 2235–60.
30. Hayden, "Drone Warfare."

Hayden refers to a "dial" as a range of proportionate responses that allow leaders multiple options to use the technology for discriminate targeting. Earlier we discussed this "dial" as the product of soldiers' moral senses of maturity and efficacy that allow them to develop the capacity to operate within the morally "gray" areas they experience as the "fog of war" or the "chaos of combat." The "dial" has different ethical and moral effects throughout the chain of command.

From the operational to tactical levels, mission command orders allow Airmen to focus their attention upon their vocational competence to deploy drones rather than the moral consequences upon their character. This focus upon the moral sense of fidelity to one's mission and unit diffuses responsibility and accountability for what happens after the attack. The commander of a Predator Squadron, Lieutenant Colonel Mark McCurley, describes standards for the *esprit de corps*, competence, and character of his Airmen after completing a significant UAV mission. "The young men and women standing on the tarmac listening to the JOC [Joint Operations Center] commander were the ones to do it. Their actions have changed the face of war forever. They remain anonymous by choice. They fiercely defend one another, their communities, and the nation while watching over our heroes on the ground. They ask for no reward beyond the simple acknowledgement of the contributions to our overall war effort."[31]

This positive focus is possible because these Airmen do not have a "proximal" link to the target. However, sensor imagery between aircraft and control stations creates a tangible image that closes proximity and reinforces drone crews' moral senses of responsibility and accountability. Lieutenant Colonel Bruce Black, a former Air Force drone pilot states, "A Predator pilot has been watching his target, knows them intimately, knows where they are, and knows what's around them."[32] In this proximity, drone crews become acutely aware of the existing moral boundaries linking their vocation with their humanity. Airman Heather Linebaugh, a former drone imagery analyst speaks about the moral effects from her proximity to targets. "How many women and children have you seen incinerated by a Hellfire missile? How many men have you seen crawl across a field, trying to make it to the nearest compound for help while bleeding out from severed legs? . . . When you are exposed to it over and over again it becomes like a small video, embedded in your head, forever on repeat, causing psychological pain and suffering that many people will hopefully never experience."[33]

31. McCurley and Mauer, *Hunter Killer*, 343.

32. Chatterjee, "American Drone Operators Are Quitting."

33. Ibid.

Drone crews operate under a national command authority that politically, ethically and legally legitimizes their warrior skills. However, their moral conscience may not accept the vocational consequences. Thus, the moral senses active within their practice of DCV generates a moral dissonance that unites them with soldiers like Hugh Thompson. Where are the points of inflection within DCV where men and women believe they are acting like soldiers, instead of like warriors or pirates?

Unlike My Lai, the above Airmen are not placed in a position where they are infantrymen ordered to participate in an obvious criminal operation that nullifies everything they have learned as professional soldiers. However, similar to My Lai, these men and women voluntarily serve in a position where they must make choices within morally gray situations where they do not control the orders, the targeting, or the outcomes. Still, they must deal with the moral consequences.

The Air Force has published a series of studies on drone pilot stress. These studies conclude that as much as half of these men and women experience high operational stress and exhibit "high anxiety, depression, or stress severe enough to affect them in their personal lives."[34] One pilot described his condition, "It's like when your engine temperature gauge is running just below the red area on your car's dashboard, but instead of slowing down and relieving the stress on the engine, you put the pedal to the floor."[35] The resulting mental and emotional fatigue produces symptoms of post-traumatic stress.

However, these studies did not ask drone crews the reasons *why* they felt this way, or the moral reasoning behind their racing thoughts. Drone crew member Brandon Bryant's narrative provides a description of his growing moral dissonance forming after participating in a targeted killing. "It was horrifying to know how easy it [the targeted killing] was. I felt like a coward because I was halfway across the world and the guy never even knew I was there. I felt like I was haunted by a legion of the dead. My physical health was gone, and my mental health was crumbled. I was in so much pain I was ready to eat a bullet myself."[36]

The influence of moral dissonance upon Bryant's life provides a basis for including moral injury as a vocational risk affecting drone crews. Like a warrior, Bryant acted with competence and killed his enemy. However, moral dissonance from this event leaves him feeling less like a soldier and more like a pirate, even to the point of suicide. Bryant is not simply

34. Ibid.
35. Ibid.
36. Ibid.

experiencing post-traumatic stress, he is dealing with a moral injury that negates his self-worth. This injury is an extension of the DCV that braids his professional character with his humanity. Like Hugh Thompson and the other soldiers mentioned throughout this book, Bryant is voicing a moral sense of fidelity that binds him to the values he uses to own responsibility and accountability of his moral agency. Also, he is using moral senses of maturity and efficacy to process the lingering soul sorrow expressed in his war narratives. In doing so, he is naming the source of his moral dissonance and taking the first steps necessary on a healing journey. This is a prime example of the assimilation and accommodation necessary to transform a harmful combat narrative into a healing narrative that re-engages veterans into life after combat.

Bibliography

Adams, Sarah. "Cost of War: Veterans Remember USS Indianapolis, Shark Attacks." *NPR.org.* July 26, 2015. http://www.npr.org/2015/07/26/425904134/cost-of-war-veterans-remember-uss-indianapolis-shark-attacks.

Aiuppa-Denning, Laura, et al. *Preventing Psychological Disorders in Service Members and Their Families: An Assessment of Programs.* Washington, DC: National Academies, 2014.

Alda, Alan, dir. "Goodbye, Farewell, and Amen." *M*A*S*H*, season 11, episode 16. February 28, 1983.

Allen, Scott. "Gettysburg at 50: The Great Reunion of 1913." *Mentalfloss.com.* July 3, 2013. http://mentalfloss.com/article/28128/gettysburg-great-reunion-1913.

Allman, Mark J. *Who Would Jesus Kill? War, Peace, and the Christian Tradition.* Winona, MN: Anselm Academic, 2008.

Ambrose, Stephen E. *Band of Brothers.* New York: Simon & Schuster, 1992.

American Psychological Association. "The Critical Need for Mental Health Professionals Trained to Treat Post-Traumatic Stress Disorder and Traumatic Brain Injury." http://www.apa.org/about/gr/issues/military/critical-need.aspx.

Anderson, Jon R. "Warfighter's Paradox." *Air Force Times*, June 30, 2014.

Anderson, Robert, and David Kohn. "Return to My Lai." *CBSNews.com.* December 6, 1999. http://www.cbsnews.com/news/return-to-my-lai.

Aquinas, Thomas. *Summa Theologica.* Translated by Fathers of the English Dominican Province. 5 vols. Westminster, MD: Christian Classics, 1948.

Armstrong, Karen. *Fields of Blood.* New York: Knopf, 2014.

Augustine. *Against the Academics.* Translated by John O'Meara. Ancient Christian Writers 12. Westminster, UK: Newman, 1951.

———. *The City of God, Books I–VII.* Translated by Demetrius B. Zema and Gerald G. Walsh. Fathers of the Church 8. Washington, DC: Catholic University of America Press, 2008.

———. *The City of God, Books VIII–XVI.* Translated by Demetrius B. Zema and Gerald G. Walsh. Fathers of the Church 14. Washington, DC: Catholic University of America Press, 2008.

———. *The Immortality of the Soul.* Translated by Ludwig Schopp. Fathers of the Church 4. Washington, DC: Catholic University of America Press, 2002.

———. *On the Trinity.* In *Nicene & Post Nicene Fathers*, vol. 3, edited by Phillip Schaff. Grand Rapids: Eerdmans, 1890.

———. *The Retractions.* Translated by Mary Inez Bogan. Fathers of the Church 60. Washington, DC: Catholic University of America Press, 1999.

Bachelor, David L. "Death Shadow: Christianity and Posttraumatic Stress." PhD diss., Trinity Theological Seminary, 2012.

———. *The Sacraments of War: The Sword and the Warrior Wash*. San Antonio: published by the author, 2014.

Balch, Dennis R., and Robert W. Armstrong. "Ethical Marginality: The Icarus Syndrome and Banality of Wrongdoing." *Journal of Business Ethics* 92 (2010) 291–303.

Barclay, William. *The Gospel of Luke*. Philadelphia: Westminster, 1975.

Barnes, Christopher M., and Keith Leavitt. "Moral Disengagements: When Will Good Soldiers Do Bad Things?" *Military Review* 90 (2010) 46–51.

Barrett, Clark C. *Finding "the Right Way": Toward an Army Institutional Ethic*. Strategic Studies Institute. Carlisle, PA: Government Printing Office, 2012.

Bartone, Paul, et al. "To Build Resilience: Leader Influence on Mental Illness." *Defense Horizons* 69 (2009) 1–8.

Battaglia, Bryan B. "The Enlisted Force and Profession of Arms." *JFQ* 62 (2011) 18–19.

Bauernfiend, O. "Strateoumai." In *Theological Dictionary of the New Testament*, edited by Gerhard Kittel and Gerhard Freidrich. Abridged in 1 vol. Translated and edited by Geoffrey Bromily. Grand Rapids: Eerdmans, 1985.

Bell, Daniel M., Jr. "The Drone Wars and Just War." *Journal of Lutheran Ethics* 14 (2014) n.p. https://www.elca.org/JLE/Articles/71.

———. *Just War as Christian Discipleship: Recentering the Tradition in the Church rather than in the State*. Grand Rapids: Brazos, 2009. Kindle edition.

Bigelow, Kathryn, dir. *The Hurt Locker*. Written by Mark Boal. Film. Voltage Pictures, 2008.

Biggar, Nigel. *In Defense of War*. Oxford: Oxford University Press, 2013.

Bilton, Michael. "Hugh Thompson." *Guardian*, January, 11, 2006. https://www.theguardian.com/news/2006/jan/11/guardianobituaries.usa.

Bolt Ernest, ed. "Vietnam Veteran John Kerry's Testimony before the Senate Foreign Relations Committee, April 22, 1971." https://facultystaff.richmond.edu/~ebolt/history398/JohnKerryTestimony.html.

Bonhoeffer, Dietrich. *Ethics*. Minneapolis: Fortress, 2005.

———. *God Is in the Manger: Reflections on Advent and Christmas*. Edited by Janna Riess. Translated by O. C. Dean Jr. Louisville: Westminster John Knox, 2010.

Bonura, Dean. *Beyond Trauma: Hope and Healing for Warriors; A Guide for Pastoral Caregivers on PTSD*. Bloomington, IN: WestBow, 2016. Kindle edition.

Boros, Crina, et al. "Analysis: A Few Thousand Dollars—the Price of Life for Civilians Killed in War Zones." Thomson Reuters Foundation News, July 16, 2014. http://news.trust.org//item/20140716123155-r35zd.

Bradley, J. Peter. "When Loyalty to Comrades Conflicts with Military Duty." In *Aspects of Leadership: Ethics, Law, and Spirituality*, edited by Carroll Connoly and Paulo Tripodi, 111–36. Quantico, VA: Marine Corps University Press, 2012.

Bradley, James. *Flags of Our Fathers: Heroes of Iwo Jima*. New York: Delacourt, 2001.

Brock, Rita Nakashima, and Gabriella Lettini. *Soul Repair: Recovering from Moral Injury after War*. New York: Random House, 2012. Kindle edition.

Brooks, David. "The Moral Injury." *New York Times*, February 17, 2015. https://www.nytimes.com/2015/02/17/opinion/david-brooks-the-moral-injury.html.

Brotherton, Marcus. *We Who Are Alive and Remain: Untold Stories from the Band of Brothers*. New York: Berkeley Caliber, 2009.

Bumiller, Elisabeth. "Air Force Drone Operators Report High Level of Stress." *New York Times*, December 18, 2011. http://www.nytimes.com/2011/12/19/world/asia/air-force-drone-operators-show-high-levels-of-stress.html.

Burtness, James M. *Consequences: Morality, Ethics, and the Future.* Minneapolis: Fortress, 1999.

Bury, Patrick. *Call Sign Hades.* London: Simon and Schuster, 2010.

Carey, Benedict. "Study Finds Suicidal Tendencies Are Evident Before Deployment." *New York Times*, March 3, 2014.

Carroll, James. "A Nation's PTSD: Decades After the Vietnam War, the Wounds Are Still Very Real." *Boston Globe*, August 19, 2013.

Cartwright, Mark. "Centurion." *Ancient History Encyclopedia.* July 4, 2014. http://www.ancient.eu/Centurion.

Caster, Brian. "Still Fighting, and Dying, in the Forever War." *New York Times*, March 9, 2017. https://www.nytimes.com/2017/03/09/opinion/sunday/still-fighting-and-dying-in-the-forever-war.html.

Caswell, Bryan. "Honor of Manhood: Joshua Lawrence Chamberlain and Notions of Martial Masculinity." *Gettysburg College Journal of the Civil War Era* 6 (2016). http://cupola.gettysburg.edu/cgi/viewcontent.cgi?article=1064&context=gcjcwe.

CBS News. "A Medal of Honor Recipient's Ongoing Burden." *CBSNews.com.* May 1, 2016. http://www.cbsnews.com/news/a-medal-of-honor-recipients-ongoing-burden.

Chamberlain, Joshua Lawrence. "Speech at the Dedication of the Second 20th Maine Monument at Gettysburg." October 3, 1889. http://www.joshualawrencechamberlain.com/maineatgettysburg.php.

———. "The Two Souls of Man and Their Relation to His Deeds of Heroism." *Springfield Republican*, June 1, 1897. http://www.joshualawrencechamberlain.com/twosouls.php.

Chatterjee, Pratrap. "American Drone Operators Are Quitting in Record Numbers." *Nation*, March 5, 2015. http://www.thenation.com/article/american-drone-operators-are-quitting-record-numbers.

Chein, Jason M., et al. "Peers Increase Adolescent Risk Taking by Enhancing Activity in the Brain's Reward Circuitry." *Developmental Science* 14 (2011) 1–10.

Chief of Defense Staff. *Duty with Honour: The Profession of Arms in Canada 2009.* Ontario: Canadian Defense Academy Press, 2009.

Chu, Judy Y., and Carol Gilligan. *When Boys Become Boys.* New York: New York University Press, 2014.

Clark, James. "5 Badass Quotes from Marine General Mattis." *Task & Purpose*, June 24, 2016. http://taskandpurpose.com/5-badass-quotes-marine-general-james-mattis.

Collins, Jim. *Good to Great.* New York: Harper Business, 2001.

Collins, Tim. "Tim Collins' Iraq War Speech in Full." *Telegraph*, October 19, 2008. http://www.telegraph.co.uk/comment/3562917/Colonel-Tim-Collins-Iraq-war-speech-in-full.html.

Cooper-White, Pamela. "Reenactors: Theological and Psychological Reflections on 'Core Selves,' Multiplicity, and the Sense of Cohesion." In *In Search of Self: Interdisciplinary Perspectives on Personhood*, edited by J. Wentzel Van Huyssteen and Erik P. Wiebe, 141–62. Grand Rapids: Eerdmans, 2011.

Couch, Dick. *A Tactical Ethic.* Annapolis: Naval Institute Press, 2010.

Couch, Dick, and William Doyle. *Navy SEALs: Their Untold Story*. New York: Morris, 2014. Kindle edition.

Currier, Joseph M., et al. "How Do Morally Injurious Events Occur?" *Traumatology* 21 (2015) 1–11.

———. "The Role of Moral Emotions in Military Trauma." *Review of General Psychology* 18 (2014) 249–62.

Davies, Roy W. *Service in the Roman Army*. Edited by David Breeze and Valerie A. Maxfield. New York: Columbia University Press, 1989.

Debuse, Mark R. *The Citizen-Officer Ideal: A Historical and Literary Inquiry*. Vice Admiral James B. Stockdale Center for Ethical Leadership Occasional Papers. Annapolis: US Naval Academy, 2008.

Dempsey, Martin E. *America's Military: A Profession of Arms*. Washington, DC: Joint Chiefs of Staff, 2010.

———. *Joint Education White Paper*. Washington, DC: Joint Chiefs of Staff, 2012.

———. *Mission Command White Paper*. Washington, DC: Joint Chiefs of Staff, 2012.

Denton-Borhaug, Kelly. "Sacrifice, Moral Injury, and the Work of Healing after War." *Caring Connections* 10 (2013) 24–27. http://www.lutheranservices.org/sites/default/files/images/pdfs-CaringConnections/CaringConnections_Winter2013.pdf.

Dewey, Larry. *War and Redemption*. Burlington: Ashgate, 2004.

Dokoupil, Tony, and Alison Snyder. "A New Theory of PTSD and Veterans: Moral Injury." *Newsweek*, December 3, 2012.

Doolin, Drew T. "Healing Hidden Wounds: The Mental Health Crisis of America's Veterans." *JFQ* 54 (2009) 74–80. http://www.dtic.mil/dtic/tr/fulltext/u2/a515579.pdf.

Dreazen, Yochi. *The Invisible War: Love and Loss in an Era of Endless War*. New York: Crown, 2014.

Dreschler, K. D., et al. "An Exploration of the Viability and Usefulness of the Construct of Moral Injury in War Veterans." *Traumatology* 17 (2011) 8–13.

Eberle, J., and Rick Rubel, "Religious Conviction in the Profession of Arms." *Journal of Military Ethics* 11 (2012) 171–85.

Eckman, Nathan. "What It Means to Be a Veteran without the Experience of War." *War Horse News*, August 12, 2016. http://taskandpurpose.com/means-veteran-without-experience-war.

Esty-Kendall, Jud, producer. "The Death That Ended His War: 'I Felt That . . . I Failed My Family.'" *NPR.org*, November 6, 2015. http://www.npr.org/2015/11/06/454719333/the-death-that-ended-his-war-i-felt-that-i-failed-my-family.

Fadiman, Anne. *The Spirit Catches You and You Fall Down: A Hmong Child, Her American Doctors, and the Collision of Two Cultures*. New York: Farrar, Straus and Giroux, 1997.

Fick, Nathaniel. *One Bullet Away*. Boston: Houghton Mifflin, 2005.

Fifteenth Alabama Company G. "One Last Battle." http://15thalabamaavi.tripod.com/id10.html.

Figley, Charles, and William P. Nash. *Combat Stress Injury: Theory, Research, and Management*. Psychological Stress Series. New York: Taylor and Francis, 2011.

Finkel, David. *The Good Soldiers*. New York: Crichton, 2009.

———. *Thank You for Your Service*. New York: Picador, 2013. Kindle edition.

Fisher, Michael P., and Terry L. Schell. *The Role and Importance of the "D" in PTSD*. Washington, DC: Rand, 2013.

Foster, Gregory D. "One War at a Time." *America Magazine*, November 17, 2008. https://www.americamagazine.org/issue/676/article/one-war-time.

Fowler, James. *Stages of Faith: The Psychology of Human Development and the Quest for Meaning*. New York: HarperOne, 1995.

Fox, Ashley. "Alejandro Villanueva's Long NFL Path." *ESPN.com*, May 22, 2014. http://www.espn.com/nfl/story/_/page/hotread140522/army-veteran-alejandro-villanueva-pursues-nfl-dream-philadelphia-eagles-three-tours-afghanistan.

Frame, Tom, ed. "The Influence of Religious Conviction." In *Moral Injury: Unseen Wounds in an Age of Barbarism*, 235–50. Sydney: University of New South Wales Press Press, 2015.

———. Introduction to *Moral Injury: Unseen Wounds in An Age of Barbarism*, 1–17. Sydney: University of New South Wales Press, 2015.

———. Postscript to *Moral Injury: Unseen Wounds in An Age of Barbarism*, 251–61. Sydney: University of New South Wales Press Press, 2015.

Frederick, Jim. *Black Hearts: One Platoon's Descent into Madness in Iraq's Triangle of Death*. New York: Broadway Paperbacks, 2010.

Friedman, Matti. *Pumpkinflowers: A Soldier's Story*. Chapel Hill: Alogonquin, 2016. Kindle edition.

Fromm, Peter D. "Warriors, the Army Ethos, and the Sacred Trust of Soldiers." *Military Review*, special edition (2010) 19–26. http://www.armyupress.army.mil/Portals/7/military-review/Archives/English/MilitaryReview_20100930ER_art006.pdf.

Fromm, Peter, and Douglas Pryer Cutright. "The Myths We Soldiers Tell Ourselves (and the Harm These Myths Do)." *Military Review* (2013) 57–68.

Fussell, Paul. *Wartime*. New York: Oxford University Press, 1989.

Gambrill, Guy. "Combat Veterans and Criminality: The Case of Audie Murphy." USJAG blog, May 10, 2016. http://www.usjag.org/combat-veterans-criminality-case-audie-murphy/#sthash.qfeXCkri.dpuf.

Gentile, Mary C. *Giving Voice to Values*. New Haven: Yale University Press, 2010. Kindle edition.

George, Rose. *Ninety Percent of Everything*. New York: Metropolitan, 2013.

Gibbons, Thomas J. "An Overview of Ethics Instruction in Senior-Level Professional Military Education." Paper presented to the International Society of Military Ethics Annual Conference, University of Notre Dame, October 2016.

Gibbons-Neff, Thomas. "Haunted by Their Decisions in War." *Washington Post*, March 8, 2015.

Gibson, David, and Judy Malana. "Spiritual Injuries: Wounds of the American Warrior on the Battlefield of the Soul." In *Aspects of Leadership: Ethics, Law, and Spirituality*, edited by Carroll Connelly and Paulo Tripodi, 343–76. Quantico, VA: Marine Corps University Press, 2012.

Gilligan, Carol. *In a Different Voice: Psychological Theory and Women's Development*. Cambridge: Harvard University Press, 1993.

———. *Joining the Resistance*. Cambridge: Polity, 2011.

Goleman, Daniel, et al. *Primal Leadership: Realizing the Power of Emotional Intelligence*. Boston: Harvard Business Review Press, 2013.

Gompert David C., and Richard L. Kugler. "Lee's Mistake: Learning from the Decision to Order Pickett's Charge." *Defense Horizons* 54 (2006) 1–8.

Gourevich, Philip. *We Wish to Inform You that Tomorrow We Will Be Killed with Our Families*. New York: Picador USA, 1998.

Gray, J. Glenn. *The Warriors: Reflections on Men in Battle*. New York: Harcourt and Brace, 1959.

Groenewald, Sonja. "And He Never Came Home." *Lutheran*, March 21, 1990, 14–16.

Grossman, David. *On Combat: The Psychology and Physiology of Deadly Conflict in War and in Peace*. 3rd ed. Belleville: PPCT Research Publications, 2012. Kindle edition.

————. *On Killing: The Psychological Cost of Learning to Kill in War and Society*. Boston: Little, Brown, 1999. Kindle edition.

Guntzel, Jeff Severns. "Beyond PTSD to Moral Injury." *OnBeing.org*, with Krista Tippett, March 14, 2013. https://onbeing.org/blog/beyond-ptsd-to-moral-injury.

Guntzel, Jeff Severns, et al. "Invisible Injury: Beyond PTSD." Illustrated story. *Public Insight Network*. June 21, 2013. https://www.publicinsightnetwork. org/2013/06/21/invisible-injury-beyond-ptsd-illustrated-story.

Gussow, Mel. "Anton Myrer, 73, Whose Novels Focused on War and Nostalgia." *New York Times*, January 23, 1996. https://mobile.nytimes.com/1996/01/23/arts/ anton-myrer-73-whose-novels-focused-on-war-and-nostalgia.html.

Gwinn, Christopher. "Joshua Chamberlain, Little Round Top, and the Memorial that Never Was." Gettysburg National Military Park blog. January 30, 2014. https:// npsgnmp.wordpress.com/2014/01/30/joshua-chamberlain-little-round-top-and-the-memorial-that-never-was.

Haidt, Jonathan. "The Psychology of Morality and Character Development." Public briefing for the New York University Stern School of Business, Center for the Army Profession and Ethic, n.d. Same briefing given to the Army Chief of Staff's Army Professional Annual Symposium, West Point, NY, July 30–31, 2014.

————. *The Righteous Mind: Why Good People Are Divided by Politics and Religion*. New York: Pantheon, 2012. Kindle edition.

Hall, Major Jeff. Personal interview with the author, 2014.

Hallett, Michael, "Cultivating Sailor Ethical Fitness." *Naval War College Review* 69 (2016) 93–106.

Hayden, Michael V. "Drone Warfare: Precise, Effective, Imperfect." Matt Crowe's blog, February 21, 2016. From the *New York Times* Opinion page, February 19, 2016. https://mattcroweahhha.wordpress.com/2016/02/19/drone-warfare-precise-effective-imperfect-by-michael-v-hayden.

Hersh, Seymour M. "The Scene of the Crime: A Reporter's Journey to My Lai and the Secrets of the Past." *New Yorker*, March 30, 2015. http://www.newyorker.com/ magazine/2015/03/30/the-scene-of-the-crime.

Hicks, Robert M., and Randy Petersen. *Returning Home / Practical Advice for War Veterans, Their Families, and Friends*. Grand Rapids: Revell, 1991.

Historium. "How to Become a Roman Centurion." *Historium.com* discussion forum. Posted March 17, 2012. http://historum.com/ancient-history/39373-how-become-roman-centurion.html.

Hoge, Charles W. M. D. *Once a Warrior Always a Warrior: Navigating the Transition from Combat to Home—Including Combat Stress, PTSD, and mTBI*. Guilford, CT: Globe Pequot, 2010.

Hoge, Charles W., et al. "Combat Duty in Iraq and Afghanistan, Mental Health Problems and Barriers to Care." *New England Journal of Medicine* 351 (2004) 13–22.

Holloway, Marjan, and Shannon Branlund. *Deployment Related Factors, Mental Health, and Suicide: Review of the Literature.* Bethesda: Department of Medical & Clinical Psychology Uniformed Services, University of the Health Sciences, 2011.

Holmes, Richard. *Acts of War: The Behavior of Men in Battle.* New York: Free Press, 1985.

Honig, Jan Willem, and Norbert Both. *Srebrenica: Record of a War Crime.* New York: Penguin, 1997.

Hood, Galvin, director. *Eye in the Sky.* Film. Written by Guy Hibbert. Entertainment One / Raindog Films, 2016.

Huang, Hsin-Hsin. "Combat Exposure, Agency, Perceived Threat, Guilt, and Posttraumatic Stress Disorder among Iraq and Afghanistan War Veterans." PhD diss., University of Missouri–St. Louis, 2010.

Huang, Hsin-Hsin, and Susan Kashubeck-West. "Exposure, Agency, Perceived Threat, and Guilt as Predictors of Posttraumatic Stress Disorder in Veterans." *Journal of Counseling & Development* 93 (2015) 3–13.

Huntley, [Staff Sergeant]. "Integrity Case Exercise." Interview, 2014. West Point, Center for the Army Profession and Ethic. http://cape.army.mil/case-studies/vcs-single. php?id=65&title=ssg-huntley.

Isaac, Logan. "For What It's Worth: Recasting Just War Theory as a Pastoral Framework." *Syndicate* 2 (2015). https://syndicate.network/symposia/theology/killing-from-the-inside-out/#logan-isaac.

Jaffe, G. "Criminals or Victims?" *Washington Post*, September 21, 2014. http://www. washingtonpost.com/sf/national/2014/09/20/criminal-or-victim/?utm_term=. b09026b3fd03.

Janoff-Bulman, Ronnie. *Shattered Assumptions: Towards a New Psychology of Trauma.* NewYork: Free Press, 1992.

Jelinek, Pauline. "'I'm a Monster': Some Veterans Carry 'Moral Injuries' of Guilt." *Seattle Times*, February 23, 2013. http://www.seattletimes.com/seattle-news/health/im-a-monster-some-veterans-carry-moral-injuries-of-guilt.

Jensen, Wollom A., and James M. Childs Jr. *Moral Warriors, Moral Wounds: The Ministry of the Christian Ethic.* Eugene, OR: Cascade, 2016.

Jones, Serene. *Trauma and Grace: Theology in a Ruptured World.* Louisville: Presbyterian, 2009.

Jones, Tony. *The New Christians: Dispatches for the Emergent Frontier.* San Francisco: Josey-Bass, 2008.

———. *The Sacred Way.* Grand Rapids: Zondervan, 2005.

Jordan, Bryant. "Army Surgeon General: Sleepy Soldiers as Impaired as Drunk Soldiers." *Military.com*, October 15, 2014. http://www.military.com/daily-news/2014/10/15/army-surgeon-general-sleepy-soldiers-as-impaired-as-drunk.html.

Junger, Sebastian. *War.* New York: Twelve, 2010.

Kahneman, Daniel. *Thinking, Fast and Slow.* New York: Farrar, Straus, and Giroux, 2011.

Kaplan, Susan. "The Military Is Going Beyond PTSD to Help Soldiers Who Have Suffered a Moral Injury." Public Radio International, *The World*, December 27, 2013. https://www.pri.org/stories/2013-12-27/military-going-beyond-ptsd-help-soldiers-who-have-suffered-moral-injury.

Kavanagh, Jennifer. *Stress and Performance: A Review of the Literature and Its Applicability to the Military.* Washington, DC: Rand, 2005.

Kashtan, Miki. "Moral Dissonance." *Psychology Today*, July 27, 2013. https://www.psychologytoday.com/blog/acquired-spontaneity/201307/moral-dissonance.

Kass, Leon R. "The Wisdom of Repugnance." *New Republic*, June 2, 1997. https://web.stanford.edu/~mvr2j/sfsu09/extra/Kass2.pdf.

Kaurin, Pauline. "The Moral Drill Sergeant: On Teaching the Grunts to Do the Right Thing." *International Society for Military Ethics*. 2000. http://isme.tamu.edu/JSCOPE00/Kaurin00.html.

Keegan, John. *The Face of Battle*. New York: Penguin, 1976.

Kem, Jack. *The Use of the "Ethical Triangle" in Military Decision Making*. Fort Leavenworth: US Army Command and General Staff College, 2006. https://www.cgscfoundation.org/wp-content/uploads/2016/04/Kem-UseoftheEthicalTriangle.pdf.

Kennedy, Kelly. "All the Warning Signs Were There, But Could Anyone Have Saved 1st Sgt. Jeff McKinney?" *Army Times*, June 9, 2008. https://www.cross-x.com/topic/35653-the-tragic-story-of-1st-sgt-jeff-mckinney.

———. *They Fought for Each Other: The Triumph and Tragedy of the Hardest Hit Unit in Iraq*. New York: Saint Martin's, 2010.

Kidder, Rushworth. *How Good People Make Tough Choices*. New York: HarperCollins, 2009.

Kime, Patricia. "5 Questions: Philosopher Explores Warriors' Moral Anguish." *MilitaryTimes.com*, November 16, 2015. http://www.militarytimes.com/story/military/benefits/health-care/2015/11/16/questions-philosopher-explores-warriors-moral-anguish/75709512.

King, Tim. "Reunion at Site of My Lai Massacre: Survivor Duc Tran Van and Photographer Ron Haeberle." *Salem News*, July 12, 2012. http://www.salem-news.com/articles/july142012/my-lay-duc-haeberle-tk.php.

Kingseed, Cole C. *Conversations with Major Dick Winters*. New York: Berkeley Caliber, 2014.

Kirkland, Faris. "Combat Psychological Trauma." *Military Review* 78 (1998) 47–49.

Klann, Gene. *Crisis Leadership: Using Military Lessons, Organizational Experiences, and the Power of Influence* . . . Greensboro, NC: Center for Creative Leadership, 2003.

Klay, Phil. *Redeployment*. New York: Penguin, 2014.

Klebold, Sue. *A Mother's Reckoning*. New York: Broadway, 2016. Kindle edition.

Kolb, Robert, and Robert Wengert, eds. *The Book of Concord: The Confessions of the Evangelical Lutheran Church*. Minneapolis: Fortress, 2000.

Krakauer, Jon. *Where Men Win Glory*. New York: First Anchor, 2009.

Kroesen, Frederick J. "The Combat Soldiers' Dilemma." *Army*, January 2012.

Krueger, Gerald P. *Sustained Military Performance in Continuous Operations: Combat Fatigue, Rest and Sleep Needs*. Fort Rucker: US Army Aeromedical Research Laboratory, 1991.

Krulak, Chales C. "Message from the Commandant: Marines Don't Do That." *Marine Corps Association and Foundation*, September 1995. https://www.mca-marines.org/leatherneck/message-commandant-marines-dont-do#.

———. "The Strategic Corporal: Leadership in the Three Block War." *Marines*, January 1999. http://www.au.af.mil/au/awc/awcgate/usmc/strategic_corporal.htm.

Krulak, Victor H. *First to Fight: An Inside View of the US Marine Corps*. New York: Pocket Books, 1984.

Kudo, Timothy. "How We Learned to Kill." *New York Times*, February 27, 2015. https://www.nytimes.com/2015/03/01/opinion/sunday/how-we-learned-to-kill.html?_r=0.

Kuz, Martin. "He Left the War without the War Leaving Him." *Stars and Stripes* 6 (2014). https://www.stripes.com/army-sgt-issac-sims-left-the-war-in-iraq-but-it-didn-t-leave-him-1.311753#.WUbopcbMwnU.

Kyle, Chris, et al. *American Sniper*. New York: HarperCollins, 2012. Kindle edition.

Lagouranis, Tony, and Allen Mikaelian. *Fear Up Harsh: An Army Interrogator's Dark Journey through Iraq*. New York: NAL Caliber, 2007.

Lang, Daniel. *Casualties of War*. New York: Pocket, 1969.

Lange, Dirk. *Trauma Recalled: Liturgy, Disruption, and Theology*. Minneapolis: Fortress, 2010.

Leavitt, Keith, and Walter J. Sowden. "Automatic Ethics: What We Take for Granted Matters." *Military Review*, special edition (2010) 86–89.

Lee, Michelle Yee Hee. "The Missing Context behind the Widely Cited Statistic That There Are 22 Veteran Suicides a Day." *Washington Post*, February 4, 2015. https://www.washingtonpost.com/news/fact-checker/wp/2015/02/04/the-missing-context-behind-a-widely-cited-statistic-that-there-are-22-veteran-suicides-a-day.

Lerner, Michael. *Embracing Israel and Palestine*. Berkeley: Tikkun, 2012.

Lifton, Robert Jay. *Home from the War: Leaning from Vietnam Veterans*. New York: Other, 1973.

———. "Understanding the Traumatized Self: Imagery, Symbolization, and Transformation." In *Human Adaption to Extreme Stress: From Holocaust to Vietnam*, edited by John P Wilson et al., 7–31. New York: Plenium, 1988.

Linden, Michael, et al. *Posttraumatic Embitterment Disorder*. Cambridge: Hogrefe & Huber, 2007.

Lindsay, Drew. "'Something Dark and Bloody': What Happened at My Lai?" *Historynet.com*. August 7, 2012. http://www.historynet.com/something-dark-and-bloody-what-happened-at-my-lai.htm.

Linehan, Adam. "Why I Think Lt Clint Lorance Is a Murderer." *Task & Purpose*, February 21, 2017. http://taskandpurpose.com/think-lt-clint-lorance-murderer.

Litz, Bret, et al. *Adaptive Disclosure: A New Testament for Military Trauma, Loss, Moral Injury*. New York: Guilford, 2016.

———. "Adaptive Disclosure Talk." PowerPoint presentation and discussion. 2014. www.med.navy.mil/sites/.../1430_Litz%20Adaptive%20Disclosure%20Talk.pptx.

———. "Moral Injury and Moral Repair in War Veterans: A Preliminary Model and Intervention Strategy." *Clinical Psychology Review* 29 (2009) 696–705.

Longacre, Edward G. *Joshua Chamberlain: The Soldier and the Man*. Cambridge, MA: Da Capo, 1999.

Lloyd, James. "The Roman Army." *Ancient History Encyclopedia*. April 30, 2013. http://www.ancient.eu/Roman_Army.

Ludwig, Daniel C., and Clinton O. Longnecker. "The Bathsheba Syndrome: The Ethical Failure of Successful Leaders." *Journal of Business Ethics* 12 (1993) 265–73.

Luther, Martin. *Can a Soldier Too Be Saved?* In *Luther's Works*, edited by Helmut Lehman and Robert C Schulz, 46:93–137. Philadelphia: Fortress, 1967.

Macera, Catherine A., et al. "Posttraumatic Stress Disorder after Combat Zone Deployment among Navy and Marine Corps Men and Women." *Journal of Women's Health* 3 (2014) 495–505.

Maguen, Shira, and Brett Litz. "Moral Injury in Veterans of War." *PTSD Research Quarterly* 23 (2012) 1–4.

Makos, Adam. *A Higher Call*. New York: Berkley Caliber, 2012.

Marin, Peter. "Living in Moral Pain." VFPUK.org (Veterans for Peace UK). Originally published in *Psychology Today*, November 1981. http://vfpuk.org/2013/living-in-moral-pain-by-peter-marin.

Marlantes, Karl. *What It Is Like to Go to War*. New York: Atlantic Monthly Press, 2011.

Marshall, George C. "The Nobel Peace Prize 1953—Presentation Speech." *NobelPrize.org*, April 28, 2017. http://www.nobelprize.org/nobel_prizes/peace/laureates/1953/press.html.

———. "Speech at Trinity College, June 15, 1941." In *The Papers of George Catlett Marshall*, vol. 2, *We Cannot Delay*. Baltimore: Johns Hopkins University Press, 1986. http://marshallfoundation.org/library/digital-archive/speech-at-trinity-college.

Martin, Rachel. "For Many Returning Vets, 'Moral Injury' Just as Difficult." *NPR.org*, February 3, 2013. http://www.npr.org/2013/02/03/170979886/for-returning-vets-winning-the-moral-victory-just-as-difficult.

Martin, David, reporter. "The Good, the Bad, and the Ugly." CBS News report on General Stanley McChrystal (video), 10:00. January 6, 2013. https://www.youtube.com/watch?v=OAoyXWAAais.

Marty, Peter W. *The Anatomy of Grace*. Minneapolis: Fortress, 2008.

Mattis, James. *Ethical Challenges in Contemporary Conflict: The Afghanistan and Iraq Cases*. Annapolis: US Naval Academy, 2004.

Maxwell, Mark David. "Targeted Killing, the Law, and Terrorists: Feeling Safe?" *Joint Force Quarterly* 64 (2012) 123–30.

McAllister, Charles K. "The Lion of the Union: The Pelvic Wound of Joshua Lawrence Chamberlain." *Journal of Urology* 163 (2000) 713–16.

McChrystal, Stanley, et al. *Team of Teams: New Rules of Engagement for a Complex World*. New York: Portfolio/Penguin, 2015.

McCurley, T. Mark, and Kevin Mauer. *Hunter Killer: Inside America's Unmanned Air War*. New York: Dutton, 2015.

McDaniel, Dick. "William Calley Apologizes for the My Lai Massacre." *Columbus Ledger Enquirer*, January 5, 2009.

McMaster, H. R. *Dereliction of Duty*. New York: Harper Perennial, 1997.

Meagher, Rober Emmet. *Killing from the Inside Out: Moral Injury and Just War*. Eugene, OR: Cascade, 2014. Kindle edition.

Michaels, Jim. "Marines Misidentified One Man in Iconic 1945 Iwo Jima Photo." *USA Today*, June 23, 2016. http://www.usatoday.com/story/news/world/2016/06/23/flag-raiser-marine-iwo-jima-photo/86254440.

Miller N. L., et al. "Fatigue and Its Effect on Performance in Military Environments." Chapter 12 of *Performance Under Stress*, edited by Peter A. Hancock and James L. Szalma. Burlington, VT: Ashgate, 2008. https://pdfs.semanticscholar.org/c9d4/2c575262abc92d414fffa3926816476f3b01.pdf.

Montagne, Renee. "Wounded in Combat, US Troops Go Back for a Proper Exit." *National Public Radio*, February 10, 2015. http://www.npr.org/templates/transcript/transcript.php?storyId=361155634.

Montgomery, Nancy. "Good Character Is No Longer a Defense: Military Lawyers Are Losing the 'Good Soldier' Defense." *Stars and Stripes*, February 9, 2015.

Moody, Steve. "On Combat: The Psychology and Physiology of Deadly Combat in War and Peace." *Snakevscrane.com*, July 24, 2012. http://www.snakevscranewingchun.com/on-combat.

Moore, Harold G., and Joseph L. Galloway. *We Are Soldiers Still: A Journey Back to the Battlefields of Vietnam*. New York: Harper Perennial, 2008.

———. *We Were Soldiers Once and Young*. New York: Random House, 1992.

Moore, S. K. *Military Chaplains as Agents of Peace*. Lanham: Lexington, 2013.

Morris, David J. *The Evil Hours: A Biography of Post-Traumatic Stress Disorder*. Boston: Houghton Mifflin Harcourt, 2015.

Mosely, Alexander. "Just War Theory." *Internet Encyclopedia of Philosophy*. http://www.iep.utm.edu/justwar.

Murphy, Audie. *To Hell and Back*. New York: Holt, 1949.

Nash, William P. "Trauma, Loss, and Moral Injury: Different Approacches for Prevention and Treatment." Armed Forces Public Health Conference, March 23, 2011. http://wwwpdhealth.mil/educaton/2011_Presentations/AFPCH%20 1120Trauma%20Loss,%20and%20Moral%%20Injury.pdf.

———. "U.S. Marine Corps and Navy Combat and Operational Stress Continuum Model: A Tool for Leaders." In *Combat and Operational Behavioral Health*, edited by Elspeth Cameron Ritchie, 107–21. Washington, DC: Office of the Surgeon General, 2011.

Nash, W. P., et al. "Psychometric Evaluation of the Moral Injury Events Scale." *Military Medicine* 178 (2013) 646–52.

Nolan, Keith W. *Ripcord*. San Marin: Presidio, 2000.

O'Connor, Richard B. *Collateral Damage: How Can the Army Best Serve a Soldier with Post-Traumatic Stress Disorder?* Land Warfare Papers 71. Arlington, VA: Institute of Land Warfare, 2009.

O'Donnell, Patrick. *Give Me Tomorrow*. Cambridge: DeCapo, 2010.

Olson, Keith. *Counseling Teenagers*. Loveland, CO: Group, 1984.

Palmer, Joseph M. *They Don't Receive Purple Hearts: A Guide to an Understanding and Resolution of the Invisible Wound of War Known as Moral Injury*. Northbrook, IL: Military Outreach USA, 2015.

Palmer, Laura. *Shrapnel in the Heart: Letters and Remembrances from the Vietnam Veterans Memorial*. New York: Vintage, 1987.

Park, Crystal et al., *Trauma, Meaning, and Spirituality; Translating Research into Clinical Practice*. Washington DC: American Psychiatric Association, 2017.

Peers, W. R. *The My Lai Inquiry*. New York: Norton, 1979.

Perry, Mark. *Conceived in Liberty: Joshua Chamberlain, William Oates, and the American Civil War*. New York: Penguin, 1997.

Perzo, Andrew. "Gen. Patton Struck Two Soldiers in August 1943." *AmericanPress.com*, August 14, 2014. http://www.americanpress.com/Gen—Patton-struck-two-soldiers-in-August-1943.

Pew Research Center. "'Nones' on the Rise: One-in-Five Adults Have No Religious Affiliation." Pew Forum on Religion and Public Life, October 9, 2012. http://www.pewforum.org/files/2012/10/NonesOnTheRise-full.pdf.

———. "U.S. Public Becoming Less Religious." Pew Forum on Religion and Public Life, November 3, 2015. http://www.pewforum.org/2015/11/03/u-s-public-becoming-less-religious.

Philipps, David. *Lethal Warriors: When the New Band of Brothers Came Home.* New York: Palgrave Macmillan, 2010.

Phillips, David. "Audie Murphy Petition Draws Major Endorsements: Murphy; A Pioneer in PTSD Awareness." *Warfoto.com*, September 9, 2013. http://www. warfoto.com/AudieMurphy.htm.

————. "Presidential Medal of Freedom Petition for Audie Leon Murphy." https:// www.ipetitions.com/petition/audiemurphy.

Phillips, Joshua. *None of Us Were Like This Before: American Soldiers and Torture.* London: Verso, 2010. Kindle edition.

Philpott, Daniel. *Just and Unjust Peace.* Oxford: Oxford University Press, 2012.

Pierce, Albert C. "Chairman's Conference on Military Professionalism: An Overview." *Joint Force Quarterly* 62 (2011) 8–9.

————. *War, Strategy vs. Ethics, Ethics and Strategy.* Fleet Admiral Chester W. Nimitz Memorial Lectureship in National Security Affairs, University of California, Berkeley, March 6, 2002. http://rcnsc.dodlive.mil/files/2013/11/Strategy-Ethics. pdf.

Plato. *The Republic.* Edited by C. D. C Reeve. Translated by G. M. A. Grube. Cambridge, MA: Hackett, 1992.

Porter, John. *If I Make My Bed in Hell.* Grand Rapids: Word, 1969.

"Pontius Pilate." *BiblicalTraining.org.* 2015. https://www.biblicaltraining.org/library/ pontius-pilate.

Preston, Andrew. *Sword or the Spirit, Shield or Faith: Religion in American War and Diplomacy.* New York: Random House, 2012.

Pryer, Douglas A. "Moral Injury: What Leaders Don't Mention When They Talk about War." *Army*, September 2014, 34–36.

Pyle, David. "What the Pastor Owes the Sheepdogs." Paper presented at National Defense University's Institute of National Security Ethics and Leadership, Washington, DC, June 26, 2009.

Ramsey, Paul. *The Essential Paul Ramsey: A Collection.* Edited by William Werphehowski and Stephen D. Crocco. New Haven: Yale University Press, 1994.

Regan, Geoffrey. *Blue on Blue: A History of Friendly Fire.* New York: Avon, 1995.

Reichberg, Gregory M., and Henrik Syse, eds. *Religion, War, and Ethics: A Sourcebook of Textual Traditions.* New York: Cambridge University Press, 2014.

Remarque, Erich Maria. *All Quiet on the Western Front.* New York: Fawcett, 1982.

Reppenhagen, Garrett. "I Was an Amerian Sniper, and Chris Kyle's War Was Not My War." *Salon*, February 1, 2015. http://www.salon.com/2015/02/01/i_was_an_ american_sniper_and_chris_kyle%E2%80%99s_war_was_not_my_war.

Ricoeur, Paul. "The Hermeneutics of Symbols and Philosophical Reflection: I." Translated by Denis Savage. In *The Conflict of Interpretations: Essays in Hermeneutics, I*, edited by Don Ihde, 328–32. Evanston: Northwestern University Press, 1974.

————. *The Symbolism of Evil.* Translated by Emerson Buchanan. Boston: Beacon, 1967.

Rielly, Robert. "The Inclination for War Crimes." *Military Review*, May–June 2010, 17–23.

Ritchie, Elisabeth Cameron. "Moral Injury: A Profound Sense of Alienation and Shame." *Nation*, April 17, 2013. http://nation.time.com/2013/04/17/moral-injury- a-profound-sense-of-alienation-and-abject-shame.

Roberts, Sam. "Charles Liteky, 85, Dies; Returned Medal of Honor in Protest." *New York Times*, January 23, 2017. https://www.nytimes.com/2017/01/23/us/charlie-liteky-dead-returned-medal-of-honor.html?_r=0.

Romer, Daniel. "Adolescent Risk Taking, Impulsivity, and Brain Development: Implications for Prevention." *Developmental Psychobiology* 52 (2010) 263–76.

Romesha, Clinton. *Red Platoon: A True Story of American Valor*. New York: Penguin, 2016. Kindle edition.

Rondeau, Ann E. "Identity in the Profession of Arms." *Joint Forces Quarterly* 62 (2013) 10–14.

Sajer, Guy. *The Forgotten Soldier*. Washington, DC: Potomac, 2000.

Samet, Elizabeth. *No Man's Land: Preparing for War and Peace in Post-9/11 America*. New York: Farrar, Straus, and Giroux, 2014.

———. *Soldier's Heart: Reading Literature through Peace and War at West Point*. New York: Farrar, Straus, and Giroux, 2007.

———. "When Is War Over?" *New York Times*, November 21, 2014. https://www.nytimes.com/2014/11/23/opinion/sunday/when-is-a-war-over.html?_r=0.

Self, Nate. *Two Wars: One Hero's Fight on Two Fronts—Abroad and Within*. Carol Stream, IL: Tyndale, 2008.

Scarry, Elaine. *The Body in Pain: The Making and Unmaking of the World*. Oxford: Oxford University Press, 1985.

Shane, Leo, III. "Living through Nine Suicides." *Stripes.com*. September 11, 2013. https://www.stripes.com/living-through-nine-suicides-1.240240#.WUcprcbMwnU.

Shanker, Andrew, and Richard A. Oppel Jr. "War's Tough Guys, Hesitant to Seek Healing." *New York Times*, June 5, 2014. https://www.nytimes.com/2014/06/06/us/politics/wars-elite-tough-guys-hesitant-to-seek-healing.html?_r=0.

Shay, Jonathan. *Achilles in Vietnam: Combat Trauma and the Undoing of Character*. New York: Scribner, 1994.

———. Interview with Religion and Ethics Newsweekly. PBS.org, March 11, 2011. www.pbs.org/wnet/religionandethics/2011/03/11/...jonathan-shay...interview/6384.

———. *Odysseus in America: Combat Trauma and the Trials of Homecoming*. New York: Scribner, 2002. Kindle edition.

———. "Trust: Touchstone for a Practical Military Ethos." In *Spirit, Blood and Treasure*, edited by Donald Vandergriff, 14–16. San Marin, CA: Presidio, 2001.

Shay, Jonathan, and Kerry Haynes. "Understanding Moral Injury and PTSD." US Army Chaplain webinar, January 4, 2017.

Sheldon, George G. *Their Last Words: A Tribute to Soldiers Who Lost Their Lives in Iraq*. New York: Berkeley, 2005.

Sherman, Nancy. *Afterwar: Healing Moral Wounds of Our Soldiers*. Oxford: Oxford University Press, 2015. Kindle edition.

———. *The Fabric of Character: Aristotle's Theory of Virtue*. Reprint. Oxford: Clarendon, 2004. Kindle edition.

———. "The Moral Logic of Survivor Guilt." *New York Times*, July 3, 2011. https://opinionator.blogs.nytimes.com/2011/07/03/war-and-the-moral-logic-of-survivor-guilt.

———. *Stoic Warriors: The Ancient Philosophy behind the Military Mind*. New York: Oxford University Press, 2005. Kindle edition.

———. *The Untold War: Inside the Hearts, Minds, and Souls of Our Soldiers*. New York: Norton, 2010. Kindle edition.

Sherman, William Tecumseh. Letter to the mayor and council of Atlanta, September 12, 1864. *Official Records of the Union and Confederate Armies, Series I—Volume XXXIX/2 Civil War.* Edited by Robert N. Scott. http://history.furman.edu/benson/docs/atlanta1.htm.

Sieff, Kevin. "In Afghanistan, Redeployed U.S. Soldiers Still Coping with Demons of Post-Traumatic Stress." *Washington Post,* August 18, 2013. https://www.washingtonpost.com/world/in-afghanistan-redeployed-us-soldiers-still-coping-with-demons-of-post-traumatic-stress/2013/08/18/27c18e96-0058-11e3-8294-0ee5075b840d_story.html?utm_term=.33cb1e3f4325.

——. "These Wounded U.S. Veterans Wanted Closure, Find It Back in Afghanistan." *Washinton Post,* May 23, 2014. https://www.washingtonpost.com/world/asia_pacific/these-wounded-us-vets-wanted-closure-they-found-it-back-in-afghanistan/2014/05/23/ab34be44-ae2f-11e3-a49e-76adc9210f19_story.html?utm_term=.31b9e1b8cbcc.

Sippola, John, et al. *Welcome Them Home, Help Them Heal: Pastoral Care and Ministry with Service Members Returning from War.* Duluth, MN: Whole Person Associates, 2009.

Sledge, Benjamin. "The Conversation about War and Our Veterans We Refuse to Have." *Bullshitist,* May 27, 2016. https://bullshit.ist/the-conversation-about-war-and-our-veterans-we-refuse-to-have-a95c26972aee.

Sledge, E. B. *With the Old Breed at Peleliu and Okinawa.* New York: Ballantine, 1981.

Snider, Don M., et al. *The Army's Professional Military Ethic in an Era of Persistent Conflict.* Professional Military Ethics Monograph Series. Center for the Army Profession and Ethic, 2009.

Snider, Don M., and Alexander P. Shine. *A Soldier's Morality, Religion, and Our Professional Ethic: Does the Army's Culture Facilitate Integration, Character Development, and Trust in the Profession?* Carlisle: Strategic Studies Institute and US Army War College Press, 2014.

Soergel, Matt. "Charlie Liteky: 'He Was Our Quarterback, and Quarterbacks Save the World.'" *NCMAF/ECVAC Newsletter* 4.1, April 19, 2009. http://jacksonville.com/news/metro/2009-04-18/story/charlie-liteky-he-was-our-quarterback-and-quarterbacks-save-world.

Solzhenitsyn, Aleksandr. *Gulag Archipelago.* New York: Harper and Row, 1973.

Spadaro, Antonio. "The Church Is a Field Hospital Where Wounds Are Treated." *La Stampa,* September 19, 2013. http://www.lastampa.it/2013/09/19/vaticaninsider/eng/the-vatican/antonio-spadaro-interviews-francis-the-church-is-a-field-hospital-where-wounds-are-treated-ZrRM4dLcOYJ2bpR8x9gvWI/pagina.html.

Spielberg, Steven, dir. *Saving Private Ryan.* Written by Robert Rodat. Film. DreamWorks / Paramount Pictures, 1998.

Stark, Rodney. *The Rise of Christianity: How the Obscure, Marginal Jesus Movement Became the Dominant Religious Force in the Western World in a Few Centuries.* New York: HarperCollins, 1996.

Steenkamp, Maria M., and William P. Nash. "Post-Traumatic Stress Disorder: Review of the Comprehensive Soldier Fitness Program." *American Journal of Preventive Medicine* 44 5 (2013) 507–12.

Steinberg, Laurence. "Risk Taking in Adolescence: New Perspectives from Brain and Behavioral Science." *Current Directions in Psychological Science* 16 (2007) 55–59.

Steinberg, Laurence, and Ann Levine. *You and Your Adolescent: The Essential Guide for Ages 10 to 25*. New York: Harper Perennial, 1990.

Stockdale, James B. *Courage Under Fire: Testing Epictetus's Doctrines in a Laboratory of Human Behavior*. Stanford: Hoover Institute, 1993.

————. *Master of My Fate: A Stoic Philosopher in a Hanoi Prison*. Annapolis: US Naval Academy, 2001.

————. *Thoughts of a Philosophical Fighter Pilot*. 5th ed. Stanford: Hoover Institute, 1995.

Stout, Jeffrey. *Flight from Authority: Religion, Morality, and the Quest for Autonomy*. South Bend, IN: University of Notre Dame Press, 1987.

Stracqualursi, Veronica. "Outgoing Joint Chiefs Chairman Martin Dempsey Reflects on His Toughest Day on the Job." *ABC News*, September 6, 2015. http://abcnews.go.com/Politics/outgoing-joint-chiefs-chairman-martin-dempsey-reflects-toughest/story?id=33557061.

Strasser, Steven, ed. *The Abu Ghraib Investigations: The Official Reports of the Independent Panel and the Pentagon on the Shocking Prisoner Abuse in Iraq*. New York: Public Affairs, 2004.

Swain, Richard. "Reflection on an Ethic of Officership." *Parameters*, spring 2007, 4–20.

Sweeney, Patrick J., Sean T. Hannah, and Don M. Snider. "The Domain of the Human Spirit in Cadet Development at West Point." In *The Warrior's Character*, edited by Don M. Snider and Lloyd J. Mathews. New York: McGraw Hill, 2013. http://isme.tamu.edu/ISME07/Snider07.html.

Sweeney, Patrick J., Jeffrey E. Rhodes, and Bruce Boling. "Spiritual Fitness: A Key Component of Total Force Fitness." *Joint Forces Quarterly* 66 (2012) 35–41.

Tacitus, Gaius Cornelius. *The Agricola and the Germania*. Neeland, 2009. Kindle edition.

Tagubu, Antonio M. *Ethical Leadership: Your Challenge, Your Responsibility*. Annapolis: Center for the Study of Professional Military Ethics, US Naval Academy, 2005.

Tanielian, Terri. "Assessing Combat Exposure and Post-Traumatic Stress Disorders in Troops and Estimating the Costs to Society." Testimony presented before the House Veterans' Affairs Committee, Subcommittee on Disability Assistance and Memorial Affairs, March 24, 2009. http://www.rand.org/content/dam/rand/pubs/testimonies/2009/RAND_CT321.pdf.

Tapper, Jake. *The Outpost: An Untold Story of American Valor*. New York: Little, Brown, 2012.

Taub, Amanda. "Moral Injury—the Quiet Epidemic of Soldiers Haunted by What They Did during Wartime." *Vox*, May 25, 2015. http://www.vox.com/2015/5/7/8553043/soldiers-moral-injury[5/13/2015.

Taylor, Charles. *Sources of the Self: The Making of the Modern Identity*. Boston: Harvard University Press, 1992.

Thompson, Hugh. *Moral Courage in Combat: The My Lai Story*. Annapolis: Center for the Study of Professional Military Ethics, US Naval Academy, 2003.

Thweat, Lee. Personal interview with the author, February 2017.

Tick, Edward. *War and the Soul*. Wheaton, IL: Quest, 2005.

————. *Warrior's Return: Restoring the Soul after War*. Boulder, CO: Sounds True, 2014. Kindle edition.

Townsend, Tim. "How Military Chaplains Are Finding New Ways to Treat Vets with Invisible Wounds." *Washington Post*, April 10, 2015. https://www.washingtonpost.

com/news/acts-of-faith/wp/2015/04/10/how-military-chaplains-are-finding-new-ways-to-treat-vets-with-invisible-wounds/?utm_term=.5d518eff336c.

Tracy, Jared. "Ethical Challenges in Stability Operations." *Military Review* 89 (2009) 84–86.

Trice, Michael Reid. *Encountering Cruelty: The Fracture of the Human Heart*. Studies in Systematic Theology 6. Leiden: Brill, 2011.

US Air Force. *Basic Doctrine*. Department of the Air Force. Volume 1. Washington, DC: Government Printing Office, 2015.

———. *Disaster Mental Health Response & Combat and Operational Stress Control*. Department of the Air Force. Instruction 44–153. Washington, DC: Government Printing Office, 2014.

US Army. *The Army Profession*. ADRP 1. Department of the Army. Washington, DC: Government Printing Office, 2015.

———. *Army 2020 Generating Health & Discipline in the Force: Ahead of the Strategic Reset*. Department of the Army. Washington, DC: Government Printing Office, 2012.

———. *The Army Profession*. Center for the Army Professional Ethic. West Point: Center for the Army Professional Ethic, 2017. http://cape.army.mil/repository/brochures/army-profession-pamphlet.pdf.

———. *Combat and Operational Stress Control Manual for Leaders and Soldiers*. Department of the Army. FM 22–51. Washington, DC: Government Printing Office, 2009.

———. *Epidemiologic Consultation no. 14-HK-OBIU-09: Investigation of Homicides at Fort Carson, Colorado November 2008–May 2009*. Center for Health Promotion and Preventive Medicine. Washington, DC: Government Printing Office, 2009.

———. *Honorable Retaliation, Video Case Study Presented by Staff Sergeant Huntley*. Center for the Army Professional Ethic. West Point: Center for the Army Professional Ethic, 2014. http://cape.army.mil/case-studies/vcs-single.php?id=19&title=honorable-retaliation.

———. *Mental Health Advisory Team Study 1–9, Operation Iraqi Freedom 05–07*. Office of the Surgeon General Multi National Forces Iraq and US Army Medical Command. Washington, DC: Government Printing Office, 2006–2008.

———. "Ready and Resilient: Achieving Personal Readiness. Optimizing Performance." *army.mil* (November 30, 2016). https://www.army.mil/readyandresilient.

———. *Report of the Department of the Army Review of the Investigations into the My Lai Incident: Volume I*. Department of the Army. Washington, DC: Government Printing Office, 1970.

———. *The U.S. Army Human Dimension Concept*. TRADOC Pamphlet 525-3-7. Department of the Army. Washington, DC: Government Printing Office, 2014.

———. *TRADOC Sergeant Audie Murphy Club*. Training and Doctrine Command. Regulation 600–14. Department of the Army. Washington, DC: Government Printing Office, 1999. http://www.armystudyguide.com/content/audie_murphy_study_guide/audie_murphy_information/tradoc-reg-60014-tradoc-s.shtml.

———. *Unified Land Operations*. ADP 3-0. Department of the Army. Washington, DC: Government Printing Office, 2011.

US Army Chief of Chaplains. *Ministering to Families Affected by Military Deployment: Resources for America's Clergy*. 4th ed. Department of the Army. Washington, DC: Government Printing Office, 2008.

US Coast Guard. *Operations*. Department of the Coast Guard. Publication 3-0. Washington, DC: Government Printing Office, 2012.

US Department of Defense. *The Armed Forces Officer*. Washington, DC: Potomac Books, 2007.

———. *Desired Leader Attributes for Joint Force 2020*. Joint Chiefs of Staff. Washington, DC: Government Printing Office, 2013.

———. *Maintenance of Psychological Health in Military Organizations*. Instruction 6490.5. Washington, DC: Government Printing Office, 2011.

———. *The Armed Forces Officer Edition of 1950*. US Department of Defense. Washington, DC: Government Printing Office, 1950.

———. *The Noncommissioned Officer and Petty Officer: Backbone of the Armed Forces*. Department of Defense. Washington, DC: National Defense University Press, 2014.

———. Officer Professional Military Education Policy (OPMEP). CJCSI 1800.01D. Joint Chiefs of Staff. Washington, DC: Government Printing Office, 2012.

———. *2012 Demographics Profile of the Military Community*. Office of the Under Secretary of Defense. Washington, DC: Government Printing Office, 2012.

US Department of Veteran Affairs. "DSM-5 Criteria for PTSD." National Center for PTSD. http://www.ptsd.va.gov/professional/PTSD-overview/dsm5_criteria_ptsd.asp.

———. "Suicide Risk and Risk of Death Among Recent Veterans." https://www.publichealth.va.gov/epidemiology/studies/suicide-risk-death-risk-recent-veterans.asp#sthash.3mup6oC4.dpuf.

US Forces Afghanistan. *Money as a Weapon System*. USFOR-A Pub 1-06. Department of Defense. Washington, DC: Government Printing Office, 2012.

US House of Representatives. *Another Crossroads? Professional Military Education Two Decades after the Goldwater-Nichols Act and the Skelton Panel*. Committee on Armed Services and Subcommittee on Oversight & Investigations. Washington, DC: Government Printing Office, 2010.

US Joint Forces Command. *Final Report: Symposium of Ethical Decision Making and Behavior in High Performing Teams Sustaining Future Force Success*. Department of Defense. Washington, DC: Government Printing Office, 2010.

———. *Joint Operations*. Joint Publication 3-0. Joint Chiefs of Staff. Washington, DC: Government Printing Office, 2011.

US Marine Corps. *Leading Marines*. MCWP 6-11. Department of the Navy. Washington, DC: Government Printing Office, 2014.

———. *Marine Corps Operational Doctrine*. MCDP 1-0. Department of the Navy. Washington, DC: Government Printing Office, 2011.

———. "Marine Ethics Stand Down Training." Department of the Navy. Washington, DC, 2012.

US Naval Academy. "Comparative Warfare Ethics: Traditional and Contemporary Perspectives." Annapolis: US Naval Academy, 2014.

———. *Moral Courage: An Evening in Honor of Vice Admiral James B. Stockdale*. Department of the Navy. Annapolis: Government Printing Office, 1999.

US Naval Institute. "Died of Wounds." *blog.usni.org*. November 2010.

US Navy. *Combat and Operational Stress Control*. NTTP 1-15M and MCRP 6-11C. Department of the Navy. Washington, DC: Government Printing Office, 2010.

———. *Naval Warfare.* Vol. NDP 1. Department of the Navy. Washington, DC: Government Printing Office, 2010.

US Special Operations Command. *Doctrine for Special Operations.* Publication 1. Department of Defense. Washington, DC: Government Printing Office, 2011.

Urasano, Robert J., et al. "On Behalf of the Army Study to Assess Risk and Resilience in Service Members (ASTARRS)." *Psychiatry* 77 (2014) 107–19.

Verkamp, Bernard J. *The Moral Treatment of Returning Warriors in Early Medieval and Modern Times.* Scranton: University of Scranton Press, 2006.

Veterans and PTSD. "Veterans Statistics: PTSD, Depression, TBI, Suicide." September 20, 2015. http://www.veteransandptsd.com/PTSD-statistics.html.

Volf, Miroslav. *Free of Charge: Giving and Forgiving in a Culture Stripped of Grace.* Grand Rapids: Zondervan, 2005.

Waggoner, Martha. "Retired Marine Sniper from Taliban Urination Video Found Dead." *Washington Times,* August 15, 2014. http://www.washingtontimes.com/news/2014/aug/15/marine-who-urinated-on-corpses-in-afghanistan-dies.

Walker, Keith. *A Piece of My Heart: The Stories of Twenty-Six American Women Who Served in Vietnam.* San Francisco: Presidio, 1985.

Wallace, Mark I. *The Second Naiveté: Barth, Ricoeur, and the New Yale Theology.* Macon, GA: Mercer University Press, 1995.

Wallace, Willard. *The Soul of the Lion: A Biography of Joshua L. Chamberlain.* Gettysburg: Stan Clark Military Books, 1960.

Wallis, Lucy. "Is 25 the New Cut Off for Adulthood?" *BBC News,* September 23, 2013. http://www.bbc.com/news/magazine-24173194.

Walzer, Michael. *Arguing about War.* New Haven: Yale University Press, 2004.

———. *Just and Unjust Wars: A Moral Argument with Historical Illustrations.* New York: Basic, 1977; 5th ed., 2015. Citations of front matter and intro are the 5th ed.

Wangelin, Bethany C., and Peter W. Tuerk. "PTSD in Active Combat Soldiers: To Treat or Not to Treat." *Neurosciences* 42 (2014) 161–70.

Washington, George. "Letter to the New York Provincial Congress." June 26, 1775. https://founders.archives.gov/documents/Washington/03-01-02-0019.

Welker, Kevin. "The Tragedy of Heroism: Charles W. Whittlesey." Society of the Honor Guard, Tomb of the Unknown Soldier. December 1, 2013. https://tombguard.org/column/2013/12/the-tragedy-of-heroism-charles-w-whittlesey.

White, John, and Alletta Cooper, producers. "For Decades, He Carried Guilt for Another Soldier's Death." *NPR.org,* April 9, 2016. http://www.npr.org/2016/04/09/473536609/for-decades-he-carried-guilt-for-another-soldiers-death.

White, Josh, and Thomas Ricks. "Top Brass Won't Be Charged Over Abuse: Army Finds Officers Responsible, but Not Culpable in the Abu Ghraib Scandal." *Washington Post,* August 27, 2004. http://www.washingtonpost.com/wp-dyn/articles/A36943-2004Aug26.html.

Wiener, Nancy H., and Jo Hirschmann. *Maps and Meaning: Levitical Models for Contemporary Care.* Minneapolis: Fortress, 2014.

Wilson, Timothy D. *Redirect: The Surprising New Science of Psychological Change.* Frederick: Highbridge, 2011.

Wink, Walter. *Engaging the Powers: Discernment and Resistance in a World of Domination.* Minneapolis: Fortress, 1992.

Winston, Morton. "Moral Patients." *An Ethics of Global Responsibility* (blog). http://ethicsofglobalresponsibility.blogspot.com/2008/02/moral-patients.html.

Wong, Leonard. *Developing Adaptive Leaders: The Crucible Experience of Operation Iraqi Freedom*. Carlisle, PA: US Army War College Press, 2004.

Wong, Leonard, and Stephen J. Gerras. *Lying to Ourselves: Dishonesty in the Army Profession*. Carlisle, PA: US Army War College Press, 2015.

Wood, David. "A Warrior's Moral Dilemma." *Huffington Post*, 2014. http://projects.huffingtonpost.com/moral-injury.

Wright, Evan. *Generation Kill*. New York: Putnam, 2004.

Wynn, Phillip. *Augustine on War and Military Service*. Minneapolis: Fortress, 2013.

Zarembo, Alan. "Nearly 1 in 5 Had Mental Illness Before Enlisting in Army, Study Says." *Los Angeles Times*, March 3, 2014. http://www.latimes.com/nation/la-me-army-mental-illness-20140304-story.html.

Zizek, Slavoi. "The Christian-Hegelian Comedy." In *The Artist's Joke*, edited by Jennifer Higgie, 216–20. London: Whitechapel, 2007.

Zust, Jeff. "The Ethical Land Navigation Model." *NCO Journal* 12 (2003) 26–28.

———. "Do the Right Thing: The NCO Role in Unit Ethics Training." *NCO Journal* 13 (2004) 16–17.

———. *White Paper: The Four Systems for Ethical Reasoning*. Washington, DC: National Defense University, 2014.